D1217343

CAMBRIDGE ENGLISH CLASSICS

Satires

and

Miscellaneous Poetry

and Prose

———

Samuel Butler

SAMUEL BUTLER

Born Feb. 161$\frac{2}{3}$
Died Sept. 1680

SAMUEL BUTLER

SATIRES
AND
MISCELLANEOUS POETRY
AND PROSE

EDITED BY
RENÉ LAMAR, M.A.

CAMBRIDGE :
at the University Press
1928

Cambridge University Press
Fetter Lane, London

New York
Bombay, Calcutta, Madras
Toronto
Macmillan

Tokyo
Maruzen-Kabushiki-Kaisha

PRINTED IN GREAT BRITAIN

NOTE

THIS third volume of Butler's *Complete Works* contains, under the comprehensive title of *Satires and Miscellaneous Poetry and Prose*, all his writings that were not included in the late A. R. Waller's editions of *Hudibras* (1905) and *Characters and Passages from Note-Books* (1908). Among so many compositions, verse and prose, some undoubtedly genuine, others more or less boldly fathered upon him, my task has been first to separate the wheat from the chaff, and secondly, when several texts were available, to determine which version the author himself would have most likely selected for printing. The problems that offered themselves, and the way they were solved, will appear more clearly if I present, under the form of a bibliography, the mass of materials that I had to examine. The MSS. left by Butler and Thyer, together with the *Genuine Remains* published by the latter, an industrious and trustworthy editor, will naturally fall into one group, while the works, of which the genuineness has been rightly or wrongly questioned, will be separately discussed.

A.

I. MANUSCRIPTS.

The only MSS. of Butler that are now available are those acquired in 1885 by the British Museum. They are contained in two folio volumes:

I. Add. MSS. 32625: Literary remains of Samuel Butler, author of *Hudibras*; consisting of miscellaneous collections and fragments in verse and prose, written in Butler's own hand. ff. 236.

NOTE

The compositions in verse are:

1. Collection of short pieces and tentative lines on various subjects, viz: *Wit and Folly, Modern War, Cowardise, Nature, Truth, Learning, Conscience, Love, Honor, Magique, Astrology, Religion, Marriage, Chymistry, Hope, Government, Cruelty, Custome, Antiquity, Popery, Opinion, Folly, Trade, Time, Arts and Sciences, Geomancy, Treachery, Rebellion, Gluttony, Absurdities, Fortune, Feare, Pride, Stinke, Virtuoso, Law, The World, Fanatiques, Theft, Women, Poetry, History, Nonsense, Avarice, Sidrophel, Injustice, Vice, Wealth, Lust, Writers, Physique, Zeal, Courage, Prelates, Infancy, Additions to Hudibras, Vulgarity, Morality.* fol. 2. (See *Poetical Thesaurus*, pp. 151–294, *Appendix*, pp. 399–465, and alternative readings.)

2. *On Phil. Nyes thanksgiving Beard—a fragment.* fol. 82. (See pp. 489–490.)

3. Ballads. fol. 84. (See pp. 105–112.)

4. Various pieces, more or less disconnected, including parts of the satires and fragments printed by Thyer, viz: *Upon Critics who judge of modern Plays precisely by the Rules of the Antients,* and *Satyr upon the Imperfection and Abuse of human Learning.* fol. 86. (See pp. 60–62, 68–81, and alternative readings.)

5. Sketch of a passage in *Hudibras* (III, iii, 621), differing from the printed text. fol. 139. (See *Hudibras's Visit to the Lawyer,* pp. 463–464.)

The compositions in prose are:

6. Miscellaneous observations and reflections on various subjects. fol. 190, printed by A. R. Waller in *Characters and Passages from Note-Books,* 1908, pp. 270–480.

At folio 86, there is the draft of a letter to his sister on the education of her son. (See p. 399.)

II. Add. MSS. 32626. Transcripts and extracts from original compositions in verse and prose of Samuel Butler, by Robert Thyer. ff. 154.

1. "Verses taken into Hudibras, or tending to explain passages in it," fol. 3, partly printed in 1822 by the editor of the second edition of the *Genuine Remains,* pp. 260 sqq.

NOTE

2. "Miscellaneous pieces in verse," fol. 21, partly printed by Thyer in the *Genuine Remains*.

3. "Thoughts in his Commonplace Collection" in verse, fol. 42, partly printed by Thyer.

4. Sixty-six "Characters," in prose, published by A. R. Waller, pp. 197–267.

[A large portion of the British Museum MSS. was never printed by Thyer. He apparently thought that much of them was not good enough to be published in the *Genuine Remains*; and he also omitted a number of verses which, on account of their coarseness, would have been out of place in his edition. The purpose of the present collection of texts is different: the prose compositions were printed by A. R. Waller in their entirety, and the same course has been followed in this volume, which contains the rest of the MSS.

The volume numbered 32625 is all that has come down to us of the papers bequeathed by the poet to his friend William Longueville. It is part of Butler's Commonplace-Book which in 1793 belonged to James Massey, of Rosthern, near Knutsford, Cheshire. That we have not all of it is evidenced by a statement of T. R. Nash, editor of *Hudibras*, who at that time could read in it part of an unfinished tragedy of Nero. The pages of the verse section in the MS. (such as remains) generally consist of two closely written columns in which the poet entered similes and thoughts as they occurred to him, thereafter working them up into more or less finished pieces (from fol. 2 to fol. 82), some under headings mentioned above (from fol. 86 to fol. 139), others without special indication.

With the exception of the sixty-six "Characters" in prose, No. 32626 is nothing but a transcript of the preceding MS., made by Thyer with a view to selecting the material for the *Genuine Remains*. As he could hardly publish No. 32625 in its undigested form, he undertook to classify the best passages as indicated above, modernizing the spelling, supplying the punctuation, and occasionally altering the text when he thought it unsatisfactory.

My rule has been to follow Butler's MS. as faithfully as possible. Only because some folios of No. 32625 are missing did I use Thyer's MS. in the few instances set forth in the textual notes. Yet, in view of the confusion of the entries, which of course were never meant for publication, I had to discriminate between them if I wished to be complete without doing a great injustice to the author. So, the sketches and thoughts in verse conveying sense by themselves have been retained in the *Poetical Thesaurus*. But the tentative lines and fragments left in

NOTE

the rough, together with the variants of, and allusions to, *Hudibras*, have been transferred into the Appendix under the proper headings.]

2. THE "GENUINE REMAINS."

I. THE / GENUINE REMAINS / IN / VERSE and PROSE / OF / Mr. SAMUEL BUTLER, / AUTHOR of HUDIBRAS. / Published from the / ORIGINAL MANU-SCRIPTS, formerly in the / Possession of W. LONGUE-VILLE, Esq; / With NOTES / By R. THYER, / Keeper of the Public Library at MANCHESTER. / IN TWO VOL-UMES. // LONDON: Printed by J. and R. Tonson, in the Strand. / MDCCLIX. / 2 vol. pp. 429, 512. in 8⁰.

[Part of the *Genuine Remains* were printed by A. R. Waller in *Characters and Passages from Note-Books* (pp. 1–193). For the remaining pieces, published in this volume, see textual notes.]

The following compositions had been printed before Thyer's edition:

1. TO THE / MEMORY / OF THE / MOST RE-NOWNED / DU-VALL: / A Pindarick Ode. // By the Author of *Hudibras*. / *LONDON*: / Printed for *H. Brome*, at the Gun in St *Paul*'s / Church-yard, at the West-end. 1671. / pp. 13 in 4⁰. (*Bodleian Library*: Wood 372 (11).)

[Cf. Thyer's *Genuine Remains*, 1, p. 145: "This Ode, which is the only genuine Poem of *Butler*'s among the many spurious ones father'd upon him in what is call'd *his Remains*, was published by the Author himself, under his own Name, in the Year 1671, in Three Sheets 4to; and agreeable to this I find it in his own Handwriting among his Manuscripts, with some little Addition, and a few verbal Alterations, as the Reader may observe, in comparing it with the Copy already printed. That pains-taking Critic Mr *Anthony Wood*, has however, in his *Athenæ*, acquainted us—'that though it is said in the Title to have been written by the Author of Hudibras, yet some curious Persons, at that Time thought otherwise'—And upon this hypothetical nameless Authority ventures to rob our Poet of his Property, and bestows it upon Dr. *Walter Pope*, Astronomy-Professor of *Gresham* College, who happened, it seems, to be a Wit as well as an Astronomer. What led to the suspicion of its being Dr. *Pope*'s was a Pamphlet published by

viij

NOTE

him the Year before upon the Same Occasion, call'd—'*The Memoirs of Mr Du Val, with his last Speech and Epitaph*'."

Reprinted in the *Posthumous Works*, IV, pp. 1–6.]

2. TWO / LETTERS, / One from *John Audland a* QUAKER, / TO / WILLIAM PRYNNE. / The Other, / WILLIAM PRYNNES / ANSWER, // *By the* AUTHOR *of* // HUDIBRAS. // LONDON, / Printed for *Jonathan Edwin* at the *Three Roses* in / *Ludgate* Street. 1672. / pp. 12 fol. (*British Museum*: 4139 h. 1.)

[Reprinted in the *Posthumous Works*, IV, pp. 91–102.]

3. THE / PLAGIARY / EXPOSED: / OR AN / OLD ANSWER / TO A / NEWLY REVIVED CALUMNY / Against the MEMORY of / King CHARLES I. / Being a / REPLY / To a Book intitled / King *Charles*'s CASE, / Formerly written by *John Cook* of *Grays* Inn, Barrister; / and since Copied out under the Title of Collonel / *Ludlow*'s LETTER, // Written by Mr. *Butler*, the Author of *Hudibras*. // LONDON: Printed for *Tho. Bennet* at the Half-Moon in / S. *Pauls* Churchyard. MDCXCI. / pp. 20. in 4°. (*British Museum*: E. 1969 (9).)

[Reprinted in *The Somers Collection of Tracts*, 1809–1815, vol. V, pp. 237 and 246, under the following titles: "*King Charles's Case Truly stated: In Answer to Mr. Cook's pretended Case of that blessed Martyr. By Mr. Samuel Butler Author of Hudibras*" and "*The Character of King Charles I. By Mr. Butler.*" The same pamphlet had often been reprinted in a book entitled: "*The secret history of the Calves head club, compleat: or the Republicans unmask'd; wherein is fully shewn the religion of the Calves-head heroes in their anniversary thanksgiving songs on the thirtieth of January by them called Anthems for the years* 1693, 1694, 1695, 1696, 1697, 1698, 1699, *etc.…with reflections thereupon.…To which is annext, A vindication of the Royal Martyr, King Charles I. Wherein are laid open The Republicans Mysteries of Rebellion.* Written in the Time of the Usurpation by the Celebrated Mr. Butler, Author of Hudibras…London." See also the *Posthumous Works*, IV, pp. 55–57.]

II. THE / GENUINE REMAINS / OF / SAMUEL BUTLER. / WITH NOTES, / BY ROBERT THYER, / KEEPER OF THE PUBLIC LIBRARY, MANCHES-

NOTE

TER. / A NEW EDITION, CORRECTED AND EN-
LARGED. / IN TWO VOLUMES. / Vol. I / LONDON:
/ PRINTED FOR CHARLES BALDWYN. / Newgate
Street. / 1822. / pp. 416 in 4°. (*New York Public Library*:
KZ Draper Collection.)

[The second volume was never published on account of Baldwyn's
failure in 1823.]

B.

I. THE "POSTHUMOUS WORKS."

I. Posthumous WORKS / *In* PROSE *and* VERSE, /
Written in the time of the Civil Wars / and Reign of K. Charles
II. by / Mr. Samuel Butler, / Author of HUDIBRAS. /
FROM / Original MSS. and Scarce and / Valuable Pieces
formerly printed. / WITH / a Key to HUDIBRAS / by Sir
Roger L'Estrange. // LONDON, / Printed for R. Smith and
G. Strahan at / the *Royal Exchange*, Jonas Brown without /
Temple bar; and Sold by J. Morphew near / *Stationers-hall*.
1715 / pp. 279. in 12°. (*British Museum*: 12270 a. 10.)

II. THE SECOND VOLUME / OF THE / Posthu-
mous WORKS / OF / Mr *SAMUEL BUTLER,* / Author
of HUDIBRAS. / Written in the Time of the GRAND /
REBELLION, and at the Be-/ginning of the RESTORA-
TION. / Being a Collection of *Satyrs, Speeches,* and / *Re-
flections* upon those Times. / WITH / A KEY to the II. and
III. / Parts of HUDIBRAS, / By Sir *Roger L'Estrange*. //
LONDON, Printed for SAM. BRISCOE, and Sold by *R.
Smith* and *G. Strahan* at the / *Royal Exchange*; *J. Browne*
without / *Temple-bar*; *J. Graves in* St *James's* / *Street*, and *J.
Morphew* near *Stationers-Hall*. 1715. / pp. 292. in 12°. (*British
Museum*: 1066 a. 6.)

[There were several editions of this volume, the third one containing
a few more poems.]

III. THE / THIRD and last VOLUME / OF / Posthumous WORKS, / Written by / Mr. *SAMUEL BUTLER,* /
Author of HUDIBRAS. / Part Written in the Time of the /

NOTE

USURPATION and the rest in the / Reign of King CHARLES II. // To which is added, *The Coffin for the* / GOOD OLD CAUSE. Publish'd just / before the RESTORATION. // By Sir Samuel Luke. // LONDON: Printed for SAM. BRISCOE, / *G. Strahan* at the *Exchange, R. Smith, J. Brown, A. Dod* without *Temple-bar* and *J. Morphew* near *Stationers-Hall.* 1717. / pp. 240. in 12°. (*British Museum*: 629 a. 24.)

IV. The Posthumous / WORKS / OF / Mr. *SAMUEL BUTLER,* / (Author of *HUDIBRAS*) / *Compleat in One VOLUME*: / Written in the Time of the Grand / Rebellion, and in the Reign of King / CHARLES II. / BEING / A Collection of SATIRES, SPEECHES, and / REFLECTIONS upon those Times. / Publish'd from / Original MSS. and Scarce and Valuable Pieces / formerly Printed. / To which is added, / A Key to HUDIBRAS by Sir Roger L'Estrange. // The Fourth Edition Corrected. // Adorn'd with Cuts. // LONDON: / Printed for and Sold by RICHARD BALD-WIN, at the / *Blue Bible* in *St Paul's Churchyard* 1732. / pp. 336, in 12°. (*British Museum*: 1078 f. 5.)

2. MISCELLANEOUS PIECES.

The following pieces have been attributed to Samuel Butler. Those that were published in the *Posthumous Works* are marked with an asterisk.

*I. TWO / SPEECHES / Made in the House of / PEERS, / On Munday the 19 of *December*, / For, and Against / Accomodation. / The one by the Earl of *Pembroke*, / the other by the Lord *Brooke*. / The latter Printed by the Order of the / House of / COMMONS. / *Hen. Elsinge, Cler. Parl. D. Com.* // *London*, Printed for Joh. Thompson. / 1642. / [10 Jan.] (*British Museum*: E. 84 (35).)

[Only the Speech of the Earl of Pembroke was reprinted in the *Posthumous Works*, IV, pp. 159–161. Obviously it was not written by Butler. It had been published already in 1707 with "THE / POETICAL WORKS / Of the Honourable / Sir *Charles Sedley* Baronet, / AND HIS / SPEECHES in PARLIAMENT, /

NOTE

WITH / *Large Additions never before made Publick.* / Published
from the Original M.S. by Capt. AYLOFFE, / a near Relation of
the Authors. / With a NEW MISCELLANY of Poems by several /
of the most *Eminent Hands.* // And a Compleat Collection of all the
Remarkable Speeches / in both *Houses of Parliament*: / ... / from
the year 1641, to the Happy Union of *Great Britain*: By several Lords
and Commoners... / *London,* Printed for SAM. BRISCOE, and Sold by
B. Bragg / at the *Raven in Pater-noster-Row.* 1707 /."]

II. A / LETTER / FROM / MERCURIUS CIVICUS
/ TO / MERCURIUS RUSTICUS: / OR, / LONDONS
CONFESSION / but not Repentance. / SHEWING, / That
the beginning and the obstinate / pursuance of this accursed
horrid / Rebellion is principally to be ascribed / *to that Rebellious
City.* //—*En quò discordia Cives?* / *Perduxit miseros: Virg. Egl.*
I. // Printed, 1643. / pp. 33 in 12°. (*Bodleian Library*: C. 14. 4
Linc.)

[Reprinted in *Somers Tracts,* vol. IV, p. 50, where it is attributed to
Butler.]

*III. The EARLE of / PEMBROKE'S / SPEECH /
In the House of / PEERES, / Upon Debate of the *Citie*'s Petition
for a / *Personall Treaty,* to be had with His / MAJESTY in
London. / And also upon debate of those Reasons / given by
their Lordships unto the / Commons, for not sending the /
three Propositions before a / TREATY. // Printed in the yeer,
1648. / July 20th / (*British Museum*: E. 453 (30).)

[Reprinted in the *Poetical Works of Sir Charles Sedley,* p. 57, and
in *Somers Tracts,* vol. VII, p. 79, where it is attributed to Sedley.]

*IV. HOSANNA: / OR, / A Song of Thanks-giving, /
Sung by the Children of *Zion,* / AND / Set forth in three notable
Speeches at *Grocers* / Hall, on the late Solemn Day of Thanks-
giving, / Thursday June 7. 1649. / The first was spoken by
Alderman *Atkins.* / The *Second* by Alderman *Isaac Pennington.*
/ The third by *Hugh Peters* (not Alderman, but) *Clericus in
cuerpo* // *Risum Teneatis Amici*? // Printed in the Yeer 1649 /
[June 12] (*British Museum*: E. 559 (11).)

[Reprinted in *Somers Tracts,* vol. VII, p. 52. The Speech of Alderman Isaac Pennington has been omitted in the *Posthumous Works.*]

NOTE

*V. THE / Last Will and Testament / OF THE / Earl of Pembroke. / [1650] (*British Museum*: 1890 e. 4 (40*).)

[Reprinted in *The Poetical Works of Sir Charles Sedley*, p. 71, and in *Somers Tracts*, vol. VII, p. 89, where it is attributed to Sedley.]

*VI. A SEASONABLE / SPEECH, / *Made by* / Alderman Atkins / In the / RUMP-PARLIAMENT. // Printed in the Year, 1660. / [1659 Jan. 20] (*British Museum*: E. 1013 (15).)

[Reprinted in *Somers Tracts*, vol. VII, p. 101.]

*VII. MOLA ASINARIA: / OR, / The Unreasonable and Insupportable / BURTHEN / Now press'd upon / The Shoulders of this groaning NATION: / BY / The headless Head, and unruly Rulers, that usurp upon / the Liberties and Priviledges of the oppressed People. / Held forth in a / REMONSTRANCE / To all those that have yet sound and impartial / Ears to hear, and duly weighed in the Scales of / Equity and Justice. // By *William Prynne*, Bencher of / *Lincolns-Inne*. // Wherein is demonstrated, / What Slavery the Nation must subject it self / to, by allowing the lawfulness and usurped / Authority of the pretended / LONG PARLIAMENT / Now unlawfully and violently held at WESTMINSTER // *Jusq; datum Sceleri* // Printed at *London*, in the Year MDCLVIX. / [May 31] (*British Museum*: E. 985 (4).)

[This parody is ascribed to Butler by Anthony Wood. Cf. *Athenæ Oxonienses*, ed. P. Bliss, 1813–1820, vol. III, p. 874.]

VIII. THE / ACTS / AND / MONUMENTS / Of our late / PARLIAMENT: / OR, / A Collection of the *Acts*, *Orders*, *Votes* / and *Resolves* that hath passed in / the HOUSE. // BY / *J. Canne* Intelligencer Generall. // LONDON: / Printed according to Order, 1659. / [October 19] pp. 8 in 4°. (*British Museum*: E. 1000 (19).)

[Reprinted in 1710 by "J. Baker at the Black Boy in Paternoster Row" and attributed to "S. Butler, author of Hudibras." See also *Harleian Miscellany*, London, 1810, vol. VII, p. 53; and *Somers Tracts*, vol. VII, p. 98.]

NOTE

IX. A / CONTINUATION / OF THE / ACTS / AND / MONUMENTS / Of our late / PARLIAMENT: / OR, / A Collection of the *Acts, Orders, Votes,* / and *Resolves* that hath passed in / the HOUSE. // From *June* 9 to *July* 7. 1659. // By *J. Canne* Intelligencer Generall. // LONDON: / Printed according to Order, 1659. / [Nov. 14] pp. 9 in 4°. (*British Museum*: E. 1010 (4).)

*X. THE / Assembly-man; // Written in the Year 1647. // ... // LONDON: / Printed for Richard Marriot, and are to be sold at his / shop under St. *Dunstans* Church in *Fleet-street,* / 166⅔. / (*British Museum*: 4103 e. 12.)

[The address to the Reader is signed J.[ohn] B.[irkenhead], and there is no doubt that Sir John Birkenhead is the actual author. In the *Posthumous Works* the pamphlet is given as "written by Mr. Samuel Butler, and Sir John Birkenhead, in the Year 1647." It was reprinted in *Somers Tracts*, vol. v, p. 487.]

*XI. A / PROPOSAL / HUMBLY OFFERED / For the / FARMING / OF / Liberty of CONSCIENCE. // Printed in the Year 1663. / [By B. G.] pp. 16 in 4°. (*Library of Congress*: Miscellaneous Pamphlets, vol. 127.)

[Reprinted in "Wit and Loyalty / REVIV'D / In a Collection of some smart / SATYRS / In Verse and Prose on the late TIMES. // By Mr. *Abraham Cowley,* / Sir *J. Berkenhead* / and the Ingenious Author of *Hudibras*, etc.... // LONDON Printed, for W. Davis. 1682/." and in *Somers Tracts*, vol. VII, p. 494.]

XII. HUDIBRAS / on Calamy's Imprisonment, and Wild's Poetry / *To the Bishops.* / [1663.] ss. (*British Museum*: Lutt. II, 28.)

[Reprinted in "Miscellaneous WORKS, / Written by His Grace, / GEORGE, Late Duke of *Buckingham*... / Also *State-Poems* on the Late Times, by / *Mr. Dryden,* / *Sir George Etherege,* / *Sir Fleetwood Sheppard,* / *Mr. Butler,* Author of *Hudibras*,... // LONDON: ... / 1704. /" under this title: "*An* EPISTLE *to the* Bishops, / *on* Calamy's *being released from* / *Imprisonment, and* Wild's *Poetry.*/" It is also to be found in the common-place book of George Sacheverell (*British Museum*: Add. MSS. 28758 f. 106), who does not give the name of the author. We may be certain, however, that Butler is not responsible for it, if one is to believe the following lines in the poem entitled: "*On the ANSWER*

NOTE

to | *Dr. WILDS POEM;* | *UPON* | *Mr.* CALAMY'S *Imprisonment.* || LONDON, Printed for R. B. 1663 |" addressed to the small poet who had made use of the name of Hudibras:

> But oh! bold Bard with brazen Front,
> That durst put Hudebras upon't!
> And filch away that Authors Fame,
> By counterfeiting of his Name;
> Not as Bathillus did, who put
> His Name to Virgill's Verses; but
> With far more impudence and shame,
> Thou hast to thine put Virgill's name....]

*XIII. Comprehensive, tho' Compendious / CHAR-ACTER / of the late / ROYAL MARTYR / King CHARLES I *of ever-blessed Memory.* / DELINEATED by One of the most EMINENT DIVINES / OF THE / CHURCH of ENGLAND. // HIS / EPITAPH. / By the Celebrated / Mr BUTLER. / [1670?] ss. fol. (*British Museum*: 105 f. 17 (30).)

*XIV. A New Ballad of King *Edward* and *Jane Shore.* / To the Tune of, *St George for England and the Dragon.* / London, 1671 / ss. with woodcuts. (*British Museum*: Rox. III. 258.)

*XV. The GENEVA BALLAD. To the Tune of 48 / LONDON / Printed for *Henry Brome*, at the Gun at the West-end of St. *Pauls* Churchyard. 1674. / ss. fol. (*British Museum*: Lutt. II. 87.)

[Reprinted in W. Walker Wilkin's *Political Ballads of the Seventeenth and Eighteenth Centuries*, p. 202. This popular ballad, often reprinted, was not composed by S. Butler, as is shown by another one entitled *An Answer to the Geneva Ballad*, where the real author is alluded to as follows:

> Of all the *Drolsters* in the Town
> Of *Popish*, or of *Hobbian* Race,
> None draggs *Religion* up and down,
> Or doth the Gospel such *disgrace*
> As *Spruce* with Coat *Canonical*
> Whose *Conscience* eccho's *have at all*,
> Would a *fat Benefice* but fall.

NOTE

He whom the Ruder *Witts* adore
And count his vile *Lampoons* Divine;
Who *Pimps* in Rhime for the *Old Whore*
And fain would patch up *Dagon's* shrine,
  A sacred *Proteus* one that can
  Blend *Gospel* with the *Alchoran*
  And takes *Texts* from *Leviathan*...etc.]

XVI. CYDIPPE / Her Answer to / ACONTIUS. /
By Mr. BUTLER. /

[In "OVID'S / EPISTLES, / TRANSLATED / BY / SEVERAL
HANDS. // ... LONDON, // ...1680. /" Reprinted in R. B.
Johnson's edition of *S. Butler's Poetical Works*. "ACONTIUS / TO /
CYDIPPE" had been translated by Mr R. Duke. Dryden wrote the
preface to the volume and probably obtained the translations from their
respective authors, as to whom therefore he is not likely to have been
mistaken.]

*XVII. *Mercurius Menippeus*. // THE / LOYAL
SATYRIST, / OR, / HUDIBRAS / IN / PROSE. / Written
by an unknown Hand in the / time of the late Rebellion. But
never / till now published. // *Si Cato reddatur, Cæsareanus erit.*
// LONDON, / Printed for *Jos. Hindmarsh* at the Sign of the
Black Bull / near the Royal Exchange in *Cornhill.* 1682. /
pp. 24 in 4º. (*British Museum*: 8122 d. 72.)

[Reprinted in the *Posthumous Works*, IV, pp. 142–159, with the
addition of doggerel lines, under the title of *Memoirs of the Years* 1649
and 50. See also *Somers Tracts*, vol. VII, p. 66, where this pamphlet is
attributed either to Butler or to Birkenhead. Internal evidence shows
that Butler did write it. Cf. Textual Notes.]

*XVIII. THE / MORNING'S SALUTATION: / Or,
a Friendly / CONFERENCE / Between a / PURITAN
PREACHER / AND A / Family of his Flock, / Upon the
30th of January. // By Mr. Butler. / Author of HUDIBRAS,
// DUBLIN: / Re-Printed by *Daniel Thompson* in *Cole's
Alley*, / *Castle-Street.* 1714 / pp. 8, in 8º. (*British Museum*:
11631 a. 63 (11).)

XIX. A SATYR against MARRIAGE. / By Mr.
Butler, the Author of *Hudibras.*

NOTE

[In "THE / GROVE; / OR, A / COLLECTION / OF / ORI-
GINAL POEMS, / TRANSLATIONS, &c. / BY W. WALSH,
Esq; / Dr. J. DONNE. / Mr. DRYDEN, Mr. HALL of Hereford,
/ The Lady E. M; / Mr. BUTLER, / Author of *Hudibras*... //
LONDON: 1721. /" This satire is not that of the *Genuine Remains*,
nor the piece entitled *Against Matrimony* in the *Posthumous Works*.]

Of the preceding compositions, the Reader will find
in this book only those that may be ascribed to Butler
upon sufficient grounds. It does not mean that all the
pieces left out are spurious. But I have made it my rule
not to include anything that does not present positive
evidence of, or trustworthy witnesses to, its genuineness. Therefore, few pieces of Group B—three altogether—have been added to the genuine remains of
Group A: *Cydippe her Answer to Acontius* and *Mola
Asinaria*... have been accepted as Butler's on the
authority of Dryden and Anthony Wood; whereas,
in *Mercurius Menippeus*...*Memoirs of the Years* 1649
and 50, a careful comparison of the text with other
productions of Butler, particularly with his hitherto
unpublished MSS., has enabled me to point out similes,
expressions and ideas, so distinctively peculiar to the poet
that his being the author of the pamphlet is no longer
a matter of doubt. It may be safely asserted, however,
that no valuable composition has been omitted. The
so-called *Posthumous Works* are nothing but an attempt to pass under the name of Butler, together with
several of his works previously printed, worthless verse
and prose falsely attributed to him, anonymous tracts
issued in the time of the civil wars, and even compositions that were known to have been written by James
Shirley, John Birkenhead and others. That the same
publishers did not scruple to print the *Speeches* and the
Last Will and Testament of the Earl of Pembroke both
in Sedley's *Poetical Works* and in Butler's *Posthumous*

NOTE

Works, shows well enough what credit they deserved; and the author of *Hudibras* will lose nothing by the fact that I have discarded so much nonsense and ribaldry sold by crafty tradesmen under his name.

A large portion of this volume is reprinted from Thyer's *Genuine Remains* or from original editions. The remaining pieces are printed, many of them for the first time, from the Butler MSS. in the British Museum. The arrangement of the book in *Formal Satires*, *Pindaric Odes*, etc. . . . is entirely my own. Misprints in the *Genuine Remains* and other editions have been corrected. Except when obviously eccentric, Butler's spelling and "pointing" have been retained. But, when the lack of punctuation would have unnecessarily puzzled the Reader, it has been silently supplied.

RENÉ LAMAR

Pau,
30 *August* 1927

CONTENTS

CONTENTS

CONTENTS

ERRATA

p. 107, l. 14 *for* Sat *read* Sate
p. 110, l. 48 *for* Bearde *read* Beard
p. 110, l. 50 *for* near *read* neare
p. 110, l. 53 *for* brass *read* bras
p. 111, l. 86 *for* at Top *read* at the Top
p. 154, l. 6 *for* Is *read* Are

FORMAL SATIRES

THE
ELEPHANT
IN THE
MOON

A LEARN'D *Society* of late,
The Glory of a foreign State,
Agreed, upon a Summer's *Night*,
To search the *Moon* by her own Light;
To take an Invent'ry of all   5
Her real Estate, and personal;
And make an accurate Survey
Of all her Lands, and how they lay,
As true as that of *Ireland*, where
The sly Surveyors stole a Shire;   10
T' observe her Country, how 'twas planted,
With what sh' abounded most, or wanted;
And make the proper'st Observations,
For settling of new Plantations,
If the *Society* should incline   15
T' attempt so glorious a Design.
    This was the Purpose of their meeting,
For which they chose a Time as fitting;
When, at the Full, her radiant Light
And Influence too were at their Height.   20
And now the lofty Tube, the Scale
With which they Heav'n itself assail,
Was mounted full against the *Moon*;
And all stood ready to fall on,
Impatient who should have the Honour   25
To plant an Ensign first upon her.
    When one, who for his deep Belief
Was *Virtuoso* then in chief,
Approv'd the most profound, and wise
To solve Impossibilities,   30
Advancing gravely, to apply
To th' optick glass his judging Eye,

Cry'd—Strange!—then reinforc'd his Sight
Against the *Moon* with all his Might,
And bent his penetrating Brow, 35
As if he meant to gaze her through.
When all the rest began t' admire,
And, like a Train, from him took Fire,
Surpriz'd with Wonder, beforehand,
At what they did not understand, 40
Cry'd out, impatient to know what
The Matter was, they wonder'd at.

Quoth he,—Th' Inhabitants o' th' *Moon*,
Who, when the *Sun* shines hot at Noon,
Do live in Cellars underground 45
Of eight Miles deep, and eighty round,
(In which at once they fortify
Against the Sun, and th' Enemy)
Which they count Towns and Cities there,
Because their People's civiler 50
Than those rude Peasants, that are found
To live upon the upper Ground,
Call'd *Privolvans*, with whom they are
Perpetually in open War;
And now both Armies, highly 'nrag'd; 55
Are in a bloody Fight engag'd;
And many fall on both Sides slain,
As by the Glass 'tis clear, and plain.
Look quickly then, that every one
May see the Fight, before 'tis done. 60

With that a great Philosopher,
Admir'd, and famous far and near,
As one of singular Invention,
But universal Comprehension,
Apply'd one Eye, and half a Nose 65
Unto the optick Engine close.
For he had lately undertook
To prove, and publish in a Book,
That Men, whose nat'ral Eyes are out,
May, by more pow'rful Art, be brought 70
To see with th' empty Holes as plain,
As if their Eyes were in again:

And, if they chanc'd to fail of those,
To make an Optick of a Nose;
As clearly it may, by those that wear   75
But Spectacles, be made appear;
By which both Senses being united
Does render them much better sighted.
This great Man, having fix'd both Sights
To view the formidable Fights,   80
Observ'd his best, and then cry'd out,—
The Battle's desperately fought:
The gallant *Subvolvani* rally,
And from their Trenches make a Sally
Upon the stubborn Enemy,   85
Who now begin to rout and fly.
   These silly ranting *Privolvans*,
Have every Summer their Campains,
And muster, like the warlike Sons
Of *Raw-head* and of *Bloody-bones*,   90
As numerous as *Soland* Geese
I' th' Islands of the *Orcades*,
Couragiously to make a Stand,
And face their Neighbours Hand to Hand;
Until the long'd-for Winter's come,   95
And then return in Triumph home,
And spend the rest o' th' Year in Lies,
And vapouring of their Victories.
From th' old *Arcadians* th' are believ'd
To be, before the *Moon*, deriv'd;   100
And when her Orb was new created,
To people her, were thence translated.
For, as th' *Arcadians* were reputed
Of all the *Grecians* the most stupid,
Whom nothing in the World could bring   105
To civil Life, but fiddling,
They still retain the antique Course,
And Custom of their Ancestors;
And always sing, and fiddle to
Things of the greatest Weight they do.   110
   While thus the learn'd Man entertains
Th' Assembly with the *Privolvans*;

Another of as great Renown,
And solid Judgment in the *Moon*;
That understood her various Soils,   115
And which produc'd best *Genet-moyles*;
And in the Register of Fame
Had enter'd his long-living Name;
After he had por'd long and hard
In th' Engine, gave a Start, and star'd—   120
    Quoth he,—A stranger Sight appears
Than e're was seen in all the Spheres,
A Wonder more unparallel'd,
Than ever mortal Tube beheld.
An *Elephant* from one of those   125
Two mighty Armies is broke loose,
And with the Horrour of the Fight
Appears amaz'd, and in a Fright;
Look quickly, lest the Sight of us
Should cause the startled Beast t' imboss.   130
It is a large one, far more great
Than e'er was bred in *Afric* yet;
From which we boldly may infer,
The *Moon* is much the fruitfuller.
And, since the mighty *Pyrrhus* brought   135
Those living Castles first, 'tis thought,
Against the *Romans*, in the Field,
It may an Argument be held
(*Arcadia* being but a Piece,
As his Dominions were, of *Greece*,)   140
To prove, what this illustrious Person
Has made so noble a Discourse on;
And amply satisfy'd us all
Of th' *Privolvans* Original.
That *Elephants* are in the *Moon*,   145
Though we had now discover'd none,
Is easily made manifest;
Since, from the greatest to the least,
All other Stars and Constellations
Have Cattle of all sorts of Nations;   150
And Heaven, like a *Tartar*'s Horde,
With great and numerous Droves is stor'd:

And, if the *Moon* produce by Nature
A People of so vast a Stature,
'Tis consequent, she shou'd bring forth   155
Far greater Beasts too, than the Earth;
(As by the best Accounts appears
Of all our great'st Discoverers)
And, that those monstrous Creatures there
Are not such Rarities as here.   160
   Mean while the rest had had a Sight
Of all Particulars o' th' Fight;
And ev'ry Man with equal Care,
Perus'd of th' *Elephant* his Share,
Proud of his Int'rest in the Glory   165
Of so miraculous a Story:
When one, who for his Excellence
In height'ning Words and shad'wing Sense,
And magnifying all he writ
With curious microscopick Wit,   170
Was magnify'd himself no less
In home and foreign Colleges,
Began, transported with the Twang
Of his own Trillo, thus t' harangue.
   Most excellent and *virtuous* Friends,   175
This great Discovery makes amends
For all our unsuccessful Pains,
And lost Expence of Time and Brains.
For, by this sole Phænomenon,
We've gotten Ground upon the *Moon*;   180
And gain'd a Pass, to hold dispute
With all the Planets that stand out;
To carry this most *virtuous* War
Home to the Door of every Star,
And plant th' Artillery of our Tubes   185
Against their proudest Magnitudes;
To stretch our Victories beyond
Th' Extent of planetary Ground;
And fix our Engines, and our Ensigns
Upon the fixt Stars vast Dimensions,   190
(Which *Archimede*, so long ago,
Durst not presume to wish to do)

7

And prove, if they are other Suns,
As some have held Opinions;
Or Windows in the Empyreum,   195
From whence those bright Effluvias come
Like Flames of Fire (as others guess)
That shine i' the Mouths of Furnaces.
Nor is this all, we have atchiev'd,
But more, henceforth to be believ'd,   200
And have no more our best Designs,
Because they're ours, believ'd ill Signs.
T' out-throw, and stretch, and to enlarge
Shall now no more be laid t' our Charge;
Nor shall our ablest *Virtuosos*   205
Prove Arguments for Coffee-houses;
Nor those Devices, that are laid
Too truly on us, nor those made,
Hereafter gain Belief among
Our strictest Judges, right or wrong;   210
Nor shall our past Misfortunes more
Be charg'd upon the ancient Score:
No more our making old Dogs young
Make Men suspect us still i' th' Wrong;
Nor new-invented Chariots draw   215
The Boys to course us, without Law;
Nor putting Pigs t' a Bitch to nurse,
To turn 'em into Mungrel-Curs,
Make them suspect, our Sculs are brittle,
And hold too much Wit, or too little: 220
Nor shall our Speculations, whether
An Elder-stick will save the Leather
Of Schoolboy's Breeches from the Rod,
Make all we do appear as odd.
This one Discovery's enough,   225
To take all former Scandals off—
But, since the World's incredulous
Of all our Scrutinies, and us;
And with a Prejudice prevents
Our best and worst Experiments;   230
(As if th' were destin'd to miscarry,
In consort try'd, or solitary)

And since it is uncertain, when
Such Wonders will occur agen,
Let us as cautiously contrive,   235
To draw an exact Narrative
Of what we every one can swear,
Our Eyes themselves have seen appear;
That, when we publish the Account,
We all may take our Oaths upon't.   240
    This said, they all with one Consent,
Agreed to draw up th' Instrument,
And, for the gen'ral Satisfaction,
To print it in the next *Transaction*.
But, whilst the Chiefs were drawing up   245
This strange Memoir o' th' Telescope,
One, peeping in the Tube by Chance,
Beheld the *Elephant* advance,
And, from the West-side of the *Moon*,
To th' East was in a Moment gone.   250
This b'ing related gave a Stop
To what the rest were drawing up;
And every Man amaz'd anew,
How it could possibly be true,
That any Beast should run a Race   255
So monstrous, in so short a Space,
Resolv'd, howe'er, to make it good,
At least, as possible as he cou'd;
And rather his own Eyes condemn,
Than question what h' had seen with them.   260
    While all were thus resolv'd; a Man,
Of great Renown there, thus began—
'Tis strange, I grant! But who can say
What cannot be; what can, and may?
Especially at so hugely vast   265
A Distance, as this Wonder's plac't;
Where the least Error of the Sight
May show Things false, but never right:
Nor can we try them so far off,
By any sublunary Proof.   270
For who can say, that *Nature* there
Has the same Laws, she goes by here?

Nor is it like, she has infus'd
In every Species, there produc'd,
The same Efforts, she does confer   275
Upon the same Productions here:
Since those with us, of several Nations,
Have such prodigious Variations;
And she affects so much to use
Variety, in all she does.   280
Hence may b' infer'd, that, tho' I grant
We've seen i' th' *Moon* an *Elephant*,
That *Elephant* may differ so
From those upon the Earth below,
Both in his Bulk, and Force, and Speed,   285
As being of a diff'rent Breed;
That, tho' our own are but slow-pac't,
Theirs there may fly, or run as fast;
And yet be *Elephants* no less,
Than those of *Indian* Pedigrees.   290
  This said, another of great Worth,
Fam'd for his learned Works put forth,
Look'd wise, then said—All this is true,
And learnedly observ'd by you:
But there's another Reason for't,   295
That falls but very little short
Of mathematick Demonstration,
Upon an accurate Calculation,
And that is—As the *Earth* and *Moon*
Do both move contrary upon   300
Their Axes, the Rapidity
Of both their Motions cannot be,
But so prodigiously fast,
That vaster Spaces may be past,
In less Time than the *Beast* has gone,   305
Though h' had no Motion of his own;
Which we can take no Measure of,
As you have clear'd by learned Proof.
This granted, we may boldly thence
Lay claim to a nobler Inference;   310
And make this great Phænomenon
(Were there no other) serve alone,

To clear the grand Hypothesis
Of th' Motion of the *Earth* from this.
 With this they all were satisfy'd,   315
As Men are wont o' th' bias'd Side,
Applauded the profound Dispute;
And grew more gay and resolute
By having overcome all doubt,
Than if it never had fall'n out;   320
And, to compleat their Narrative,
Agreed t' insert this strange Retrieve.
 But, while they were diverted all
With wording the Memorial,
The Footboys, for Diversion too,   325
As having nothing else to do,
Seeing the *Telescope* at leisure,
Turn'd *Virtuosos* for their Pleasure;
Began to gaze upon the *Moon*,
As those they waited on, had done,   330
With Monkeys Ingenuity,
That love to practise, what they see;
When one, whose Turn it was to peep,
Saw something in the Engine creep;
And, viewing well, discover'd more,   335
Than all the Learn'd had done before.
Quoth he,—A little Thing is slunk
Into the long star-gazing Trunk;
And now is gotten down so nigh,
I have him just against mine Eye.   340
 This being overheard by one,
Who was not so far overgrown
In any virtuous Speculation,
To judge with mere Imagination,
Immediately he made a Guess   345
At solving all Appearances,
A Way far more significant,
Than all their Hints of th' *Elephant*;
And found, upon a second View,
His own Hypothesis most true;   350
For he had scarce apply'd his Eye
To th' Engine, but immediately

He found, a *Mouse* was gotten in
The hollow Tube, and shut between
The two Glass-windows in Restraint   355
Was swell'd into an *Elephant*;
And prov'd the virtuous Occasion,
Of all this learned Dissertation.
And, as a Mountain heretofore
Was great with Child, they say, and bore   360
A silly *Mouse*; this *Mouse*, as strange,
Brought forth a Mountain, in Exchange.
   Mean while, the rest in Consultation
Had penn'd the wonderful Narration;
And set their Hands, and Seals, and Wit   365
T' attest the Truth of what th' had writ;
When this accurst Phænomenon
Confounded all th' had said or done.
For 'twas no sooner hinted at,
But th' all were in a Tumult strait,   370
More furiously enrag'd by far,
Than those that in the *Moon* made War,
To find so admirable a Hint,
When they had all agreed t' have seen't,
And were engag'd to make it out,   375
Obstructed with a paultry Doubt.
When one, whose Task was to determin,
And solve th' Appearances of Vermin;
Wh' had made profound Discoveries
In Frogs, and Toads, and Rats, and Mice;   380
(Tho' not so curious, 'tis true,
As many a wise Rat-catcher knew)
After he had with Signs made Way
For something great he had to say
           —This Disquisition   385
Is, half of it, in my Discission:
For, though the *Elephant*, as *Beast*,
Belongs of Right to all the rest,
The *Mouse*, b'ing but a *Vermin*, none
Has Title to, but I alone;   390
And therefore hope, I may be heard,
In my own Province, with Regard.

It is no Wonder, w' are cry'd down,
And made the Talk of all the Town,
That rants and swears, for all our great   395
Attempts, we have done nothing yet,
If ev'ry one have Leave to doubt,
When some great Secret's half made out;
And, 'cause perhaps it is not true,
Obstruct, and ruin all we do.   400
As no great Act was ever done,
Nor ever can, with Truth alone;
If nothing else but Truth w' allow,
'Tis no great Matter what we do.
For Truth is too reserv'd, and nice,   405
T' appear in mix'd Societies;
Delights in solit'ry Abodes,
And never shews her self in Crowds;
A sullen little Thing, below
All Matters of Pretence and Show;   410
That deal in Novelty, and Change,
Not of Things true, but rare and strange,
To treat the World with what is fit,
And proper to its nat'ral Wit;
The World, that never sets Esteem   415
On what Things are, but what they seem;
And, if they be not strange and new,
Th' are ne'er the better for b'ing true.
For, what has Mankind gain'd by knowing
His little Truth, but his Undoing,   420
Which wisely was by Nature hidden,
And only for his Good forbidden?
And, therefore, with great Prudence does,
The World still strive to keep it close;
For if all secret Truths were known,   425
Who would not be once more undone?
For Truth has always Danger in't,
And here, perhaps, may cross some Hint,
We have already agreed upon,
And vainly frustrate all we've done;   430
Only to make new Work for *Stubs*,
And all the *academick* Clubs.

How much then ought we have a Care,
That no Man know above his Share;
Nor dare to understand, henceforth,   435
More than his Contribution's worth:
That those, wh' have purchas'd of the *College*
A Share, or half a Share of Knowledge,
And brought in none, but spent Repute,
Should not b' admitted to dispute;   440
Nor any Man pretend to know
More than his Dividend comes to?
For Partners have been always known
To cheat their publick Int'rest prone;
And, if we do not look to ours,   445
'Tis sure to run the self-same Course.
    This said, the whole Assembly allow'd
The Doctrine to be right, and good;
And, from the *Truth* of what th' had heard,
Resolv'd to give *Truth* no Regard,   450
But, what was for their Turn, to vouch,
And either find, or make it such:
That 'twas more noble to create
Things like Truth, out of strong Conceit,
Than, with vexatious Pains and Doubt,   455
To find, or think t' have found her out.
    This b'ing resolv'd, they, one by one,
Review'd the Tube, the *Mouse*, and *Moon*;
But still, the narrower they pry'd,
The more they were unsatisfy'd,   460
In no one Thing, they saw, agreeing;
As if th' had sev'ral Faiths of seeing.
Some swore, upon a second View,
That all th' had seen before was true,
And that they never would recant   465
One Syllable of th' *Elephant*;
Avow'd, his Snout could be no *Mouse*'s,
But a true *Elephant*'s Proboscis.
Others began to doubt, and waver,
Uncertain which o' th' two to favour;   470
And knew not whether to espouse
The Cause of th' *Elephant*, or *Mouse*.

Some held no Way so orthodox
To try it, as the *Ballot-Box*;
And, like the Nation's Patriots,   475
To find, or make, the Truth by Votes.
Others conceiv'd it much more fit
T' unmount the Tube, and open it;
And, for their private Satisfaction,
To re-examine the Transaction;   480
And after explicate the rest,
As they should find Cause for the best.
    To this, as th' only Expedient,
The whole Assembly gave Consent:
But, e're the Tube was half let down,   485
It clear'd the first Phænomenon:
For, at the End, prodigious Swarms
Of Flies, and Gnats, like Men in Arms,
Had all past Muster, by mischance,
Both for the *Sub*, and *Privolvans*.   490
This, b'ing discover'd, put them all
Into a fresh, and fiercer Brawl,
Asham'd, that Men so grave and wise
Should be chaldes'd by Gnats and Flies,
And take the feeble Insects' Swarms   495
For mighty Troops of Men at Arms;
As vain as those, who when the *Moon*
Bright in a crystal River shone,
Threw Casting-nets as su'tly at her,
To catch and pull her out o' th' Water.   500
But, when they had unscrew'd the Glass,
To find out, where th' Impostor was,
And saw the *Mouse*, that by mishap,
Had made the *Telescope* a Trap,
Amaz'd, confounded, and afflicted,   505
To be so openly convicted,
Immediately they get them gone,
With this Discovery alone:
That those who greedily pursue
Things wonderful, instead of true;   510
That in their Speculations chuse
To make Discoveries strange News;

And Nat'ral History a Gazette
Of Tales stupendous, and far-fet;
Hold no Truth worthy to be known,   515
That is not huge, and over-grown,
And explicate Appearances,
Not as they are, but as they please,
In vain strive Nature to suborn,
And, for their Pains, are paid with Scorn.   520

THE
ELEPHANT
IN THE
MOON
IN
LONG VERSE

A VIRTUOUS, learn'd *Society*, of late
The Pride and Glory of a foreign State,
Made an Agreement on a Summer's Night,
To search the *Moon* at full, by her own Light;
To take a perfect Invent'ry of all   5
Her real Fortunes, or her Personal;
And make a geometrical Survey,
Of all her Lands, and how her Country lay,
As accurate as that of *Ireland*, where
The sly *Surveyor* 's said t' have sunk a Shire: 10
T' observe her Country's Climate, how 'twas planted,
And what she most abounded with, or wanted;
And draw Maps of her prop'rest Situations
For settling, and erecting new Plantations;
If ever the *Society* should incline   15
T' attempt so great, and glorious a Design:
A Task in vain, unless the German Kepler
Had found out a Discovery to people her,
And stock her Country with Inhabitants
Of military Men, and Elephants.   20
For th' Ancients only took her for a Piece
Of red-hot Iron, as big as Peloponese,
Till he appear'd; for which, some write, she sent
Upon his Tribe as strange a Punishment.

This was the only Purpose of their Meeting,   25
For which they chose a Time, and Place most fitting;
When, at the *Full*, her equal Shares of Light
And *Influence* were at their greatest Height.

And now the lofty *Telescope*, the *Scale*,
By which they venture *Heav'n* itself t' assail,   30
Was rais'd, and planted full against the *Moon*;
And all the rest stood ready to fall on,
Impatient, who should bear away the Honour
To plant an Ensign, first of all, upon her.

　　When one, who, for his solid deep Belief,   35
Was chosen *Virtuoso* then in chief;
Had been approv'd the most profound, and wise
At solving all Impossibilities,
With Gravity advancing, to apply
To th' *Optick-glass* his penetrating Eye,   40
Cry'd out,—O strange!—then reinforc'd his Sight
Against the *Moon* with all his Art and Might;
And bent the Muscles of his pensive Brow,
As if he meant to stare and gaze her thro',
While all the rest began as much t' admire,   45
And, like a Powder-train, from him took Fire,
Surpriz'd with dull Amazement beforehand
At what they would, but could not understand;
And grew impatient to discover, what
The Matter was, they so much wonder'd at.   50

　　Quoth he,—The old Inhabitants o' th' *Moon*,
Who, when the *Sun* shines hottest about Noon,
Are wont to live in Cellars under ground,
Of eight Miles deep, and more than eighty round,
In which at once they use to fortify   55
Against the Sun-beams, and the Enemy,
Are counted Borough-Towns and Cities there,
Because th' Inhabitants are civiler
Than those rude Country Peasants, that are found,
Like Mountaineers, to live on th' upper Ground,   60
Nam'd *Privolvans*, with whom the others are
Perpetually in state of open War.
And now both Armies, mortally enrag'd,
Are in a fierce and bloody Fight engag'd;
And many fall on both Sides kill'd and slain,   65
As by the *Telescope* 'tis clear and plain.
Look in it quickly then, that every one
May see his Share before the Battle's done.

At this, a famous great Philosopher,
Admir'd, and celebrated, far and near   70
As one of wond'rous singular Invention,
And equal universal Comprehension,
By which he had compos'd a Pedlars Jargon,
For all the World to learn, and use in Bargain,
An universal canting Idiom,   75
To understand the swinging Pendulum,
And to communicate, in all Designs,
With th' Eastern *Virtuoso-Mandarines,*
Apply'd an optick Nerve, and half a Nose
To th' End and Center of the Engine, close: 80
For he had, very lately, undertook
To vindicate, and publish in a Book,
That Men, whose native Eyes are blind, or out,
May by more admirable Art, be brought
To see with empty Holes as well and plain,   85
As if their Eyes had been put in again.

This great Man, therefore, having fix'd his Sight
T' observe the bloody formidable Fight,
Consider'd carefully, and then cry'd out,
—'Tis true, the Battle's desperately fought;   90
The gallant *Subvolvans* begin to rally,
And from their Trenches valiantly sally,
To fall upon the stubborn Enemy,
Who fearfully begin to rout and fly.

These paltry domineering *Privolvans*   95
Have, every Summer-season, their Campains;
And muster, like the military Sons
Of *Raw-head*, and victorious *Bloody-bones*,
As great and numerous as *Soland-geese*
I' th' *Summer-Islands* of the *Orcades*,   100
Couragiously to make a dreadful Stand
And boldly face their Neighbour's Hand to Hand.
Until the peaceful, long'd-for Winter's come;
And then disband, and march in Triumph Home;
And spend the rest of all the Year in Lies,   105
And vap'ring of their unknown Victories.

From th' old *Arcadians* they have been believ'd
To be, before the *Moon* herself, deriv'd;

And, when her Orb was first of all created,
To be from thence, to people her, translated.   110
For as those People had been long reputed
Of all the *Peloponesians*, the most stupid,
Whom nothing in the World could ever bring
T' endure the civil Life, but Fiddling;
They ever since retain the antique Course,   115
And native Frenzy of their Ancestors;
And always use to sing, and fiddle to
Things of the most important Weight they do.
　　While thus the *Virtuoso* entertains
The whole Assembly with the *Privolvans*,   120
Another Sophist, but of less Renown,
Though longer Observation of the Moon;
That understood the Diff'rence of her Soils,
And which produc'd the fairest *Gennet-moyles*;
But for an unpaid Weekly Shillings Pension,   125
Had fin'd for Wit, and Judgment, and Invention;
Who, after poring tedious and hard
In th' *Optic-Engine*, gave a Start, and star'd,
And thus began—A stranger Sight appears,
Than ever yet was seen in all the *Spheres*;   130
A greater Wonder, more unparallel'd
Than ever mortal *Tube*, or *Eye* beheld;
A mighty *Elephant* from one of those
Two fighting Armies is at length broke loose,
And with the desp'rate Horror of the Fight   135
Appears amaz'd, and in a dreadful Fright:
Look quickly, lest the only Sight of us
Should cause the startled Creature to imboss.
It is a large one, and appears more great
Than ever was produc'd in *Africk* yet;   140
From which we confidently may infer,
The *Moon* appears to be the fruitfuller.
And since, of old, the mighty *Pyrrhus* brought
Those living Castles first of all, 'tis thought,
Against the *Roman* Army in the Field;   145
It may a valid Argument, be held,
(The same *Arcadia* being but a Piece,
As his Dominions were, of antique *Greece*)

To vindicate, what this illustrious Person
Has made so learn'd, and noble a Discourse on; 150
And giv'n us ample Satisfaction all
Of th' ancient *Privolvans* Original.
  That *Elephants* are really in the Moon,
Although our Fortune had discover'd none,
Is easily made plain, and manifest, 155
Since from the greatest *Orbs*, down to the least,
All other Globes of *Stars* and *Constellations*
Have Cattle in 'em of all Sorts and Nations;
And *Heav'n* like a *northern Tartar*'s Horde,
With numerous and mighty Droves is stor'd. 160
And, if the *Moon* can but produce by Nature
A People of so large, and vast a Stature,
'Tis more than probable, she should bring forth
A greater Breed of Beasts too, than the *Earth*;
As by the best Accounts we have, appears 165
Of all our crediblest Discoverers;
And, that those vast and monstrous Creatures there
Are not such far-fet Rarities, as here.
  Meanwhile th'*Assembly* now had had a Sight
Of all distinct Particulars o' th' Fight; 170
And every Man with Diligence and Care
Perus'd, and view'd of th'*Elephant* his Share,
Proud of his equal Int'rest in the Glory
Of so stupendous, and renown'd a Story,
When one, who for his Fame and Excellence 175
In heightening of *Words*, and shadowing *Sense*,
And magnifying all, he ever writ,
With delicate, and *Microscopick* Wit,
Had long been magnify'd himself no less
In foreign and domestick *Colleges*, 180
Began at last (transported with the Twang
Of his own Elocution) thus t' harangue.
  Most *virtuous*, and incomparable Friends,
This great Discov'ry fully makes amends
For all our former unsuccessful Pains, 185
And lost Expences of our Time and Brains:
For, by this admirable Phænomenon,
We now have gotten Ground upon the *Moon*;

And gain'd a Pass t' engage, and hold Dispute
With all the other *Planets*, that stand out;   190
And carry on this brave and *virtuous* War
Home to the Door of th' obstinatest Star;
And plant th' Artillery of our *Optick Tubes*
Against the proudest of their Magnitudes;
To stretch our future Victories beyond   195
The uttermost of Planetary Ground;
And plant our warlike Engines, and our Ensigns
Upon the fix'd *Stars* spacious Dimensions,
To prove, if they are other *Suns*, or not,
As some *Philosophers* have wisely thought,   200
Or only Windows in the *Empyreum*,
Through which those bright Effluvias use to come;
Which *Archimede*, so many Years ago,
Durst never venture, but to wish to know.
Nor is this all, that we have now atchiev'd,   205
But greater Things!—Henceforth to be believ'd,
And have no more our best, and worst Designs,
Because th' are ours, suspected for ill Signs.
T' out-throw, and magnify, and to enlarge
Shall, henceforth, be no more laid to our charge;   210
Nor shall our best and ablest *Virtuosos*
Prove Arguments again for *Coffee-Houses*;
Nor little Stories gain Belief among
Our criticalest Judges right or wrong:
Nor shall our new-invented Chariots draw   215
The Boys to course us in 'em, without Law:
Make Chips of Elms produce the largest Trees,
Or sowing Saw-dust furnish Nurseries:
No more our heading Darts (a swinging one!)
With Butter only harden'd in the Sun;   220
Or Men that use to whistle loud enough
To be heard by others plainly five Miles off,
Cause all the rest, we own, and have avow'd
To be believ'd as desperately loud.
Nor shall our future Speculations, whether   225
An Elder-stick will render all the Leather
Of School-boys Breeches proof against the Rod,
Make all we undertake appear as odd.

This one Discovery will prove enough
To take all past and future Scandals off: 230
But since the *World* is so incredulous
Of all our usual Scrutinies and us,
And with a constant Prejudice prevents
Our best, as well as worst Experiments,
As if they were all destin'd to miscarry,   235
As well in Concert try'd, as solitary;
And that th'*Assembly* is uncertain, when
Such great Discoveries will occur agen,
'Tis reas'nable, we should, at least, contrive
To draw up as exact a Narrative   240
Of that which every Man of us can swear,
Our Eyes themselves have plainly seen appear;
That when 'tis fit to publish the *Account*,
We all may take our several Oaths upon't.

    This said, the whole *Assembly* gave Consent   245
To drawing up th' authentick Instrument;
And, for the *Nation*'s general Satisfaction,
To print, and own it in their next *Transaction*.
But while their ablest Men were drawing up
The wonderful Memoir o' th' *Telescope*,   250
A Member peeping in the *Tube*, by chance,
Beheld the *Elephant* begin t' advance,
That from the West-by-North Side of the *Moon*
To th' East-by-South was in a Moment gone.
This, being related, gave a sudden Stop   255
To all, their *Grandees* had been drawing up;
And every Person was amaz'd a-new,
How such a strange Surprizal should be true;
Or any Beast perform so great a Race,
So swift and rapid, in so short a Space,   260
Resolv'd, as suddenly, to make it good,
Or render all as fairly as they cou'd;
And rather choose their own Eyes to condemn,
Than question, what they had beheld with them.

    While every one was thus resolv'd, a *Man*   265
Of great Esteem, and Credit, thus began;
—'Tis strange, I grant! but who, alas! can say,
What cannot be, or justly can, and may,

Especially at so hugely wide and vast
A Distance, as this Miracle is plac't,   270
Where the least Error of the *Glass*, or Sight,
May render Things amiss, but never right?
Nor can we try them, when th' are so far off,
By any equal sublunary Proof:
For who can justify, that *Nature* there   275
Is ty'd to the same Laws, she acts by here?
Nor is it probable, she has infus'd
Int' every Species, in the *Moon* produc'd,
The same Efforts, she uses to confer
Upon the very same Productions here: 280
Since those upon the *Earth*, of several Nations,
Are found t' have such prodigious Variations;
And she affects so constantly to use
Variety in every Thing she does.

    From hence may be inferr'd, that, tho' I grant,   285
We have beheld i' th' *Moon* an *Elephant*,
That *Elephant* may chance to differ so
From those with us, upon the *Earth* below,
Both in his Bulk, as well as Force and Speed,
As b'ing of a different Kind and Breed,   290
That, tho' 'tis true, our own are but slow pac'd,
Their's there, perhaps, may fly, or run as fast,
And yet be very *Elephants*, no less
Than those deriv'd from *Indian* Families.

    This said, another *Member* of great Worth,   295
Fam'd for the learned Works he had put forth,
In which the mannerly, and modest Author
Quotes the Right Worshipful, his elder Brother,
Look'd wise a while, then said—All this is true,
And very learnedly observ'd by you;   300
But there's another nobler Reason for't,
That rightly 'bserv'd, will fall, but little, short
Of solid *mathematick* Demonstration,
Upon a full, and perfect Calculation;
And that is only this—As th' *Earth* and *Moon*   305
Do constantly move contrary upon
Their several Axes, the Rapidity
Of both their Motions cannot fail to be

So violent, and naturally fast,
That larger Distances may well be past,   310
In less Time than the *Elephant* has gone,
Altho' he had no Motion of his own,
Which we on *Earth* can take no Measure of;
As you have made it evident by Proof.
This granted, we may confidently hence   315
Claim Title to another Inference;
And make this wonderful *Phænomenon*
(Were there no other) serve our Turn alone,
To vindicate the grand Hypothesis,
And prove the Motion of the *Earth* from this.   320
     This said, th' *Assembly* now was satisfy'd,
As Men are soon upon the biast Side;
With great Applause receiv'd th' admir'd Dispute,
And grew more gay, and brisk, and resolute,
By having (right or wrong) remov'd all doubt,   325
Than if th' Occasion never had fall'n out;
Resolving to compleat their Narrative,
And punctually insert this strange Retrieve.
     But, while their *Grandees* were diverted all
With nicely wording the *Memorial*,   330
The *Footboys* for their own Diversion too,
As having nothing, now, at all to do,
And when they saw the *Telescope* at leisure,
Turn'd *Virtuosos*, only for their Pleasure;
With Drills and Monkeys Ingenuity,   335
That take Delight to practice all they see,
Began to stare and gaze upon the *Moon*,
As those they waited on, before had done.
When one, whose Turn it was, by chance to peep,
Saw something in the lofty *Engine* creep;   340
And, viewing carefully, discover'd more
Than all their *Masters* hit upon before.
Quoth he,—O strange! a little Thing is slunk
On th' Inside of the long star-gazing *Trunk*;
And now is gotten down so low and nigh,   345
I have him here directly 'gainst mine Eye.
     This chancing to be overheard by one,
Who was not, yet, so hugely overgrown

In any *philosophic* Observation,
As to conclude with mere Imagination;   350
And yet he made immediately a Guess
At fully solving all Appearances,
A plainer Way, and more significant,
Than all their Hints had prov'd o' th' *Elephant*;
And quickly found upon a second View,   355
His own Conjecture, probably, most true:
For he no sooner had apply'd his Eye
To th' *optick Engine*, but immediately
He found a small *Field-Mouse* was gotten in
The hollow *Telescope*, and shut between   360
The two Glass-Windows, closely in restraint,
Was magnify'd into an *Elephant*;
And prov'd the happy *virtuous* Occasion
Of all this deep and learned Dissertation.
And as a mighty *Mountain* heretofore,   365
Is said t' have been begot with Child, and bore
A silly *Mouse*, this captive *Mouse*, as strange,
Produc'd another *Mountain* in Exchange.
    Mean while the *Grandees*, long in Consultation,
Had finish'd the miraculous *Narration*,   370
And set their Hands, and Seals, and Sense, and Wit
T' attest and vouch the Truth of all th' had writ;
When this unfortunate *Phænomenon*
Confounded all they had declar'd and done.
For 'twas no sooner told, and hinted at,   375
But all the rest were in a Tumult straight,
More hot and furiously inrag'd, by far,
Than both the *Hosts*, that in the *Moon* made War,
To find so rare and admirable a Hint,
When they had all agreed, and sworn t' have seen't, 380
And had engag'd themselves to make it out,
Obstructed with a wretched paultry Doubt.
    When one, whose only Task was to determin,
And solve the worst Appearances of *Vermin*;
Who oft' had made profound Discoveries   385
In *Frogs* and *Toads*, as well as *Rats* and *Mice*
(Though not so curious and exact, 'tis true
As many an exquisite *Rat-catcher* knew)

After he had a while with Signs made way
For something pertinent, he had to say,   390
At last prevail'd—Quoth he—this Disquisition
Is, the one half of it, in my *Discission*:
For tho', 'tis true, the *Elephant*, as *Beast*,
Belongs, of nat'ral Right, to all the Rest;
The *Mouse*, that's but a paultry *Vermin*, none   395
Can claim a Title to, but I alone;
And therefore humbly hope, I may be heard
In my own Province freely, with Regard.

    It is no Wonder, that we are cry'd down,
And made the Table-talk of all the *Town*,   400
That Rants and Vapours still, for all our great
Designs and Projects, we've done nothing yet,
If every one have Liberty to doubt,
When some great Secret's more than half made out,
Because, perhaps, it will not hold out true,   405
And put a stop to all w' Attempt to do.
As no great Action ever has been done,
Nor ever's like to be by *Truth alone*,
If nothing else but only *Truth* w' allow
'Tis no great Matter what w' intend to do;   410
For Truth *is always too reserv'd and chaste,*
T' indure to be by all the Town embrac'd,
A solitary Anchorite *that dwells,*
Retir'd from all the World in obscure Cells,
Disdains all great *Assemblys*, and defies   415
The Press and Crowd of mix'd *Societies*,
That use to deal in Novelty and Change,
Not of things true, but great, and rare, and strange;
To entertain the *World* with what is fit
And proper for its Genius, and its Wit;   420
The *World*, that's never found to set Esteem
On what Things are, but what th' appear, and seem;
And, if they are not wonderful and new,
Th' are ne're the better for their being true.
For what is Truth, or Knowledge, but a Kind   425
Of Wantonness and Luxury o' th' Mind,
A Greediness and Gluttony o' the Brain,
That longs to eat forbidden Fruit again,

And grows more desp'rate, like the worst Diseases,
Upon the nobler Part (the Mind) it seizes?   430
And what has *Mankind* ever gain'd by knowing
His little Truths, unless his own Undoing,
That prudently by *Nature* had been hidden,
And, only for his greater Good, forbidden?
And therefore with as great Discretion does   435
The *World* endeavour still to keep it close:
For if the Secrets of all Truths were known,
Who would not, once more, be as much undone?
For *Truth* is never without Danger in't,
As here it has depriv'd us of a Hint,   440
The whole *Assembly* had agreed upon,
And utterly defeated all w' had done,
By giving Foot-Boys leave to interpose
And disappoint, whatever we propose,
For nothing but to cut out Work for *Stubs*,   445
And all the busy *Academick* Clubs,
For which they have deserv'd to run the Risks
Of Elder-sticks, and penitential Frisks.
How much then ought we have a special Care,
That none presume to know above his Share,   450
Nor take upon him t' understand, henceforth,
More than his *weekly Contribution*'s worth:
That all those, that have purchas'd of the *College*
A half, or but a quarter Share of *Knowlege*,
And brought none in themselves, but spent Repute, 455
Should never be admitted to dispute;
Nor any *Member* undertake to know
More than his equal *Dividend* comes to?
For *Partners* have perpetually been known,
T' impose upon their publick Int'rest, prone;   460
And, if we have not greater Care of ours,
It will be sure to run the self-same Course.
    This said, the whole *Society* allow'd
The Doctrine to be orthodox, and good;
And from th' apparent *Truth* of what th' had heard, 465
Resolv'd, henceforth, to give *Truth* no Regard,
But what was for their Interests to vouch,
And either find it out, or make it such:

That 'twas more admirable to create
Inventions like *Truth* out of strong Conceit,   470
Than with vexatious Study, Pains, and Doubt,
To find, or but suppose t' have found it out.
　This b'ing resolv'd, th' Assembly, one by one,
Review'd the *Tube*, the *Elephant*, and *Moon*;
But still the more, and curiouser they pry'd,   475
They but became the more unsatisfy'd,
In no one Thing, they gaz'd upon, agreeing,
As if th' had different Principles of seeing.
Some boldly swore, upon a second View,
That all they had beheld before, was true,   480
And damn'd themselves, they never would recant
One syllable, th' had seen, of th' *Elephant*;
Avow'd his Shape and Snout could be no *Mouse*'s,
But a true nat'ral *Elephant*'s Proboscis.
Others began to doubt as much, and waver,   485
Uncertain which to disallow, or favour;
Until they had as many cross Resolves,
As Irishmen *that have been turn'd to Wolves,*
And grew distracted, whether to espouse
The Party of the *Elephant*, or *Mouse*.   490
　Some held, there was no Way so orthodox,
As to refer it to the *Ballot-Box*;
And, like some other Nation's *Patriots*,
To find it out, or make the *Truth*, by Votes.
Others were of Opinion, 'twas more fit   495
T' unmount the *Telescope*, and open it,
And for their own, and all Men's Satisfaction
To search, and re-examin the *Transaction*;
And afterward to explicate the rest,
As they should see Occasion for the best.   500
　To this, at length, as th' only *Expedient*,
The whole *Assembly* freely gave Consent:
But, 'ere the *optic Tube* was half let down,
Their own Eyes clear'd the first *Phænomenon*:
For, at the upper End, prodigious Swarms   505
Of busy *Flies* and *Gnats*, like Men in Arms,
Had all past Muster in the *Glass* by chance,
For both the *Peri-* and the *Subvolvans*.

This b'ing discover'd, once more put them all
Into a worse, and desperater Brawl,   510
Surpriz'd with Shame, that *Men so grave and wise*
Should be trepann'd by *paultry Gnats and Flies*;
And to mistake the feeble *Insects* swarms
For Squadrons, and Reserves of Men in Arms:
As politick as those, who, when the *Moon*   515
As bright and glorious in a River shone,
Threw Casting-nets, with equal Cunning at her
To catch her with, and pull her out o' th' Water.

But when at last, they had unscrew'd the Glass,
To find out where the sly Impostor was,   520
And saw 'twas but a *Mouse*, that by mishap
Had catch'd himself, *and them*, in th' *optick Trap*,
Amaz'd, with Shame confounded, and afflicted
To find themselves so openly convicted,
Immediately made haste to get them gone,   525
With none, but this Discovery alone:

That *learned Men*, who greedily pursue
Things, that are rather wonderful than true,
And, in their nicest Speculations, choose
To make their own Discoveries strange News,   530
And Nat'ral Hist'ry rather a Gazette
Of Rarities stupendous, and far-fet;
Believe no Truths are worthy to be known,
That are not strongly vast, and overgrown;
And strive to explicate Appearances,   535
Not as they're probable, but as they please,

In vain endeavour *Nature* to suborn,
And, for their Pains, are justly paid with *Scorn*.

SATYR UPON THE ROYAL SOCIETY

A LEARNED Man, whom once a Week
   A hundred *Virtuoso's* seek,
And like an Oracle apply to,
T' ask Questions, and admire, and lye to,
Who entertain'd them all of Course   5
(As Men take Wives for better or worse)
And past them all for Men of Parts,
Though some but Sceptics in their Hearts:
For when they're cast into a Lump,
Their Talents equally must jump;   10
As Metals mixt, the rich and base
Do both at equal Values pass.
   With these the ord'nary Debate
Was after News, and Things of State,
Which Way the dreadful *Comet* went   15
In sixty-four, and what it meant?
What Nations yet are to bewail
The Operation of its Tail;
Or whether *France*, or *Holland* yet,
Or *Germany* be in its Debt?   20
What Wars and Plagues in *Christendom*
Have happened since, and what to come?
What *Kings* are dead, how many *Queens*
And *Princesses* are poison'd since;
And who shall next of all by Turn   25
Make Courts wear black, and Tradesmen mourn?
What Parties next of Foot, or Horse
Will rout, or routed be of Course?
What *German* Marches, and Retreats
Will furnish the next Month's *Gazettes*?   30
What pestilent Contagion next,
And what Part of the World infects?
What dreadful *Meteor*, and where
Shall in the Heavens next appear;
And when again shall lay Embargo   35
Upon the Admiral, the good Ship *Argo*?

FORMAL SATIRES

Why *Currents* turn in Seas of Ice
Some thrice a Day, and some but twice;
And why the *Tides* at Night and Noon
Court, like *Caligula*, the Moon?   40
What is the nat'ral Cause why *Fish*,
That always drink, do never piss;
Or whether in their Home the Deep
By Night or Day they ever sleep?
If *Grass* be green, or *Snow* be white,   45
But only as they take the Light?
Whether Possessions of the *Devil*,
Or mere Temptations do most evil?
What is't, that makes all *Fountains* still
Within the Earth to run up Hill;   50
But on the Outside down again,
As if th' Attempt had been in vain?
Or what's the strange magnetic Cause,
The *Steel* or *Loadstone*'s drawn, or draws,
The Star, the Needle, which the Stone   55
Has only been but touch'd upon?
Whether the North-Star's Influence
With both does hold Intelligence;
(For red-hot Ir'n, held tow'rds the Pole,
Turns of it self to't, when 'tis cool)   60
Or whether Male and Female screws
In th' Ir'n and Stone th' Effect produce?
What makes the Body of the *Sun*,
That such a rapid Course does run,
To draw no Tail behind through th'Air,   65
As *Comets* do, when they appear,
Which other *Planets* cannot do,
Because they do not burn, but glow?
Whether the *Moon* be Sea, or Land,
Or Charcoal, or a quench'd Firebrand;   70
Or if the dark Holes that appear,
Are only Pores, not Cities there?
Whether the *Atmosphere* turn round,
And keep a just Pace with the Ground;
Or loiter lazily behind,   75
And clog the Air with Gusts of Wind?

Or whether *Crescents in the Wane*
(For so an Author had it plain)
Do burn quite out, or wear away
Their Snuffs upon the Edge of Day?   80
Whether the *Sea* increase, or waste,
And, if it do, how long 'twill last;
Or if the *Sun* approaches near
The Earth, how soon it will be there?
   These were their learned Speculations   85
And all their constant Occupations;
To measure *Wind*, and weigh the *Air*,
And turn a *Circle* to a *Square*;
To make a *Powder of the Sun*,
By which all Doctors should b' undone   90
To find the *North-west* Passage out,
Although the farthest Way about;
If Chymists from a *Rose*'s Ashes
Can raise the *Rose* itself in Glasses;
Whether the Line of *Incidence*   95
Rise from the Object, or the Sense?
To stew th' *Elixir* in a Bath
Of Hope, Credulity, and Faith;
To explicate by subtle Hints
The Grain of *Diamonds* and *Flints*,   100
And in the Braying of an *Ass*
Find out the Treble and the Base;
If *Mares* neigh *alto*, and a *Cow*
A double *Diapason* low.

*   *   *   *   *

SATYR UPON THE WEAKNESS
AND MISERY OF MAN

WHO would believe, that wicked *Earth*,
  Where *Nature* only brings us forth,
To be found guilty, and forgiven,
Should be a Nursery for *Heaven*;
When all, we can expect to do,   5
Will not pay half the Debt we owe,
And yet more desperately dare,
As if that wretched Trifle were
Too much for the eternal Pow'rs,
Our great and mighty Creditors,   10
Not only slight what they enjoin,
But pay it in adulterate Coin?
We only in their Mercy trust,
To be more wicked and unjust:
All our *Devotions*, *Vows*, and *Pray'rs*   15
Are our own Interest, not theirs:
Our *Off'rings*, when we come t' adore,
But begging Presents, to get more:
The purest Business of our *Zeal*
Is but to err, by meaning well,   20
And make that Meaning do more harm,
Than our worst Deeds, that are less warm:
For the most wretched and perverse
Does not believe himself, he errs.
  Our holy'st Actions have been   25
Th' Effects of Wickedness and Sin;
Religious Houses made Compounders
For th' horrid Actions of the *Founders*;
Steeples, that totter'd in the Air,
By *Letchers* sin'd into Repair;   30
As if we had retain'd no Sign,
Nor Character of the divine
And heav'nly Part of human Nature,
But only the coarse earthy Matter.
Our universal Inclination   35
Tends to the worst of our Creation,

As if the *Stars* conspir'd t' imprint
In our whole Species, by Instinct,
A fatal Brand, and Signature
Of nothing else, but the Impure.   40
The best of all our Actions tend
To the preposterousest End,
And, like to *Mungrels*, we're inclin'd
To take most to th' ignobler Kind;
Or *Monsters*, that have always least   45
Of th' human Parent, not the Beast.
Hence 'tis we've no Regard at all
Of our best half Original;
But, when they differ, still assert
The Int'rest of th' ignobler Part;   50
Spend all the Time we have upon
The vain Capriches of the one,
But grudge to spare one Hour, to know
What to the better Part we owe.
As in all compound Substances   55
The greater still devours the less;
So, being born and bred up near
Our earthy gross Relations here,
Far from the ancient nobler Place
Of all our high paternal Race,   60
We now degenerate, and grow
As barbarous, and mean, and low,
As modern *Grecians* are, and worse,
To their brave nobler Ancestors.
Yet, as no Barbarousness beside   65
Is half so barbarous as Pride,
Nor any prouder Insolence
Than that, which has the least Pretence,
We are so wretched, to profess
A Glory in our Wretchedness;   70
To vapour sillily, and rant
Of our own Misery, and Want,
And grow vain-glorious on a Score,
We ought much rather to deplore,
Who, the first Moment of our Lives,   75
Are but condemn'd, and giv'n Reprieves;

And our great'st Grace is not to know,
When we shall pay 'em back, nor how,
Begotten with a vain Caprich,
And live as vainly to that Pitch.   80
    Our *Pains* are real Things, and all
Our *Pleasures* but fantastical;
Diseases of their own Accord,
But *Cures* come difficult and hard;
Our noblest *Piles*, and stateliest *Rooms*   85
Are but Out-houses to our *Tombs*;
Cities, though e're so great and brave,
But mere Ware-houses to the *Grave*;
Our *Bravery*'s but a vain Disguise,
To hide us from the World's dull Eyes,   90
The Remedy of a Defect,
With which our Nakedness is deckt;
Yet makes us swell with Pride, and boast,
As if w' had gain'd by being lost.
    All this is nothing to the Evils,   95
Which *Men*, and their confed'rate *Devils*
Inflict, to aggravate the Curse
On their own hated Kind, much worse;
As if by *Nature* th' had been serv'd
More gently, than their Fate deserv'd,   100
Take pains (in Justice) to invent,
And study their own Punishment;
That, as their *Crimes* should greater grow,
So might their own *Inflictions* too.
Hence bloody *Wars* at first began,   105
The artificial *Plague* of Man,
That from his own Invention rise,
To scourge his own Iniquities;
That if the *Heav'ns* should chance to spare
Supplies of constant poison'd Air,   110
They might not, with unfit Delay,
For lingering Destruction stay;
Nor seek Recruits of *Death* so far,
But plague themselves with *Blood* and *War*.
    And if these fail, there is no good,   115
Kind *Nature* ere on Man bestow'd,

But he can easily divert
To his own Misery and Hurt;
Make that, which *Heaven* meant to bless
Th' ungrateful World with, gentle *Peace*   120
With *Luxury* and *Excess*, as fast
As *War* and *Desolation*, waste;
Promote Mortality, and kill,
As fast as Arms, by sitting still;
Like *Earthquakes* slay without a Blow,   125
And only moving overthrow;
Make *Law* and *Equity* as dear,
As *Plunder* and *Free-quarter* were,
And fierce Encountres at the *Bar*
Undo as fast, as those in *War*;   130
Enrich *Bawds*, *Whores*, and *Usurers*,
Pimps, *Scriv'ners*, *silenc't Ministers*,
That get Estates by being undone
For *tender Conscience*, and have none;
Like those, that with their Credit drive   135
A Trade without a Stock, and thrive;
Advance Men in the *Church* and *State*
For being of the meanest Rate,
Rais'd for their *double-guil'd* deserts,
Before *Integrity* and *Parts*;   140
Produce more grievious Complaints
For *Plenty*, than before for *Wants*,
And make a *rich* and fruitful Year
A greater Grievance, than a *dear*;
Make Jests of greater Dangers far,   145
Than those they trembl'd at in *War*;
Till, unawares, they've laid a Train
To blow the *Publick* up again;
Rally with *Horror*, and in Sport
Rebellion and Destruction court,   150
And make *Fanatics*, in Despight
Of all their *Madness*, reason right,
And vouch to all they have foreshown,
As other *Monsters* oft have done.
Although from *Truth* and *Sense* as far,   155
As all their other *Maggots* are:

For Things said false, and never meant,
Do oft prove true by accident.
    That *Wealth*, that bounteous *Fortune* sends
As presents to her dearest Friends,   160
Is oft laid out upon a Purchase
Of two Yards long in *Parish Churches*;
And those too happy Men that bought it,
Had liv'd, and happier too, without it.
For what does vast *Wealth* bring, but *Cheat*,   165
Law, *Luxury*, *Disease*, and *Debt*,
Pain, *Pleasure*, *Discontent*, and *Sport*
An easy-troubled Life, and short?
    But all these *Plagues* are nothing near
Those far more cruel and severe,   170
Unhappy Man takes Pains to find,
T' inflict himself upon his *Mind*;
And out of his own Bowels spins
A Rack and Torture for his Sins:
Torments himself, in vain, to know   175
That most, which he can never do;
And the more strictly 'tis denied,
The more he is unsatisfied;
Is busy in finding *Scruples* out,
To languish in eternal *Doubt*,   180
Sees *Spectres* in the Dark, and *Ghosts*,
And starts, as Horses do at Posts;
And, when his Eyes assist him least,
Discerns such subtle Objects best:
On hypothetic *Dreams* and *Visions*   185
Grounds everlasting Disquisitions,
And raises endless Controversies
On vulgar *Theorems* and *Hearsays*:
Grows positive and confident
In Things so far beyond th' Extent   190
Of human Sense, he does not know,
Whether they be at all, or no;
And doubts as much in Things, that are
As plainly evident, and clear:
Disdains all useful Sense, and plain,   195
T' apply to th' Intricate and Vain;

And cracks his Brains in plodding on
That, which is never to be known;
To pose himself with Subtleties,
And hold no other Knowledge wise;   200
Although, the subtler all Things are,
They're but to *nothing* the more near:
And the less Weight they can sustain,
The more he still lays on in vain;
And hangs his *Soul* upon as nice   205
And subtle *Curiosities*,
As one of that vast Multitude,
That on a Needle's Point have stood:
Weighs *right* and *wrong*, and *true* and *false*
Upon as nice and subtle *Scales*,   210
As those that turn upon a Plane
With th' hundredth Part of half a Grain;
And still the subt[i]ler they move,
The sooner false and useless prove.
So *Man*, that thinks to force and strain   215
Beyond its natural Sphere his *Brain*,
In vain torments it on the Rack,
And, for improving, sets it back;
Is ign'rant of his own Extent,
And that to which his Aims are bent,   220
Is lost in both, and breaks his *Blade*
Upon the *Anvil*, where 'twas made:
For as *Abortions* cost more Pain
Than *vig'rous Births*; so all the vain
And weak Productions of Man's Wit,   225
That aim at Purposes unfit,
Require more Drudgery, and worse
Than those of strong and lively Force.

SATYR UPON THE LICENTIOUS
AGE OF CHARLES THE 2D

'TIS a strange *Age* we've liv'd in, and a lewd
    As 'ere the *Sun* in all his Travels view'd;
An *Age* as vile, as ever *Justice* urg'd,
Like a fantastic *Letcher*, to be scourg'd:
Nor has it scap'd, and yet has only learn'd,   5
The more 'tis plagu'd to be the less concern'd.
Twice have we seen two dreadful Judgments rage,
Enough to fright the stubborn'st-hearted Age;
The one to mow vast Crowds of People down,
The other (as then needless) half the *Town*;   10
And two as mighty Miracles restore,
What both had ruin'd and destroy'd before:
In all as unconcern'd, as if th' had been
But Pastimes for Diversion to be seen.
Or, like the Plagues of *Ægypt*, meant a Curse,   15
Not to reclaim us, but to make us worse.
    Twice have Men turn'd the *World* (that silly Blockhead!)
The wrong Side outward, like a *Jugler*'s Pocket,
Shook out Hypocrisy, as fast and loose,
As e're the *Dev'l* could teach, or Sinners use,   20
And on the other Side at once put in
As impotent Iniquity, and Sin.
As Sculls, that have been crack'd, are often found
Upon the wrong Side to receive the Wound,
And, like Tobacco-pipes at one End hit,   25
To break at th' other still that's opposite:
So Men, who one Extravagance would shun,
Into the contrary Extreme have run;
And all the Difference is, that, as the first
Provokes the other Freak to prove the worst;   30
So, in return, that strives to render less
The last Delusion, with its own Excess;
And, like two unskill'd *Gamesters*, use one Way
With bungling t' help out one another's Play.
For those, who heretofore sought private Holes,   35
Securely in the Dark to damn their Souls,

Wore Vizards of Hypocrisy, to steal
And slink away, in Masquerade, to *Hell*,
Now bring their Crimes into the open *Sun*,
For all Mankind to gaze their worst upon,   40
As *Eagles* try their Young against his Rays,
To prove, if they're of generous Breed, or base;
Call *Heav'n* and *Earth* to witness, how they've aim'd
With all their utmost Vigour to be damn'd,
And by their own Examples, in the View   45
Of all the World, striv'd to damn others too:
On all Occasions sought to be as civil,
As possible they cou'd, t' his Grace the *Devil*,
To give him unnecessary Trouble,
Nor in small Matters use a Friend so noble,   50
But with their constant Practice done their best
T' improve, and propagate his Interest.
For Men have now made Vice so great an Art,
The matter of Fact's become the slightest Part;
And the debauched'st Actions they can do,   55
Mere Trifles, to the Circumstance and Show.
For 'tis not what they do, that's now the Sin,
But what they lewdly affect, and glory in;
As if prepost'rously they would profess
A forc'd Hypocrisy of Wickedness: 60
And Affectation, that makes good Things bad,
Must make affected Shame accurst, and mad;
For Vices for themselves may find Excuse,
But never for their Complement, and Shews.
That, if there ever were a Mystery   65
Of moral secular Iniquity,
And that the *Churches* may not lose their Due
By being encroach'd upon, 'tis now, and new.
For Men are now as scrupulous, and nice,
And tender-conscienc'd of low paltry Vice,   70
Disdain as proudly to be thought to have
To do in any Mischief, but the brave,
As the most scrup'lous *Zealot* of late Times
T' appear in any, but the horrid'st Crimes;
Have as precise and strict Punctilios   75
Now to appear, as then to make no Shows;

And steer the World by disagreeing Force
Of diff'rent Customs 'gainst her nat'ral Course.
So pow'rful's ill Example to incroach,
And Nature, spite of all her Laws, debauch;   80
Example, that imperious *Dictator*
Of all that's good, or bad to human Nature;
By which the World's corrupted, and reclaim'd,
Hopes to be sav'd, and studies to be damn'd;
That reconciles all Contrarieties,   85
Makes Wisdom Foolishness, and Folly wise,
Imposes on Divinity, and sets
Her Seal alike on Truths, and Counterfeits;
Alters all Characters of Virtue and Vice,
And passes one for th' other in Disguise,   90
Makes all Things, as it pleases, understood,
The Good receiv'd for Bad, and Bad for Good;
That slyly counter-changes Wrong and Right,
Like white in Fields of black, and black in white,
As if the Laws of Nature had been made   95
Of purpose, only to be disobey'd;
Or Man had lost his mighty Interest,
By having been distinguish'd from a Beast;
And had no other Way but Sin and Vice,
To be restor'd again to *Paradise*.   100
    How copious is our Language lately grown,
To make blaspheming Wit, and a Jargon?
And yet how expressive and significant,
In *Damme* at once to curse, and swear, and rant?
As if no way exprest Mens Souls so well,   105
As damning of them to the Pit of *Hell*;
Nor any Asseveration were so civil,
As mortgaging Salvation to the *Devil*;
Or that his Name did add a charming Grace,
And Blasphemy a Purity to our Phrase.   110
For what can any Language more enrich,
Than to pay Souls for vitiating Speech;
When the great'st Tyrant in the World made those
But lick their Words out, that abus'd his Prose?
What trivial Punishments did then protect   115
To publick Censure a profound Respect,

When the most shameful Penance and severe,
That could b' inflicted on a *Cavaliere*
For infamous Debauch'ry, was no worse,
Than but to be degraded from his Horse,   120
And have his Livery of Oats and Hay,
Instead of cutting Spurs off, ta'n away?
They held no Torture then so great as Shame,
And, that to slay was less than to defame;
For just so much regard, as Men express   125
To th' censure of the Publick, more or less,
The same will be return'd to them again,
In Shame or Reputation, to a Grain:
And, how perverse so'ere the World appears,
'Tis just to all the Bad it sees, and hears.   130
And, for that Virtue, strives to be allow'd
For all the Injuries, it does the Good.

    How silly were their *Sages* heretofore
To fright their *Heroes* with a *Syren-Whore?*
Make 'em believe a *Water-witch* with Charms   135
Could sink their Men of War, as easy as Storms,
And turn their Mariners, that heard them sing,
Into Land-porpusses, and Cod, and Ling;
To terrify those mighty Champions,
As we do Children now with *Bloody-bones*;   140
Until the subtlest of their Conjurors
Seal'd up the Labels to his Soul, his Ears,
And ty'd his deafen'd Sailors (while he pass'd
The dreadful Lady's Lodgings) to the Mast,
And rather venture drowning, than to wrong   145
The Sea-pugs chaste Ears with a bawdy Song:
To b' out of Countenance, and like an Ass,
Not pledge the Lady *Circe* one Beer-glass;
Unmannerly refuse her Treat and Wine,
For fear of being turn'd into a Swine;   150
When one of our heroic Advent'rers now
Would drink her down, and turn her int' a Sow.

    So simple were those Times, when a grave *Sage*
Could with an Oldwive's-Tale instruct the Age;
Teach Virtue, more fantastick Ways and nice,   155
Than ours will now endure t' improve in vice,

Made a dull Sentence, and a moral Fable
Do more, than all our Holdings-forth are able;
A forc'd obscure Mythology convince,
Beyond our worst Inflictions upon Sins.   160
When an old Proverb, or an End of Verse
Could more, than all our Penal Laws, coerce;
And keep Men honester than all our Furies
Of Jailors, Judges, Constables, and Juries;
Who were converted then with an old Saying,   165
Better than all our Preaching now, and praying.
What Fops had these been, had they liv'd with us,
Where the best Reason's made ridiculous;
And all the plain and sober Things we say,
By Raillery are put beside their Play?   170
For Men are grown above all Knowledge now,
And, what they're ignorant of, disdain to know;
Engross Truth (like *Fanatics*) underhand,
And boldly judge, before they understand,
The self-same Courses equally advance   175
In spiritual, and carnal Ignorance;
And, by the same Degrees of Confidence,
Become impregnable against all Sense;
For, as they outgrew *Ordinances* then,
So would they now *Morality* agen.   180
Tho' Drudgery and Knowledge are of Kin,
And both descended from one Parent Sin;
And therefore seldom have been known to part,
In tracing out the Ways of Truth, and Art;
Yet they have *North-west* Passages to steer   185
A short Way to it, without Pains or Care.
For, as implicit Faith is far more stiff,
Than that which understands its own Belief;
So those, that think, and do but think, they know,
Are far more obstinate, than those that do,   190
And more averse, than if they'd ne'er been taught
A wrong Way, to a right one to be brought;
Take Boldness upon Credit beforehand,
And grow too positive to understand;
Believe themselves as knowing, and as famous,   195
As if their Gifts had gotten a *Mandamus*,

A *Bill of Store* to take up a Degree,
With all the Learning to it, Custom-free;
And look as big, for what they bought at Court,
As if they'd done their Exercises for't.   200

SATYR UPON GAMING

W HAT Fool would trouble *Fortune* more,
    When she has been too kind before;
Or tempt her to take back again,
What she had thrown away in vain;
By idly vent'ring her good Graces 5
To be dispos'd of by *Alms-Aces*;
Or settling it in Trust to Uses,
Out of his Pow'r, on *Trays* and *Deuses*:
To put it to the Chance, and try,
I' th' Ballot of a Box and Dye, 10
Whether his Money be his own,
And lose it, if he be o'erthrown;
As if he were betray'd, and set
By his own Stars to every Cheat,
Or wretchedly condemn'd by Fate 15
To throw Dice for his own Estate;
As Mutineers, by fatal Doom,
Do for their Lives upon a Drum?
For what less Influence can produce,
So great a Monster as a *Chowse*; 20
Or any two-leg'd Thing possess
With such a brutish Sottishness?
Unless those tutelary Stars,
Intrusted by *Astrologers*
To have the Charge of Man, combin'd 25
To use him in the self-same Kind;
As those, that help'd them to the Trust,
Are wont to deal with others just.
For to become so sadly dull
And stupid, as *to fine* for Gull, 30
(Not, as in Cities, to b' excus'd,
But to be judg'd fit to be us'd)
That, whoso'ere can draw it in
Is sure inevitably t' win;
And, with a curs'd half-witted Fate, 35
To grow more dully desperate,

UPON GAMING

The more 'tis made a common Prey,
And cheated foppishly at Play,
Is their Condition: Fate betrays
To Folly first, and then destroys.   40
For what, but Miracles, can serve
So great a Madness to preserve;
As his, that ventures Goods and Chattles
(Where there's no Quarter giv'n) in Battles,
And fights with Money-bags as bold,   45
As Men with Sand-bags did of old:
Puts Lands, and Tenements, and Stocks
Into a paultry Jugler's Box;
And, like an Alderman of *Gotham*,
Embarketh in so vile a Bottom: 50
Engages blind and senseless Hap
'Gainst *High*, and *Low*, and *Slur* and *Knap*,
(As *Tartars* with a Man of Straw
Encounter Lions, Hand to Paw)
With those, that never venture more,   55
Than they had safely 'nsur'd before;
Who, when they knock the Box and shake,
Do, like the *Indian* Rattle-Snake,
But strive to ruin, and destroy
Those that mistake it for fair Play: 60
That have their *Fulhams* at command,
Brought up to do their Feats at hand;
That understand their Calls and Knocks,
And how to place themselves i' th' Box;
Can tell the Oddses of all Games,   65
And when to answer to their Names;
And, when he conjures them t' appear,
Like Imps are ready every where;
When to play foul, and when run fair
(Out of Design) upon the Square;   70
And let the greedy Cully win,
Only to draw him further in:
While those, with which he idly plays,
Have no regard to what he says;
Although he *Jernie* and blaspheme,   75
When they miscarry, Heav'n and them;

47

And damn his Soul, and swear, and curse,
And crucify his Saviour worse
Than those *Jew*-Troopers, that threw out,
When they were raffling for his Coat;   80
Denounce Revenge, as if they heard,
And rightly understood, and fear'd,
And would take heed another Time,
How to commit so bold a Crime;
When the poor Bones are innocent   85
Of all he did, or said or meant,
And have as little Sense almost,
As he that damns them, when h' has lost:
As if he had rely'd upon
Their Judgement, rather than his own;   90
And that it were their Fault, not his,
That manag'd them himself amiss:
And gave them ill Instructions, how
To run, as he would have them do,
And then condemns them sillily   95
For having no more Wit than he.

SATYR UPON OUR RIDICULOUS
IMITATION OF THE FRENCH

WHO would not rather get him gone
    Beyond th' intolerablest *Zone*;
Or steer his Passage through those Seas,
That burn in Flames, or those that freeze,
Than see one *Nation* go to School,   5
And learn of another, like a Fool?
To study all its Tricks and Fashions
With epidemic Affectations;
And dare to wear no Mode or Dress,
But what they, in their Wisdom, please;   10
As *Monkies* are, by being taught
To put on Gloves and Stockings, caught:
Submit to all that they devise,
As if it wore their Liveries;
Make ready and dress th' Imagination,   15
Not with the Cloaths, but with the Fashion;
And change it, to fulfil the Curse
Of *Adam*'s Fall, for new, though worse;
To make their Britches fall and rise
From middle Legs to middle Thighs,   20
The *Tropics* between which the Hose
Move always as the Fashion goes:
Sometimes wear Hats like Pyramids,
And sometimes flat like Pipkin's Lids
With broad Brims sometimes like Umbrellas,   25
And sometimes narrow as *Punchinello*'s:
In coldest Weather go unbrac't,
And close in hot, as if th' were lac't:
Sometimes with Sleeves and Bodies wide,
And sometimes straiter than a Hide: 30
Wear Peruques, and with false grey Hairs
Disguise the true ones, and their Years;
That, when they're modish, with the young
The old may seem so in the Throng:
And as some Pupils have been known,   35
In time to put their Tutors down;

So ours are often found t' have got
More Tricks, than ever they were taught:
With sly Intrigues and Artifices
Usurp their Poxes, and their Vices;   40
With Garnitures upon their Shoes,
Make good their Claim to gouty Toes;
By sudden Starts, and Shrugs, and Groans
Pretend to Aches in their Bones,
To Scabs and Botches, and lay Trains   45
To prove their Running of the Reins;
And, lest they should seem destitute
Of any Mange, that's in Repute,
And be behind hand with the Mode
Will swear to *Chrystallin* and *Node*;   50
And, that they may not lose their Right,
Make it appear how they came by't:
Disdain the Country, where th' were born,
As Bastards their own Mothers scorn;
And that which brought them forth contemn, 55
As it deserves for bearing them:
Admire whate'er they find abroad,
But nothing here, though e'er so good.
Be *Natives* wheresoe'er they come,
And only *Foreigners* at home;   60
To which th' appear so far estrang'd,
As if th' had been i' th' Cradle chang'd;
Or from beyond the Seas convey'd
By *Witches*—not born here, but laid;
Or by outlandish fathers were   65
Begotten on their Mothers here,
And therefore justly slight that Nation,
Where th' have so mungrel a Relation;
And seek out other Climates, where
They may degenerate less than here;   70
As Woodcocks, when their Plumes are grown,
Born on the Winds Wings and their own,
Forsake the Countries, where th' are hatcht,
And seek out others, to be catcht:
So they more nat'rally may please   75
And humor their own Geniuses,

Apply to all Things, which they see
With their own Fancies best agree;
No matter how ridiculous,
'Tis all one, if it be in use;   80
For nothing can be bad or good,
But as 'tis *in* or *out* of Mode;
And as the Nations are that use it,
All ought to practise, or refuse it:
T' observe their postures, move, and stand   85
As they give out the Word o' Command;
To learn the dullest of their Whims
And how to wear their very Limbs;
To turn and manage every Part,
Like *Puppets*, by their Rules of Art;   90
To shrug discreetly, act, and tread,
And politicly shake the Head,
Until the Ignorant (that guess
At all Things by th' Appearances)
To see how Art and Nature strive,   95
Believe them really alive,
And that th' are very Men, not Things
That move by *Puppet-work* and Springs;
When truly all their Feats have been
As well perform'd by *Motion-men*,   100
And the worst Drols of *Punchinellos*
Were much th' ingeniouser Fellows;
For, when they're perfect in their Lesson,
Th' Hypothesis grows out of Season,
And, all their Labour lost, they're fain   105
To learn new, and begin again:
To talk eternally and loud,
And altogether in a Crowd,
No matter what, for in the Noise
No Man minds what another says: 110
T' assume a Confidence beyond
Mankind, for solid and profound;
And still the less and less they know,
The greater Dose of that allow:
Decry all Things; for to be wise   115
Is not to know, but to despise,

And deep judicious Confidence
Has still the Odds of Wit and Sense,
And can pretend a Title to
Far greater Things than they can do: 120
T' adorn their *English* with *French* Scraps,
And give their very Language Claps;
To *Jernie* rightly, and renounce
I' th' pure and most approv'd of Tones,
And, while they idly think t' enrich,   125
Adulterate their native Speech;
For though to smatter Ends of *Greek*,
Or *Latin* be the Rhetorique
Of Pedants counted, and vain-glorious,
To smatter *French* is meritorious;   130
And to forget their Mother-Tongue,
Or purposely to speak it wrong,
A hopeful Sign of Parts and Wit,
And that th' improve and benefit;
As those, that have been taught amiss   135
In liberal Arts and Sciences,
Must all th' had learnt before in vain
Forget quite, and begin again.

SATYR UPON DRUNKENNESS

'TIS pity *Wine*, which Nature meant
  To Man in Kindness to present;
And gave him kindly to caress,
And cherish his frail Happiness,
Of equal Virtue to renew   5
His wearied Mind, and Body too,
Should (like the Cyder-tree in *Eden*,
Which only grew, to be forbidden)
No sooner come to be enjoy'd,
But th' Owner's fatally destroy'd;   10
And that, which she for Good design'd,
Becomes the Ruin of Mankind,
That for a little vain Excess
Runs out of all its Happiness,
And makes the Friend of Truth and Love   15
Their greatest Adversary prove;
T' abuse a Blessing she bestow'd
So truly essential to his Good;
To countervail his pensive Cares,
And slavish Drudgery of Affairs;   20
To teach him Judgment, Wit, and Sense,
And, more than all these, Confidence;
To pass his Times of Recreation
In choice and noble Conversation,
Catch Truth and Reason unawares,   25
As Men do Health in wholesome Airs;
(While Fools their Conversants possess
As unawares with Sottishness)
To gain Access a private Way
To Man's best Sense, by his own Key,   30
Which painful Judgers strive in vain
By any other Course t' obtain;
To pull off all Disguise, and view
Things as th' are natural, and true;
Discover *Fools* and *Knaves*, allow'd   35
For *wise* and *honest* in the Crowd;

With innocent and virtuous Sport
Make short Days long, and long Nights short,
And Mirth the only Antidote
Against Diseases, ere th' are got;   40
To save Health harmless from th' Access
Both of the Med'cine, and Disease;
Or make it help itself, secure
Against the desperat'st Fit, the Cure.
   All these sublime Prerogatives   45
Of Happiness to human Lives
He vainly throws away, and slights
For Madness, Noise, and bloody Fights;
When nothing can decide, but Swords
And Pots, the Right or Wrong of Words,   50
Like *Princes* Titles; and he's outed
The Justice of his Cause, that's routed.
   No sooner has a Charge been sounded,
With—*Son of a Whore*, and—*damn'd confounded*
And the bold Signal giv'n, the *Lye*,   55
But instantly the Bottles fly;
Where Cups and Glasses are small Shot,
And Cannon-ball a Pewter-pot.
That Blood, that's hardly in the Vein,
Is now remanded back again;   60
Tho' sprung from Wine of the same Piece,
And near a-kin, within Degrees,
Strives to commit Assassinations
On its own natural Relations;
And those Twin-spirits so kind-hearted,   65
That from their Friends so lately parted,
No sooner several Ways are gone,
But by themselves are set upon,
Surpriz'd like Brother against Brother,
And put to th' Sword by one another: 70
So much more fierce are civil Wars,
Than those between mere Foreigners;
And Man himself with Wine possest
More savage than the wildest Beast.
For Serpents, when they meet to water,   75
Lay by their Poyson and their Nature:

And fiercest Creatures, that repair,
In thirsty Desarts, to their rare
And distant River's Banks to drink,
In Love and close Alliance link,   80
And from their Mixture of strange Seeds
Produce new, never heard of Breeds,
To whom the fiercer Unicorn
Begins a large Health with his Horn;
As Cuckolds put their Antidotes,   85
When they drink Coffee, into th' Pots.
While Man, with raging Drink inflam'd,
Is far more savage and untam'd;
Supplies his Loss of Wit and Sense
With Barbarousness and Insolence;   90
Believes himself, the less he's able
The more heroic and formidable;
Lays by his Reason in his Bowls,
As *Turks* are said to do their Souls,
Until it has so often been   95
Shut out of its Lodging, and let in,
At length it never can attain
To find the right Way back again;
Drinks all his Time away, and prunes
The End of 's Life, as *Vignerons*   100
Cut short the Branches of a Vine,
To make it bear more Plenty o' Wine;
And that, which Nature did intend
T' enlarge his Life, perverts t' its End.
    So *Noah*, when he anchor'd safe on   105
The Mountain's Top, his lofty Haven,
And all the Passengers, he bore,
Were on the new World set ashore,
He made it next his chief Design
To plant, and propagate a *Vine*,   110
Which since has overwhelm'd and drown'd
Far greater Numbers, on dry Ground,
Of wretched Mankind, one by one,
Than all the *Flood* before had done.

SATYR UPON MARRIAGE

SURE Marriages were never so well fitted,
As when to Matrimony Men were committed,
Like Thieves, by Justices; and to a Wife
Bound, like to good Behaviour, during Life:
For then 'twas but a civil Contract made,   5
Between two Partners, that set up a Trade;
And if both fail'd, there was no Conscience,
Nor Faith invaded, in the strictest Sense;
No Canon of the Church, nor Vow was broke,
When Men did free their gall'd Necks from the Yoke;   10
But when they tir'd, like other horned Beasts,
Might have it taken off, and take their Rests,
Without b'ing bound in Duty to shew Cause,
Or reckon with divine, or human Laws.
    For since, what use of Matrimony has been,   15
But to make Galantry a greater Sin?
As if there were no Appetite, nor Gust,
Below Adultery, in modish Lust;
Or no Debauchery were exquisite,
Until it has attain'd its perfect Height.   20
For Men do now take Wives to nobler Ends,
Not to bear Children, but to bear 'em Friends,
Whom nothing can oblige at such a Rate,
As these endearing Offices of late.
For Men are now grown wise, and understand   25
How to improve their Crimes, as well as Land;
And if th' have Issue, make the Infants pay
Down for their own Begetting on the Day,
The Charges of the Gossiping disburse,
And pay beforehand (ere they're born) the Nurse;   30
As he that got a Monster on a Cow,
Out of Design of setting up a Show.
For why should not the Brats for all account,
As well as for the Christ'ning at the Fount,
When those that stand for them, lay down the Rate   35
O' th' Banquet and the Priest, in Spoons and Plate?

UPON MARRIAGE

The antient *Romans* made the State allow,
For getting all Men's Children above two:
Then married Men to propagate the Breed,
Had great Rewards for what they never did,   40
Were privileg'd, and highly honour'd too,
For owning what their Friends were fain to do;
For, so th' had Children, they regarded not
By whom (good Men) or how they were begot.
To borrow Wives (like Money) or to lend,   45
Was then the civil Office of a Friend,
And he, that made a Scruple in the Case,
Was held a miserable Wretch, and base;
For when th' had Children by 'em, th' honest Men
Return'd 'em to their Husbands back agen.   50
Then for th' Encouragement and Propagation
Of such a great Concernment to the Nation,
All People were so full of Complacence,
And civil Duty to the public Sense,
They had no Name t' express a Cuckold then,   55
But that which signify'd all married Men;
Nor was the Thing accounted a Disgrace,
Unless among the dirty Populace,
And no Man understands on what account
Less civil Nations after hit upon't: 60
For to be known a Cuckold can be no
Dishonour, but to him that thinks it so;
For, if he feel no Shagrin, or Remorse,
His Forehead's shot-free, and he's ne'er the worse,
For Horns (like horny *Calluses*) are found   65
To grow on Sculls, that have receiv'd a Wound,
Are crackt, and broken; not at all on those
That are invulnerate, and free from Blows.
What a brave Time had Cuckold-makers then,
When they were held the worthiest of Men,   70
The real Fathers of the Commonwealth,
That planted Colonies in *Rome* itself?
When he, that help'd his Neighbours, and begot
Most *Romans*, was the noblest Patriot.
For, if a brave Man, that preserv'd from Death   75
One Citizen, was honour'd with a Wreath;

He, that more gallantly got three or four,
In Reason must deserve a great deal more.
Then, if those glorious Worthies of old *Rome*,
That civiliz'd the World th' had overcome,   80
And taught it Laws and Learning, found this Way
The best to save their Empire from Decay;
Why should not these, that borrow all the Worth
They have from them, not take this Lesson forth,
Get Children, Friends, and Honour too, and Money   85
By prudent managing of Matrimony?
For, if 'tis honourable by all confest,
Adultery must be worshipful at least;
And these Times great, when private Men are come
Up to the Height and Politic of *Rome*.   90
All By-blows were not only free-born then,
But like *John Lilborn*, free-begotten Men;
Had equal Right and Privilege with these,
That claim by Title of the four Seas.
For being in Marri'ge born, it matters not,   95
After what Liturgy they were begot;
And if there be a Difference, they have
Th' Advantage of the Chance in proving brave,
By b'ing engender'd with more Life and Force,
Than those begotten the dull Way of Course.   100
　　The *Chinese* place all Piety and Zeal,
In serving with their Wives the Commonweal,
Fix all their Hopes of Merit, and Salvation,
Upon their Women's Supererogation,
With solemn Vows their Wives and Daughters bind,   105
Like *Eve* in Paradise, to all Mankind;
And those, that can produce the most Gallants,
Are held the pretiousest of all their Saints,
Wear Rosaries about their Necks to con
Their Exercise of Devotion on;   110
That serve them for Certificates to show,
With what vast Numbers they have had to do:
Before th' are marry'd, make a Conscience
T' omit no Duty of Incontinence;
And she, that has been oftenest prostituted,   115
Is worthy of the greatest Match reputed.

UPON MARRIAGE

But, when the conqu'ring *Tartar* went about
To root this orthodox Religion out,
They stood for Conscience, and resolv'd to dye,
Rather than change the antient Purity   120
Of that Religion, which their Ancestors,
And they had prosper'd in so many Years;
Vow'd to their Gods to sacrifice their Lives;
And dye their Daughters Martyrs, and their Wives,
Before they would commit so great a Sin   125
Against the Faith they had been bred up in.

UPON
CRITICS
Who judge of
MODERN PLAYS
Precisely by the
RULES of the ANTIENTS

WHO ever wil Regard Poetique Fury,
   When it is once found Idiot by a Jury?
And evry Peart, and Arbitrary Fool
Can all Poetique Licence over-Rule?
Assume a Barbrous Tyranny, to Handle   5
The Muses, worse then Ostro-goth, or Vandal?
Make 'em submit to verdict and Report
And stand (or Fall) to th' orders of a Court.
Much lesse, Be sentenc'd by the Arbitra[r]y
Proceedings of a witless Plagiary   10
That forge's old Records, and Ordinances
Against the Right and Property of Fancys
More False, and Nice, then weighing of the weather
To th' Hundredth Atom, of the lightest Feather,
Or measuring of Aire upon Pernassus   15
With Cilinders of Torricellian Glasses;
Reduce all Tragedy by Rules of Art
Back, to its Antique Theater, a Cart,
And make 'em hence forth keep the beaten Roades
Of Reverend Choruses, and Episodes;   20
Reforme and Regulate a Puppet-Play
According to the tru and antient way:
That not an Actor shal Presume to Squeek
Unless he hav a Licence for't, in Greek;
Nor Whittington Henceforward, sel his Cat in   25
Plaine vulgar English, without Mewing Latin:
No Pudding shalbe sufferd to be witty
Unles it be in Order to Raise Pitty;

UPON CRITICS

Nor Devil in the Puppet-play, b' allowd
To Rore and Spit fire, but to fright the Crowd,   30
Unless some God, or Dev'l chance t' have Piques
Against an Antient Family of Greeks;
Others may have Leave to tremble, and take warning,
How such a Fatal Progeny th' are Born in.
For none but such for Tragedy are fitted   35
That have been Ruind only to be Pittyd;
And only those held Proper to Deterre
Wh' have had th' Il Luck, against their wils to erre.
Whence only such as are of Midling Sizes
Between Morality and venial vices   40
Are Qualifyd to be Destroyd by Fate
For other Mortals to take warning at.
    As if the Antique Laws of Tragedy
Did with our own Municipall agree
And servd like Cobwebs but t' insnare the weake   45
And give Diversion to the Great to break;
To make a lesse Delinquent to be brought
To Answer for a Greater Persons Fault
And suffer all the worst, the worst Approver
Can, to excuse, and save himself, Discover.   50
    No longer shal Dramatiques be confind
To draw tru Images, of al Mankinde,
To Punish in Effigie Criminals,
Reprieve the Innocent, and hang the False;
But a Club-Law [to] execute, and kill,   55
For nothing, whom so ere they Please, at will:
To terrify Spectators from committing
The Crimes, they did, and sufferd for, unwitting.
    These are the Reformations of the Stage,
Like other Reformations of the Age: 60
On Purpose to Destroy all wit and sense
As th' other did all Law, and Conscience.
No better then the Laws of British Plays
Confirmd in th' Antient good King Howels Days
Who made a Gen'ral Councel Regulate   65
Mens catching women by the—you know what,
And set down in the Rubrick, at what time
It should be counted Legal, when a Crime;

Declare when 'twas, and when 'twas not a sin
And on what days it went out, or came in.   70
    An English Poet should be tryd b' his Peres
And not by Pedants, and Philosophers
Incompetent to Judge Poetique Fury,
As Butchers are forbid to b' of a Jury;
Beside the most Intollerable wrong   75
To try their Matter in a Forrain Tongue
By Forrain Jury men, like Sophocles
Or Tales falser then Euripides;
When not an English Native dares appear
To be a witnes for the Prisoner,   80
When all the Laws they use t' Arraigne, and try
The Innocent and wrongd Delinquent by
Were made b' a Forraine Laweyer and his Pupils
To put an End to all Poetique Scruples,
And by th' Advice of Virtuosi-Tuscans   85
Determind al the Doubts of Socks and Buskins;
Gave Judgment on all Past and Future Plays,
As is Apparent by Speronys Case,
Which Lope Vega first began to steale,
And after him the French Filou Corniele;   90
And since our English Plagiarys Nim
And steal their farfet Criticismes, from him,
And, by an Action falsly layd of Trover,
The Lumber, for their Proper Goods Recover;
Enough to furnish al the Lewd Impeachers   95
Of witty Beumonts Poetry, and Fletchers,
Who, for a few Misprisions of wit,
Are chargd by those, who ten times worse commit;
And for Misjudging some unhappy scenes
Are censurd for't, with more unlucky sense;   100
When all their worst miscarriages Delight
And please more then the Best, that Pedants write.

SATYR UPON PLAGIARIES

WHY should the World be so averse
　　To *Plagiary* Privateers,
That all Mens Sense and Fancy seize,
And make free Prize of what they please?
As if, because they huff and swell,　　　5
Like Pilferers full of what they steal,
Others might equal Pow'r assume,
To pay 'em with as hard a Doom;
To shut them up, like Beasts in Pounds,
For breaking into others Grounds;　　　10
Mark 'em with Characters and Brands,
Like other Forgers of Mens Hands;
And in Effigie hand and draw
The poor Delinquents by *Club-Law*;
When no Inditement justly lies,　　　15
But where the Theft will bear a Price.

　For though *Wit* never can be learn'd
It may b' assum'd and own'd, and earn'd;
And, like our noblest Fruits, improv'd,
By b'ing transplanted and remov'd:　　　20
And as it bears no certain Rate,
Nor pays one Peny to the *State*,
With which it turns no more t' account
Than *Virtue*, *Faith*, and *Merit*'s wont;
Is neither Moveable, nor Rent,　　　25
Nor Chattel, Goods, nor Tenement;
Nor was it ever pass'd b' Entail,
Nor settled upon Heirs Male;
Or if it were, like ill-got Land,
Did never fall t' a second Hand;　　　30
So 'tis no more to be engross'd,
Than Sun-shine, or the Air inclos'd;
Or to Propriety confin'd,
Than th' uncontrol'd and scatter'd Wind.

　For why should that which Nature meant　35
To owe its Being to its Vent;

That has no Value of its own,
But as it is divulg'd and known;
Is perishable and destroy'd,
As long as it lies unenjoy'd,   40
Be scanted of that lib'ral Use,
Which all Mankind is free to choose,
And idly hoarded, where 'twas bred,
Instead of being dispers'd and spread?
And the more lavish and profuse,   45
'Tis of the nobler general Use;
As Riots, though supply'd by Stealth,
Are wholesome to the *Commonwealth*;
And Men spend freelier what they win,
Than what th' have freely coming in.   50
    The World's as full of curious Wit,
Which those, that father, never writ,
As 'tis of Bastards, which the Sot
And Cuckold owns, that ne'er begot;
Yet pass as well, as if the one   55
And th' other By-blow were their own.
For why should he that's impotent
To judge, and fancy, and invent,
For that Impediment be stopt
To own, and challenge, and adopt,   60
At least th' expos'd, and fatherless
Poor Orphans of the Pen, and Press,
Whose Parents are obscure, or dead,
Or in far Countries born and bred.
    As none but *Kings* have Pow'r to raise   65
A Levy, which the Subject pays;
And, though they call that Tax a Loan,
Yet, when 'tis gather'd, 'tis their own:
So he, that's able to impose
A Wit-excise on Verse or Prose;   70
And, still the abler Authors are,
Can make them pay the greater Share,
Is *Prince* of Poets of his Time,
And they his Vassals, that supply him;
Can judge more justly of what he takes   75
Than any of the best he makes;

UPON PLAGIARIES

And more impartially conceive
What's fit to chuse, and what to leave.
For Men reflect more strictly upon
The sense of others, than their own;   80
And Wit, that's made of Wit and Slight,
Is richer than the plain downright:
As Salt, that's made of Salt's more fine,
Than when it first came from the Brine;
And Spirits of a nobler Nature,   85
Drawn from the dull ingredient Matter.
    Hence mighty *Virgil*'s said of old,
From Dung to have extracted Gold;
(As many a Lout and silly Clown,
By his Instructions since has done)   90
And grew more lofty by that means,
Than by his Livery Oats and Beans;
When from his Carts and Country Farms
He rose a mighty Man at Arms;
To whom th' Heroics ever since   95
Have sworn Allegiance as their *Prince*,
And faithfully have in all Times
Observ'd his Customs in their Rhimes.
    'Twas counted Learning once and Wit
To void but what some Author writ;   100
And what Men understood by rote
By as implicit Sense to quote.
Then many a magisterial Clerk
Was taught, like singing Birds i' th' Dark;
And understood as much of Things,   105
As th' ablest Blackbird what it sings;
And yet was honour'd and renown'd,
For grave, and solid, and profound.
Then why should those, who pick and choose
The best of all the best compose,   110
And join it by *Mosaic* Art,
In graceful Order, Part to Part,
To make the whole in Beauty suit,
Not Merit as compleat Repute
As those, who with less Art and Pains   115
Can do it with their native Brains,

And make the home-spun Business fit
As freely with their Mother Wit?
Since what by Nature was deny'd
By Art and Industry's supply'd,   120
Both which are more our own, and brave
Than all the Alms, that Nature gave.
For what w' acquire by Pains and Art
Is only due t' our own Desert;
While all th' Endowments she confers,   125
Are not so much our own, as hers,
That, like good Fortune, unawares
Fall not t' our Virtue, but our Shares;
And all we can pretend to merit,
We do not purchase, but inherit.   130
　　　Thus all the great'st Inventions, when
They first were found out, were so mean,
That th' Authors of them are unknown,
As little things they scorn'd to own;
Until by Men of nobler Thought   135
Th' were to their full Perfection brought.
This proves that *Wit* does but rough-hew,
Leaves *Art* to polish, and review;
And that a Wit at second Hand
Has greatest Int'rest and Command: 140
For to improve, dispose, and judge
Is nobler than t' invent, and drudge.
　　　Invention's humorous and nice,
And never at Command applies;
Disdains t' obey the proudest Wit,   145
Unless it chance to b' in the Fit;
(Like *Prophecy*, that can presage
Successes of the latest Age,
Yet is not able to tell when
It next shall prophecy agen)   150
Makes all her Suitors course and wait
Like a proud Minister of State,
And, when she's serious in some Freak,
Extravagant, and vain, and weak,
Attend her silly, lazy Pleasure,   155
Until she chance to be at leisure:

UPON PLAGIARIES

When 'tis more easy to steal Wit;
To clip, and forge, and counterfeit,
Is both the Business and Delight,
Like hunting Sports, of those that write;   160
For Thievery is but one Sort,
The Learned say, of hunting Sport.
    Hence 'tis, that some, who set up first
As raw, and wretched, and unverst;
And open'd with a Stock as poor,   165
As a healthy Beggar with one Sore;
That never writ in Prose or Verse,
But pick'd, or cut it, like a Purse;
And at the best could but commit
The *Petty-Larceny* of Wit;   170
To whom to write was to purloin,
And printing but to stamp false Coin;
Yet after long and sturdy 'ndeavours
Of being painful Wit-receivers,
With gath'ring Rags and Scraps of Wit,   175
As Paper's made, on which 'tis writ,
Have gone forth Authors, and acquir'd
The *right*—or *wrong* to be admir'd;
And arm'd with Confidence incurr'd
The Fool's good Luck, to be preferr'd.   180
    For as a Banker can dispose
Of greater Sums, he only owes,
Than he, who honestly is known
To deal in nothing but his own:
So whose'er can take up most,   185
May greatest Fame and Credit Boast.

SATYR UPON THE IMPERFECTION AND ABUSE OF HUMAN LEARNING
PART 1ST

IT is the Noblest Act of Human Reason,
To Free it selfe, from Slavish Prepossession,
Assume the Legall Right to Disingage,
From all, it had Contracted under Age:
And not its Ingenuity, and wit,   5
To all it was Imbu'd with first, submit,
Take Tru, or False, For Better, or for worse:
To Have, or t' Hold, indifferently, of Course.
    For Custom, though but Usher of the Schoole
Where Nature breede's the Body up, and Soul,   10
Usurpe's a Greater Pow'r, and Interest,
O're Man, the Heir of Reason, then Brute Beast;
That by two Different Instincts is Led,
Born to the one and by the other Bred.
And Traine's him up, with Rudiments more False   15
Then Nature do's, her Stupid Animals.
And that's one Reason, why more Care's bestowd
Upon the body, then the Soule's allow'd:
That is not found to understand, and know,
So Subtly as the Body's found to Grow.   20
    Though Children, without Study, Paines, or thought,
Are Languages, and vulgar Notions taught:
Improve their Nat'ral Talents without Care,
And Apprehend, before they are aware:
Yet as all Strangers never leave the Tones,   25
They have been usd of children to Pronounce,
So most Mens Reason never can outgrow
The Discipline, it first Receiv'd to know
But render words, they first began to con,
The End of all that's after to be known;   30
And set the Helps of Education back,
Worse then (without it) Man could ever lack.
Who therefor, finde's, The Artificialst Fooles
Have not been changd i' th' Cradle but the Schooles:
Where Error, Pædantry, and Affectation   35
Run them, behind Hand, with their Education.

And all alike are taught Poetique Rage
When Hardly one's fit for it, in an Age.
   No sooner are the Organs of the Braine
Quick to Receive, and stedfast to Retaine   40
Best knowledges; But All's layd out upon
Retriving of the Curse of Babilon,
To make Confounded Languages Restore
A Greater Drudgery, then it Bard before.
And therefor those Imported from the East,   45
Where first the[y] were Incurd, are held the Best,
Although conveyd in worse Arabian Pothookes
Then Gifted Tradsmen Scratch in Sermon Notebooks;
Are Really but Paines, and Labour lost
And not worth half the Drudgery they cost,   50
Unles, like Raritys, as th' have been brought
From foraine Climats, and as Dearly bought;
When those who had no other but their own
Have all Succeeding Eloquence outdon;
As Men that wink with one eie see more tru   55
And take their Aime much better then with two.
For the more Languages a man can speake,
His Talent has but sprung the Greater Leak:
And for the Industry, H' has spent upon't,
Must ful as much some other way Discount.   60
The Hebrew, Chalde, and the Syriac
Do (like their Letters) set mens Reason back:
And turn's their wits, that strive to understand it,
(Like those that write the Character[s],) Left-Handed.
Yet He that is but able to express   65
No Sense at all, in Severall Languages,
Will Pass for Learneder, then Hee that's known
To Speake the Strongest Reason, in but one.
   These are the modern Arts of Education
With all the Learned of Mankind in Fashion,   70
But Practicd only with the Rod and whip,
As Riding Schools inculcate Horsmanship
Or Romish Penitents let out their Skins
To beare the Penaltys of others Sins.
When Letters at the first were meant for Play   75
And only usd to Passe the time away:

When th' Ancient Greeks, and Romans had no name
T" express a Schoole, and Play-hous, but the same;
And in their Languages so long agone,
To study or be Idle, was all one.   80
For nothing more Preserv's men in their wits,
Then giving of them, leave to Play by fits,
In Dreames to sport, and Ramble with all Fancies,
And waking, little less Extravagancies:
The Rest, and Recreation of tyr'd Thought,   85
When 'tis Run down with Care, and overwrought:
Of which, who ever do's not freely take
His Constant Share, is never Broad awake,
And when he wants an equal Competence
Of both Recruits, Abates as much of Sense.   90
   Nor is their Education worse design'd,
Then Nature (in her Province) Prove's unkind.
The Greatest Inclinations, with the least
Capacitys, are Fatally Possest,
Condemnd to Drudge, and Labour, and take Paines,   95
Without an equal Competence of Braines:
While those she has Indulgd in Soul, and Body,
Are most averse to Industry, and Study.
And th' Activst Fancies share as loose Alloys,
For want of Equal weight to Counterpoyse: 100
But when those Great conveniences meet,
Of equal Judgment, Industry, and wit;
The one but strives the other to Divert:
While Fate, and Custom, in the Feud take Part
And Schollers by Prepostrous over doing,   105
And under-Judging, All their Projects Ruine:
Who, though the understanding of Mankind
Within so streit a Cumpasse is confin'd,
Disdain the Limits Nature set's to Bound
The wit of Man, and vainly Rove beyond.   110
When Bravest Souldiers scorn, until th' are got
Close to the Enemy, to mak[e] a Shot,
Yet Great Philosophers delight to stretch
Their Talents most, at things beyond their Reach:
And Proudly think t' unriddle ev'ry Cause   115
That Nature use's, by their own By-laws

THE ABUSE OF LEARNING

When 'tis not only Impertinent, but Rude,
When she deny's Admission, to intrude:
And, all their Industry is but to Erre
Unless they have free Quarentine from her: 120
Whence 'tis, the World the less has understood
By striving to know more, then 'tis allow'd.
  For Adam with the Loss of Paradise
Bought knowledg at too Desperate a Price;
And ever since that Miserable Fate   125
Learning did never Cost an Easier Rate:
For though the most Divine, and Sovraine Good
That Nature has upon Mankind bestowd,
Yet it has Prov'd a Greater Hinderance
To th' Interests of Truth then Ignorance,   130
And therefore never Bore so high a valew
As when it was Contemptible and shallow,
Had Academy[s], Schooles, and Colledges,
Endowd for its Improvment, and Increase:
With Pomp, and Shew, was introduced with Maces,   135
More than a Roman Magistrate, had Fasces;
Impowrd with Statute, Privilege, and Mandate,
T' assume an Art, and after understand it,
Like Bills of Store, for taking a Degree,
With all the Learning to it, Custome-free,   140
And own Professions, which they never took
So much Delight in, as to Read one Book:
Like Princes had Prerogative to Give
Convicted Malefactors, a Reprive.
And having but a little Paultry wit   145
More then the world, Reduct, and Govern'd it:
But Scornd, as soon as 'twas but understood,
As Better is a Spightful fo to Good.
And now has nothing left for its Support,
But what the Darkest times Provided for't.   150
    Man has a natural Desire to know,
But th' one Half, is for Intrest, Th' other show,
As Scrivners take more Paines to learn the Slight
Of making knots, then all the Hands they write.
So all his Study is not to Extend   155
The Bounds of Knowledg, but some vainer End;

71

T' appeare and Pass for Learned, though his Clame
Will Hardly Reach beyond the Empty Name.
For most of those that Drudg, and Labour Hard
Furnish their understandings by the yard   160
As a French Library by th' whole is,
So much an Ell, for Quartos, and for Folios,
To which they are but Indexes themselvs,
And understand no further then the shelvs,
But smatter with their Titles, and Editions   165
And Place them, in their Classical Partitions:
When all a Student know's of what he Read's
Is not in 's own, but under Gen'rall Heads
Of Common Places, not in his own Powr,
But like a Dutchmans Money, i' th' Cantore,   170
Where all he can make of it, at the Best,
Is hardly three Per Cent, for Interest:
And whether he wil ever get it out,
Into his own Possession, is a Doubt.
Affect's all Books of Past, and modern Ages,   175
But Read's no further then the Title Pages,
Only to con the Authors Names by Rote,
Or at the Best, those of the Books they wrot.
Enough to challenge Intimate Acquaintance,
With all the Learned Moderns, and the Antients.   180
As Roman Noble men were wont to Greet
And complement the Rabble in the Street:
Had Nomenclators in their Traines to clame
Acquaintance, with the Meanest, by his Name;
And by so cheap, contemptible, a Bribe   185
Trepand the Suffrages, of every Tribe.
So learned Men, by Authors Names unknown,
Have Gaind no smal Improvement to their own.
For He's esteemd the Learnedst of all others,
That has the Largest Catalogue of Authors.   190

FRAGMENTS
of an intended
SECOND PART
of the foregoing
SATYR

[MENS] Talents Grow more Bold and Confident,
  The further th' are beyond their Just Extent.
As Smattrers Prove more Arrogant and Peart
The less they truly understand an Art;
And, where th' ave least Capacity to doubt,   5
Are wont t' appear more Peremptory, and Stout;
While those that Know the Mathematique Lines
Where Nature all the wit of Man Confines,
And when it keep's within it's Bounds, and where
It Act's beyond the Limits of it's Sphere,   10
Injoy an Absoluter free Command
O're all they have a Right to understand,
Then those that falsly venture to Incroach
Where Nature has denyd the[m] all Approach;
And still the more they strive to understand,   15
Like Great Estates, run furthest Behinde Hand;
Will undertake the Univers to Fathom,
From Infinite, down to a Single Atom,
Without a Geometrique Instrument,
To take their own Capacity's Extent;   20
Can tell as Easy how the world was made
As if they had been brought up to the Trade,
And whether Chance, Necessity, or Matter
Contrivd the whole œconomy of Nature;
When all their Wits to understand the World   25
Can never tell why a Pigs Tayle is Curld
Or give a Rational Accompt, why Fish
That always use to Drink, do never Pisse.

  What Mad Phantastique Gambols have been P[l]ayd
By th' antique Greek Forefathers of the Trade?   30

73

That were not much Inferior to the Freaks
Of all our Lunatique, Fanatique Sects:
The First and Best Philosopher of Athens,
Was Crackt, and Ran stark-staring mad with Patience;
And had no other way to shew his wit,   35
But when his Wife was in her Scolding Fit:
Was after in the Pagan Inquisition,
And sufferd Martyrdom for no Religion.
Next him, his Scholler striving to Expell
All Poets, his Poetique Common-weal,   40
Exild himself, and al his Followers,
Notorious Poets only Bating verse.
The Stagyrite, unable to Expound
The Euripus, leapt int' it, and was Drownd:
So he, that put his Eies out, to Consider,   45
And Contemplate on Natural things, the steadier:
Did but himself for Idiot convince,
Tho Reverenct by the Learned ever since.
Empedocles, to be esteemd a God,
Leapt into Ætna with [his] Sandals shod,   50
That b'ing blown out, discoverd what an Ass,
The Great Philosopher, and Jugler was,
That to his own New Deity sacrifict
And was himself the victime, and the Priest.
The Cynique coynd False Money, and for feare   55
Of being Hangd for't, turnd Philosopher:
Yet with his Lanthorn went by Day to finde
One Honest Man in th' Heap of all Mankind;
An Idle Freak, he needed not have don,
If he had known himself to be but one.   60
With swarms of Magots of the self-same Rate,
The Learned of all Ages celebrate:
Things that are properer for Knights-bridg-Colledge,
Then th' Authors, and Originals of Knowledg;
More Sottish then the two Fanatiques trying   65
To mend the World, by Laughing or by Crying:
Or he, that laughd until he chokd his whistle,
To Rally on an Ass, that eate a Thistle.
That th' Antique Sage, who was Gallant t' a Goose
A Fitter Mistres could not Pick and Chuse   70

THE ABUSE OF LEARNING

Whose Tempers, Inclinations, Sense, and wit
Like two Indentures, did agree so fit.

   The Antient Sceptiques constantly Denyd,
What they maintaind, and thought they Justifyd:
For when Th' Affirmd, That Nothing's to be known, 75
They did but what they sayd, before, Disowne:
And, [like] Polemiques of the Post, Pronounce
The same things, to be true, and False at once.
   These Follies had such Influence on the Rabble,
As to Ingage them in Perpetual Squabble;   80
Divided Rome, And Athens, into clans
Of Ignorant Mechanique Partizans:
That to maintaine their Own Hypotheses,
Broke one anothers Block-heads, and the Peace.
Were often set by Officers i' th' Stocks   85
For Quarrelling about a Paradox,
When Pudding-wives were launchd in cockquen stooles,
For Falling-foul on Oyster-womens Schooles:
No Herb-women sold Cabbages, or Inions
But to their Gossips of their own Opinions,   90
A Peripatetique Cobler scornd to sole
A Pair of Shoos of any other Schoole
And Porters of the Judgment of the Stoiques
To go on Errand of the Cyrenaiques,
That us'd t'encounter in Athletique Lists   95
With Beard to Beard and Teeth and Nailes to Fists:
Like modern Kicks, and Cufs among the Youth
Of Academiques, to maintaine the Truth:
But, in the Boldest Feates of Arms, the Stoique,
And Epicureans, were the most Heroique,   100
That stoutly venturd breaking of their Necks,
To vindicate the Intrests of their Sects.
And stil behavd themselves as Resolute
In waging Cuffs, and Bruises, as Dispute,
Until with wounds, and Bruises, which th' had got, 105
Some Hundred were kild Dead, upon the Spot:
When al their Quarrels (rightly understood)
Were but to prove Disputes, the Sovrain Good.

Distinctions, that had been at first Design'd
To Regulate the Errors of the Minde,   110
By b'ing too Nicely over-straind, and vext,
Have made the Comment, harder then the Text;
And do not now (like Carving) hit the Joynt,
But break the Bones, in Pieces, of a Poynt:
And with Impertinent Evasions, force   115
The Clearest Reason, from it's Native Course—
That argue things s' uncertaine, 'tis no Matter
Whether they are, or never were in Nature,
And venture to Demonstrate when th' are slurd
And Palmd, a Fallacy upon a Word.   120
For Disputants (As Sword-men use to fence,
With Blunted Foyles) Dispute with Blunted Sense,
And as th' [are] wont to Falsify a Blow,
Use nothing else to Pass upon the Foe.
Or if they venture further to attack,   125
Like Bowlers, strive to Beat away the Jack:
And when they finde themselves, too hardly Prest-on,
Prævaricate, and change the State o' th' Question,
The Noblest Science of Defence, and Art,
In Practice now with all that Controvert;   130
And th' only Mode of Prizes, from Bear-garden
Down to the Schooles, in giving Blows, or warding.

As old Knights Errant in their Harnes fought
As Safe as in a Castle, or Redout,
Gave one another Desperat Attaques   135
To storme the Counter Scarps upon their Backs,
So Disputants Advance, and Post their Armes
To storm the works of one anothers Tearms,
Fall Foul on some extravagant Expression
But nere Attempt the maine Designe and Reason—   140
So some Polemiques, use to Draw their Swords
Against the Language only, and the words;
As He, who fought at Barriers with Salmasius
Ingagd with nothing but his Style, and Phrases,
Wav'd to assert the Murther of a Prince,   145
The Author of False Latin to Convince;
But Layd the Merits of the Cause aside,

By those who understood 'em to be try'd;
And counted Breaking Priscians Head a thing
More Capital then to behead a King,   150
For which H' has been admir'd by all the Learnd
Or Knavs concernd, and Pedants unconcern'd.

   Judgement is but a Curious Pair of Scales,
That turn's with th' Hundredth Part of True, or False
And still the more 'tis usd, is wont, t' abate   155
The Subtlety, and Nicenes of it's weight.
Untill 'tis False, and will not Rise, nor Fall;
Like those that are less Artificiall,
And therefore Students, in their way of Judging,
Are faine to swallow many a Senseles Gudgeon: 160
And by their over-underst[and]ing loose
Its Active Faculty with too much use.
For Reason, when too Curiously 'tis Spun,
Is but the next of all Removd from none:
   It is Opinion governs all Mankind   165
As wisely as the Blinde, that leads the Blinde:
For as those Sur-names are Esteemd the Best
That signify, in all things else, the Least,
So men Pass fairest in the worlds Opinion,
That have the least of Truth and Reason in 'em.   170
Truth would undo the world, if it Possest
The Meanest of its Right, and Interest.
Is but a titular Princes, whose Authority
Is always under-age, and in Minority;
Has al things don, and carryd in her Name,   175
But most of all, where she can lay no Clame.
As far from Gayety, and Complesance,
As Greatness, Pride, Ambition, Ignorance.
And therefore has surrenderd her Dominion
Ore all Mankind, to barbarous opinion.   180
That in her Right, usurps the Tyrannys
And Arbitrary Government of Lyes—
   As no Tricks on the Rope, but those that Break
Or come most Near to breaking of a Neck
Are worth the Sight: so nothing Go's for wit,   185
But Nonsense, or the next of al to it.

For Nonsense being neither False, nor tru,
A Little wit to any thing may Screw.
And when it has a while been usd of Course
Wil stand as well in virtu, Powr and Force   190
And Pass for Sense t' all Purposes as good
As if it had at first been understood.
For Nonsense, has the Amplest Priviledges
And more then all the Strongest Sense, oblige's.
That furnishes the Schools, with Tearms of Art   195
The Mysterys of Science, to Impart.
Supplys all Seminarys, with Recruites
Of endless Controversys, and Disputes,
For Learned Nonsense has a Deeper Sound
Then Easy Sense, and go's for more Profound.   200

The greatest writers commonly Compile,
At Charge of Nothing, but the words and Style.
And all the Nicest Critiques of the Learnd
Believe themselves in Nothing else concernd.
For as it is the Garniture and Dress   205
That all things weare in Books and Languages
And all Mens Qualitis are wont t' appeare
According to the Habits that they weare,
'Tis Probable to be the Fittest Test,
Of all the ingenuity o' th' Rest: 210
The Lives of Trees Ly chiefly in their Barks,
And all the wit i' th' Styles of Learned Clerks,
Hence 'twas, the Antient Roman Politicians
Went to the Schooles of Forrain Rhetoricians
To learn the Art of Patrons (in Defence   215
Of Intrest, and their Clients) Eloquence:
When Consuls, Censors, Senators, and Prætors,
With great Dictators, usd t' apply to Rhetors:
To heare the Greater Magistrate, o' th' School,
Give Sentence in his Haughty Chair-Curule.   220
And those who Mighty Nations over-came,
Were fain to say their Lessons, and declame.
    Words are but Pictures, tru or False Designd
To Draw the Lines, and Features of the Minde,
The Characters and artificial Draughts   225

THE ABUSE OF LEARNING

T' express the inward Images of thoughts;
And Artists say a Picture may be good
Altho the Moral be not understood;
Whence some Infer, They may Admire a Style,
Though all the Rest be ere so Mean and vile: 230
Applaud th' outsides of words, but never minde,
With what Fantastique Taudery th' are Lyn'd.
    So Orators, Inchanted with the Twang
Of their own Trillos, take Delight t' Harangue;
Whose Science, like a Juglers Box, and Balls   235
Convey's, and Counterchanges Tru, and False.
Cast's Mists before their Audiences eies,
To Pass the one, for th' other in Disguise:
And like a Morice-Dancer drest with Bells,
Only to serve for Noyse, and Nothing else,   240
Such as a Carryer make's his Cattle weare
And Hang's for Pendents in a Horses Eare:
For if the Style and Language beare the Test,
No matter what become's, of all the Rest:
The Ablest orator, to save a word,   245
Would throw all Sense, and Reason, over boord.
    Hence 'tis that nothing else, but Eloquence,
Is tyd to such a Prodigal Expence;
That Lay's out Halfe the wit, and Sense it uses
Upon the other halfes, as vain excuses.   250
For all Defences, and Apologies,
Are but Specifique's, t' other Frauds and Lies;
And th' Artificiall wash of Eloquence,
Is dawbd in vaine, upon the Clearest Sense.
Only to staine the Native Ingenuity,   255
Of æqual Brevity, and Perspicuity.
While all the Best, and Sobrest, Feats he does;
Are when he Coughs, or Spits, or Blows his Nose,
Handles no Poynt, so evident, and cleare
(Beside his white Gloves) as his Handkercher;   260
Unfold's the Nicest Scruple, so Distinct,
As if his Talent had been wrapd-up in't
(Unthriftily) and now he went about
Henceforward to Improve, and put it out.

For Pædants are a Mungrel Breed that Sojorn   265
Among the Ancient writers, and the modern;
And while their studys are between the one,
And th' other spent, have nothing of their own;
Like Spunges, are both Plants, and Animals
And equally to both their Natures false.   270
For whether 'tis their want of Conversation,
Inclines them to al Sorts of Affectation:
Their Sedentary Life, and Melancholy,
The Everlasting Nursery of Folly;
Their Poring upon Black and White too subtly   275
Has turnd the Insides of their Brains to Motly,
Or squandring of their wits, and time, upon
Too many things, has made them fit for none,
Their Constant over-straining of the minde
Distort[s] the Braine, as Horses break their winde;   280
Or Rude Confusions of the things they Read
Get up like noxious vapours in th[e] Head,
Untill they have their Constant wanes, and Fuls
And Changes, in the Insides of their Skuls;
Or venturing beyond the reach of wit   285
Had rendred them for al things else unfit;
But never bring the world and Books together
And therefore never Rightly Judg of either;
Whence multitudes of Revrend men and Critiques
Have got a kinde of Intellectual Riquets,   290
And by th' Immoderate Excess of Study
Have found the Sickly Head t' outgrow the Body.
    For Pedantry is but a Corn, or wart
Bred in the Skin of Judgment, Sense, and Art,
A Stupifyd Excrescence, like a Wen   295
Fed by the Peccant Humors of Learnd Men,
That never Grows from Natural Defects
Of Downright and untutord Intellects,
But from the over curious and vain
Distempers of an Artificial Brain—   300
    So Hee that once stood for the Learnedst man,
Had Read-out Little-Britain, and Duck-Lane,
Worn out his Reason, and Reducd his Body
And Brain to nothing, with Perpetual Study:

Kept Tutors of all Sorts, and virtuosos,   305
To Read all Authors to him, with their Glosses,
And made his Laqueis (when he walkd) Beare Folios
Of Dictionarys, Lexicons, and Scolios
To be Read to him evry way, the winde
Should chance to sit before him, or Behind: 310
Had read out all the imaginary Duels
That had been fou[gh]t by Consonants and vowel[s];
Had Crackt his Scul, to find out Proper-Places,
To lay up all Memoires of things in Cases,
And Practicd all the Tricks upon the Carts   315
To Play with Packs of Sciences and Arts,
That serve t' improve a Feeble Gamsters Study
That venture's at Grammatique Beast, or Noddy;
Had Read-out all the Catalogues of wares
That come in Dry fats o're, from Francfort-faires,   320
Whose Authors use t' articulate their Surnames
With Scraps of Greek, more Learned then the Germans:
Was wont to scatter Books in evry Roome
Where they might best bee seen, by all that come,
And lay a Train, that natrally should force   325
What he designd, as if it fel of Course.
And all this; with a worse Success then Cardan,
Who bought both Bookes and Learning at a Bargain
When lighting on a Philosophique Spel,
Of which he never Knew one Syllable,   330
Presto be gone! H' unriddled all he Read
As if he had to nothing else been Bred.

PINDARIC ODES

UPON AN

HYPOCRITICAL NONCONFORMIST

I

THERE'S nothing so absurd, or vain,
 Or barbarous, or inhumane,
But if it lay the least Pretence
To Piety and Godliness,
Or tender-hearted Conscience;   5
And Zeal for *Gospel-Truths* profess,
Does sacred instantly commence;
And all, that dare but question it, are strait
Pronounc'd th' Uncircumcis'd, and Reprobate:
As Malefactors, that escape, and fly   10
 Into a Sanctuary for Defence,
 Must not be brought to Justice thence,
Although their Crimes be ne'er so great and high;
 And he, that dares presume to do't,
 Is sentenc'd and deliver'd up   15
 To *Satan*, that engag'd him to't,
For vent'ring wickedly to put a Stop
To his Immunities and free Affairs,
 Or meddle saucily with theirs,
That are employ'd by him; while he and they   20
Proceed in a *religious* and a *holy* Way.

II

 And as the *Pagans* heretofore
 Did their own Handyworks adore,
And made their Stone and Timber Deities,
Their Temples, and their Altars of one Piece,   25
 The same *Outgoings* seem t' inspire
 Our modern self-will'd Edifier,

8 5

That out of Things as far from Sense, and more,
 Contrives new Light and Revelation,
 The Creatures of th' Imagination,   30
 To worship and fall down before;
 Of which his crack'd Delusions draw
 As monstrous Images and rude,
As ever *Pagan*, to believe in, hew'd;
 Or Madman in a Vision saw;   35
 Mistakes the feeble Impotence,
 And vain Delusions of his Mind,
 For spiritual Gifts and Offerings,
 Which *Heaven*, to present him, brings;
 And still, the further 'tis from Sense,   40
 Believes it is the more refin'd,
And ought to be receiv'd with greater Reverence.

III

But as all Tricks, whose Principles
 Are false, prove false in all Things else,
 The dull and heavy Hypocrite   45
 Is but in Pension with his Conscience,
 That pays him for maintaining it
 With zealous Rage and Impudence,
 And as the one grows obstinate,
 So does the other rich and fat;   50
Disposes of his Gifts and Dispensations,
  Like spiritual Foundations,
Endow'd to pious Uses, and design'd
To entertain the Weak, the Lame, and Blind,
But still diverts them to as bad, or worse,   55
Than others are by unjust Governors:
 For, like our modern *Publicans*,
  He still puts out all Dues,
He owes to *Heaven*, to the *Devil* to use,
And makes his godly Interest great Gains;   60
 Takes all, the brethren (to recruit
 The Spirit in him) contribute
And, to repair and edify his spent
And broken-winded outward Man, present
For painful holding forth against the Government.   65

AN HYPOCRITICAL NONCONFORMIST

IV

The subtle Spider never spins,
But on dark Days, his slimy Gins;
Nor does our *Engineer* much care to plant
  His spiritual Machines,
Unless among the Weak and Ignorant,   70
  Th' Inconstant, Credulous, and Light,
  The Vain, the Factious, and the Slight,
That in their Zeal are most extravagant:
For Trouts are tickled best in muddy Water;
And still the muddier he finds their Brains,   75
  The more he's sought, and follow'd after;
  And greater *Ministrations* gains;
  For talking idly is admir'd,
  And speaking Nonsense held inspir'd;
  And still, the flatter and more dull   80
His Gifts appear, is held more *powerful*:
  For Blocks are better cleft with Wedges,
  Than Tools of sharp and subtle Edges;
  And dullest Nonsense has been found
By some to be the solid'st, and the most profound. 85

V

A great *Apostle* once was said
With too much Learning to be mad;
But our great *Saint* becomes distract,
  And only with too little crackt;
Crys moral Truths and human Learning down,   90
And will endure no Reason, but his own.
  For 'tis a Drudgery and Task,
Not for a *Saint*, but *Pagan* Oracle,
To answer all Men can object, or ask;
  But to be found impregnable,   95
And with a sturdy Forehead to hold out,
In spight of Shame or Reason resolute,
Is braver than to argue and confute.
  As he, that can draw Blood, they say,
From Witches, takes their magic Pow'r away: 100

So he, that draws Blood int' a *Brother*'s Face,
Takes all his Gifts away, and Light, and Grace.
For while he holds, that nothing is so damn'd
    And shameful, as to be asham'd,
      He never can b' attack'd,   105
But will come off; for Confidence well back'd,
    Among the weak and prepossest,
Has often *Truth* with all her *Kingly* Pow'r opprest.

VI

    It is the Nature of late Zeal,
    'Twill not be subject, nor rebel,   110
    Nor left at large, nor be restrain'd,
    But where there's something to be gain'd;
    And that b'ing once reveal'd defies
    The Law with all its Penalties;
      And is convinc'd, no Pale   115
O' th' *Church* can be so sacred as a Jail.
For as the *Indians* Prisons are their Mines;
    So he has found are all Restraints
      To thriving and free-conscienc'd *Saints*;
For the same Thing enriches that confines;   120
And, like to *Lully*, when he was in hold,
He turns his baser Mettals into Gold;
Receives returning and retiring Fees
For holding-forth, and holding of his Peace,
And takes a Pension to be Advocate,   125
And standing *Counsel* 'gainst the *Church* and *State*
    For gall'd and tender Consciences;
Commits himself to Prison, to trepan,
    Draw in, and spirit all he can;
    For Birds in Cages have a Call,   130
    To draw the wildest into Nets,
    More prevalent and natural,
Than all our artificial Pipes and Counterfeits.

VII

His slipp'ry Conscience has more Tricks
Than all the juggling Empirics,   135

And ev'ry one another contradicts;
 All Laws of Heav'n and Earth can break,
And swallow Oaths, and Blood, and Rapine easy;
 And yet is so infirm and weak,
 'Twill not endure the gentlest Check,   140
But at the slightest Nicety grows queasy;
 Disdains Controul, and yet can be
 No where, but in a Prison, free;
 Can force it self, in spight of God,
 Who makes it free as Thought at Home,   145
 A Slave and Villain to become,
 To serve its Interests abroad.
And though no *Pharisee* was ere so cunning
 At tithing *Mint* and *Cummin*;
No dull Idolater was ere so flat   150
 In Things of deep and solid Weight;
Pretends to Charity and Holiness,
 But is implacable to Peace,
 And out of *Tenderness* grows *obstinate*.
And though the Zeal of God's House eat a *Prince*   155
 And *Prophet* up (he says) long since,
 His cross-grain'd peremptory Zeal
Would eat up God's House, and devour it at a Meal.

VIII

 He does not pray, but prosecute,
 As if he went to Law, his Suit;   160
 Summons his Maker to appear,
 And *answer* what he shall *prefer*;
 Returns him back his Gift of Prayer,
 Not to *petition*, but *declare*;
  Exhibits cross Complaints   165
Against him for the Breach of Covenants,
 And all the Charters of the *Saints*;
Pleads guilty to the Action, and yet stands
 Upon high Terms, and bold Demands;
 Excepts against him and his Laws,   170
And will be judge himself in his own Cause;
 And grows more saucy and severe

Than th' *Heathen Emp'ror* was to *Jupiter*,
That us'd to wrangle with him, and dispute;
And sometimes wou'd speak softly in his Ear,   175
    And sometimes loud, and rant, and tear,
And threaten, if he did not grant his Suit.

IX

    But when his painful Gifts h' employs
    In holding-forth, the Virtue lies
    Not in the Letter of the Sense,   180
    But in the spiritual Vehemence,
The Pow'r, and Dispensation of the Voice,
    The zealous Pangs and Agonies,
    And heav'nly turnings of the Eyes;
The Groans, with which he piously destroys,   185
    And drowns the Nonsense in the Noise:
And grows so loud, as if he meant to force
    And take in *Heav'n* by Violence;
    To fright the *Saints* into Salvation,
    Or Scare the *Devil* from Temptation;   190
    Until he falls so low and hoarse,
        No kind of carnal Sense,
Can be made out of what he means:
But as the antient *Pagans* were precise
To use no short-tail'd Beast in Sacrifice,   195
He still conforms to them, and has a Care,
T' allow the largest Measure to his paltry Ware.

X

    The ancient *Churches*, and the best
    By their own Martyrs Blood increas'd;
    But he has found out a new Way,   200
    To do it with the Blood of those,
    That dare his *Church*'s Growth oppose,
Or her imperious Canons disobey;
    And strives to carry on the Work,
Like a true primitive reforming *Turk*,   205
With holy Rage, and edifying War,
    More safe and pow'rful Ways by far:

For the *Turk*'s Patriarch *Mahomet*
Was the first great *Reformer*, and the Chief
    Of th' ancient *Christian* Belief,   210
    That mix'd it with new Light, and Cheat,
    With Revelations, Dreams, and Visions,
    And *apostolic* Superstitions,
To be held forth, and carry'd on by War;
And his Successor was a *Presbyter*   215
With greater Right, than *Haly* or *Abubeker*.

XI

For as a *Turk*, that is to act some Crime
    Against his Prophet's holy Law,
    Is wont to bid his Soul withdraw,
    And leave his Body for a Time: 220
So, when some horrid Action's to be done,
    Our *Turkish* Proselite puts on
Another Spirit, and lays by his own;
    And when his over-heated Brain
Turns giddy, like his Brother *Mussulman*,   225
He's judg'd inspir'd, and all his Frenzies held
    To be prophetic, and reveal'd.
The one believes all Madmen to be Saints,
Which th' other crys him down for, and abhors,
And yet in Madness all Devotion plants,   230
    And where he differs most concurs;
    Both equally exact and just
    In Perjury, and Breach of Trust;
    So like in all Things, that one Brother
    Is but a Counterpart of th' other;   235
    And both unanimously damn,
    And hate (like two that Play one Game)
Each other for it, while they strive to do the same.

XII

Both equally design to raise
    Their *Churches* by the self-same Ways;   240
    With War and Ruin to assert
Their Doctrine, and with Sword and Fire convert;

To preach the Gospel with a Drum,
And for convincing overcome;
And, though in worshipping of God all Blood   245
  Was by his own Laws disallow'd,
Both hold no holy Rites to be so good:
  And both to propagate the Breed
  Of their own *Saints* one way proceed;
For Lust and Rapes in War repair as fast,   250
  As Fury and Destruction waste;
  Both equally allow all Crimes
  As lawful Means to propagate a Sect;
For Laws in War can be of no Effect,
And Licence does more good in *Gospel-times*.   255
Hence 'tis, that holy Wars have ever been
  The horrid'st Scenes of Blood and Sin;
  For when *Religion* does recede
From her own Nature, nothing but a Breed
Of Prodigies and hideous Monsters can succeed.   260

UPON MODERN CRITICS

I

'TIS well, that equal *Heav'n* has plac'd
   Those Joys above, that, to reward
The Just and virtuous, are prepar'd,
Beyond their reach, until their Pains are past;
Else Men would rather venture to possess   5
   By force, than earn their Happiness;
   And only take the Dev'ls advice,
As *Adam* did, how soonest to be wise,
   Though at th' expence of *Paradise*.
For, as some say, to fight is but a base   10
Mechanic Handy-work, and far below
   A gen'rous Spirit t' undergo:
   So 'tis to take the Pains to know,
Which some, with only Confidence and Face,
   More easily and ably do;   15
For daring Nonsense seldom fails to hit,
Like scatter'd Shot, and pass with some for Wit.
Who would not rather make himself a Judge,
   And boldly usurp the Chair,
   Than with dull Industry and Care   20
   Endure to study, think, and drudge
For that, which he much sooner may advance
With obstinate, and pertinacious Ignorance?

II

For all Men challenge, tho' in spite
Of *Nature* and their *Stars*, a Right   25
   To censure, judge, and know;
Tho' she can only order who
Shall be, and who shall ne'er be wise:
Then why should those, whom she denies
Her favour and good graces to,   30
Not strive to take Opinion by surprize,
And ravish, what it were in vain to woo?

For he, that desp'rately assumes
The censure of all Wits and Arts,
Tho' without Judgment, Skill, and Parts,   35
Only to startle and amuse,
And mask his Ignorance (as *Indians* use
    With gawdy colour'd Plumes
Their homely nether Parts t' adorn)
Can never fail to captive some,   40
That will submit to his oraculous Doom,
    And rev'rence what they ought to scorn;
    Admire his sturdy confidence
For solid Judgment, and deep Sense;
And credit purchas'd without Pains or Wit,   45
Like stolen Pleasures, ought to be most sweet.

III

Two Self-admirers, that combine
Against the World, may *pass a Fine*
Upon all Judgment, Sense, and Wit,
And settle it, as they think fit,   50
On one another, like the Choice
Of *Persian* Princes by one Horse's Voice.
    For those fine Pageants, which some raise,
    Of false and disproportion'd Praise,
T' enable whom they please t' appear,   55
And pass for what they never were,
In private only b'ing but nam'd,
Their Modesty, must be asham'd,
    And not endure to hear;
And yet may be divulg'd and fam'd,   60
And own'd in public every where:
So vain some Authors are to boast
Their want of Ingenuity, and club
    Their affidavit Wits, to dub
Each other but a *Knight o' th' Post*,   65
    As false as suborn'd Perjurers,
That vouch away all right, they have to their own Ears.

UPON MODERN CRITICS

IV

But when all other Courses fail,
There is one easy Artifice,
That seldom has been known to miss, 70
To cry all Mankind down, and rail:
For he, whom all Men do contemn,
May be allow'd to rail again at them,
 And in his own Defence
To outface Reason, Wit, and Sense, 75
And all, that makes against himself, condemn;
 To snarle at all Things right or wrong,
Like a mad Dog, that has a Worm in's Tongue;
Reduce all Knowledge back of Good and Evil,
 T' its first Original the *Devil*; 80
And, like a fierce *Inquisitor* of Wit,
To spare no Flesh, that ever spoke, or writ;
 Tho' to perform his Task as dull,
As if he had a Toad-stone in his Scull,
 And could produce a greater Stock 85
Of Maggots than a pastoral Poet's Flock.

V

The feeblest Vermin can destroy,
As sure as stoutest Beasts of Prey;
And only with their Eyes and Breath
Infect, and poyson Men to death: 90
But that more impotent Buffoon,
That makes it both his Bus'ness, and his Sport
 To rail at all, is but a Drone,
That spends his Sting on what he cannot hurt,
Enjoys a kind of Letchery in Spight, 95
Like o'ergrown Sinners, that in whipping take Delight,
Invades the Reputation of all those,
 That have, or have it not to lose;
And if he chance to make a Difference,
 'Tis always in the wrongest Sense: 100
 As rooking Gamesters never lay
 Upon those Hands, that use fair Play;

But venture all their Bets
Upon the Slurs, and cunning Tricks of ablest Cheats.

VI

Nor does he vex himself much less 105
    Than all the World beside,
Falls sick of other Mens Excess,
Is humbled only at their Pride,
And wretched at their Happiness;
Revenges on himself the Wrong, 110
    Which his vain Malice and loose Tongue
To those, that feel it not, have done;
And whips and spurs himself, because he is outgone;
    Makes idle Characters and Tales,
    As counterfeit, unlike, and false, 115
As Witches Pictures are of Wax and Clay
To those, whom they would in Effigie slay.
And as the *Devil*, that has no Shape of's own,
    Affects to put the ugliest on,
And leaves a Stink behind him, when he's gone; 120
So he, that's worse than nothing, strives t' appear
    I' th' likeness of a Wolf or Bear,
    To fright the weak; but, when Men dare
Encounter with him, stinks, and vanishes to air.

TO THE

HAPPY MEMORY

Of the most

Renown'd

DU-VAL

I

'TIS true, to compliment the Dead
　　Is as impertinent and vain,
As 'twas of old to call them back again,
　　Or, like the *Tartars*, give them Wives
　　With Settlements, for After-lives:　　　　　5
For all that can be done, or said,
　　Tho' ere so noble, great, and good,
By them is neither heard, nor understood.
　　All our fine Slights, and Tricks of Art,
First to create, and then adore Desert,　　　10
　　And those Romances, which we frame,
　　To raise ourselves, not them, a Name,
In vain are stuft with ranting Flatteries,
And such as, if they knew, they would despise.
For as those Times the Golden Age we call,　15
In which there was no Gold in Use at all,
　　So we plant Glory and Renown,
　　Where it was ne'er deserv'd, nor known,
　　But to worse Purpose many Times,
　　To flourish o'er nefarious Crimes,　　　　20
And cheat the World, that never seems to mind,
How good, or bad Men die, but what they leave behind.

PINDARIC ODES

II

And yet the brave *Du-Val*, whose Name
Can never be worn out by Fame,
That liv'd, and dy'd, to leave behind   25
A great Example to Mankind;
That fell a public Sacrifice,
From Ruin to preserve those few,
Who, tho' born false, may be made true,
And teach the World to be more just, and wise,   30
    Ought not, like vulgar Ashes, rest
    Unmention'd in his silent Chest,
Not for his own, but public Interest.
He, like a pious Man, some Years before
    Th' Arrival of his fatal Hour,   35
    Made ev'ry Day he had to live,
To his last Minute a Preparative;
    Taught the wild *Arabs* on the Road
    To act in a more gentle Mode,
Take Prizes more obligingly than those   40
    · Who never had been bred *Filous*;
And how to hang in a more graceful fashion,
Than e'er was known before to the dull *English* Nation.

III

In *France* the Staple of new Modes,
Where Garbs and Miens are currant Goods,   45
That serves the ruder *Northern* Nations
With Methods of Address and Treat;
Prescribes new Garnitures and Fashions,
And how to drink, and how to eat
No out-of-fashion Wine or Meat;   50
    To understand Cravats and Plumes,
And the most modish from the old Perfumes;
    To know the Age and Pedigrees
    Of Poynts of *Flandres* or *Venise*;
Cast their Nativities, and to a Day   55
Foretel how long they'll hold, and when decay;

TO THE MEMORY OF DU-VAL

T'affect the purest Negligences
  In Gestures, Gaits, and Miens,
  And speak by *Repartee-rotines*
Out of the most authentic of Romances;   60
And to demonstrate with substantial Reason,
What Ribbands all the Year are in, or out of Season.

IV

In this great Academy of Mankind
  He had his Birth, and Education;
Where all Men are s' ingeniously inclin'd,   65
  They understand by Imitation,
Improve untaught, before they are aware,
As if they suck'd their Breeding from the Air,
  That naturally does dispense
To all a deep and solid Confidence,   70
  A Virtue of that precious Use,
  That he, whom bounteous *Heav'n* endues
But with a mod'rate Share of it,
Can want no Worth, Abilities, or Wit.
  In all the deep *Hermetic* Arts,   75
  (For so of late the Learned call
  All Tricks, if strange and mystical)
  He had improv'd his nat'ral Parts,
  And with his magic Rod could sound
  Where hidden Treasure might be found.   80
He, like a *Lord o' th' Manor*, seiz'd upon
  What ever happen'd in his Way,
    As lawful *Weft* and *Stray*,
And after by the *Custom* kept it as his own.

V

From these first Rudiments he grew   85
To nobler Feats, and try'd his Force
Upon whole Troops of Foot and Horse,
Whom he as bravely did subdue;
Declar'd all *Caravans*, that go
Upon the *King*'s Highway, the Foe;   90

Made many desperate Attacks
Upon itinerant Brigades
Of all Professions, Ranks, and Trades,
On Carriers Loads, and Pedlars Packs,
Made 'em lay down their Arms, and yield   95
And, to the smallest Piece, restore
All, that by Cheating they had gain'd before;
And after plunder'd all the Baggage of the Field.
In every bold Affair of War
He had the chief Command, and led them on;   100
For no Man is judg'd fit to have the Care
Of others Lives, until h' has made it known,
How much he does despise, and scorn his own.

VI

Whole Provinces 'twixt Sun and Sun
Have by his conqu'ring Sword been won;   105
And mighty Sums of Money laid,
For Ransom, upon every Man,
And Hostages deliver'd till 'twas paid.
Th' Excise and Chimney-*Publican*,
The *Jew*-Forestaller and Enhancer,   110
To him for all their Crimes did answer.
He vanquish'd the most fierce and fell
Of all his Foes, the *Constable*;
And oft had beat his Quarters up,
And routed him, and all his Troop.   115
He took the dreadful *Lawyer*'s Fees,
That in his own allow'd Highway
Does Feats of Arms as great as his,
And, when th' encounter in it, wins the Day:
Safe in his Garison the *Court*,   120
Where meaner Criminals are sentenc'd for't,
To this stern Foe he oft gave Quarter,
But as the *Scotchman* did t' a *Tartar*,
That he, in Time to come,
Might in return from him receive his fatal Doom.   125

TO THE MEMORY OF DU-VAL

VII

He would have starv'd this mighty Town,
And brought its haughty Spirit down,
Have cut it off from all Relief,
And, like a wise and valiant Chief
   Made many a Fierce Assault   130
Upon all Ammunition Carts,
And those that bring up Cheese, and Malt,
Or Bacon, from remoter Parts;
No Convoy e'er so strong with Food
   Durst venture on the desp'rate Road: 135
He made th' undaunted *Waggoner* obey,
And the fierce *Higler* Contribution pay,
   The savage *Butcher* and stout *Drover*
Durst not to him their feeble Troops discover;
   And, if he had but kept the Field,   140
   In Time had made the City yield;
For great Towns, like to Crocodiles, are found,
I' th' Belly aptest to receive a mortal Wound.

VIII

But when the fatal Hour arriv'd,
   In which his Stars began to frown,   145
   And had in close Cabals contriv'd
To pull him from his Height of Glory down;
   And he, by numerous Foes opprest,
   Was in th' enchanted Dungeon cast,
     Secur'd with mighty Guards,   150
   Lest he by Force or Stratagem
Might prove too cunning for their Chains, and them,
And break thro' all their Locks, and Bolts, and Wards,
   Had both his Legs by Charms committed
     To one another's Charge,   155
   That neither might be set at large,
And all their Fury and Revenge outwitted.
   As Jewels of high Value are
   Kept under Locks with greater Care,
     Than those of meaner Rates;   160
So he was in Stone Walls, and Chains, and Iron Grates.

IX

Thither came *Ladies* from all Parts,
To offer up close Prisoners their Hearts,
    Which he receiv'd as Tribute due,
And made them yield up *Love* and *Honour* too;   165
    But in more brave heroic ways,
    Than e'er were practis'd yet in Plays:
For those two spightful Foes, who never meet
    But full of hot Contests, and Piques
    About Punctilios, and mere Tricks,   170
Did all their Quarrels to his Doom submit;
    And far more generous and free,
In Contemplation only of him did agree,
    Both fully satisfy'd; the one
    With those fresh Lawrels he had won,   175
    And all the brave renowned Feats,
    He had perform'd in Arms;
The other with his Person, and his Charms:
    For just as Larks are catch'd in Nets,
    By gazing on a Piece of Glass;   180
So while the Ladies view'd his brighter Eyes,
    And smoother polish'd Face,
Their gentle Hearts, alas! were taken by Surprize.

X

Never did bold *Knight*, to relieve
Distressed *Dames*, such dreadful Feats atchieve,   185
    As feeble *Damsels*, for his Sake,
    Would have been proud to undertake;
    And bravely ambitious to redeem
    The World's Loss, and their own,
Strove who should have the Honour to lay down,   190
    And change a Life with him:
    But finding all their Hopes in vain
    To move his fix'd determin'd Fate,
    Their Life itself began to hate,
    As if it were an Infamy   195
    To live, when he was doom'd to die;

Made loud Appeals and Moans,
To less hard-hearted Grates and Stones;
Came swell'd with Sighs, and drown'd in Tears,
To yield themselves his Fellow-sufferers;   200
And follow'd him, like Prisoners of War
Chain'd to the lofty Wheels of his triumphant Car.

BALLADS

A

BALLAD

AS close as a Goose
Sate the Parlament house
  To hatch this Royal Gul;
After much Fiddle-Faddle,
The Eg prov'd adle,   5
  And Oliver came forth Nol.

Yet old Queen Madge,
Though things do not Fadge,
  Wil serve to be Queen of a May-pole;
Two Princes of Wales,   10
For Whitsun-Ales,
  And her Grace Mayd-Marrian Claypool.

In a Robe of Cow-hide
Sat yesty Pride,
  With his Dagger and his slinge;   15
H' was the pertinentst Pere
Of al that were there,
  T' advise with such a King.

A great Philosopher
Had a Goose for his Lover,   20
  That followd him day and night:
If it be a True Story
Or but an Allegory,
  It may be both ways right.

Strickland and his Son,   25
Both cast into one,
  Were meant for a Single Baron;
But when they came to sit,
There was not wit
  Enough in them both, to serve for [one].   30

Wherfore 'twas thought good
To ad Honeywood;
   But when they came to trya[l,]
Each one prov'd a Fool,
Yet three Knaves in the whole,   35
   And that made up a Pere-royal.

A
BALLAD

PART I

DRAW neare, good People, al draw neare,
   And hearken to my Ditty;
      A stranger Thing
      Then this I sing
   Came never to this City.   5

Had you but seen this monster,
   You would not give a Farthing
      For the Lyons in th' Grate,
      Nor the Mountaine Cat,
   Nor the Bears in Paris-Garden.   10

You would defy the Pageants
   Are born before the Mayor;
      The strangest shape,
      You ere did Gape
   Upon in Bartlemew-fayr!   15

His Face is round and decent,
   As is your Dish or Platter,
      On which there grow's
      A thing like a Nose,
   But, indeed, it is no such matter.   20

On both sides of th' aforesayd
   Are eies, but th' are not matches,
      Ore which there are
      To be seen two fayr
   And large, wel-grown Mustaches.   25

Now this with admiration
   Dos al beholders strike,
      That a Beard should grow
      Upon a Things Brow,
   Did ye ever see the like?   30

He has no Scul, 'tis well known
  To thousands of beholders;
    Nothing, but a Skin,
    Dos keep his braines in
From Running about his shoulders.   35

On both sides of his Noddle
  Are straps o' th' very same lether;
    Ears are imply'd
    But th' are mere hide
Or morsels of Tripe, chuse ye whether.   40

Between these two extendeth
  A slit from eare to eare
    That, evry howr,
    Do's gape to devour
The Sowce that grows so neare.   45

Beneath, a Tuft of Bristles
  As rough as a Frees-Jerkin;
    If it had been a Bearde,
    'Twould have serv'd a heard
Of Goats, that are of his near kin.   50

Within, a Set of Grinders
  Most sharp and keen, Corroding
    Your Ir'n and brass
    As easy as,
That you would do a Pudding.   55

But the strangest thing of al is,
  Upon his Rump there groweth
    A great long Tayl,
    That useth to Trayle
Upon the Ground, as he goeth.   60

PART II

This monster was begotten
  Upon one of the witches,
    B' an Imp that came to her,
    Like a Man, to woo her,
With black Dublet and breeches.   65

When he was whelpd, for certaine,
  In divers sevral Cuntrys,
    The Hogs and swine
    Did grunt and whine,
  And the Ravens Croakd upon Trees.   70

The windes did blow, the Thunder
  And lightning lowdly rumbled;
    The Dogs did howl,
    The hollow Tree in th' Owl—
  'Tis a good hors that nere stumbled.   75

As soon as he was brought forth,
  At th' midwife's Throat he flew,
    And threw the Pap
    Down in her Lap;
  They say 'tis very true.   80

And up the wals he clamberd,
  With Nayles most sharp and keen,
    The Prints whereof,
    I' th' Bords and the Roofe,
  Are yet for to be seen.   85

And out at Top o' th' Chimny
  He vanishd, seen of none;
    For they did winke,
    Yet by the Stinke
  Knew which way he was gone.   90

The Country round about there
  Became like to a wilder-
    ness; for the sight
    Of him did fright
  Away men, women, and children.   95

Long did he there Continue,
  And al those Parts much harmed,
    Til a wise-woman, which
    Some cal a white witch,
  Him into a Hogsty charmed.   100

There when she had him shut fast,
  With brimstone and with Niter
    She singd the Claws
    Of his left Paws,
  With the tip of his Tayl, and his right eare. 105

And with her Charmes and Oyntments
  She made him Tame as a Spaniel;
    For she usd to ride
    On his back astride,
  Nor did he do her any il.   110

But, to the admiration
  Of al both far and neare,
    He hath been shown
    In evry Town,
  A[nd] eke in evry Shere.   115

And now, at length, he's brought
  Unto fayr London Citty,
    Where, in Fleetstreet,
    All those may see't,
  That wil not believe my ditty.   120

God save the king, and Parlament,
  And eke the Princes highness;
    And quickly send
    The wars an end,
  As here my Song has   125

Finis.

MOCK ENCOMIUMS

To the Honourable

EDWARD HOWARD, Esq;

Upon his incomparable

POEM

of the

BRITISH PRINCES

SIR,

    You've obliged the *British* Nation more
Than all their Bards could ever do before,
And at your own Charge, Monuments more hard
Than Brass, or Marble, to their Fame have rear'd:
For as all warlike Nations take delight   5
To hear how brave their Ancestors could fight,
You have advanc'd to wonder their Renown,
And no less virtuously improv'd your own.
For 'twill be doubted, whether you do write,
Or they have acted at a nobler hight.   10
You of their ancient *Princes* have retriev'd
More than the Ages knew, in which they liv'd;
Describ'd their Customs, and their Rites anew,
Better than all their *Druids* ever knew:
Unriddled their dark Oracles, as well,   15
As those themselves, that made them, could foretell.
For as the *Britons* long have hop'd in vain,
Arthur would come to govern them again;
You have fulfill'd that Prophecy alone,
And in this Poem plac'd him on his Throne.   20
Such magic Pow'r has your prodigious Pen,
To raise the Dead, and give new Life to Men.
Make rival *Princes* meet in Arms, and Love,
Whom distant Ages did so far remove:
For as Eternity has neither past,   25
Nor future, (Authors say) nor first, nor last,

But is all instant; your eternal Muse
All Ages can to any one reduce.
Then why should you, whose Miracle of Art
Can Life at Pleasure to the Dead impart,   30
Trouble in vain your better busied Head
T' observe what Time they liv'd in, or were dead?
For since you have such arbitrary Power,
It were defect in Judgment to go lower,
Or stoop to Things so pitifully lewd,   35
As use to take the vulgar Latitude.
There's no Man fit to read what you have writ,
That holds not some Proportion with your Wit:
As Light can no Way but by Light appear,
He must bring *Sense*, that understands it here.   40

A
PALINODIE
To the Honourable
EDWARD HOWARD, Esq;
Upon his incomparable
BRITISH PRINCES

IT is your Pardon, Sir, for which my *Muse*
Thrice humbly thus, in form of Paper, sues;
For having felt the dead Weight of your Wit,
She comes to ask Forgiveness, and submit,
Is sorry for her Faults, and, while I write,   5
Mourns in the Black, does Penance in the White:
But such is her Belief in your just Candor,
She hopes you will not so misunderstand her,
To wrest her harmless Meaning to the Sense
Of silly Emulation, or Offence.   10
No; your sufficient Wit does still declare
Itself too amply, they are mad that dare
So vain and senseless a Presumption own,
To yoak your vast Parts in comparison.
And yet, you might have thought upon a Way   15
T' instruct us, how you'd have us to obey,
And not command our Praises, and then blame
All that's too great, or little for your Fame.
For who could choose but err, without some Trick
To take your Elevation to a Nick?   20
As he, that was desir'd, upon occasion,
To make the *Mayor* of *London* an Oration,
Desir'd his Lordship's Favour, that he might
Take Measure of his Mouth, to fit it right;
So, had you sent a Scantling of your Wit,   25
You might have blam'd us, if it did not fit;
But 'tis not just t' impose, and then cry down
All that's unequal to your huge Renown;

For he, that writes below your vast Desert,
Betrays his own, and not your Want of Art.   30
Praise, like a Robe of State, should not fit close
To th' Person 'tis made for, but wide and loose,
Derives its Comeliness from being unfit,
And such have been our Praises of your Wit,
Which is so extraordinary, no Height   35
Of Fancy but your own can do it right;
Witness those glorious Poems you have writ
With equal Judgment, Learning, Art, and Wit,
And those stupendious Discoveries,
You've lately made of Wonders in the Skies.   40
For who but from yourself did ever hear,
The Sphere of Atoms was the Atmosphere?
Who ever shut those Straglers in a Room,
Or put a Circle about Vacuum,
What should confine those undetermin'd Crowds,   45
And yet extend no further than the Clouds?
Who ever could have thought, but you alone,
A Sign, and an Ascendant were all one?
Or how 'tis possible the Moon should shrowd
Her Face, to peep at *Mars*, behind a Cloud;   50
Since Clouds below are so far distant plac'd,
They cannot hinder her from being barefac'd?
Who ever did a Language so enrich,
To scorn all little Particles of Speech?
For though they make the Sense clear, yet th' are found   55
To be a scurvy Hindrance to the Sound;
Therefore you wisely scorn your Stile to humble,
Or for the Sense's Sake to wave the Rumble,
Had *Homer* known this Art, h' had ne'er been fain
To use so many Particles in vain,   60
That to no Purpose serve, but (as he hap's
To want a Syllable) to fill up Gaps.
You justly coin new Verbs to pay for those,
Which in Construction you o'ersee, and lose:
And by this Art do *Priscian* no Wrong   65
When you break 's Head, for 'tis as broad as long.
These are your own Discoveries, which none
But such a Muse as yours could hit upon,

A PALINODIE TO E. HOWARD

That can in spight of Laws of Art, or Rules
Make Things more intricate than all the Schools   70
For what have Laws of Art to do with you,
More than the Laws with honest Men and true?
He that's a Prince in Poetry should strive
To cry 'em down, by his Prerogative,
And not submit to that, which has no Force   75
But o'er Delinquents, and Inferiors.
Your Poems will indure to be try'd
I' th' Fire like Gold, and come forth purify'd,
Can only to Eternity pretend,
For they were never writ to any End.   80
All other Books bear an uncertain Rate,
But those you write are always sold by Weight,
Each Word and Syllable brought to the Scale,
And valu'd to a Scruple in the Sale.
For, when the Paper's charg'd with your rich Wit,   85
'Tis for all Purposes and Uses fit,
Has an abstersive Virtue to make clean
Whatever Nature made in Man obscene.
Boys find b' Experiment, no Paper-kite,
Without your Verse, can make a noble Flight.   90
It keeps our Spice, and Aromatics sweet;
In *Paris* they perfume their Rooms with it;
For burning but one Leaf of yours, they say,
Drives all their Stinks and Nastiness away.
Cooks keep their Pyes from burning with your Wit,   95
Their Pigs and Geese from scorching on the Spit:
And Vintners find their Wines are ne'er the worse,
When Ars'nick's only wrap'd up in the Verse.
These are the great Performances, that raise
Your mighty Parts above all reach of Praise,   100
And give us only Leave t' admire your Worth,
For no Man, but yourself, can set it forth,
    Whose wond'rous Pow'r's so generally known,
    Fame is the Echo, and her Voice your own.

A
PANEGYRIC
UPON
Sir JOHN DENHAM'S
Recovery from his Madness

SIR, you've outliv'd so desperate a Fit,
As none could do, but an immortal Wit;
Had yours been less, all Helps had been in vain,
And thrown away, tho' on a less sick Brain:
But you were so far from receiving Hurt,   5
You grew improv'd, and much the better for't.
As when th' *Arabian* Bird does sacrifice,
And burn himself in his own Country's Spice;
A Maggot first breeds in her pregnant Urn,
Which after does to a young *Phœnix* turn: 10
So your hot Brain, burnt in its native Fire,
Did Life renew'd, and vig'rous Youth acquire;
And with so much Advantage, some have guest,
Your *After-wit* is like to be your best;
And now expect far greater Matters of ye,   15
Than the bought *Cooper's Hill*, or borrow'd *Sophy*:
Such as your *Tully* lately drest in Verse,
Like those he made himself, or not much worse;
And *Seneca*'s dry Sand unmixt with Lime,
Such as you cheat the *King* with, botch'd in Rhime.   20
Nor were your Morals less improv'd; all Pride,
And native Insolence quite laid aside;
And that ungovern'd Outrage, that was wont
All, that you durst with Safety, to affront.
No *China* Cupboard rudely overthrown;   25
Nor Lady tip'd, by being accosted, down;
No *Poet* jeer'd, for scribbling amiss,
With Verses forty times more lewd than his:
Nor did your Crutch give Battle to your *Duns*,
And hold it out, where you had built, a Sconce;   30

Nor furiously laid *Orange-Wench* aboard,
For asking what in Fruit and Love you'd scor'd;
But all Civility and Complacence,
More than you ever us'd, before or since.
Beside, you never over-reach'd the *King*   35
One Farthing, all the while, in reckoning,
Nor brought in false Accompt, with little Tricks
Of passing broken Rubbish for whole Bricks;
False mustering of Workmen by the Day,
Deduction out of Wages, and dead Pay   40
For those that never liv'd; all which did come,
By thrifty Management, to no small Sum.
You pull'd no Lodgings down, to build them worse;
Nor repair'd others, to repair your Purse,
As you were wont; till all you built appear'd   45
Like that, *Amphion* with his Fiddle rear'd:
For had the Stones (like his) charm'd by your Verse
Built up themselves, they could not have done worse:
And, sure, when first you ventur'd to *survey*,
You did design to do't no other way.   50
    All this was done before those Days began,
In which you were a wise and happy Man.
For who e'er liv'd in such a Paradise,
Until fresh Straw and Darkness op'd your Eyes?
Who ever greater Treasure could command,   55
Had nobler Palaces, and richer Land,
Than you had then, who could raise Sums as vast,
As all the Cheats of a *Dutch* War could waste,
Or all those practis'd upon public Money?
For nothing, but your Cure, could have undone ye.   60
For ever are you bound to curse those Quacks,
That undertook to cure your happy Cracks;
For, tho' no Art can ever make them sound,
The tamp'ring cost you Threescore Thousand Pound.
How high might you have liv'd, and play'd, and lost,   65
Yet been no more undone by being chowst,
Nor forc'd upon the *King*'s Accompt to lay
All, that in serving him, you lost at Play?
For nothing, but your Brain, was ever found
To suffer Sequestration, and Compound.   70

MOCK ENCOMIUMS

Yet you've an Imposition laid on Brick,
For all you then laid out, at *Beast*, or *Gleek*:
And, when you've rais'd a Sum, strait let it fly,
By understanding low, and vent'ring high;
   Until you have reduc'd it down to Tick,
   And then recruit again from Lime and Brick.

75

TRANSLATIONS

BOILEAU

SATYR

on

RHYME

GREAT famous Wit, whose rich and easy Vein,
   Free, and unus'd to Drudgery and Pain,
Has all *Apollo*'s Treasure at command,
And, how good Verse is coin'd, dost understand;
In all Wit's Combats Master of Defence,   5
Tell me, how dost thou pass on Rhime and Sense?
'Tis said th' apply to thee, and in thy Verse
Do freely range themselves as Volunteers;
And without Pain, or pumping for a Word,
Place themselves fitly of their own Accord.   10
I, whom a lewd Caprich (for some great Crime
I have committed) has condemn'd to rhime,
With slavish Obstinacy vex my Brain
To reconcile 'em, but, alas! in vain.
Sometimes I set my Wits upon the Rack,   15
And, when I would say *white*, the Verse says *black*.
When I would draw a brave Man to the Life,
It names some Slave, that pimps to his own Wife;
Or base Poltroon, that would have sold his Daughter,
If he had met with any to have bought her.   20
When I would praise an Author, the untoward
Damn'd Sense, says *Virgil*, but the Rhime—
In fine, whate'er I strive to bring about,
The contrary (spight of my Heart) comes out.
Sometimes, enrag'd for Time and Pains misspent,   25
I give it over tir'd, and discontent;
And, damning the dull Fiend a thousand Times,
By whom I was possest, forswear all Rhimes;
But having curst the Muses, they appear,
To be reveng'd for't, e're I am aware.   30
Spight of myself, I strait take fire agen,
Fall to my Task with Paper, Ink, and Pen,

And breaking all the Oaths I made, in vain
From Verse to Verse, expect their Aid again.
But if my Muse, or I were so discreet,   35
T' endure, for Rhime's Sake, one dull Epithet,
I might, like others, easily command
Words without Study, ready and at Hand,
In praising *Chloris*, Moons, and Stars, and Skies
Are quickly made to match her Face, and Eyes;—   40
And Gold, and Rubies, with as little Care,
To fit the Colour of her Lips, and Hair;
And mixing Suns, and Flow'rs, and Pearl, and Stones,
Make 'em serve all Complexions at once,
With these fine Fancies, at hap-hazard writ,   45
I could make Verses without Art or Wit,
And, shifting forty times the Verb and Noun,
With stol'n Impertinence patch up mine own.
But, in the Choice of Words, my scrup'lous Wit
Is fearful to pass one, that is unfit;   50
Nor can endure to fill up a void Place,
At a Line's End, with one insipid Phrase;
And, therefore, when I scribble twenty Times,
When I have written four, I blot two Rhimes.
May he be damn'd, who first found out that Curse,   55
T' imprison, and confine his Thoughts in Verse;
To hang so dull a Clog upon his Wit,
And make his Reason to his Rhime submit.
Without this Plague, I freely might have spent
My happy Days with Leisure and Content;   60
Had nothing in the World to do, or think,
Like a fat Priest, but whore, and eat, and drink;
Had past my Time as pleasantly away,
Slept all the Night, and loiter'd all the Day.
My Soul, that's free from Care, and Fear, and Hope,   65
Knows how to make her own Ambition stoop,
T' avoid uneasy Greatness, and Resort,
Or for Preferment following the Court.
How happy had I been, if, for a Curse,
The Fates had never sentenc'd me to Verse?   70
But, ever since this peremptory Vein
With restless Frenzy first posses'd my Brain,

SATYR ON RHYME

And that the Devil tempted me, in spite
Of my own Happiness, to judge, and write,
Shut up against my Will, I waste my Age   75
In mending this, and blotting out that Page;
And grow so weary of the slavish Trade,
I envy their Condition, that write bad.
O happy *Scudery*! whose easy Quill
Can, once a Month, a mighty Volume fill.   80
For, though thy works are written in despite
Of all good Sense, impertinent, and slight,
They never have been known to stand in need
Of Stationer to sell, or Sot to read.
For, so the Rhime be at the Verse's End,   85
No matter whither all the rest do's tend.
Unhappy is that Man, who, spite of 's Heart,
Is forc'd to be ty'd up to Rules of Art.
A Fop that scribbles, does it with Delight,
Takes no Pains to consider, what to write;   90
But, fond of all the Nonsense he brings forth,
Is ravish'd with his own great Wit and Worth.
While brave and noble Writers vainly strive
To such a Height of Glory to arrive:
But still, with all they do unsatisfy'd,   95
Ne'er please themselves, though all the World beside.
And those, whom all Mankind admire for Wit,
Wish for their own Sakes, they had never writ,
Thou then, that see'st how ill I spend my Time,
Teach me for Pity, how to make a Rhime;   100
And, if th' Instructions chance to prove in vain,
Teach—how ne'er to write again.

OVID

CYDIPPE
HER ANSWER TO
ACONTIUS

IN silent fear I read your Letter o're;
  Lest I shou'd Swear, as I had done before!
Nor had I read, but I fear'd t' engage
By my neglect the peevish Goddess Rage:
In vain I deck her Shrine, her Rites attend,   5
The partial Goddess still remains your Friend.
A Virgin rather shou'd a Virgin Aid,
But where I seek Relief I am betray'd!
I languish, and the Cause of my Disease
As yet lies hid, no Medicine gives me Ease.   10
In how much pain do I this Letter write!
To my weak Hand my sicklier thoughts indite:
What anxious fear alas afflicts me too,
Lest any but my trusty Nurse shou'd know!
To gain me time to write, the door she keeps,   15
And whispering tells the Visitants—*She Sleeps*.
Worse ills I could not for your sake sustain,
Tho' you had merit equal to my Pain.
Your Love betrays, my Beauty proves my Snare,
I had been happy had I seem'd less Fair: 20
Whilst with your Rival you contend to raise
My Beauty's Fame, I perish by your Praise:
Whilst neither will admit the others Claim,
The Chase is hinder'd, and both miss the Game.

   My Nuptial day draws on, my Parents press   25
The Sacred Rites, my blooming years no less.
But whilst glad *Hymen* at my door attends,
Grim Death waits near to force me from his Hands.
Some call my Sickness Chance, and some pretend
The Gods this Lett to cross my Nuptials send;   30

CYDIPPE TO ACONTIUS

Whilst by severer Censure you are guest,
By *Philtra's* to have wrought upon my Breast.
If then your love such mischief can create,
What Misery is reserv'd for her you Hate!
   Wou'd I to *Delos* ne'r had found the way,   35
At least not found it on that fatal Day!
When in our Port our Anchors first we weigh'd,
Th' unwilling vessel still i' th' Harbour stay'd;
Twice did cross winds beat back our flagging Sails;
Said I, cross winds? no! those were prosp'rous Gales!   40
Those winds alone blew fair, that back convey'd
Our Ship, and those that oft our Passage stay'd.
Yet I to see fam'd *Delos* am in pain,
And fondly of each hind'ring blast complain.
By *Tenos* Isle, and *Mycone* we Steer'd,   45
At last fair *Delos'* winding Cliffs appear'd;
And much I fear lest now the *Fairy* Shore,
Shou'd vanish, as 'tis said t' have done before.
At night we Land, soon as the day return'd
My platted Tresses are with Gemms adorn'd,   50
Then to attend the Sacred Rites we go,
And pious Incense on each Altar throw,
My Parents there at their Devotion stay;
My Nurse and I through all the Temple stray:
We view each Court, and each, fresh wonder brings;   55
Pictures, and Statues, Gifts of Ancient Kings.
But whilst into these Rarities I pry'd,
I am my self by sly *Acontius* spy'd.
Thence to the inmost Temple we remove,
The place that should a Sanctuary prove.   60
Yet there I find the Apple with this Rhime—
Ah! me, I'd like to have Sworn the second time!
The Name of Wedlock I no sooner read,
But through my Cheeks a troubled blush was spread.
Why didst thou cheat an unsuspecting Maid?   65
I shou'd have been intreated, not betray'd:
Is then the Goddess bound to take thy part?
And ratifie an Oath without the heart?
The will consents, but that was absent there;
I read indeed the Oath, but did not swear.   70

Yet cannot I deny that I suspect
Diana's Rage this sickness do's inflict;
Glad *Hymen* thrice did to our Courts repair,
Thrice frighted fled to find Death planted there.
Thin Cov'rings on my Feaverish Limbs are spread,   75
My Parents mourn me as already Dead.
What have I done to merit this distress,
That read but words whose fraud I cou'd not guess!
Do thou, ev'n thou from whom my suff'rings spring,
T' appease the Goddess Rage thine Off'rings bring.   80
When will those hands that writ the fatal Rhime
Bear Incense to remove my pain, thy Crime!
   Nor think that thy rich Rival, tho' allow'd
To Visit, is of greater Favours proud.
By me he sits, but still just distance keeps,   85
Restless as I, talks seldom, often weeps:
Blushing he takes a kiss, and leaves a tear,
And once his Courage serv'd to Cry—My Dear.
But from his arms still by degrees I creep,
And to prevent discourse pretend to sleep.   90
He finds, but wou'd his Sense o' th' flight disguise,
He checks his Tongue, but chides me with his Eyes.
With grief he wasts, and I with Feavours pine
'Tis we that suffer, but th' Offence was thine.
   You write for leave to come and see me here,   95
Yet know your former visit cost me dear.
Why wouldst thou hither come, thou canst but see
The double Trophies of thy Cruelty.
My flesh consum'd, my Cheeks of bloodless hue,
Such as I once did in thy Apple view.   100
Shou'dst see me now thou wou'dst repent thy cheat,
Nor think me worth such exquisite Deceit.
To *Delos* back with greater haste wou'dst go,
And beg the Goddess to release my Vow.
On new designs thy fancy wou'dst imploy,   105
Contrive new Oaths the former to destroy.
   No Means have been omitted to procure
My health, but still my Feav'rish fits endure.
We ask'd the Oracle what caus'd my pains?
The Oracle of broken Vows complains!   110

CYDIPPE TO ACONTIUS

The Gods themselves on your behalf declare:
What hast thou done to merit this their care?
But so it is—and I at last incline,
Since that thou art their choice, to make thee Mine.
Already to my Mother I've declar'd,   115
How by your Cunning I have been insnar'd.
I've done, and what I have already said,
I fear is more than will become a Maid.
My thoughts are now confus'd, and can indite
No more, my feeble hand no more can write.   120
Nor need I more subscribe, but this, Be True!
And (since it must be so) *my Dear, Adieu!*

MISCELLANEOUS PIECES

REPARTEES

between

CAT and PUSS

at a

CATERWALLING

In the Modern Heroic Way

IT was about the middle Age of Night,
  When half the Earth stood in the other's Light;
And Sleep, Death's Brother, yet a Friend to Life,
Gave weary'd Nature a Restorative:
When Puss, wrapt warm in his own native Furs,   5
Dreamt soundly of as soft and warm Amours,
Of making Galantry in Gutter-tiles,
And sporting on delightful Fagot-piles;
Of bolting out of Bushes in the dark,
As Ladies use at Midnight in the Park;   10
Or seeking in tall Garrets an Alcove,
For Assignations in th' Affairs of Love.
At once his Passion was both false and true,
And the more false, the more in earnest grew.
He fancy'd, that he heard those amorous Charms,   15
That us'd to summon him to soft Alarms,
To which he always brought an equal Flame,
To fight a Rival, or to court a Dame:
And, as in Dreams Love's Raptures are more taking,
Than all their actual Enjoyments waking,   20
His amorous Passion grew to that Extream,
His Dream itself awak'd him from his Dream.
Thought he, what Place is this! or whither art
Thou vanish'd from me, Mistress of my Heart?
But now, I had her in this very Place,   25
Here, fast imprison'd in my glad Embrace,
And, while my Joys beyond themselves were rapt,
I know not how, nor whither thou'rt escap'd:

Stay, and I'll follow thee—With that he leap'd
Up from the lazy Couch on which he slept;   30
And, wing'd with Passion, through his known Purlieu,
Swift as an Arrow from a Bow, he flew,
Nor stop'd, until his Fire had him convey'd,
Where many an Assignation h' had enjoy'd;
Where finding, what he sought, a mutual Flame,   35
That long had stay'd and call'd, before he came,
Impatient of Delay, without one Word,
To lose no further Time, he fell aboard;
But grip'd so hard, he wounded what he lov'd;
While she, in Anger, thus his Heat reprov'd.   40
C. Forbear, foul Ravisher, this rude Address,
Canst thou at once both injure and caress?
P. Thou hast bewitch'd me with thy pow'rful Charms,
And I, by drawing Blood, would cure my Harms.
C. He, that does love, would set his Heart a Tilt,   45
Ere one Drop of his Lady's should be spilt.
P. Your Wounds are but without, and mine within;
You wound my Heart, and I but prick your Skin:
And while your Eyes pierce deeper than my Claws,
You blame th' Effect, of which you are the Cause.   50
C. How could my guiltless Eyes your Heart invade,
Had it not first been by your own betray'd?
Hence 'tis, my greatest Crime has only been
(Not in mine Eyes, but yours) in being seen.
P. I hurt to love, but do not love to hurt.   55
C. That's worse than making Cruelty a Sport.
P. Pain is the Foil of Pleasure, and Delight,
That sets it off to a more noble Height.
C. He buys his Pleasure at a Rate too vain,
That takes it up beforehand of his Pain.   60
P. Pain is more dear than Pleasure, when 'tis past.
C. But grows intolerable, if it last.
P. Love is too full of Honour, to regard
What it enjoys, but suffers, as reward.
What Knight durst ever own a Lover's Name,   65
That had not been half murther'd by his Flame?
Or Lady, that had never lain at Stake,
To Death, or force of Rivals for his Sake?

BETWEEN CAT AND PUSS

C. When Love do's meet with Injury and Pain,
Disdain's the only Med'cine for Disdain.   70
P. At once I'm happy, and unhappy too,
In being pleas'd, and in displeasing you.
C. Prepost'rous Way of Pleasure, and of Love,
That contrary to its own End would move!
'Tis rather Hate, that covets to destroy;   75
Love's Business is to love, and to enjoy.
P. Enjoying and destroying are all one,
As Flames destroy that which they feed upon.
C. He never lov'd at any gen'rous Rate,
That in th' Enjoyment found his Flame abate.   80
As Wine (the Friend of Love) is wont to make
The Thirst more violent, it pretends to slake;
So should Fruition do the Lovers fire,
Instead of lessening, inflame Desire.
P. What greater Proof, that Passion do's transport,   85
When, what I would dye for, I'm forc'd to hurt?
C. Death among Lovers is a Thing despis'd,
And far below a sullen Humour priz'd.
That is more scorn'd, and rail'd at than the Gods,
When they are crost in Love, or fall at odds.   90
But since you understand not what you do,
I am the Judge of what I feel, not you.
P. Passion begins indifferent to prove,
When Love considers any Thing but Love.
C. The Darts of Love (like Lightning) wound within, 95
And, though they pierce it, never hurt the Skin;
They leave no Marks behind them, where they fly,
Though through the tend'rest Part of all, the Eye;
But your sharp Claws have left enough to shew,
How tender I have been, how cruel you.   100
P. Pleasure is Pain, for when it is enjoy'd,
All it could wish for was but to b' allay'd.
C. Force is a rugged Way of making Love.
P. What you like best, you always disapprove.
C. He that will wrong his Love will not be nice,   105
T' excuse the Wrong he does, to wrong her twice.
P. Nothing is wrong, but that which is ill meant.
C. Wounds are ill cured with a good intent.

REPARTEES

P. When you mistake that for an Injury,
I never meant, you do the Wrong, not I.   110
C. You do not feel yourself the Pain you give;
But 'tis not that alone, for which I grieve;
But 'tis your want of Passion that I blame,
That can be cruel, where you own a Flame.
P. 'Tis you are guilty of that Cruelty,   115
Which you at once outdo, and blame in me:
For while you stifle, and inflame Desire,
You burn, and starve me in the self-same Fire.
C. It is not I, but you, that do the Hurt,
Who wound yourself, and then accuse me for't: 120
As Thieves, that rob themselves 'twixt Sun and Sun,
Make others pay for what themselves have done.

UPON
PHILIP NYE'S
THANKSGIVING BEARD

A BEARD is but the Vizard of a Face,
   That *Nature* orders for no other Place;
The Fringe and Tassel of a Countenance,
That hides his Person from another Man's;
And, like the *Roman* Habits of their Youth,   5
Is never worn until his perfect Growth;
A Privilege, no other Creature has,
To wear a nat'ral Mask upon his Face,
That shifts its Likeness, every Day he wears,
To fit some other Persons Characters;   10
And by its own Mythology implies,
That Men were born to live in some Disguise.
   This satisfy'd a *reverend Man*, that clear'd
His disagreeing Conscience by his Beard.
H' had been prefer'd i' th' Army, when the *Church*   15
Was taken with a Why not? in the lurch;
When Primate, Metropolitan, and Prelates
Were turn'd to Officers of Horse, and Zealots,
From whom he held the most Pluralities
Of Contributions, Donatives, and Salaries;   20
Was held the chiefest of those spiritual Trumpets,
That sounded Charges to their fiercest Combats,
But in the desperatest of Defeats
Had never blown as opportune Retreats;
Until the *Synod* order'd his Departure   25
To *London*, from his caterwalling Quarter,
To sit among 'em, as he had been chosen,
And pass, or null things, at his own disposing;
Could clap up Souls in *Limbo* with a Vote,
And for their Fees discharge, and let them out;   30
Which made some *Grandees* bribe him with the Place
Of holding-forth upon *Thanksgiving-Days*,

PHILIP NYE'S BEARD

Whither the *Members*, two and two abrest,
March'd to take in the Spoils of all—the Feast;
But by the way repeated the *Oh-hones*   35
Of his wild *Irish* and chromatic Tones,
His frequent and pathetic *hums* and *haws*,
He practis'd only t' animate the *Cause*,
With which the *Sisters* were so prepossest,
They cou'd remember nothing of the rest.   40
  He thought upon it, and resolv'd to put
His *Beard* into as wonderful a Cut,
And, for the further Service of the Women,
T' abate the Rigidness of his Opinion;
And, but a Day before, had been to find   45
The ablest *Virtuoso* of the Kind,
With whom he long and seriously confer'd
On all Intrigues, that might concern his *Beard*;
By whose Advice he sat for a Design
In little drawn, exactly to a Line: 50
That, if the Creature chance to have Occasion
To undergo a *Thorough-reformation*,
It might be born conveniently about,
And by the meanest Artist copy'd out.
  This done, he sent a Journeyman Sectary,   55
H' had brought up to retrieve, and fetch, and carry,
To find out one, that had the greatest Practice,
To prune, and bleach the Beards of all *Fanatics*,
And set their most confus'd Disorders right,
Not by a new Design, but newer Light;   60
Who us'd to shave the *Grandees* of their Sticklers,
And crop the Worthies of their *Conventiclers*;
To whom he shew'd his new-invented Draught,
And told him, how 'twas to be copy'd out.
  Quoth he, 'tis but a false, and counterfeit,   65
And scandalous Device of human Wit,
That's absolutely forbidden in the *Scripture*,
To make of any carnal thing the Picture.
  Quoth th' other *Saint*, you must leave that to us,
T' agree what's lawful, or what scandalous: 70
For, till it is determin'd by our Vote,
It's either lawful, scandalous, or not;

Which, since we have not yet agreed upon,
Is left indiff'rent to avoid or own.

    Quoth he, my Conscience never shall agree   75
To do it, till I know what 'tis to be;
For, though I use it in a lawful Time,
What, if it after should be made a Crime.

    'Tis true, we fought for Liberty of Conscience
'Gainst human Constitutions in our own Sense;   80
Which I'm resolv'd perpetually t' avow,
And make it lawful, whatsoe'er we do;
Then do your Office with your greatest Skill,
And let th' Event befall us, how it will.

    This said, the nice *Barbarian* took his Tools,   85
To prune the *Zealot*'s Tenets, and his Jowles;
Talk'd on as pertinently, as he snipt,
A hundred times for every Hair he clipt;
Until the *Beard* at length began t' appear,
And reassume its antique Character,   90
Grew more and more itself, that Art might strive,
And stand in Competition with the Life:
For some have doubted, if 'twere made of Snips
Of Sables glew'd and fitted to his Lips;
And set in such an artificial Frame,   95
As if it had been wrought in *Filograin*,
More subtly fil'd and polisht than the Gin,
That *Vulcan* caught himself a Cuckold in;
That *Lachesis*, that spins the Threads of Fate,
Could not have drawn it out more delicate.   100

    But b'ing design'd and drawn so regular,
T' a scrup'lous Punctilio of a Hair,
Who cou'd imagine, that it shou'd be portal
To selfish, inward-unconforming Mortal?
And yet it was, and did abominate   105
The least Compliance in the *Church* or *State*;
And from it self did equally dissent,
As from *Religion*, and the *Government*.

PROLOGUE
TO THE
QUEEN OF ARRAGON,
Acted before the Duke of *York*,
Upon his Birth-Day

SIR, while so many Nations strive to pay
   The Tribute of their Glories to this Day,
That gave them Earnest of so great a Sum
Of Glory (from your future Acts) to come;
And which you have discharg'd at such a rate,   5
That all succeeding Times must celebrate:
We, that subsist by your bright Influence,
And have no Life, but what we own from thence,
Come humbly to present you, our own way,
With all we have (beside our Hearts) a *Play*.   10
But as devoutest Men can pay no more
To *Deities*, than what they gave before;
We bring you only, what your great Commands
Did rescue for us from ingrossing Hands,
That would have taken out *Administration*   15
Of all departed *Poets* Goods i' th' Nation;
Or, like to *Lords of Manors*, seiz'd all Plays,
That come within their Reach, as *Wefts* and *Strays*;
And claim'd a Forfeiture of all past Wit,
But that your Justice put a stop to it.   20
'Twas well for us, who else must have been glad
T' admit of all, who now write new, and bad:
For still the wickeder some Authors write,
Others to write worse are encourag'd by't.
And though those fierce *Inquisitors* of Wit,   25
The *Critics*, spare no Flesh, that ever writ;
But just as *Tooth-draw'rs* find among the Rout
Their own Teeth work in pulling others out;
So they, decrying all of all that write,
Think to erect a Trade of judging by't.   30

TO THE QUEEN OF ARRAGON

Small Poetry, like other Heresies,
By being persecuted multiplies:
But here th' are like to fail of all Pretence;
For he, that writ this Play, is dead long since,
And not within their Pow'r: for Bears are said   35
To spare those, that lie still, and seem but dead.

EPILOGUE

Upon the same.

To the DUTCHESS.

MADAM, the Joys of this great Day are due,
No less than to your *royal Lord*, to you;
And, while three mighty *Kingdoms* pay your Part,
You have, what's greater than them all, his *Heart*,
That Heart, that, when it was his Country's Guard,　5
The Fury of two Elements out-dar'd;
And made a stubborn haughty Enemy
The Terror of his dreadful Conduct fly;
And yet you conquer'd it—and made your Charms
Appear no less victorious, than his Arms:　10
For which you oft' have triumph'd on this Day,
And many more to come *Heav'n* grant you may.
But, as great *Princes* use, in solemn Times
Of Joy, to pardon all, but heinous Crimes;
If we have sin'd, without an ill Intent,　15
And done below what really we meant,
We humbly ask your Pardon for't, and pray
You would forgive, in Honour of the Day.

AN EPISTLE to a FRIEND

A FRAGMENT

THIS Night we are met at the Globe of Purpose
   To Drink, and to write to thy Gentle Corpus;
Where, having got Sack, Pen, Paper, and Inke,
I wish I could write as easy as thinke;
But th' best way of all to put us in,   5
I think, is with Drinking first to begin.
Here's a Health to thy self, and thy second Part,
The wine's not so neare, as y' are both to my Heart,
And that's not very far of[f], Pardy!
For I feel it warme my Pericardy.   10
This Night w' intend to sup, and lodge at Kingston,
Where wee shal want a Poet, unles thou bring'st one.

*   *   *   *   *   *   *   *

TO THOMAS ....

THOMAS, thou art so great a Drunkard,
 Th' art able to o'relay a Dung-cart.
Thomas thou art all Ale, thy Skin
Hath nothing else but ale therein.
That Scull of thine, instead of Braines,   5
Is Stuft with half a Peck of Graines,
[Thy] Heart, thy liver, and thy Lungs,
Is made of that, that stoppeth Bungs;
Thou dost not drink at any club
But tun Ale int' another Tub   10
Which Learned Brewers call a Fat,
And none can say but thou art that;
Thence it Run's out at a Small Tap,
That ha's indured man' a Clap;
But now 'tis safe enough, No whore   15
Can ever hurt it any more,
Unless she could shoot Pox at distance
A Furlung of[f], for such Resistance
Thy Belly makes—Belly said I?
No, Thomas, I confess I ly.   20
It was a Belly once, but now
It is a Tun, and like to grow
As mighty, if our hopes it answer,
As that at Heidleburg, thy Grandsire.

TRIPLETS
UPON
AVARICE

AS Miners their own Laws Injoyn
  To weare no Pockets in the Mine
For feare they should the Oare Purloyn;

So he that Toyles, and Labours hard
To Gaine, and what he Gets has Spard,   5
Is from the use of all Debard.

And tho he can Produce more Spankers
Than all the usurers, and Bankers,
Yet after more and More he Hankers.

And after all his Paines are don   10
Has nothing he can call his own
But a meare Livelyhood alone.

EPIGRAM

ON A

CLUB of SOTS

THE jolly Members of a toping Club,
   Like Pipestaves, are but hoop'd into a Tub;
And in a close Confederacy link,
For nothing else, but only to hold Drink.

DESCRIPTION OF HOLLAND

A CUNTRY that Draw[s] fifty foot of Water,
  In which Men live, as in the Hold of Nature;
And when the Sea dos in upon them break
And Drown a Province, dos but Spring a Leak;
That always Ply the Pump, and never think   5
They can be Safe, but at the Rate they stink;
That Live as if they had been Run on Ground,
And when they dy, are cast away, and Drownd;
That dwel in Ships, like Swarms of Rats, and Prey
Upon the Goods all Nations Fleets Convey,   10
And, when their Merchants are Blown up and Crackt,
Whole Towns are cast away in Storms, and wrackt;
That feed like Canibals on other Fishes
And serve their Coussen Germans up in Dishes:
A Land that Rides at Anchor, and is moord,   15
In which they do not live, but go abourd.

POETICAL THESAURUS

WIT AND FOLLY

A MAN of Quick and Active wit
For Drudgery is more unfit,
Compard to those of Duller Parts,
Then Running Nags to draw in Carts.

Have wee not Built a Stately Colledge
T' instruct Four Nations in all knowledge
(Who now are Barbarus and Rude)
As soon as once they are subdu'de?
But what or where these Nations are
Wee know as little as they care
Nor when the Busnes wilbe don
Unles th' are Colonies i' th' Moon.

Fooles (like Philosophers) disdain
All that's Impossible t' obtain,
And b'ing incapable of wit
Dispise, and undervalew it;
And as the Greeks by Hors, and Bul,
Discrib'd what s'ever 's great, and Full:
So he that would discribe their wit
By Horse and Bull must blazon it.

——None but Sots
Would put the Moon out for her Spots.

                              No Asse
'Ere knew what kinde of Beast he was.

Wit beare's no Rate but as it pleases:
So Pearels in Fishes, are Diseases,
And Perfumes of the Richest Sents
In Beasts but sores, or excrements.

Fancy in the Darke see's best
When outward eies Discern the least.

        As we finde Small Partys are
The fittest for Surprize in ware,
So Feeble wits in Consultations
Are best at Cavils and evasions.

WIT AND FOLLY

Wit and Prayse (like Salt and sweet
In Cookery) can never meete.

The Lives of th' old Philosophers of Greece,
Were but their Apothegm's and Repartee's.
For all their Actions Historys discover,
Is what they us'd so often to say over.

Dancers jog down all their wit
Out of their Heads, into their Feet.

The Ignorant and wise
Are to each other of a Size;
And both as nat'rally contemne
The wise, th' Ignorant, and they them.

Great wits have only been Preferd
In Princes Traines to be interd;
And, when they cost them nothing, Placd
Among their Followers not the last;
But, while they livd, were far enough
From al Admittances kept of[f].

Wit
Wil neither Love, nor money get.

As Salt Rust[s] swords; so too much wit
Debases valour when they meet.

Th' one Half of wit's maintaind by Folly
That finde's it Fresh supplys to Rally;
For wit's unable to Invent
What Idiots naturally vent.

Wits who have little enough t' ingage,
Are cold, before their time, to th' Stage.

For these take measure of their own,
That Cry all others Talent down.
And by their own false Standards, try
All others Ingenuity.

One who had wanted long
A Sphincter Mussle to his Tongue.

WIT AND FOLLY

So great a Thief, hee'd cut the wit
From under a Smal Poets feet.

All Prophesies that Rhime and Quible
Are truer the[n] the Leaves of Sibil.

Too much or too little Ingenuity and wit
Do only render th' owners fit
For Nothing, but to be undon
Much easier, then if th' had none.

    Like Philosophers, A wittall
Is with his Parts Content though ere so little;
For hee believs, that has the least,
Hee's better furnishd then the best.

In th' Age of Turnaments, and Tilting
All wit in Stiching lay and Quilting;
When Men did weare their Prettyst Jests
Imbroderd on their Backs and Brests,
And None Invok'd a Muse or Phœbus,
But to be Inspird with a Rebus;
And He was Held the subtlest witted,
Whose Motto, and Imprese best Fitted.
From hence came Clinch, at first, and Quibble,
At which the Revrend Men still Nibble,
And hold their wit and Parts undon
In overseeing of a Pun.
When all our venerable Benches
Gave Judgment and Pronouncd in Clinches,
And he, who was but at a Loss,
Was Counted very Dull and Gross;
And none so worthy to sit there,
As those who on a Poynt could Jeare.
Next after these came Ends of Latin,
Though now 'tis held but idle Prating,
But then the Greates[t] Hight of Art
To have most Sentences by Heart.

For Nature never gave to Mortall yet
A Free and Arbitrary Pow'r of wit,
But bound him to the Good Behavior for't
That he should never use it to do hurt.

WIT AND FOLLY

Most men are so unjust to looke upon
Anothers wit as Enemy t' his own.

For wit and Fancy, like a Diamond,
The more exact, and curious, 'tis ground,
Is forcd, for evry Caract, to abate,
As much in valew, as it wants in weight.

It is a harder thing for men to Rate
Their own Parts at an æqual estimate,
Then cast up Fractions, in th' Account of heaven,
Of time, and motion, and Adjust them eaven:
For modest Persons, never had a tru
Particular, of all, that is their Due.

All wit do's but Divert men from the Road,
In which things vulgarly are understood,
And Force Mistake and Ignorance to own
A Better Sense, then commonly is known.

For Men Learn sooner then they can Imagin,
Take Folly and Ill habits by Contagion,
And, as the Persons they converse with Hap,
Catch Ignorance or Reason like a Clap
And Propagate the epidemique Ach
Which all the Rest of one another catch.

As no Edge is accounted sharp and keene
That by the subtlest Eie is to be seen,
So no wit for Acute should be Allowd
That's Plaine, and Easy to be understood.

For those get least, that take the greatest Pains,
But least of all i' th' Drudgery of Brains,
A Natral Sign of weaknes, as an Ant
Is more Laborius then an Elephant,
And Children are more busy at their Play
Then men that wisest pas their time away.

LEARNING

FOR what do's all Philosophy
    But teach men Learnedly to Ly?
From false Grounds solidly t' infer
And how Judiciously to erre,
To universalls strech all Art
Untill 'tis Lame in evry Part.

What Nature had to human eies denyd,
He with the optiques of his minde discry'd.

Bookes and Schooles
Made Few men wise, but worlds of Fooles.

The History of Learning is so Lame;
That 'tis unknown, from whence, at first it came:
Or who Invented it; For th' old Ægyptian
Do's only, claime a Title, by Præsc[r]iption,
Time out of Minde; and the untutord Græcians,
Were taught their Alphabet, by th' old Phœnicians.
Whence some are Confident, The Hebrew-Jew
Has better Right, to challeng, as his Due.
Derivd from Adam: As their own Samboscer
(The Rabins write) His Tutor was, and usher;
Till many Ages after, Greece, and Rome,
Were into Full Possession of it come.
Whence some have thought; 'Twas but to call to minde
Some Notions, left, in th' other world Behinde;
And quite forgotten, in our Passage hither,
Untill we Had Collected them, together.

The Noblest Sense was never Learnt, nor taught
But into this world with the owner brought
As Naturally as a Part, or Limbe,
That was Begotten, and grew up with him.
From whence it was, The Antient world was wont
T' ascribe Invention to some Gods Account.
For there's no Liberal Art, nor Document
That teache's how to Fancy and Invent.

LEARNING

That's but a Natural Freehold of Merit
Which only those wh' are born to can Inherit.
Yet when The Freest Judgment, and first Starts
Of Reason are the Signes of greatest Parts
Some think they are but dainty Fruits that Drop,
By Beast, or vermine to be Eaten up.

The Faults of Language, are the variations,
Of Dialects, and Moods, and Declinations,
With æqual wants of Syntax, to Reduce,
And make hang together, in their use.
In which, the Nat'rall Temper of the Greek
Is both the most Luxuriant, and to seeke.
And yet their Sages, who are known, s' absurd,
To put their Stress of Reason, on a word,
Could never express exactly what they meant
Untill they had Destroyd the Argument.

In all mistakes, The Strickt, and Regular,
Are found, to be the Desperatst ways to Erre:
And worst to be avoyded, as a wound
Is sayd to be, the harder Curd, that's Round:
For Error and mistake the less th' Appeare
In th' End are found to be the Dangrouser;
As no Man mind's those Clocks that use to go
Apparently to[o] over fast, or slow.

More Proselyts, and Converts, use t' accrew
To false Perswasions, then the Right, and true.
For Error, and Mystake, are Infinite
But Truth has only one way, to b' in the Right.
As Numbers may t' Infinity be Grown
But never be Reducd to less then one.

The Stoiques believd, the Gods could do no good
Nor Hurt, themselvs, but as the Fates allowd;
But when they stickled for it, in their Porch,
The Fates forsooke and left them in the lurch,
Exposd them to maintaine it with the losses
Of some mens lives, and others Eies, and Noses,
And provd their own opinions, by their Fall,
That some Mens virtu is an Animal.

LEARNING

The Epicureans had no persuasion
T' Imploy the Gods upon this worlds Creation;
Believ'd 'twas Modeld not by Artifice
But Fortune, and Haphazard, piece by piece;
And to afflict 'em for their Ignorance
Believd themselvs as Justly made by Chance,
Until th' Athenians for their Principles
Chargd them with luxury, and nothing else.

So He that offers Nature best to know,
Deny's the God[s], H' had made his Prayers to.
Begs Venus t' use her Interest with Mars
To Leave his Battles (for a while) and wars
And, for his Patron Memmius, Intercede
To be at leasure, what he sayd, to Read,
But Presently conclude[s], The Gods Forbear
To medle with our little Intrests here,
And, when he makes the Heavy thing[s] ascend,
Because the greatest Trees do upward tend,
Forgot that Trees grow upward to their Hight
When all the thin Attracted Parts are light.

So he that put his Son to Socrates
To learn to Prove, what ever, he should please,
To pay his Debts with Arguments, chose rather
To shew his skil in Beating of his Father,
And after answer for it, in a Court,
As he Design'd, and was acquitted for't.

                              [Learned Men]
Are wont to fortify the weakest Places
Of all their Studies with the Hardest Phrases,
Tho wholly unconcernd in Truth or Falshood
But as they Chance to fall out for the Souls good
But always Pin a Hebrew Alphabet
Upon the Hangings where they use to eat;
With Prints of Hieroglyphiques on the wals,
With Kircher Box of whistles and Catcals,
And many a Talismanical Device
To Root out vermine with, and Rats and mice;
Whose most Extempral and Careles Act
Is stiffer then an antique Cataphract.

LEARNING

No mathematician ever was Esteemd
That had not been for Conjurer condemnd.

The Metaphysique's but a Puppet Motion
That go's with Screw's, the Notion of a Notion,
The Copy of a Copy, and Lame Draught
Unnaturally taken from a thought;
That Counterfets all Pantomimique Tricks
And Turnes the Eies, like an old Crucifix.
That Counter Changes, whatsoe're it calls
B' another Name, and make's it tru, or False.
Turns truth to falshood, Falshood into Truth
By vertu of the Babilonians Tooth.

For Reason is not only found to Grow,
But wast's, and weares out, with the Body too.
Is Sickly, and In health, and Sleeps, and wakes,
And whatsoere the Body feeles Partakes.
When all their Reason[s] have but one Result,
And that's Instinct, or Quality occult,
That understand when Reason's at its Height,
And when again Impertinent and slight;
When it Approaches next to Demonstration,
And when no Nearer then Imagination.

If greatest Masters, ere they reachd their Height,
Had not in Bungling, found as much Delight
As After in their greatest Mastery,
They never had Arrivd at that Degree.

The Best Authority, instead of Reasons,
Is but a Kind of Statute with Defeasance:
For things that are Imperiously sayd
Are but the sooner to be disobeyd.

For all Inventions that the world Contains
Were not by Reason first found out, but chance;
But Pass for theirs, who had the Luck to light
Upon them by Mistake, or oversight.

A Language Dead can never be Restord
So much to Life, to own a New made word;
Were Tully now alive, Hee'd be to seek
In all our Latin Tearms of Art, and Greek.

LEARNING

Would never understand one word of Sense,
The most Irrefragables[t] Schoolman means;
As if the Schooles Designd their Tearms of Art
Not to Advance a Science, but Divert;
As Hocus-Pocus Conjures, to amuse
The Rabble, from observing what he do's.

The world had never been a St[r]aw the worse
If it had never had Philosophers.

For Metaphysique's but a kinde of Brandy
Drawn out of Dead-wine Leeze, t' ingage, and bandy
And yet wil serve Inceptors to Comence,
And take Degrees, much easier then with Sense,
To clabber-claw a tough and stuborn Theses
To any Nonsense, either Party Pleases:
For some Mens Fortunes like a weft or stray
Are only Gained by losing of their way.

So he that held th' Ete[r]nity of Nature
In the next place, makes mention, of First matter;
And after, to Interpret what he means,
Put's on the words a Metaphisique Sense;
Which some b' a second hand Mistake, have been
So Confident, to take their Oaths, Th' have seene.

For 'tis not strange for Disputants t' assert
What both deny (Implicitly) by Art:
The one to prove, the other, to Disclame,
When both mistake themselves; and meane the same.

The more men take upon them, and Profess
To know all things, they understand the lesse;
Who count it a Disparagment, and Shame
To heare an unknown Booke, or Authors Name,
Or aske the meaning of a word abroad,
They never heard before, nor understood,
For feare of being Suspected, For their want
Of knowing all things, weake and Ignorant,
The only course that never fayles, t' Advance,
And fortify, their Nat'rall Ignorance.

LEARNING

The Barbarousest Nations Adages
Are wittyer, then those of Rome, and Greece,
Which Pædants with their greatest Diligence
Had rather breed their Pupils to, then sense.
As Properer to fit the Idiom
Of th' Antique Parrots and Jack-daws of Rome.

The wits of Mankind are but subtle Spirits
Designd to Hunt in th' underworld like Ferrets,
But have no wings to Raise themselves and Fly
Beyond their Altitude at things too High.

For when the Circulation of the Bloud
Tho ere so easy, was not understood,
How should the world expect that things more hard
Should ever be Discoverd afterward.

ARTS AND SCIENCES

Rules

Were made for Novices, and Fooles.

The old Ægyptians stered their Boats
And Sayld down Cataracts of Spoats,
Made Spectacles t' Improve the Sight
And see i' th' Dark as wel as light.

'Tis strange how stubbornly industrious
Some men are found t' appeare Preposterous,
That spare no Drudgery, and Paines
To wast their little stock of Braines,
All Arts and Sciences perplex,
And, with a thousand idle Freakes,
The Government of Nature vex,
And like Fanatiques in their Hearts
Have visions, and New lights in Arts;
From old Designes of water-engines
Steal Gifts, and Lights of New Inventions,
Make Pumps for water, and their wit,
To Rayse 'em both so many feet,
And forge their Gimcracks at the Rate
Fanatiques use in Church, and State,
And out of Antique Theorems
New Jiggambobs of Light and Dreames.

Smattrers are more Brisk and Peart
Then those who understand an Art,
As little spa[r]kles shine more bright
Then Glowing Coales, that give 'em light,
Whose sudden Vanitys and Flashes
Are clouded by themselves with Ashes.

'Tis not the Art of Schools to understand,
But make things Hard, in stead of b'ing explaind;
And therefore Those are comonly, the Learnedst,
That only study between Jest, and Earnest:

L 2

ARTS AND SCIENCES

For when the End of Learning's to Pursue,
And trace, the Subtle steps, of false and true,
They ne're consider how they are t' Apply,
But only listen, to the Noyse and Cry,
And are so much Delighted with the Chace,
They never mind the Taking of their Preys.

  For Books are but a Kinde of Utensils
Of Turning Children upon Potters wheels,
That, when th' are ore'clogd with heavy men,
Reduce 'em natrally to Boys agen.

  For Bookes were made for Men, not Men for Bookes,
No more then Meat was made for dressing Cookes;
Are Commonly the By-blows of an Author:
Not one in Forty has an Honest Mother.

PÆDANTS

FOR Pædantry is But a Lewd Caprich
Which Pupills Catch of Tutor's like the Itch;
And many nere Recover, till th' are Men,
But still grow worse till th' are twice Boys agen;
That in the world at first was Introducd
As but the Garbe, and meen, that Schollers usd,
But since is so Inlargd it has outgrown
The usefull Part of all that's to be known,
And in its Roome Imported Affectations
Of Obsolete, and Antiquitated Fashions;
From whence the virtuoso-wit of France
Do's not oppose to knowledg, Ignorance
[But] Pædantry, as th' Horribler Defect
And Imperfection of the Intellect.
Besides the Crambe-Surfets of his Parts
Diseasd, and Cropsick, with his Nauseous Arts:
For all a Pædants Skill Ly's in his Tearms
As conjurers and witches in their Charms,
That never Speaks, But Consters, and Imbr[o]thers
The Bumbast-Stuff, with Ends of Antique Authors
More Insignificant, then Osce, and Volsce,
Or Modern Macaronique Linsy-wolse,
The Constant Pedlers Dialect, of Schoolers
Patcht up with Scraps, of Diffrent Stufs, and Cullers,
More Tawdry then a Botchers Chequerd Cushion
He Sings, and stiches with his Legs a Cross-on,
And (like a Fripprer) do's but Turn and Dress
The wrong-side out-wards sevrall Languages
Of which He smatters greater Stores at once
Then th' Antique Hundred voyces could Pronounce.
So He that usd to set the Highest valews
Upon a word, of Meane Condition, Alius,
A Paltry Epithite Prizd it beyond
The Richest Jewells meerly, for the Sound,
And Counted those the Eloquentst Clarks
That Frequentst Introduct it, in their works.

PÆDANTS

A Tru Pedantique writer in a worke
Wil manage all his matters with a Fork
And not omit the least Puntilio
That might his Breding and Good-manners show.
As Formall as a Ceremonious Author
Quote's the Right worshipful his Elder Brother.

A Pædagogue, that mounted in his Schoole
Is but a Kinde of Master of Misrule,
Is Puft up with his own conceipt, and Swels
With Pride and vanity and Nothing else,
Like Bladders in the Late Pneumatique Engine,
Blown up with nothing but their owne Extension.

And when he speak's in Languages unknown
To those that hardly understand their own,
Talke's to himself, as other madmen use,
And only is Permited to go loose.

For Pædants teach their youth, to Apprehend
And take their Lessons in at the wrong end;
And when they'r sick, have been præscribed by Leaches
For exercise, to Labour at their Breeches.

VIRTUOSO

LOGITIANS use to clap a Proposition,
    As Justices do Criminals, in Prison;
And in as Learnd Authentique Nonsense writ,
The Names of all their Moodes and figures fit;
For a Logician's one, that has been broke
To Ride and Pace his Reason by the Booke,
And by their Rules, and Precepts, and Examples,
To put his wits into a kind of Trammells.

For as the Famous Trismegist,
B' observing of a Beast that Pist,
Is sayd t' have first found out a way
To Reckon evry Howr o' th' Day,
And, when he had the water Cast,
Could tell Correctly how time Past,
So some, by Chamber Pots and Glasse[s],
Can tell as truly how time Passes;
And, as the Tides of Liquor Run,
Can Calculate the Course o' th' Sun,
And [that] More Certain and exact
Then all the Tricks i' th' Almanack.

Until our Modern Curious virtuosos,
By only knocking at the Doores of Houses,
Will, by the Sound, unriddle the Just Sum
How many Persons are in the Roome.

Take Ptolomy That Liv'd in Adrian's Days
For some Ægyptian King of th' antique Race
And Joyn him with his Colleague in the Stars
Alphonso Sovraine of Astronomers.

And when no Atom in the universe
The wit of Man (beyond the Name) can Pierce
It has (like Powder of a Diamond)
The Hardest Parts of Nature, Cut, and Ground,
And taught men to Discerp and Penetrate
All Form, and matter, simply as they say't.

VIRTUOSO

When al his wit's unable to unriddle
The wonders of the Magnete, and the Needle
That makes the Globe o' th' Earth a Thoroughfare
To pass as Quick as Light dos through the Aire
And at a Race of Motion to out-run
And beat the Jaded Horses of the Sun.

ANTIQUITY

A LITTLE wit, and Reason's Necessary
  To Qualify an able Antiquary;
Who has no Busnes for the Intellect
But to Transcrible and Copy, and Collect;
Is but an Antiquated Ghost that Haunts
The Charnel-Houses of the Antients
And calls the Dead Deponents up, to Answer
And solve all Questions of the Necromancer,
But has a Prejudice to all that's New
Though 'ere so useful, Rational, and Tru;
When al the Antients understood before
The Moderns have improvd, and somthing more.
As if Books, like a China-Potters Clay,
Prepard for th' use of After-ages lay,
And Time, that can the Hardest things devour,
Ore Feeble Age and Error had no Power,
And that which stubbornst Adamants can break
Turnd Edge against the most infirme and weake.

  The Antients Had no Folios, nor Pages
That have been since found out, by after Ages,
Were Nice of Forraine words, and Affectations,
Of Far-fet, and outlandish Imitations.
Disdaind to Copy, and Translate, and Quote,
And if they would, they Had no way to do't.
Had not so much, as Indexes, to looke,
And finde out what, they sought for, in a Booke.
Knew nothing of a Table to an Author
T' examine, and Discover what they sought for:
But had a freer way of Sense, and wit,
In all they left, of what they sayd, or writ.
Had not so many Languages to Purchace,
As Men are now Ingaged in, to no Purpose.
For if the world Grow Elder ev'ry howr
Since the Creation, then it was before,
The Modern Ages wilbe found, to bee
The Best Pretenders, to Antiquity.

ANTIQUITY

When all the Antique Globe of Heavn Contain
Was but the furniture of Sea, and Land;
And Men, and Beasts, and Birds, and Fish and Foul
Was but an Inventory of the whole;
The Orbes but Nests of Boxes, to Inclose
And Shut up Nature fast, from Breaking loose;
Whence al their Learned Men were of Opinion
Nothing could Represent them better then an Inion
That, in the Judgment of Philosophers,
[Were] Natral Types of al the universe.

    The Antients in their writings are not found
To be the least Pedantique, and Hide-bound.

    The Antients Layd up Stores of all Provisions
Of Common Places, Topiques, and Transitions.

    For most men take their Learning upon Tick,
From the Antient Roman, or the Elder Greek:
And for the Revrence due to Age, believe
It ought to have the sole Prerogative;
And therefor whatsoere it do's, or says,
The world is bound, Implicitly to Pass.
For nothing is esteemd so Learnedish
As t' Imitate the Antients, tho Amis.
Who when in Publique Roads, Th' Interd the Dead,
Mad[e] Epitaphs, for Passengers to Read,
Which wee, to Imitate Antiquity,
To Travellers through Churches now Apply,
And Dedicate to all that Pass that Roade,
To keep the Antique Custome up, and Mode.
So when the Senate, and the States of Rome
Were wont to Rayse (for Nations over-come)
Triumphal Arches, to their Emperors,
The Moderns do it to themselvs, of course:
And when an Antique Book was but a Scroule,
They usd (like Maps) about a Stick to Roule,
And for the more Convenience of their use,
Were faine to Frequent Sections to Reduce,
Things that are now Impertinent, and vaine
Which we have now no use of, yet retaine:

ANTIQUITY

The Moderns to preserve the Fashions, Reckon
The Length of all their writings by the Section.
As when the Antients counted Shepherds fit,
To Pass for Men of Quick, and Ready wit,
Though now the Ablest is as great a Dunce
As any other Sort of Rugged Clownes,
Wee to conform, write Eglogues in their Names
To vindicate the Title of their Clames,
Because No Sheep can shew so great a Stock
Of Magots, as a Pastral Poets Flock:
And Sillily have made to Sing, and Pipe,
Of all Perfections else a Standing Type:
So Aristotle was at first Debard
All Christian Schooles, yet Counted Afterward
The Schoolmens only Oracle, and Chief
Apostle of the Mystrys of Belief:
A Paradox not only against the Grain
Of all their own Opinions, but in vaine.
For why should they Reduce Belief to Proof,
If it be stronger when 'tis further off?
That's Necessary, by their own Confession,
If Faith have more Authority then Reason?

   The Antients left the world more wise and Learnd
Then After ages when their Books were burnd
And other Barbarous writers in their Places
Supplyd the world with all their Sottish Trashes.

HISTORY

TH' Ægyptian Pyramids were first Begun
 Upon the same Designe with Babilon
T' avoyd an Inundation and Deliver
The Founders from the Deluge of their River.

The Antients held no act Adul[t]erous
That was Committed in a Common house.

Medea in a Pot could Stew
Decayd old Age to youth anew,
And could with herbs and spices season
A youthfull Ragoust of old Æson;
Yet half his Cunning had she not,
That Could renew the very pot.

The British Language has no word
T' express a River but a Sword;
As if their swords much antienter
And long before their Rivers were,
And war more Natural then th' earth
Or Elements that brought them forth.

When Adam had eaten the forbidden fruite,
Of Leaves he made him a sligh[t] Summer suite;
But, being Banishd Eden for his Sins,
To labour like a Clown, h' was clad in Skins.

Lik Stow and Hollinshead who tell us where
The King did keep his Christmas evry yeare.

The Antient Jews did morne in sackcloth
As now the Christians do in black cloth.

The antient Picts made feasts
[Of] Sheperds Bums and womens brests.

For who but Fooles and Knaves possess
Those Antient Stately Pallaces,
Of Bethlem Sion, and Bridewell,
Where Princes heretofore did Dwell?

HISTORY

In Spaine
[T]hey count theyr yeares From Tubalkain,
[Th]e Patriarch of Iron Trades,
[T]hat Forgd Toled' and Bilbo-blades.

A Roman Prætor, as he led
His Army through the Gates of Rome,
    Had hornes appearing on his head:
Which was interpreted if ere he Come
    Within the wals of Rome againe
    He wilbe crownd a King and Reigne.

A great Philosopher did choke
With laughing at a Jest he broke.

        Th' Embassador of France,
Tooke out the Queen of Spain to dance
And after made a vow, and Swore
He 'd never dance with Lady more
After so great a Queen had daygned
To let him take her by the hand.

In Rome no Temple was so low
As that of Honor, built to shew
[How] Humble Honor ought to bee,
Though there 'twas all Authority.

The great Saint Lewis, king of France,
Fighting against Mahometans,
In Ægipt, in the holy war,
Was routed and made Prisoner.
The Sultan then, into whose hands
He and his Army fell, demandes
A thousand weight of gold, to free
And set them al at Liberty.
The king pay's down half o' th' nayle,
And for the other offers bayle
The Pyx, and in't the Eucharist
The Body of our Savior Christ.
The Turk considerd, and allowd
The Kings Security for good;

HISTORY

Such Credit had the Christian Zeal
In those days with an Infidell,
That wil not pass for two pence now
Among themselves, 'tis faln so low.

The Mores believe Granada Ly's
Directly under Paradise,
And that they differ both no more
Then th' upper Roomes do from the Floure.

The Antients payd respect and wonder
To Trees or Person[s] struck with Thunder.

Was not king Dor forcd by the Tartar
To Keep Swine for a year and quarter,
And after being restord againe
Injoyd a Long and glorious Reigne?

Indians of Siam (Authors write)
Instead of Black do mourn in white.

The Spartans, that were held of all the Græcians
Most thrifty of their Language, and Expressions
That could indure no length of Circumstance
Yet cald themselves Lacedæmonians.

Chineses took the Busnes most unkinde
To see their Cuntry in our Maps designd,
And mad[e] the Skirts of all the universe,
Which they mistook to be the same to theirs.

So all Inferiors of that Cuntry use
Before their Betters to Pull of[f] their shoes:
And [when] two æqualls civilly Salute,
Neither wil yeld to take the upper Foot.

So those that at the Battle of Cressy, make
Theyr Bowstrings with a Showr of Rain, to slake
Were Ignorant of Nature, to forget
They were Contracted rather by the wet.
Else th' Ingineres of Rome that strov to Rayse
A great Aguglio, firm upon his Base,
Their Cables b'ing too long, had fayld, if Nature
Had not Retrencht them, when th' were drencht in water.

HISTORY

Th' old Romans us'd to match, and pair
Their servants with great Art and Care;
Were critically exact to see
Their Statures, and their Years agree;
To match the colour of their Hair,
The black with black, and fair with fair;
And accurately fit, and size
Their Mouths, their Noses, and their Eyes;
And made them wear their Limbs, and Faces
For Liv'rys of the self-same Laces.

ABSURDITIES

DE Scudery make's Turks at Sea-shipt
Sayl through the Baltique Sea to Ægypt.

Predictions are but like Devises
At Lotterys to draw all Prizes.

Russian wives believe th' are usd
Unkindely till th' are Drubd and bruisd.

An Asse will with his long eares fray
The Flys, that tick[l]e him, away;
But Man delight's to have his eares
Blown Magots in by Flatterers.

At Saint Thomas Waterings
Where men a[re] Angled for, with Strings
And many a Tory-Navigator
Choakd like a Fish with Hemp in water.

The world has Long Indevord to Reduce
Those things to Practice, that are of no use,
And strive's to Practice things of Speculation
And bring the Practicall to Contemplation.
And by that Error, Renders both in vaine
By forcing Natures Course against the Graine.
What sort of Creature Summum Bonum was,
Philosophers Describe, so like an Ass.
If virtue were an Animall determine
Or vice, but Insects, and Imperfect vermine.
So Church Historians undertake to Tell
Where Th' Hous stands yet, of an old Parable.
And shew the Ruines of the Habitation,
Of th' Antient Morall, and Interpretation:
So most Religious Men have nothing else
In all their Historys, but Miracles;
When No Believer would Indure the Falshood
Of what they write, but only for the Souls good;
And Nature do's far greater Miracles
Then all their Deviations from her else.

ABSURDITIES

A Roman Magistrate was made Supreme,
Only to Knock a Naile into a Beame.

So that wise virtuoso Sydrophel,
Who in a Publique Tax is sayd t' appeale,
And show how much he had bee[n] over-reckond
To pay a Tenth for but a third, or second.

The Germans when a Boy do's grow
Fit for the wars: wil not allow
His manhood, til he's kickt i' th' Arse
And then he's listed for the wars.

So Russian Lambs (some write) are wont to travel,
Instead of Four-Lege's, only with a Navel:
That Rooted in the Earth, both Feeds, and Grows,
And eates the Grass on both sides as He goes.

Some Deaf men (they say) see words
If those that speake 'em have no beards;
Others can heare a violin
Holding between [their] teeth a Pin.
Like him that drew th' Invisible Mountain
Which all Philosophy do's Containe,
Or like the Painter that designd
A Noyse, or he that drew the winde.

CUSTOME

CUSTOM is (like the moone's) Inconstant, vain,
  And always shifting 'twixt the Ful and wane:
Was never known to weare one certaine face,
And twice apeare to be the same it was,
And therefore 'tis no Miracle, mens mindes
Are to themselves more various then the winds.
For as 'tis Natural for use and Custome
To Reconcile things ere s' averse and Loathsom
(As Ragusts of a Basilisque or Toad
By Custome have been Renderd wholsom food)
So use can make an obstinate Practician
Do Feats beyond an ordinary Magician;
As in Mechanique Practices the Hand
Can See, and Hear, and Judge, and understand,
And ev'ry finger in the Dark, finde out
The Subtlest Mathematique Poynt by Rote,
As Blinde men when they Play upon an Harp
Unsight unseen, can hit a Flat or Sharp;
And when that Fatal Desperate Impostume
Contagious, and Pestilential Custome
Is but Possest of any vital Part,
The Remedy is Past the Cure of Art.

  To prove by Syllogism's but to spel
A Proposition like a Syllable.

OPINION

WHO dos not know with what fierce Rage
 Opinions Tru, or False ingage?
And, 'cause they Govern all Mankind,
Like the Blindes Leading of the Blinde,
All Claime an equal Interest
Of free Dominion, ore the Rest.
And as one Shield, that fell from Heaven,
Was Counterfeited by Eleaven,
The Better to Secure the Fate
And lasting Empyre of a State;
The False are Numerous, and the tru,
(That only have the Right) but Few.
Hence Fooles, that understand them least
Are Still the Fiercest in Contest;
Unsight, unseen, espouse a Side,
At Random, like a Princes Bride,
To Damn their Soules, and Sweare and ly for
And, at a venture, Live and Dy for.

 The Great Des Cartes with long thought and Study
Had Run himself, out of his Soul, and Body:
Had Forfeted the world, and what's in't,
Till he Recoverd al, and more, b' a Hint.
For since he could not think, He did not think,
Found out, his Soul, and He were things Distinct;
When Really 'twas not his Soul, and Hee,
That differd, but his Supposd No Body.

 Opiniasters Naturally Differ
From other men, as woodd[en] legs are Stiffer
Then those of Plyant Joynts, to yeld and Bow
Which way so ever th' are Designd to Go.
That make Belief and Knowledge the same Case
Because on tick both equally wil Pass
And since th' are chargd on equal Principles
Believe they are the same in al things else.

OPINION

Opinion governs all Mankind,
Like the Blind's leading of the Blind;
For he, that has no Eyes in 's Head,
Must be b' a Dog glad to be led;
And no Beasts have so little in 'em
As that inhuman Brute, Opinion.
'Tis an infectious Pestilence,
The Tokens upon Wit and Sense,
That with a venemous Contagion
Invades the sick Imagination;
And, when it seizes any Part,
It strikes the Poyson to the Heart.
This Men of one another catch
By contact, as the Humours match;
And nothing's so perverse in Nature,
As a profound Opiniaster.

And as the Chast Penelope
Unraveld all sh' had don by day
When Night arrivd; so do's shee too,
And all sh' had don before, undo.

NONSENSE

WHAT Art have Jewellers t' Improve a Stone
Unles with Dust and Powder of its own?

For things Abhominable in Conversation,
Will Pass in Bookes, for Modish, and in Fashion:
As German Authors first found out the Trick
T' Articulate their New Nicknames in Greek,
And Mercers use to give a Rotten Stuffe
A New hard Name, to go the easier off.
That servs our modern Authors here to face
The Titles of their workes, like Copperlace.

Though Art, and Nature's no more Different,
Then Characters from things they Represent:
And when the one's exactly tru Designd
It is but copyd from the other kinde
To cheat Philosophers, who think th' are Matters
Of sevrall kindes, and Disagreeing Natures,
When Art has nothing Excellent, and Good,
But what the Laws of Nature have allowd:
Yet Learned men have sevral Scales, to weigh
All that they write, Distinct, from what they say,
As other Tradsmen, that in measures deale,
Have long to buy withall, and short to sell:
That b'ing compard together only Differ
The more Elaborate, is but the Stiffer:
Write things in Heats, which in the colder Bloud
Of Fancy are not to be understood.
The more they treat of things Methodically
Do but the [more] impertinently dally
And by Referring things that are most hard,
To Proper Heads, nere mind them afterward.
Believe that no man can be in the wrong,
That is mistaken in a Learned Tongue.
The very Sound o' th' Language is enough
To keep all ordinary Censure off.

NONSENSE

Th' Ignorant World without Distinction, lookes
On all, that Passe's on th' Accompt of Booke's;
And when there are two Scollers, that within
The Species only, hardly are of kin;
The world wil pas for men of equall knowledg,
If equally th' have Loyterd in a Colledge.

The Curiousest Judgment's apt to loose
The vigor of it's Sense, with too much use;
For Mules at once, wil Travel, Eate, and Sleep
Upon a Road, they have been usd to keep.

Was not our Cuntry-man, the Great Manage
The Noblest virtuoso of the Age?
Before Morinus, a Cadet-Physitian
Exchangd Professions, with a Mathematician,
Who spent a whole week to Convince his Brother,
But, in the End, Converted one another;
And, while the one Maintaind, what th' other doubted,
Both got the victory, yet both were Routed.

The Prince of Syracuse, whose Destind Fate
It was to Kepe a Schoole, and Rule a State,
Found that his Scepter, never was so Awd,
As when it was translated to a Rod;
And that his vassals nere were s' obedient,
As when he was Inaugurated Pedant:
Whence those that use to teach the Liberal Arts,
Are Princes al and Tyrants in their Hearts.
And look as wise as if like Prester John
Th' had been begotten al by Solomon:
For to Instruct is greater then to Rule
And no Command 's Imperious as a School.

For no Infatuations are so Bad
As theirs, who to Improve themselves, Run Mad.
As if to teach, were nothing but to Part
With something of their Native Sense, and Art;
Or put their Ingenuity to sale
To those th' Instruct, by outcry, or Retayle.

For the best Characters of Ignorance
Are vanity, and Pride, and Arrogance;

NONSENSE

As Blind men use to bear their Noses higher
Then those that have their Eiesight most Intire.

As Campanella usd to screw and wrest
His face like Theirs, to whom he then Addrest,
And allways found he had the best Success,
When best he did it, most of all to Please:
So Famous writers think their very Looks
Will ad a great Advantage to their Books;
And therefore, when they put their works in Print,
Their Pictures are the first things handled in't.

[Cardan] that Admird Italian Doctor wrot
His Parents Frenzies, when he was begot;
Told how his Sire lookd one way, and his Mother
In th' Act, when they committed him, another,
For feare of b'ing surprizd, and taken, in
So Infamous a Place, and Lewd a Sin.
That in the Eies of th' Embrio, did Imprint
The Native Signature he had, to Squint:
And how their Hugs, and Locks, had Sprain'd his Toos
They never could be fit, for any Shoos
All which Past well; because such kinde of Freakes
Had been Committed once by th' Antique Greeks;
And since, some Later writers of Romances
Have Matchd it with their Plagiary Fancies,
Whose Great Examples have been thought enough
To Justify Extravaganter Stuff.

The Antients thought, that Men and Goats drew th' Aire
To set their Longs on work, at either Eare;
But whether that were but a Flam or Tru
The Devil any of them ever knew!

TRUTH

THINGS Determind by most voyces
    Are not the Greatest Truths, but Noyses.

All wise men should be just as kinde
To Truth, as Truth to them they finde.

For Peace, and Truth are found t' unite
As Nat'rally, as to Ly and Fight;
And Therefor when they Battle wage
The Ly's the Signal to engage.

To fight for Truth, is but the Sole Dominion
Of ev'ry Idiot's Humor or Opinion,
And what it fancy's Truth, maintaine's
By ventring t' Hardest Blows, his Braine[s];
And he, whose Noddle is most tough,
Demonstrate's with the Clearest Proof.

For Naked Truth like naked women
Is Impudent, Deboshd, and Common,
A more Prodigious thing appeare
Then Truth would to a Princes eare.
For Truth and Kings have fierce Contests
About their Pow'r, and Interests;
And therefore by their Ministers
Are never sufferd to Converse
But Parted, as the Persian King
And Queen were, for the Selfsame thing
And by their servants at a Fitting,
Convenient Distance, kept from meeting.

Truth can be no older then
The first original of men
But Lying is much Antienter
Ever since the Fall of Lucifer
Who, b'ing the Patriarch of Lys,
Then Raisd those older Family[s].

TRUTH

For Truth is no Original, but Lines
Drawn Perfectly from Natures own Designes;
And t' understand Truth is not to be wise,
But to unriddle all intrigue of Lies.

And some have doubted whether Knights of the Post
Or Natural Historians Lie most,
Have no Regard to Truth in All they write,
But file their Forgerys the more Polite.

The End of Learning's only to Persue
The ways of Truth within and out of view,
To Copy out th' Originals of Nature
As Far as Human wit can Imitate her,
And draw a Scheam exactly in the minde
T' agree with that shee in the world Designd.

For Truth do's stand in Need of no Excuse;
Or if it did, 'Twould serve it to no use;
That never Suffers on its own Account,
But some things else that has been Layd upon't.

Nothing a Tryal undergoes
Without some Injury, and Loss,
And cannot be prov'd true without
The charge and trouble of the Doubt.

The World's occasions cannot be supplyd
With too much Truth and Reason on it's side;
Is fain to take in Falshood, Fraud, and Error,
To sell its own Commodities the dearer.
For Truth, that is supreme and absolute,
Must not be brought to question and dispute;
But, like the sovran pow'r of Principles
In Arts, and Sciences, try all things else,
And not to any other Pow'r alive
Submit its Int'rest, and Prerogative;
Nor suffer any other Law to try
The dictates of its high Authority.

PHYSIQUE

NO Nation has such Physical Liefhebbers
   As th' English swarme withal, among their Neighbors,
Where evryones Delight, as wel as Study,
Is to store-up all medecines, for Mans Body.
That serves them for their Natural Diversions,
And Entertainment, of al other Persons.
And this by People of all Trades, and Ranks,
As if th' had beene Design'd for Mountebanks.
For as the Antient Empriques, usd to lay
Their Patients in the Publiquest High-way,
T' have evry mans opinion, that past by,
About the Sick mans Cure, and malady,
The selfsame Course, our modern Patient[s] take,
And all they meet with, their Physicians make.
For all Pretender[s] of the virtuosos,
Turn Doctors when the[y] do but talk of Doses.
A Cook, an Host, an Herb-woman; or Nurse
Are all Licentiats in the Art, of Course,
A Barber for a Surgeon is Allowd
But turns all-Doctor, when [he] lets men Bloud,
And He, that has the least acquaintance Tampers
With Sickmen, in their very Beds, or Chambers,
Where those that are but talkative enough,
Præscribe a Medcine when they hear him cough.
No Parson did his office for the sick,
But gave it over and turnd Emperique.
So he that had been cured by Flys, that Got
By Chance, into the medcine, and the Pot,
But when the Dose was spent: He sent for more
With those black Creatures in't, he tooke before.

For universal Medcines are a Trick
That Nature never Meant, to Cure the Sick,
Unless by Death the Singular Receipt
To Root out all Diseases by the Great,
For universals deal in no one Part
Of Nature, Nor Particulars of Art,

PHYSIQUE

And therefore That French Quack that Set up Physique,
Cald his Receipt a General Specifique:
For tho In mortal Poysons, evry one,
Is Mortal universally alone:
Yet Nature never made an Antidot,
To Cure them all, as Easy as th' are Got;
Much less, among so many variations,
Of Diffrent Maladys, and Complications:
Make all the Contrarieties of Nature,
Submit themselves t' an Equall Moderator.

A Farrier is a Doctor, nere the worse,
For Shooing, and for Curing of a Horse:
That dos not only fit him, with his shoos
But when Hee's sicke, Administer a Dose.

For nothing but their own Indispositions,
Are Dangerous, and Fatall to Physitians.

For all the Good they can pretend to do
Are but for ostentation meant, and show.

The Frequentst Leprosys, and b'ing Possest
With Inmate Devils, at the same time ceast.

For to examine Pulses, or cast water,
Are but to pump Diseases hid by Nature.

For Sickmen are no Patients held until
They take the Medcine, as the Greater Ill.

Like those that catch Diseases, with Conceipt,
And Cure them, with a charme, or Amulet.

For Empriques torture worse then Hangmen,
To Rescue members from the Gangreen:
And operators slash, and Mangle,
To cure Inflamd Sores, when they Rancle.
Whose Remedys are little lesse
Then th' Insupportablest Disease,
Recover wounds with greater Cuts,
And Cure with Bullets, twisted Guts.

PHYSIQUE

Like him, who Nicely eate his Meals,
And Nonchons in a Pair of Scales.
And did not only Drink, and Eate,
But Pist, and went to stoole, by weight.

A Dog, that Grazes when hee's sick:
Is th' only Natrall Emperique.

Is't not the Greatest Art of State,
To make those wh' are so obstinate,
And mad upon their own undoing,
That nothing can Preserve from Ruine:
But by Diverting of these Freaks,
To save them, that would break their Necks?
And bring them back into their Senses,
With faire, and Plausible Pretences?
Whom all the Plainest Truth, and Reason,
Had nere been strong enough to ceaze on?
For nothing else in Nature's able,
To Rescue from it self, the Rabble,
With whom, there's Nothing Tru, or wise
Will ever Pass, but in Disguise,
And when th' are Mad, and Peremptory,
Prescribe a whimsy, or a Story:
And with mere Rallery, Impose
Health, better then the luckyst Dose:
And, with it self, Recover a Disease,
More Natral then sovrainst Recipes.

So Cardan cur'd himself of making mone
Perpetual for the Hanging of his Son,
And put an End, to all his whinneling,
By Pissing only through a wedding-Ring.

For nothing is more trite, and ordinary,
Then shifting Medcines, by th' Apothecary
That wants a Simple, in a Doctor's Bill,
And put's in those, for any other Ill.

For when the Doctor doubts of the Disease
His best opinion's Cross, or Pile, to guess.

PHYSIQUE

Whence men are brought to Desprater Dist[r]esses,
By catching Physique rather then Diseases:
Whence 'tis observd they frequently Recover
As soon as Doctors do but give them over.
For when the sickly Body, and the Soul
Do chance to fall on one another, Foul:
Their Busnes is to talke Secundum Artem
And, to Compound the Controversy, Part 'em.

For 'tis not what th' have don, but what th' have earnd
That makes the best Physitians, and most Learnd.

And when there are but one, at most in Ten
That Nature takes for Tithes, of all Sick men,
Unles it be in Epidemique Aches
When Nature makes the violentst Dispatches
The Rest miscarry, for the greatest Part,
By usinge too much, or too little Art.
And by their own Neglects, or vain Excess
Destroy themselves, instead of the Disease.

The French hold Guicciardine, the best Historian,
For treating civilly their Native Murrian:
And Placing most impartially, The Staples
Of that great Factory, at first, at Naples.

For Nature when she's bent to do her Part,
Acts more Effectuall, then the Greatest Art.
That but Diverts the Course, she meant to take,
And sets her Few, but better Medcines back:
For who can tell what Nature would have don
If sh' had been cald in to her self alone?

A Doctor's sick of evry mans Disease
And cure's himself first, with his Recipes
And when he cuts and Slashes, and Dissects
'Tis only to finde out his own Defects.

NATURE

LEAKE'S like a Tub and not a Boat:
For th' one Runs in, and th' other out.

The Sphere of Vapours rule's the Aire,
And makes the weather foul, or fayre.

The Moon do's never dare t' appeare
In Heaven while the Sun is Neare,
But still the further of[f] he goes
The more her borrowd Splendor shows,
And when shee's gotten opposite
Set's up with all her borrowd light.

Fishes with Scales are tyl'd about
Like Houses to keep water out.

An Army and a Populous Town
Infected with the Plague's all one.

Men's cornes are wont, before a Shour of Raine,
But never when th' are in't, to be in Paine.

So woodcocks that are Cullord like Dead Leaves
The Crafty Fowler easily deceives.

So in the western Sea of Spain, The Sun
Is like a Taper, put out and go's down.
That in a moment shines, and then go's out,
As th' Antients in his Sea-Bed-Chamber thought.

A single Feather breaks a Horses back
And Drops of water greatest vessels wrack.

Sleep that wearyd Life Redeemes
Is fed with vaine and Idle Dreames.

The most Divine of all the works of Nature
Was not to make Model, but the Matter;
As men may Build without Designs and Rules
But [not] without Materials, and Tooles.

A Salmon is both Bow and Arrows
That is both Shot himself and carrys.

NATURE

The Lady (like a Fishes Row) had Roome
For such a Shole of Infants in her wombe.

Nature Denys Brute Animals expression
Because they are Incapable of Reason.

Punaises have as great a Brood
I' th' Natives heads as in their wood,
And multiply no where in France
So numerous as the Peoples Braines.

Pretious Stones not only do Foretel
The Dire Effects of Poyson but Expel.

When no one Person's able t' understand
The vast stupendious uses of the Hand,
The only Engin helpes the wit of Man
To bring the world in Compass of a Span,
From Raysing mighty Fabriques on the Seas
To filing Chaines to fit the Necks of Fleas.

The Left Hand is but Deputy to th' Right
That For a Jorney man is wont t' imploy't.

The moon herself do's never steal the Light
She Pilfers from the Sun, but in the Night.

For tho the Moone's Commandres of the Seas
And all her various, Diffrent Nations sways,
She never yet, has, at the ful, been sayd
To make her Natral Subjects, Fishes mad,
Like those that, out of her Supreme Command,
Are Born, and Bred, and live upon the Land.

Weeds grow of themselvs as Natrally
As noble Plants degenerate and Dy.

All Beasts, and Foules forsake their yong,
They had been so tender of so long:
As soon, as once they have no Need
Of further Help, to shift, and Feed.

In all the yeare, The Day and Night
Have less of Darknes, then of Light

NATURE

In twilights, and the Dawnes of Suns
Besides six months of Shining Moons.
The light below, and upper-Darknes dy
The Naturall Blew Tincture of the Sky
For all the Heat, and light we finde appeare,
Extends no further then the Atmosphere:
The Rest all Darknes, only where the Moon,
And other Planets, entertaine the Sun;
That Hold no more Proportion to the whole,
Then Glo-worms Tayles, or Sparcles of a Cole.

Some guess the Earth is but a shell
And all the Inner Concave Hell
Th' Infernall Dungeons, and Dark holes
Of Reprobate Departed Soules,
Which Poets call the Stygian Lake
From whence no Traveller Comes back.

Water's the Clepsydra, to Cast
How many yeares the world wil last.

As an Arrow in the Sky
Do's, like the Bow that shot it, fly,
And make an Arch, so al things else
Conform, stil to their Principles.

Al Phænomenas
May be expounded several ways.

Nature permit's the mungrel Breed
Of Mules, No further to proceed,
For there's but one in evry Race,
Begotten between Horse and Ass:
Which makes the sons of zealous Saints,
To prove the greatest Miscreants.
And great Philosophers to think
Al fooles begot in Love, or Drink.

The Sunne-beames
When they are empty will descend
But when th' are Loaded upwards tend.

NATURE

Vermine were th' Originals of Cheats,
As Spiders first taught men the use of Nets,
And Lobsters first taught Armorers their Trade
And how the Joynts of Cuiraces are made.

A Madman's stronger in his Fits,
But Drunkard less then in his wits,
So much do Natral Parts Disdaine
To vaile t' an Artificiall Braine.

'Tis sayd of vipers when they Breed
The Femal bite's of[f] the Males head,
Which th' yong-ones back in Kinde Repay
And through her Bowels eate their way.

Prop that cannot stand alone
Grow's firm by being leand upon.

No Water of it self do's Run
Untill 'tis melted by the Sun.

The Moon, by striving to out run
And get the better of the Sun,
Is lost herself, and all her Light
Ecclips'd and vanish'd out of Sight.

That silly Meteor
Som call the Falling of a Star,
That, 'till it fals, is never seen,
Shines, and is *out*, as soon as *in*.

Without the Tale of Numbers, Birds are wont
To keep of Time, an exquisite Account
Can cast up all their Recconings, How long
They are to sit, before they hatch their yong.
And all that while, can tell at what a Clock
The Hen's expected to Relieve the Cock.
To Recreate his wearynes, and when
He is to do the same thing for the Hen.
As Time is Accuratly told by Clocks
That know not how to Reckon their own Strokes.

Female Asses are more tall
And sturdy then the silly Male.

NATURE

Nature
Do's all her work by Fire and water,
The two Divine Antagonists
By whose Contests the world subsists.

The Western Coasts of Wales, and Spaine
Exposd to th' Indian Ocean;
Have Mountaines, like Redouts, designd
To breake the Fury of the winde,
And turning of them, sevral ways,
Divert the Storms, those vast Seas Raise.

The Sun Appear's more glorious and Great
The nearer he Approaches to his Set.

As vaine as Dead men, when they have been drownd,
Swim Nat'rally, when 'tis too late, on Grownd.

The most Pacifique Seas with greatest Rage
Encounter when in Narrow streits, th' Engage.

Those Pigs the Devil did Posses
Mistook themselves, for Porc-pisces
And Ran into the Sea to finde,
And mix with others of their kinde.

Navigation, that withstood
The Mortal Fury of the Floud
And Prov'd the only Meanes to save
All Earthly Creatures, from the wave,
Ha's for it Taught the sea, and winde,
To lay a Tribute on Mankind:
That, by Degrees, has Swallowd more
Then all it Drownd, at once before.

The wounded whale dos Run on Shore
The Salt sea vexes him so Sore,
And Rather Runs himself on Ground
Then to endure the Torment of his wound.

No other members have those Graces
As Eies, and —— to be kept in Cases;
And since, no others can import
Mankind so much are kept like Jewels for't.

194

NATURE

A Stone that is but cast into a Pond
Without a Compas, make's a Circle Round.

Some Sorts of Fishes, only with the Tongue,
(As virtuoso's say) Beget their yongue.

As if the Greatest Mastery of Art
Were only against Nature to take Part,
Believe all knowledg of the Growth of Nature
To be like the Rough unpolishd Matter
And Art the Form, that bring's into being
Though Spoild with Ignorance, and over-seing.
As that Great Critique of the Trade took motion
To be a Natural thing and not a Notion.

A Horses Teeth are Ephemerides
And calculate their own Nativities.

An Ignis Fatuus against its Nature
Instead of Burning 's wont to Duck in water.

One Fish is but another Fishes vittle
By Nature and the Sea, layd up in Pickle.

The Hebrews, Spanyards and the Antique Welch
Do not Pronounce their Languages, but Belch;
And from the very Bottoms of their Throats
Fetch up their Close and Intimatest Thoughts.

All Arts and Arms of Excellence and worth
Are now the Native Products of the North,
Though their Originals were of the Growth
And Manufacture only of the South,
Which made the Ægyptians beare away the Glory
Of all Inventions (Right or wrong) in Story,
And al the learnedst Antiquarys writ
The South's the worlds left Hand the North's the Right.

Art is in vain unles it takes its Lesson
From Nature or her Secretary Reason.

For Nature gave an Ass the longer Eare
The Charming Accents of his Brays to hear.

Our Food is but a Medcin that Revive's
The Natural Consumption of our Lives.

NATURE

Nature has placd so glorious a Shew
Of other worlds and Suns within our view
That only tempt us with Desire to know
Without the Possibility of how;
And, since th' are Placd beyond our own concern,
Allows us no Capacity to Learn.

For Stars of the first Ma[g]nitude appeare
The least of all to those that view 'em here.

The Sun and water at so vast
Immeasurable a distance plac't
Are both espous'd to one another,
He nature's father, she her mother;
And by the mixtures of their seeds
Fill sea and land with various breeds.

Guns do not Hurt, by making of a noyse;
It is the Silent Bullet that destr[o]y's.

As some Affirme A Bever, and his Taile,
Is each a Diffrent Sort of Animall;
And tho they seem by Nature of one Piece,
The one is Perfect flesh, the other Fish:
And therefore in his House, The Beast do's ly
Above the waters Top, one Story high,
Altho his Tayle would mortify, and Gangreen
Without a Constant watry Cell to hang in.

Hair is the Native excrement of seed
That on the Cranion is observd to Breed,
And the[re]fore, when the Sperm do's first Decay,
The Hair fals of[f] or else turns grey:
Whence 'tis untimely Discontents and Cares
Bring men as Naturally to Grey haires.

The Motions of the Earth or Sun,
(The Lord know's which) that Turn, or Run,
Are both performd by fits, and Starts;
And so are those of Lovers Hearts:
Which though they keep no eaven Pace;
Move Tru, and Constant to one Place.

NATURE

As both the Longitude, and Latitude,
Are only by each other, understood;
And nothing else, but either Parallel
What th' other mean's can Naturally tell.
The under-Earth Degrees of Heaven show,
And only Heavn, those of Earth below.
But which move's Round; or which stands always stil,
The Learned make a Doubt, and ever will;
As much as whether Zealots use to move,
From th' Earth with us below, or Heavn, above.

So learned men, from Substance without Matter
Conclude the Greatest Myracles in Nature,
Demonstrate Artificially mere Fancies,
And Prove Eaternity b' as Hard Nunc-stances.

For if the water constantly grow lesse
And th' Earth is found as Naturally t' Increase
As virtuosos Naturally believe,
By Lands the Sea has beene observd to leave.
Besides th' Abundant Quantity, she uses
In all mixt compositions, she Produces,
Which 'tis unreasonable, and in vaine,
T' expect should ever be Returnd againe,
With other Instances as Evident,
The stock of water, wil in th' end be spent,
The ocean-seas perpetually wast
Until they are utterly Dryd up at last;
And if the Sun do's but draw neare to us
As great Philosophers believe He do's,
The Date of this worlds Charter will Expire
And all its Moveables Consume in Fire.

CHYMISTRY

A SOTTISH Chymist in Dispight of Nature
  Think's to make Gold by Penetrating Matter:
And, like a Spirit, Transubstantiate
Brass-Pots, and Kettles, into Silver Plate
Of which the greater Dose must be allowd,
To keep th' Alloy from being understood:
And therefore Ignorantly take Occasion,
To pass it for as vaine Multiplication.
In which th' Appeare as Idle and Absurd
In Sottishly Mischanging of a word.
For he that has but puzzl'd his Criss-cross-over
Is learnd enough to make a Stone-Philosopher
Who, when they undertake to Teach the Stone,
Make Solemne vows t' impart the Truth to None;
Which 'tis no Miracle but they may do,
And yet sweare only what's exactly tru.
The Ablest of their Spagirists are made,
Of Hot-braind Bank-rupts, of some other Trade.
For if but one, had got th' Hermetique Stone,
All others had for ever been undon.
The Meanest had Disdaind t' have Bought, or sold,
But turnd their Tin, and Lead, and Irn to Gold.
While all Professions else, had only serv'd
For want of Necessarys, to be stervd.
The Prices of all things had grown so Great
That None but Chymists could afford to Eate.
And when there were no other Men to Rob
Had beene Reducd to th' Indigence of Job;
And no men Held more wretchedly undon,
Then those who Newly had found the Stone:
Beside, if Fire cannot Distroy (as th' hold),
By consequence it never can make Gold,
For Art and Nature nere found out a way
To make that, which it self Cannot Destroy.

MAGIQUE

THE Devill was more Generous then Adam,
    That never Layd the Fault upon his Madam:
But like a Gallant, and Heroique Elfe,
Tooke freely all the Crime upon himself.

For Men are never certaine of strange sights,
Their Senses are so Distressed with Frights:
Especiall[y] of Specters, that forbeare,
Unless it bee in Darkest Nights, t' appeare.

For Magique is a False Spirituall slur,
And therefore subtler then the Secular:
Is more Mysterious, as it is Infernall,
And hard to [be] Disciferd then the Carnall:
Whose Intricate Designes, are better Layd,
Then those that use to be above boord playd.

For Ages, when they are Inhumane Grown,
Make worke, for Idle Sorcerers, to own:
When all extravagant, and Lewd Capricches,
Are Chargd upon the false Accompt of witches.
As if th' Indentures between Hags and Fiends
Were more Familiar then the Name Pretend's.
When some have Hangd for swimming on their Backs
And Sticking Pins, in Images of Wax.

For Men are counted Atheists that Deny,
Or doubt the Devils Infallibility:
When Cats for Nine Lives have procurd a Lease,
To serve him Co[n]stantly with Pigs and Geese.
And witches both their Soules, and Bodys give
To Please themselvs with mischief while they live;
When nothing can fall out, tho ere so Common,
But is Reducd to Prodigy, or Omen.

              [A Witch]
Is Able to outly a Proselyte,
That has been New-absolvd b' a Jesuite:

MAGIQUE

And by Confession's orderd to Deny all
He had acknowledg'd, when he comes to Tryall.
Untill the Poore Deluded Creature Dy's,
A Martyr, to the Patriarke of Lys.

The Devil first Debaucht a modest Man
To bee a Courtier quite against the Graine.
And in Defyance of his Fatall Stars
Trepand a Timorous Coward to the wars.
For when the Devill ow's some Men a Shame,
He put's-by all the Passes, that they Aime.
And with his Cloven Diabolique Foot
Kicks all the mischief down, they go about.

There Need's no other Charme, nor Conjurer,
To Rayse Infernall Spirits-up, but Feare:
That makes Men Pul their Hornes in, like a Snayle
That's both a Prisner to it selfe, and Jayle.
Draws more Phantastique Shapes, then in the Graines,
Of knotted wood; in some Men's Crazy Braines:
When all the cocks they think they see, and Bulls,
Are only in the Insides of their Sculs.

So in the stable ty'd-up Nags
Are Ridden Post, by mounted hags.

The Prophesies of Dreams Prognosticate
Mens Constitutions rather then their Fate.

GEOMANCY

                    Geomancy
Is nothing but a Trick to fancy,
That setting down a few smal Pricks
More Short then other Magique tricks,
Like throwing Dice upon the Square,
P[r]edict at Random unaware,
By which no Doubt can be so Hard,
But in a moment may be cleard.

ASTROLOGY

THE Antients held no Omen was so Dire,
  As to Spill water, when they ta[l]kd of Fire.
And that the certainst Skemes they had of thieves
Portended those that usd to weare Long sleevs:
Believd the Stars knew less of our Affairs,
And are as unconcernd as we in theirs:
Who have no way to know, Believe, or guesse
At what they should bee by Appearances.

Whether the Fixt Stars are but Holes, to pass
Th' Empyrium through, in Bright Effluvia's
Or Suns to other worlds; It is No matter
To all our own Discoverys in Nature.

For he that only look's among the Stars
To finde the Dark Events, of Peace or wars,
And not among th' Affairs of Active men,
Do's ten times, more Ridiculously then
Hee that tooke Pills for finding-out his Ass
Altho by Accident, it came to Pass.

For those are frequentst by the Stars Detected,
Whom most of all the wizard findes suspected:
Is sure to be his own significator
Whose Influence they most of all Look after.

Astrology, and Magique, Charms, and Spels
Are all that's Left, o' th' Devils Oracles:
Have acted greater Diabolique Sorcerys,
Then all the Litters of his Lapland-Nurserys.

Fooles are Familiars to themselvs,
That serve the Cunning men for elvs:
And make them only pimp, and set,
And owne the Tricks, they Counterfet.
That Hire, and Promp them to Detect,
The Parties, whom they most suspect:
And tell them first what Kinde of Men
That they may tell it them agen.

ASTROLOGY

The Factorys of Folly, and Imposture,
That with the weak, and Ignorant pas Muster:
Astrology, and all those Monstrous Fictions,
To cheat the world with Counterfet Prædictions:
That serve for nothing, if they should be tru,
But to take up misfortune, ere 'tis Due.
For Comets, and Ecclipses stil foreboad
Distruction to Mankind, but never Good:
With Chieromancy, Horoscopy, and Caball,
The Drums, and Rattles, of the Sottish Rabble
With all the vaine, Impertinent Delusion[s]
Of Frantique and Fanatique Rosi-crucians
All meant for Scarcrows false, and Counterfet,
To fright the world out of its little wit:
For all their stiff Formalitys of Arts,
Are no more Revrend, then the Beards of warts.

For did not once Astrologers perswade
Th' Inhuman Emprour Nero, to evade
The Dire Distruction, which a Star did seem,
To aime and Level Purposely at him:
To frustrat all the Black Designs of Fate,
And turn their sad Effects upon the State?

So some that passe for Deepe Astrologers
Have made great Princes Presents of New-stars,
As Virtuosos sillyly have don
And giv'n away whole Ilands in the Moon:
Although not fortifyd so Regular,
With Natrall Strength, as Castles in the Air.

Nor should their Art, or Science Mathematique
Escape the Test, which th' Antients took of Magique,
That undertake's the Universe to Fathom
From Infinite down to a single Atom.
And venturs to unriddle evry Cause
That Nature uses, by their own By-laws.
When all that's truly useful in the Art
Is no more then the mere Mechanique Part
And if they strive to aime beyond; Their Rules
Will not fit Nature and their Gresham-Schooles.

ASTROLOGY

For though the Earth be Round, yet evry Span
O' th' Superficies Rests upon a Plane,
Or else Th' Antipodes could never meet
On Equal Tearms, but with their Feet to Feet:
And neither Drake, nor Candish, nor Columbus,
Had 'ere been able al the Globe to Compas,
But evry Pacquet-Boate, or Petty Trader,
Had Sunke in th' Aire, and Founderd to Nadyr.
So those that made a Planet of the Sun,
Were Ignorant of what themselvs had don:
When there's so vast a Difference, Betwixt
The Rest and him, The world believ's He's Fixt.
And all their Notions of a Planet were
To be the Thickest Part of all it's Sphere:
Can take the Height of Stars, yet do not know
Whether they are Above 'em, or Below
Or how so many worlds upon their Centers
(With all their weight) should [be] hangd up on tenters:
Believd the Spheres, were but a Nest of Boxes
Only designd for Holding Paradoxes:
Whence that of Fire, has been so long Retrencht
Of all they had Contrivd it for, and Quencht.
Have beat their Braines, about a Freak, and worme,
To Square the Circle, they could nere Perform.
Things so absurd, Ridiculous, and wild,
That now they wil not Pass upon a Child.

The Hebrew-Kalendar did never Cast
The years Accompt up, till 'twas gone, and Past;
Which shew's they gave no Credit to the stars
Or those, that Prompted them, Astrologers.

LOVE

ALL Lovers in their Amrous fits
    Turn Poets and set up for wits,
Make all their Mistresses of Stars,
And, when their Ladys prove averse,
Confound and damne the stars for doing
Il offices to Cross their woing.
For Lover's by their Lady's kindred,
The Stars, are often Crost, and hindred.

Love is a Boy, and when it's youth
Is past, outlive's it self and truth.

The Devill has him fast enough
Whose stones are in his Cloven hoof.

Love that's the work, and Recreation
And Charter of the first Creation
From whom all Soul's of things derive
The Free Inheritance of Life
That in a short time would expire
But that 'tis lengthned by Desire.
—— For how Could Nature live
But that Love give's it a Reprive,
That has no more then one life in't
If Love did not inlarge that Stint.

All Love at first, like Gen'rous wine,
Ferment's, and Frets, until 'tis fine:
But when 'tis setled on the Lee,
And from th' Impurer matter free:
Becomes the Richer stil the older,
And Proves the Pleasanter the Colder.

As He that steal's away a Heart
Has Right to all and evry Part.

What woeman ever durst Resist
A Diamond Locket at a wrist,
Or could Refuse, th' untowardst Lover
Imbroderd and Perfumd all over?

205

LOVE

For though, the less Love Cost's of Pains
And Slavry 'tis the Clearer Gaines,
As wine (the Friend of Love) Provs Best
That Freely Runs, before 'tis Prest;
Some Lovers are Besotted most
Where most they finde their matters Crost,
As other Beasts are Sharper set
The lesse they are allowd to eat.

Victory in Armes or Love
Are Cozin-Germans one Remove.

Lov's but an Ague in the old,
Whose hot fit come[s] before the Cold.

Lovers, like wrestlers, when they do not lay
Their Hold below the Girdle, use Fair Play.

Love shoots at Random in the Darke,
Yet seldom fayles to hit his marke.

Can any Powr Pretend to aw
Love, Natures Fundamentall Law?
Or offer to give Laws t' a Lover,
They have no Jurisdiction over?
Shall He that with his Magique Bow
Strikes Hearts of Monarks through and through
Submit his own Great Laws of war,
To come t' a Trial at the Bar?
To turn Solicitor, and Prog
Suborn, Forsweare, and Pettifog?

Lovers, that are eternal Haters
Of all Impertinent Spectators,
And hee's less odious that discovers
A Statesman's Cabal, then a Lovers;
That do their Busnes best alone
And care not to be lookd upon
To fight their Duels hand to fist
And neede no Seconds to assist.
.........As those that shite
Abhor to do their Feats in sight.

LOVE

Love like Honor's Priviledgd,
And cannot be by oaths obligd,
No more then what a witnes swear's,
Is valid in his own affaires;
And Love has nothing to pretend,
But its own Interest and end.

Some have been with a look that sour
Sharp-set upon a New amoure
To set an Edge on Fancy with
As Braying of an Ass do's teeth.

For what Fond Lover can hold out
Till things are fairly brought about?
Who shew's he do's not Greatly heed her
That can have Patience to consider.

[Woman]
A most incomparable Creature
For want (especially) of a Better.

None but Lovers are so absurd
To play their false Dice, above Board.

When a Surfet of Delight
Has Duld the Lovers Appetite,
He must have time, til New Desire
Restore againe his Amorous Fire.

Platonique Love
Is from Socratical, but one Remove.

Spanish Gallants with their Lances
At once wound Bulls and Ladys Fancies;
And He subdu's the Noblest Spouse,
That widdow's most Tariffa-Cows.

Why should not some love Age, and uglines,
As wel as stinking meats and rotten cheese?

Some time he thinkes there is no trick
[O]f Love s' endearing as a kick.
Indeed 't were not amiss to venture
Men ought to knock before they enter.

LOVE

Love is to[o] great a Happines
For this world truly to possess;
Could it hold out inviolate
Against those Injurys of fate
Which all Felicitys below
By Cruel Laws are Sentencd to,
It would becom a Bliss too high
For Perishing Mortality,
Translate to earth the Joys above,
For nothing go's to heavn, but Love.

Love that's by Conversation gaind
Must by the same way be maintain'd;
Though Absence rayse the Appetite,
Like Fasting, it destroy's it quite,
When 'tis too long Continu'd.

What makes two Buls such mortal Foes
To fight to Death, but forty Cows?
What Quarrel has a Cock to Cock
But right to evry hen in th' Flock?

Can Love use so preposterous a Course
To take Possession of it's right by force?

When Love to Love returnd becomes unkinde
Desire is but the Feaver of the minde,
That in its hot fit long's to entertaine
That which injoyd do's but increase its Paine.

Love never feard what Horror might attend
In Consequence so it injoyd its end.

Passion do's never fall into Distress
But when Desire turnes Tenant to excess.

O 'tis a Happy and Heavnly Death
When a man Dy's above and a woman beneath.

Do not mine Affection sligh[t]
Cause my Locks with Age are white.

Your Brests have snow without and snow wit[hin]
While Flames of fire in your bright eies are see[n].

LOVE

That Heart must be of Horn or tuffer
That would not yeald to see you suffer.

For though some one way, some another
Yet al are Martyrs to Loves mother.

Love is so far from b'ing derivd
From Likenesses, as 'tis believd,
That it may rather seem to bee
Th' effect of Contrariety:
For all Fair women Love black men,
And black men stil Love them agen;
Low men Love women that are tall,
And they them as Fantastical;
The Bewteous for the ugly burne,
And they an equal flame return.

Expecting Love stands at a Stay
But in th' injoyment post's away.

A woman's Like a Looking glas
That entertains the shape of any face.

If Love between a Man and woman
Be nothing but Desire of union,
No Man would hang himself to fly
That which he cannot have, and Dy.

Love and Fighting is the Sum
Of all Romances from Tom Thumb
To Arthur, Gundibert, and Hudibras,
And all those worthys that De Scudry has.

Doe not unjustly blame
My guiltles brest
For vent'ring to disclose a Flame
It had so long supprest.

In its own Ashes it designd
For ever to have layn
But that my sighs like blasts [of wind]
Make it break out again.

The lylly grows not, nor the Rose
Upon your Chekes, but in my Hose.

LOVE

Love that has substance for its ground
Must be more lasting, firm and sound
Then that which has the slightest Basis
Of Airy Virtu, wit, and Graces.
Which is of such thin Subtlety
In Man it Creepes in at the eie;
But that which its extraction ownes
From Solid Gold and pretious Stones,
Must like its shining Parents, prove
As Solid and as glorious Love.

Not ten among a thousand weare
Their own Complexions nor their haire.

All Ladys what so ere that Dy
Are Fair and good in th' Elegie.

Tho Love, they say, all Natrall things subdues,
The Impotentst the Conqueror Reduce.

MARRIAGE

ADAM, who was but accessary to 's Wife,
   Was damn'd to dig and drudge for't all his life,
While Eve, subornd by the Devil to betray him,
Was sentenc'd but to love, and to obey him,
Which made her Penance, like her Crime, the worse,
Because oblig'd to do it as a Curse,
And he at liberty to love, or hate her,
Upon her good behaviour, or ill nature,
Who is not bound to do it, but at will,
Although she use him e're so well, or ill:
For there's no Slavery so desperate
As to b' impos'd upon to love, or hate.
Hence 'tis, they are no sooner made one Flesh,
And both compounded int' a civil mesh;
But Sexes next become the sole debate,
And which has greater right to this, or that;
Or whether 'tis Obedience, or Dominion
That Man can claim a title to, or Woman,
Untill the Issue has been fairly try'd,
And legally found oftest for the bride,
Who can reduce the most imperious Brave
To be her Drudge, and Utensil, and Slave:
To Husband takes the Idiot during life
And makes him but a Helper to his wife.

   The Bodys of all Animals
Are Femals, and the Souls the Males,
That Being Joynd like Man and Wife
Maintaine the Intercourse of Life.

   There's forty Femal witches sent to Jail
Condemned and Executed for one Male.

   A marrid Man com's nearest to the Dead
And to be Burryd ['s] but to go to Bed.

   A Virgin when she works upon a Bed
Do's like a Bird but Build a Nest, to Breed.

MARRIAGE

Birds go a wooing in the Spring and wed
And none but their own Lawful Spouses tread.

A widow do's but Raise up Horns to the dead,
As Antient Jews did Issue in their stead.

For evry widow is but a Reversion
That Brings a Joynter only of her Person.

      Illegal Matrimony
Is but a Pagan Ceremony
That in the Team of wedlock yoakes
Illegally an As and Ox.

A whimsy, in which evry one
Believe's he ha's found out the Stone,
The only True Receipt to marry,
And all beside himself miscarry.

One wife did Solomon more Hurt,
Then all the Madams of his Court.

The Credit of the Marriag-bed
Has been so loosly Husbanded,
Men only Deal for Ready money,
And women Sep'rate Alimoney;
And Ladys Errant, for Debauching,
Have better Tearmes, and equal Caution:
And for their Jorney-worke, and Paines,
The Chare-woemen cleare greater Gaines.

If he be a Beast that marrys,
He's one that Rides, as wel as Carry[s];
As Centaures mount at once, and Beare,
And are both Steed, and Cavaliere.

A Bargain Clubd to by a Paire
Of Dealers at a Chinese Faire,
Where hee that want's a wife or money
May give or take in matrimony.

      Virgins Marry just as Nuns;
The same thing, the same way Renounce;

MARRIAGE

Before th' have wit to understand
The Bold Attempt they take in hand;
Or having stayd, and lost their Tides,
Are out of Season grown for Brides.

And though one wife undid the Devil,
That do's not Prove al others evil.
One Mistress would have made Belpheger
In half the Time as great a Begger.

Some say that Lovers marry,
As Criminals take Sanctuary,
In Prison one another Clap,
Until they finde a way t' escape.

Agree and cleave to one another
Like John Baptista, and his Brother.

The Natural Difference
Of Temper, Humor, wit, and Sense,
And th' endles Cavils they Produce,
Make all their Quiet but a Truce.

Only with their Bodys worship,
For Souls are not Concernd in Courtship.

And yet some strive, as if the Curse
Were not enough, to make it worse.
When Ladys of the Fairst Deserts,
For Virtu, Bewty, wit, and Parts,
Will Squander al away at once
Upon as wonderful Pultrones,
And, though Disfigur'd with French Pock-holes
Th' had got by Playing at Hotcockles
Among so many, none knew who
The Lady was that gave the Blow,
Yet still th' Inhumaner they Prove
Become the Stupider in Love
Who all Inheritances owe
To th' Tenure of the Marriage-vow.

All Sorts of Vot'ries, that profes
To binde themselves Apprentices

MARRIAGE

To Heav'n, abjure with solemn vows
Not Cut, and Longtail, but a Spouse,
As th' worst of all Impediments
To hinder their Devout intents.

               [Kings]
By Proxy bring the Love Intregue
To Consummation, with one Leg
As Jews Contracted with their Hams
And marry only with their Names,
Espouse a Picture for a Queen
And take their Chance unsight unseen.

   To Love, and Honor, and obey
Things, that the Bride may sing, or Say,
And when th' are spoken by the Priest
Take 'em for th' Husband if she list.
Who when th' are virgins and but woo'd
Pass all for Gentle, soft, and Good
But with their wedding cloath[s] and Rings
Degenerat to other things.

       The Banes of Matrimony
To Aloes turne all their Honey.

   Man brought nothing of his Bliss
But woman, out of Paradise,
No Relique of his former Life
And blest Condition, but his wife
[And] as that life, and Innocence
Did never Part, before, nor since,
All that is left of both, live's now
Contracted in the marriage vow
That all his earthly loss supplys
With everlasting Paradise.
For he who rashly interlopes,
And ventures upon trading Sloops,
Besid the Danger of b'ing fird,
And blown up in the Pink he Hird,
Makes forfeture of all he beares,
And wracks the Title of his Heirs,

MARRIAGE

Of all their Right (but shame) defeats 'em,
And strives t' expose, before he gets 'em.

No virtu can disparage
A modish wit so much as marriage
That scorn it as a Paltry vanity
That has too little Inhumanit[y].

When unequal youth, and Age,
I' th' Banes of Matrimony 'ngage,
All other Matters run as Cross,
When Expectation's at a Losse,
When Feeble Impotent Fruition
Determines, in as Idle wishing.
And all the Sports of Love and Jumbling
Conclude in Miserable Tumbling;
In Driblets cannot pay th' Expence
Of Dunning Due Benevolence,
Until the Doteing Blown-up Lover
Makes all he Ha's to Feoffes over,
To pay th' Arrieres, with Use on Use,
And all from time to time accrew's.

When Love is still behind in Payment,
And turne's Platonique in th' Injoyment:
For Matrimony's a Quietus
To Love, though ever so Impetuous.

Yoaks are understood
But Characters of servitude.

In four hundred yeares, one Dozen
Of Jews produc'd six hundred thousand.

As the Romans drubd mens Bones
To th' Cadences and Moods of Tunes,
And Rack'd a Guilty Criminal
With Fiddle strings through al the Skale,
To shew, that Justice in their state
Was don in Measure, Time, and weight;
Our Ladies, with Inchanting Cords,
They set to more bewitching words,

MARRIAGE

Performe the same, and with the Charm
Their Hearts as wel as eares Disarm—
Those Passionate Croamatique Clamors
Melodious as the Ratling Hammers
By which Philosophers found out
The Alpha-bet, of evry Note
And from the Braying Tones of Asses
Invented Trebles first, and Bases.
Whence Lovers use, in all their Songs,
To treat of nothing but their wrongs,
Delight in Streames, that, as they Glide,
In Purling murmurs vex and Chide.

                          [Ladies]
Whose Soules weare nothing of their own
But what is Borrowd and put on;
That, like their watches, weare their faces
In delicate Inammeld Cases,
And all their Sense and wit as Tawdry
Except their Native Talent: Bawdry.

    Mean while, more By-blows are begot
In Matrimony then without.

    Nor can Diseases, though begot
By one, or Both, unty the knot:
For Health and Sicknes b'ing al one
Which both ingagd before, to own;
And are not with their Bodys bound,
To worship only when th' are sound:
The worst that fals can be no more
Then was provided for before.
And when both sides have shard the Hurt,
Who ever did it suffer's for't.

    The Giving of the Brid 's as fatall
As Giving Sentence, wounds, or Battle.

    'Tis Desperat t' espouse a Fool
And not be able to controll.

    For in the Factory of wives,
An Hundred break, for one that thrive's.

MARRIAGE

Andromeda was chain'd t' a Rock
On worse Tearms in the Marriage-yoake
Then but to be Devour'd by a whale,
More Gentle then the Rugged Male.

He was a Man that only Marryd
With Palisados t' arme his Forehead.
For nothing but his easy Head
Was of his Issu, brought to Bed,
As once the Thundrers Pia Mater
Is sayd t' have brought him forth a Daughter.

Sick of a fatal Pleurisy, a Bride,
The desprat'st inflammation of the side.

When Continence and Chastity in Rome
Was such a monstrous Prodigy become,
Suspected Vestals nothing could relieve
Less strange than carry'ing water in a Sieve;
Or, with their Girdles from their Wastes unbound,
Two mighty Ships that had been run on ground,
Which all the Force of Rome in vain before
Had strove to disengage and drag a shore.

So necessary then were all th' Acquests
Of Matrimony to their Interests.
For Fortune had no other way so soon
To set Men either up, or pull them down:
Which all the noblest Romans then were fain
T' assert with marks of Honour, and maintain;
When greatest Magistrates enjoy'd their Peerage
According to their elder dates of Marriage,
And married Men of all the rest took place,
Who had no Wives to shew for't, in the case;
And therefore those that us'd t' adopt their Heirs,
And for their Fathers turn'd their Fatherers,
Ne're ask'd the real Parents, if th' were got
Exactly in the legal Form, or not;
Were bound to nothing else, but that the years
Both of the new made Parents, and their Heirs
Might prove s' agreeable, they might be hop'd
To have begot, as well as to adopt.

MARRIAGE

The Dutch (of course) lay Matrimony by
Like th' extreme Unction, till they come to dye;
And, if they wed within the nick of life,
The Issue's lawful, and the Bride the Wife.
The antient Jews were bound to do the deed,
To raise their nearest Cousin-Germans seed,
Who us'd to father, after they were dead,
And own the Children gotten in their stead.

Birds hatch the Eggs they use to sit upon,
No matter whether th' are, or not, their own;
And make their Cocks themselves to sit, and brood
Upon the young ones, which they never trod.
Whence 'tis, that far more Bye-blows are begot
In Matrimony, than there are without,
As oft as Hedghogs suck the Teats of Cows
And Virgin-Pullets have been clap'd by Crows.

The antient Greeks, the Oracle profest
To be the wisest men of all the rest,
Believ'd the Globe of Earth, the Fire and Water
To be the greatest Deities in Nature,
And those more holy and devout than the others,
That marri'd with their Daughters, and Mothers.

For Matrimony's but a bargain made
To serve the Turns of Interest and Trade;
Not out of Love or kindness, but designs,
To settle Lands and Tenements like Fines;
Where Husbands are but Copy-holds, and Wives
Mere Messuages to have and t' hold for lives.

Marriage either make's or mars
More Certain then Ascendant stars.

An Error that b'ing once Committed
By death alone can be acquitted.

That Bind's the Bridegroom, and the Bride,
I' th' middle like a Fagot ty'd.

MARRIAGE

A thing that's only usd for Forme
Which none that undertake Perform.
No more Concernd then Vouchers are
In what they undertake to Sweare.

A Happines that only Lyes
Amonge the Sottish or the wise
That oversee, or else Prevent
Th' occasions of their Discontent.

WOMEN

A PARSONS wife, some Critiques use to Recon
  Half-way in Orders, like a Fœmall Deacon
That by their Husbands Copys, are ordaind,
And made their Vicars, at the Second Hand;
And by their Spirituall Callings, have their Shares
In ordering the Parishes Affairs.
And chang the Nature of their Sex, betwixt
The Clergy, and the Layety Commixt.

   The one half of the world has been begot
Against the other Parts Designe and Plot.

   The Soules of women are so small
That Some believe th' have none at all;
Or, if they have, Like Cripples, still
Th' ave but one Facu[l]ty, the Will;
The other two are quite layd by
To make up one great Tyranny:
And though their Passions have most Powr,
They are (like Turkes) but slaves the more
To th' Abs'lute will, that with a breath
Has Sovrain Powr of life and Death.
And, as it's little Intrests move,
Can turne 'em all to Hate or love,
For nothing in a Moment turn
To Frantique Love, Disdain, and Scorn,
And make that Love degenerate
T' as great extremity of Hate
And Hate againe, and Scorn, and Piques
To Flames, and Raptures, and Love-tricks.

   Our women, though they have forsworn
Virginity, like Nuns, are shorn.

   The chast Lucrecia durst not stand
The fatal thrust of Tarquins hand,
But rather let him have his will
Then feel the sharpnes of his steel;

WOMEN

But when the Feat was don and past
All remedy (I mary was't)
She did not feare to act his part,
And boldly stabd her self to th' heart.

   The Sophy give's his Bauds Commission
To Leavy, for his own Provision
The Brightest Bewtys, and to Choose
Those that are fittest for his use,
With Powr, by Privy-search, to try
Their fitnes, and Ability,
If they Rest quietly t' explore
Or in their sleeps break winde, or snore.

LUST

COMPARD with you, the Antique Dame
  Had never gaind her self, a Name,
By Breaking of the wildest Horses
Who do it better with their ——.

What's Pleasure but the Repetition
Of over-ridden, Tyrd Fruition?

   Harlotry's a Double vice
As Cissors Cutting once Cut twice.

There are more Naked, Baudy Pictures made
Of Innocent Lucrecia with her Blade,
Then all the Famous Lady Curtezans;
In History, or fabulous Romances.

Monsters got twixt Man and Beast
Stil take to th' Human-Parent least
Because the Beast, that do's but suffe[r],
Is not so Beastly as the Lover.

As Frenchmen with their Diseases
As Fraile, and tender as Punaises.

A Leacher's like a Bartl[m]ew fair Fiddle
With nothing but a lazzo in the middle.

One under Milstone, wil weare out,
Six upper-ones that Turn about.

And if she chance t' imploy a Neibor
To save herself and him the Labour
The Busnes is the better don
Then if sh' had trusted him alone.

What Lovers e're were so Capriccious
To whip their own Socratique Breeches?

  Claps that in the Getting Please
Delight as much in giving ease.

LUST

Punks made their Easy Cullys truckle
As witches Ride the Imps they suckle.

More Arts are usd to bring in a —— whore
Then to Create a French Pope heretofore.

   The Turks Seragl[i]o
Is but a kind of Bawdy Hospital,
Where Eunuch-Pimps and Virtuoso-women
Are kept with smal Allowances in Common,
Shut up and watchd in Secret Nunnerys
Beyond the Reaches of the Publique Eies,
And not allowd at Liberty to Ramble
And clap the Sex with scandalous Example.

   [Courtiers]
With costly Pride, and vanity, Proclame
Their Infamous Prerogative of Shame,
And by their Pompe, and Insolence, and Port,
The Ignorance and weaknes of the Court,
Until the very Name of Chr[i]stian
Is but a Foyl to that of Musselman.

The Antients in their times esteemd it more,
Then Punishment enough, To be a whore.
That Draw their faces after the Designe
Of th' Antient Master, Peter Aretine,
And for the Strokes and Cullor of the Paint, 'tis
All coppyd out of famous Elephantis.

HONOR

DISHONOR, tho a Negative, is Real
But Honor Nothing but a Jugler['s] Spell.
Has no more virtue in't, nor Influence
Then th' Antient Powder, of Experience:
That Smoke, the vaprous Excrement of Fire,
Do's not more Naturally strive, t' aspire.
That aime's at no Designe, but to exempt
The Mean, and Despicable, from Contempt:
And when they have no Honor of their owne
To take a Dispensation of the Crown.
A Priviledg of Pereage, and Free Grant,
T' indulge the frayl Nobles with what they want;
A Royall Bill of Store, and many times
A Pardon for th' Intollerablest Crimes
Which make's the New-Atchievments pass, instead
Of Honorable, Heroique Act, and Deed.
And servs for Compensation to Supply
The Reall wants of tru Nobility.

For those that only Clame the Priviledge
To Ride to execution, on a Sledge
Disdaine Inferiors, of less Deserts
That only are allowd to Ride in Carts.

The Turks caress a Drunken Prisoner
And Drub them, till they greater men Appeare
Then they would owne themselves, t' have been before,
To set a greater Ransom on their score.

And Painters made all Signes o' th' Saracen
As big as Gyants, tho but Little men;
Because the Christians in the holy wars
Were sometimes beat by such smal Conquerors,
To save their Credit, Drew their Heads and Faces
As fierce as Gog-magogs, or Goliasses.

HONOR

Contempt of Honor in the Great is worse
Then want of Conscience, in Inferiors.

And when there are two Persons, that within
The Species only, hardly are of kin,
A great and lesser, both lay Claims t' allyance,
With æqual Scorn of both sides, and Defyance:
For Little Familys, are sure to claime,
To be the Best Descended of the Name:
And Antient Houses, that are under Hatches
Have been Restord to Honorable by matches;
And New ones half-gentile, Half-Mungrels,
Have been erected into Great, from Dung-hills.
How many Kitchin-mayds, and homely Drudges
Have been espousd by Aldermen, and Judges?
And Whetstone-Sinners, virtuous Ladys dubd
As soon as Churchd of Child-bed-Claps, and tubd.

The Raggedst Begger is the most Clinquant,
And He the Richest that is most in want.
For those that have the Plentifullest Stores,
Of Broken Limbes, and Vermin, Scabs and Sores
And own the Greatst Variety of Patches
Are held the most Considerable Matches.
So thievs abroad are held the most Gentile
That oftest stand for Breaking on the wheel
Have don their Exercises best to Boyl,
For Forging Coyn, in Kitchen-stuf, or Oyl,
On Gibbets strivd to take their last Farewels
And Hang themselvs for their own Passing-bels;
Have undergone the French Strapado oftest
Down from the Top to Bottom and the loftiest.

All wild, but Generous Creatures, Live of Course
As if they had Agreed for better, or worse:
The Lion's constant to his only Miss
And never Leav's his Faithfull Lioness.
And she as Chast and tru, to him, agen
As virtuous Ladys use to be to Men.
The Docile and Ingenious Elephant,
T' his own, and only fœmal, is Gallant:

HONOR

And she as Tru, and Constant, to his Bed:
That first Injoyd her single Mayden-Head.
But Paltry Rams, and Bulles, and Goats, and Boars
Are never satisfyd with New Amores,
As all Pultrons with us delight to Range,
And tho but for the worst of all, to change.

THE WORLD

DIVIDE the world int' equall Halfes
The one's all Fooles, the other Knaves.

All Ovids Metamorphoses
Turn Men to Beasts, or Stones, or Trees
But seldom any where translate
The Changlings to a Better State.

Should [once] the world Resolve t' abolish
All that's Ridiculous, and Foolish,
It would have nothing left to do
T' apply in Jeast or Earnest to,
No Busnes of Importance, Play,
Or State, to pass it's time away.

Mankind's the same to Beasts and Fouls
That Devils are to Humane Soules,
Who therefor, when like Fiends th' appeare,
Avoyd and Fly with equal feare;
And to be tempted or to be tam'd
Is but to be betrayd or Damnd;
While Both have but one Reason for't,
Their own Advantages or Sport.

The world, the more it know's,
The worse and wickeder it grows.
Is but more vaine, and Foolisher
The more it turns Philosopher:
For Truth, and Reason are not fit
For all mens Tempers, nor their wit,
And knowledge honestly acquird
More hard to come by, then th' Inspird
Where Men may 'ssume with greater ease
Then Pains, and Study, what they please;
And, as they Grow more Rich by stealing
By Cheats, and Fraud then honest Dealing,
Appeare more wise by shifts and Tricks
Then Just, and solid Politiques

THE WORLD

And sooner wriggle into Trust
Then think to rise by being Just.

When al the world for Sin was drownd,
That which succeeded was not found
To be much better, then Before,
But to deserve that vengeance more.

The Greatest People and the least
Are much the same, like East and West,
For Luxury the one, as much as
The other Penury, Deboches.

What Horrid Actions would the world forbear
If Men were sure to be Immortal here?
When those that do but think, they may be so,
Such Barbrous Villanys Presume to do.

For Innocence is a Defence
For nothing else but Conscience;
'Twil not beare out the blows of Fate,
Nor Fence against the Tricks of State;
Nor from th' oppression of the Laws
Defend the Plain'st and Justest Cause;
Nor keep unspotted a good Name
Against the obloquies of fame;
Feeble as Patience, and as soon
By being blown upon undon.

If a few sober thoughts might be allowd
Free from the Sottish Madnes of the Crowd;
Or that it were not madnes now to dare
But to be less mad then our betters are,
I would say something faine, but truth and Sense
Are now become a high and bold offence,
And knowledg such forbidden fruite, [he] shows
A desprat Folly, that Speake's what he knows.
For men are grown so bad, they can indure
The —— Disease no longer, nor the Cure,
But rave like madmen in their hottest fits
'Gainst those that strive to bring them to their wits.

THE WORLD

Never for Satyr was there better times,
Wee now are got up to the hight of Crimes:
All that was don before was mean and low
To that, which evry Day produce's now.

When Death Come's to the happy and the blest
They' r turnd out; and the wretched but releast.

For to what end do's wit and Learning serve
But to bring those, that own them most, to s[t]erve?

There's nothing great, or high, or Noble,
That is not ful of glorious trouble.

Disclame the mean Applause of Ignorants
Live with thy self and thou wilt know thy wants.

As no excess can hold without supply,
Rapine is Treasurer to Luxury.

Think evry Day thy last and what remain[s]
Comes unexpectedly and is cleare gaines.

      This world is like Noahs Ark
In which few men but many Beasts imbark.

Vices, like eeles, slip through a gentle hand,
But with rough Leaves are held, or rugged Sand.

                  A Pimp
Is but a whores familiar or her Imp.

The world would be more Just, if truth, and Lys
And Right, and wrong, did beare an æqual Price;
But since Impostures are so highly Raysd,
And Fayth, and Justice equally Debasd,
Few men have Tempers, for such Paltry Gaines,
T' undo themselves, with Drudgery, and Paines.

A Place so barbarous and foul
The Devil would [not] go there for a Soul,
And, if h' had left his eies behind,
Rather then fetch 'em would be blinde.

THE WORLD

Our solemn Blacks are worn
To cloath our selves not them for whom we [mourn].

Shame and Repentance are the Constant Price
Of all our False and Idle vanities,
And our best wisdom only to esteeme
The world a vain and Short Fantastique Dreame.

For most mens Lives are nothing but Diversions
T' avoyd th' uneasinesses of their own Person's.
Had rather tumble Sisiphus his Stone
Then but indure themselvs, to be alone.

Man of all Creatures the most Fierce and wild
That ever God Made, or the Devil Spoyld.

For Mankind Naturally resents the Need
Of nothing more then what they are forbid.

There is no honest meanes of Rising high:
The Stairs of Rooms of State are built awry.

So wax, that is the worst of all things else,
Is therefore usd to serve the world in Seales,
When nothing in the world can be more fit
To be Defacd, and Forgd, and Counterfit.

Dead mens Graves
Consume and Bury their own Epitaph[s].

Life is a Game that'[s] lost before 'tis Playd
And is but not thrown up, when 'tis Injoyd.

VULGARITY

HOW various, and Innumerable
    Are those, who live upon the Rabble?
'Tis they maintaine the Church, and State,
Imploy the Priest and Magistrate,
Beare all the Charge of Government,
And pay the Publique Fines, and Rent;
Defray all Taxes, and excises,
And Impositions of all Prices;
Beare all th' expence of Peace, and war,
And pay the Pulpit, and the Bar:
Maintain all Churches, and Religions,
And give their Pastors exhibitions.
And those, who have the greatest Flocks,
Are Primitive, and orthodox.
Support all Schismatiques, and Sects,
And pay 'em for tormenting Texts.
Take all their Doctrines of[f] their Hands
And pay 'em in good Rents, and Lands;
Discharg all Costly Offices,
The Doctor's and the Lawyers fees,
The Hangmans wages, and the Scores
Of Caterpiller Baudes, and whores;
Discharge all Damages, and Costs
Of Knights, and Squires of the Posts,
All Statesmen, Cutpurses, and Padders,
And pay for all their Ropes and Ladders;
All Pettifoggers, and all Sorts
Of Mercats, Churches, and of Courts;
All Sums of Money payd or spent,
With all the charges Incident,
Layd out, or thrown away, or given,
To purchace this world, Hell, or Heaven.
For should the world but take account
To what it's Charges do amount,
One third at least of all the Sum
Is spent upon the world to Come.

VULGARITY

Nothing make's Hell s' intollerable
As the bad Company and Rabble.

All Mankind is but a Rabble
As silly and unreasonable
As those that Crowding in the Street
To see a Show or Monster meet;
Of whom no one is in the Right,
Yet all fall out about the Sight;
And when they chance t' agree, the choyce is
Still in the most and worst of Voyces;
And all the Reasons that prevayle
Are measur'd not by weight but tale.

Non live so happy and at ease
As those who mortifying profes.

The two wicked Elders Susanna would grope
While she sent out her mayd to fetch her some sope;
But when they could not make her a whore
They swore she had swiv'd with another before.

A Thief, whose Destiny's forespoke,
And sentenc'd by his hanging Look,
As soon as he's condemn'd to dye,
Looks handsome in the Rabble's eye.

MORALITY

ALL mens Intrigues, and Projects tend
 By sevrall Courses to one end,
To Compass by the Properst shows,
What ever their Designes propose;
And that which ownes the fairst Pretext
'Tis often found the Indirect'st.
Hence 'tis that Hypocrites stil paint
Much fayrer then the Real Saint,
And Knaves appeare more just, and true
Then honest men, that make less show;
The Dullest Ideots in Disguise
Appeare more knowing then the wise;
Illiterate Dunces undiscern'd
Pass in the Rabble for the Learnd;
And Cowards that can damn, and Rant
Pass muster for the Valiant.
For he that has but Impudence
To all things has a Just Pretence;
And Put amonge his wants but shame
To all the world may lay his Clame.

In Ballances the lightest end
Do's always Naturally ascend:
So in th' Affaires of Church and State
Men soonest rise for want of weight:
And as those Names are Counted best,
That signify and meane the least;
So 'tis with Persons in th' opinion
Of Church and State, that have least in 'em.

Al great Men are found to rise
As Pigeons mount with seald-up eies.

For as in great and Crowded Faires
Monsters and Puppet plays are wares,
Which in the less wil not go of[f],
Because they have not money enough:

MORALITY

So men in Princes Courts will pass,
That will not in another place.

     Most of all great Persons Fates
Deserve mens Pitty or their Hates.

     Men flatter with their Tongues, more false,
And base, then Dogs do, with their Tayles,
And creep more vilely into favour,
Then Hounds that drivel, with their Chaps, and slaver.

     To aske Forgivenes, and excuse
An Injury, and past Abuse
Is such a Plaister for a wound
As that o' th' weapon Salve is found,
That only has virtue to restore
And Cure the Hurt it did before.

     Willows are weak and yet beinge Bow'd
Have Powr to binde the stubborn'st wood.

     Mens Armes grow next their heads t' infer
Advice and Action should be neare.

     As Thistles wear the softest Down,
To hide their Prickles, till they're grown;
And then declare themselves, and tear
Whatever ventures to come near:
So a smooth Knave does greater Feats
Than one, that idly rails and threats,
And all the Mischief, that he meant
Does like a Rattle-snake prevent.

     As al men Live by one anothers Deaths
The Murthrer gaine's but what the Dead bequeaths.

AVARICE

AS he, whose destiny do's prove
    To dangle in the Aire above,
Do's loose his life for want of Air,
That only fell to be his share:
So he, whom Fate at once design'd
To Plenty and a wretched minde,
Is but condemnd to rich Distress,
And starves with Niggardly excesse.
So Ships that chance to run aground
Are oft for want of water drown'd.

[A Miser]
Who with an upright Heart Lov'd Gold,
Not to injoy but t' have, and hold,
And was it's tru, and Real Friend
Without the least Designe, or end.
Observd it only for it self
As hidden Treasure's by an Elfe.

In all the world, there is no vice
Less Prone t' excess then Avarice;
It neither cares for food, nor clothing:
Nature's Content with little, that with nothing.

FORTUNE

[DAME] Fortune some Men's Tutelar
Takes charge of them without their Care,
Do's all their Drudgery, and work,
Like Fairies, for 'em in the Dark,
Conduct's 'em Blindfold, and advances
The Naturals by blinder Chances:
While others by Desert and wit,
Could never make the Busnes hit,
But still the Better they Deserve,
Are but the Abler thought to sterve.

      Fortun[e]'s never so Perverse
As when Sh' oblige's Conquerers.
For Victorys acquir'd too soon
Are Lost as Easyly as won.

  Men at their Hight of Fortune are undon
As all Ecclipses Happen at Ful moon.

  There is no more, but a mere cast at Dice
Between the Greatest Idiot, and the wise
But Cross, and Pile between the Great, and Smal
And which shal Prove the Female, or the Male.

  For some Mens Fortunes like a weft or Stray
Are only Gaind by loosing of their way
An[d] fall from one mans, to anothers Hands
By chance and Destiny like Deodands.

  The Cunningst Gamsters are not lik[e] to win
That Put out Better Cards then they take in.

  Man is supreme Lord and Master
Of his own Ruin and Disaster,
Controuls his Fate, but nothing else
In ord'ring his own Happiness:
For all his Care and Providence
Is too too feeble a Defence,

FORTUNE

To render it secure and certain
Against the Injuries of Fortune;
And oft, in spight of all his Wit,
Is lost with one unlucky hit,
And ruin'd with a circumstance,
And mere punctilio of Chance.

As Gold, that's proof against th' Assay,
Upon the Touchstone wears away;
And, having stood the greater Test,
Is overmaster'd by the least:
So some Men, having stood the Hate
And spiteful Cruelty of Fate,
Transported with a false Caress
Of unacquainted Happiness,
Lost to Humanity and Sense,
Have fall'n as low as Insolence.

WEALTH

THE fishes of the Sea have more
    And Richer Banks of wealth in Store
With Pretious Stones of greater worth
Then all the Princes of the Earth
Brought freely in by evry Storme
But do 'em neither good nor Harme;
Which, if they were on Land, th' excess
Would bring their valew down to less
And render them as useless here
As now th' are to no purpose there;
So Dutch men to Keep up the Price
Are fain to burn vast Stores of Spice.

            Partners in Distress agree
Much better then Prosperity.

The Restles Drudgery of Fooles
That for their work mistake their Tooles
And, like the silly Prussian, eate,
And swallow Knives instead of meate,
And know no use at all for Money
But Slavery and Parcimony.

                        [Fooles]
That have no use, beside their Drudging,
For all their Miserable Curmudging,
But, for an Itch of getting more,
Will venture all they had before,
And for an Idle Flam of Hopes
Stake Necks and all to th' ods of Ropes.

The very Paint of Gold is Poyson
And Gold to some have provd as Noysom.

                    An Old Curmudgin
Grown Rich with Penury, and Drudging,
As Usurers Tooles work night and Day
And earne by Passing time away,

WEALTH

The more his Time is idly Lost
And thrown away, improv's it most
Let's out his Heralds fields of Gold
For Mortgages, to have and hold
Until h' has Raysd his Silver-Acres
Beyond th' Unconscionablest Rackers.

Men are not Limited with less, or more:
Desire and Fancy makes them Rich or Poore.

WRITERS

AS 'tis the greatest Mastry in the Art
Of Painting, to Foreshorten any Part
Then draw it out, So 'tis in Bookes, the Chief
Of all Perfections, to be Plain, and Brief.

For He that Plainly writs his Busenes down,
He is obligd to Justify and owne,
Appeares more wise, then if he did Compile
Far Greater Matters in a Polishd Style.

It is impossible to write
Satyrically, and not light
On something of him unawares
As Spaniels Casually Start Hares.

The Modern times have no Arithmetique
Of th' Antient Roman Masters, nor the Greek.

The Antients Seldom did translate a Book,
But only what was for their Purpose tooke,
And left the Rest for others to make use
Of what they Pleasd, and freely Pick and Choose.
But what is more Familiar in their Books
Then Men begetting children upon Brooks?
From which they fetch their Antique Pedigrees
And own themselves at first a Spawne of Fish.
Others derive their Races from the Gods
That Ravisht silly Virgins in the woods,
As Naturally as the Spanish Kinde
Of Running Nags ingendred by the wind.

As Cutpurses do never minde what Sum
Nor who the Person is, they take it from,
And, though their Throttles are layd down at Stake,
Know nothing if they Gold or Silver take,
Some strive the Cheapest ways to understand
And take their Notions up at second Hand.

WRITERS

All Plagiarys do but Steal, and Poch
And upon other Careless wits encroach.
Converst with wits, and Rallyers, to way lay
And Intercept, all that they Chancd to say.
Made Topiques, Indexes, and Concordances,
Of smart Reflexions, Repartees, and Fancies,
When that which may be tru enough, turn's False
When 'tis but weyd in false uneven Scales.

As He that both condemnd and stole from Hobs
Like a French Thief that murthers when he Robs.

For evry Author is a Criminall,
That by his Pere's is Bound to stand, or Fall;
And like the Laws Mediety o' th' Tongue
By Fooles, or wise men, Censurd Right or wrong;
Altho in one Epistle Dedicatory,
He Pawnes the Notes, He gatherd under Glory;
And lays out all the Inventory of Prayses,
H' had Scrapd together, in his Comon-Places:
To settle all the Property upon
Some Honorable, Singular Patrone,
Provided the Mecænas undertook
Against the Critiques, to secure his Book:
And, like a Man of Honor, kept his Promise,
To Rescue him from Zoilus, and Momus,
That when his Felonys, should be Detected,
They might by him, as vainly, be Protected;
When all the Powr he has, will not afford
A Dispensation, to one Faulty word;
A Lewd, and most Ridiculous Divice,
And yet by Custome Past for Learnd, and wise.

Next this the Præface Follows, with excuses
For all the Faults, the Author knows, but uses.
Makes his Submission to the Grave, and wise,
But the Ignorant, and Criticall De[f]y's:
Put's in his own Exceptions before Hand,
'Gainst all that shall Prætend to understand.
And like a Guilty Criminall in Books
Excepts against his Jury by their Looks

WRITERS

Only to Put in Caveats, and Demurrers
And Cuningly Assignes himself his Errors;
Calls all his Gentle Readers, Thou, and thee:
But styles himself, Our Person, us, and wee.
Makes Honorable Mention, of all others
Who've undergone the Dignity of Authors,
And never Names them, but for Honors sake,
Especially, of those that seeme to take
And have the Naturallest Inclynations
To all his own Opinions, and Perswasions.
But as the Devill blows both Hot, and Cold
So if it be His Chance to Rayle, or Scold
H' has foul words enough, for th' extirpation
Of all Good maners, in the Civillst Nation.
With Tropes, and Figures such as Western-Pugs,
Repeate upon the Thames in Dialogues.
Until the Porch grow's Bigger then the House:
As Mountaines Swel and Ly-in of a Mouse.

The Smartest of all Libels and Lampoones
Like vermin Scratch, and Bite, but break no Bones;
For all their Edges and their Claws are turnd,
As soon as once they are Dispisd, and Scornd.

For some are stil most constantly Imployd
In doing what they study to avoyd:
For to consider's nothing but to Prune
All that's superfluous, and over don,
And not impertinently to ad more
To what was too extravagant before;
And, therefore, a Judicious Authors Blots
Are more Ingenious then his first Free thoughts,
And those that understand, are modester
In telling truth, then Pedants, when they erre;
Are most severe themselvs to all they write,
As Candles tremble when they give us light.

POETRY

AS wine, that with its own weight run's, is best,
  And counted much more noble then the Prest:
So is that Poetry, whose generous Straines
Flow without servile Study, Art, or Paines.

[Poets]
Make the Gods Stickle in Heroique Actions,
And manage all Disputes in Armes by Factions,
That set the Knights together by the eares,
And part them afterwards like Dogs and Beares;
For when the Champions valiantly have fought
The Gods themselves, to part the Fray, fall out.

Things that are written in Cold bloud
Seldom prove excellently good.

Can any thing be don or sayd
That may not good, or bad be made?

Poets are Free of evry Nation
And need no Naturalization.

For why should not affected Negligence
Pass for wit here as freely as in France?

Wits that are always in the State of war
    Hold it no Crime but Lawful Prize
To plunder those that are their enemies.

For one Admirer is enough
To serve for good sufficient proof,
Though ever so extravagant
Among the weake and Ignorant.

Why should a Man aske Pardon for a fault
That's in his Power to commit or not?

For as some Critiques use to make that wit,
That never was so much as meant for it;

POETRY

[So] (to be like themselves) they'l make that pass
For Nonsense and mistake, that never was;
[Th]at like to Rookes bet on some fancyd hand,
[W]hich they like better then they understand.
[F]or what they finde not faulty they wil make,
And Damne what's written wel, and they mistake;
[F]or whatsoever is above their reach
[To] their own Low capacity they'l stretch.

It is not Poetry that makes men Poore;
For few do write, that were not so before;
For those that have writ best, had they been rich,
[Had] nere been clap'd with a Poetique itch;
Had lovd their ease too well, to take the Paines
[To u]ndergo that drudgery of Braines;
[B]ut being for all other Trades unfit,
[On]ly t' avoyd b'ing idle set up wit.

Some call it Fury, some a Muse,
That, as Possessing Devils use,
Haunts, and forsake's a man, by fits:
And when hee's *in*, h' is *out* of 's wits.

A Foolish Title, like a Foolish Look,
Is a True Symptom of a foolish Book.

He that creepes after Sense shal nere excel
In Nonsense, Fustian, nor in Doggerel.

No other Nation's so severely bent
To see offenders brought to punishment
As th' English are, for when a Thief is Caught,
To be by officers to Justice brought,
All People Crow'd to hurry him along,
As if h' had don to evry one the wrong:
So when a Poet happens to Commit
Ever so smal a Robbery of wit,
You al Cry upon him, and pursue,
As if h' had stol'n from evry one of you.

A Satyr, like a Roman Magistrate,
Has Rods before him born in state,

POETRY

To fright the Guilty from their Crimes,
And Scourge the faults of vicious Times:
For in extent of Powr a Satyr
Is absolute as a Dictator.

Who always shootes his Bolts of wit
Has ill Luck if they never hit.

Nothing more moves the just disdain of men
Then bold assumings of an Ignorant Pen.

He that would understand what you have writ
Must read it through a Microscop of wit;
For evry Line is Drawn so curious there
He must have more then eies that reads it cleare.

All Elegies are false and Satyrs true
If Prayse and Disprayse had its Due.

As Pedants when they fayl in prose or verse
Maintaine their Errors by committing worse
Tel what they learnt when they were boys at Schoole
An[d] Justify their Nonsense with a Rule.

All writers, though of Diffrent Fancies,
Do make all People in Romances,
That are distrest and discontent,
Make Songs and sing t' an Instrument;
And Poets by their Suffrings grow,
As if there were no more to do,
To make a Poet excellent,
But only want and discontent.

They, that do write in Authors Prayses,
And freely give their Friends their voyces,
Are not Confind to what is True;
That's not to give, but pay a Due:
For prayse that's true, do[es] give no more
To worth, then what it had before;
But to commend without Desert
Requires a Mastery of Art,
That set's a gloss on what's amisse,
And writes what should be, not what is.

POETRY

In Forraine Universities,
When a King's born, or wed's, or Dy's,
All other Studys are layd by,
And all apply to Poetry:
Some write in Hebrew, some in Greeke,
And some more wise in Arabique,
T' avoyd the Critique, and th' expence
Of Difficulter wit, and Sense,
And seeme more Learnedish then those
That at a greater Charge Compose.
The Doctors lead, and Students follow;
Some call him Mars, and some Apollo,
Some Jupiter, and give him th' ods
Or even tearmes of all the gods:
Then Cæsar he's nicknamd, as Duly as
He that in Rome was Christend Julius,
And was adrest to by a Crow
As pertinently long agoe;
And with more Hero's Names is Stild,
Then Saints are clubd t' an Austrian Child:
And as wit goes by Colleges,
As wel as Standing and Degrees,
He stil write's better then the rest,
Who's of the House that's Counted best.

All the wit
At Play-houses is in the Pit.

For Poets sing, and ne're speake Plain,
As those that quote their works maintain,
And no man's bound to any thing
He do's not say, but only sing.
For since the good Confessors time
No deeds are valid writ in Rhime,
Nor any held Authentique Acts
Seald with a Tooth upon the wax:
For Men did then so freely deal,
Their words were deeds, and teeth a Seal;
And 'tis not a Straw-matter whether
'Tis tru or false, or both, or neither,

POETRY

For all men write in th' Intervalls
Of Sense is neither tru nor false.

Melodious as the Bard, whose Muse
Resound's in Galleries, and Pews,
Or those Heroique Deathles sheets
Are Chanted at the Ends of Streets.

Stages are but Poets Banks
On which they play Heroique Pranks.

So Homer in th' Immortall Piques
Between the Trojans, and the Greeks,
That neither Party might Prevayl
Bring's in the Gods to stave, and Tayl.

For all Encomions are but meant to whedle
Enchant and tickle writers, like a Fiddle,
And Blow them up, with Rosen, and Horse-hair,
As Bel once, and the Idol Dragon were.

Some modern Authors have found out New ways
To hedg applause in at the end of Plays,
And cheat their Audience with a sly intrigue
By turning of an Epilogue t' a Jigge,
And, if yee clap it, as ye are always wont,
To put th' Applause upon the Plays account.
But he that makes a Conscience of his ways
Wil not defraud you of one Jot of prays,
But rather take whatever you think fit
Then use the least cheat to set of[f] his wit.

Brambles and Thorns weare Prickles to defend
Their Harsh wild Fruite against the Fingers end
While nobler Trees freely expose their Store
And as that's richer, bend their Bows the lower.

As Poets that for money write
Do but make Sale-work Coarse and slight
That for the cheapnes of the Stuff
Is like to go the better of[f].

POETRY

As al Fanatiques preach, so al men write
Out of the Strength of Gifts, and Inward light,
In Spight of Art, as Horses thorough-pac'd
Were never taught, and therefore go more fast.

As He that make's his Mark is understood
To write his Name, and 'tis in Law as good:
So he that cannot write one word of Sense
Believ's he ha's as legal a Pretence
To Scribble what he do's not understand,
As Idiots have a Title to their Land.

Some to that height of Impudence are grown
To charge on others thefts that are their own.

A Prologue is the usher of a Play
Just as an Eave is to a Holiday.

Critiques are like a kinde of Flys that breed
In wild Fig-trees, and when they'r grown up, feed
Upon the raw Fruit of the nobler kinde,
And by their nibling on the outward rinde
Open the Pores, and make way for the Sun
To rip'n it sooner then he would have don.

Some by whole Tribes and Familys do write
New Plays as th' antient Jews were wont to fight.

Al men of Judgment do not ask how soone
A thing was doing but how wel 'tis done.

Some hold it is Impossible to write
One Act without a Song, or Dance, or fight,
Or make al Different Intrigues accord
Until th' have been decided by the Sword.

For Gentlest Spectators at a Play,
That throng and Crowd to see it the first Day,
Feare nothing more then that it should prove Good
Or by the wit-inquisitors be allowd,
But chiefly those that have writ il before
And do intend to try again once more.

POETRY

Who like those kinde Spectators in the Ring
When Necks are broken at a Wrastling
No matter whose, set up their throats and Bawl
O'rejoyd when any man receive's a Fall.

    Al sorts of Ideots, like Fanatiques,
Have pow'r in Comedy, and turn Dramatiques
For just as when a Taylor make's a Suite
What neede's the Cloth or stuffe he uses to't
Should by himself be made? No more is't fit
All a man writes should be of his own wit.

    For He that steales French wit do's worse
Then he that Picks an empty Purse,
And is an Ignoranter Toney
Then he that files and clip's false money,
And vainly think's to gaine by those,
Who never had one *Souse* to loose,
Worse then a Goldfinder that rake's
For Spoones and Bodkins in a Jakes.

    No Man wants wit, for he that has the least
Believes hee's as well furnishd as the Best.

    For hee's a Poet that write's bad,
No less then he that do's excel,
As he's a Merchant that do's loose as wel
As he that thrives and grow's rich by his trade.

    As if the Plaine Expression of a Thought,
The greatest Mastry, were the greatest fault.

    For as in Tale of Dead things men are wont
To allow more in th' hundred on account
Then to the Living: So men after fate,
Have more allowd in th' hundred to their weight
Then th' had before: For Nature has Contrived,
That men are Fuller dead, then when they livd.

GOVERNMENT

THE People have as much a Negative voyce,
  To hinder making War, without their Choyce,
As Kings of Making Laws in Parlament,
No Money is as Good as *no Assent*.

For Cromwel found his Politiques Miscarry,
By trusting but one Antient Adversary:
For all his Arbitrary Empire sunk,
As soon as He Employd, and trusted Munke.

When Princes idly Lead about,
Those of their Party follow Suite,
Til others trump upon their Play,
And turn the Cards another way.

The Greatest Princes are not free from Paying
The Cost and Charges of their own betraying,
That (like Good Christians) stand faire
To take another Cuff on th' Eare,
As Jewish Prophets usd t' intreat
And beg the Favour to be Beat.

Queen Elzabeth Placd Officers to waite
In London constantly at every Gate,
To Cut the Ruffs of al that Past the Guard
That were above a Naile deep of a yard.

A womans Government is braver then,
And far more Masculine then that of men:
The Reason of the Paradox is Common;
For woemen take to Men, and men to women.

What makes all Subjects discontent
Against a Princes Government?
And Princes take as great offence
At Subjects Disobedience?
That neither, th' other can abide,
But too much reason on each side?

GOVERNMENT

The Roman Empire raysd upon
Revenge, for wrongs to Lucrece don,
Was after by a Harlot savd
From b'ing eternally inslavd;
Yet 'tis not wise t' infer from thence
All States are safe that use that meanes.

For what Do's Hist'ry use to tel us
But Tales of Subjects being Rebellious,
The vain Perfidiousnes of Lords,
And Fatall Breach of Princes words?
The Sottish Pride, and Insolence
Of Statesmen, and their want of Sense?
Their Treachery, that undo's, of Custome,
Their own-selves first, next those who trust 'em?

Our Saxon Princes spent their Reignes
In Building Abbies, Routing Danes
That puld them down, and making Saints
To fill 'em with Inhabitants.
Our Saxon Princes beat the Danes
From Pagans into Christians,
Who in Requital gave no Quarters,
But drubd the Christians into Martyrs.

David, who was himself a mighty Prince,
Diswade's the world to trust 'em for three Pins.

The most Inhumane of the Roman Emprors
Were Pædants, and Lief-hebbers in their Tempers;
And those that Prov'd the most Infernal Monsters
Began with Turning Fidlers first, and Songsters;
Were but a kind of Dabling Virtuosos
No better then Gitar-men, and Flut-douces;
And those that Prov'd the Jockys, of the Cæsars,
Forgot the Glory of their Predecessors.

The Populace
Is Head of all Republicas.

[The Rabble]
Injoy two equal Delights
In Gallowses, and walking Sprights;

GOVERNMENT

And visit once a Month of Course
The Tombe-stones of their Ancestors.

The earth is easier undermind
By Moles, and Vermine deaf and Blind
Then those that have their senses Sound
But cannot Dig so under ground.

As those that are starke Blinde, can trace
The Nearest ways from Place, to Place:
And find the Right way easier out,
Then those, that Hoodwink'd try to do't:
So Tricks of State are Managd best,
By those that are suspected least;
And greatest Finenes brought about
By Engines most unlike to do't.

Tho world believes no Man the worse,
That takes the Trecherousest Course:
But like's his Jugling as a Cheat feat
That's wittily perform'd, and neat:
And what they cannot justly gaine,
Believe's they ought by Art [t'] obtain.

Some Tyrannys have been s' extreame
To make it Criminal to dreame
When Men for sleeping were condemnd
For having traytorously dreamd.

A Good Prince is a wonder that appeare's
But once or twice in many hundred yeares.

All Churches are but th' Interests
Of Princes, and the Trades of Priests.

No Crisis is so Desperate
As Fatal Lethargies of State.
For Remedys are spent in vaine,
On those who have no sense of Paine.

Lyons are Kings of Beasts, and yet their Power
Is not to Rule and govern, but Devoure:
Such savage Kings all Tyrant[s] are, and they
No better then mere Beasts, that do obey.

GOVERNMENT

The old Burgundians cald their kings
T' accompt for cold and Backward Springs
And Punishd them if aught but wel
Their Cattle or their Corn befell.

Plato held what so ere incumbers
Or strengthens Empire comes from numbers.

Though once one Conquerd by Delay
There were no more that tryd that way.

As at th' Approach of Winter, all
The Leave's of great Trees use to fall
And leave them Naked to ingage
With Stormes and Tempests when they rage;
While Humbler Plants are found to weare
Their Fresh green Liverys all the yeare:
So, when the glorious Season's gon
With Princes, and hard times come on,
The greatst Calamitys oppress
The greatest stil, and spare the less.

Nothing's more Dul and Negligent
Then an old Lazy Government;
That knows no Interest of state,
But such as serve a Present Streit,
And to patch up, or shift, wil close,
Or breake alike with Friends or foes;
That runs behinde hand, and has spent
It's Credit to the last extent;
And the first time 'tis at a Loss
Has not one true Friend, nor one Cross.

Authority is a Disease, and Cure,
Which men can neither want nor wel indure.

'Tis sad
That those who rule the world should stil be mad.
So Puddles when the sun shines faire
In Cloudy Chariots mount the Aire,
But when a Storm is raysd, in Raine
Fall down in Ditches back againe.

GOVERNMENT

What is a Fellon
In times of Prosperous Rebellion
Such as we happily Live in?
When all are Sinners there's no Sin.

Authority like wine intoxicates
And make's mere fooles of Magistrates,
The Fumes of it invade the Braine,
And make's them giddy headed, proud and vaine:
By this the fool Commands the wise,
The Noble with the base Complys,
The Sot assume's the rule of wit
And Cowards make the Brave submit.

He that imploys men for respects,
Besides their usefulness, neglects
His service for his servants sake,
And soon wil finde his own mistake.

Authority must not admit
Relations that grow under it;
'Tis witchcraft and not powr to know
Familiars rising from below.

They that go up hil use to bow
Their bodys forward, and stoop low,
To poyse themselves, and sometimes creep,
When th' way is difficult and steep:
So those at Court that do addresse
By low ignoble offices,
Can stoop to any thing, that's base,
To wriggle into Trust and grace,
Are like to rise to greatness sooner
[Then] those that go by worth and honor.

All Acts of Grace, and Pardon, and Oblivion,
Are meant of Services, that are forgiven;
And not of Crimes, Delinquents have committed,
And Rather been Rewarded, then acquitted.
For Pastures that are newly broken up
Are wont to yeld the Plentifullest Crop,
And Flowers, that grow among a Field of corn
To weeds as bad as thorns, and thistlles turn.

LAW

FOR in all Parlaments, The Commoner[s]
  Are but a kinde of Nursery of Peres,
Where all the Disafected to the Court
Are turnd to Peres and Sons of Honor for't.

A little wit wil serve, and lesser Law
A Jury and the witnesses to aw.

One Chanc'ler may suffice to Judge a Cause
In æquity, but four t' unriddle Laws.

The Antient Fleying-off a Judges Skin
The best Specifique of the Law has been;
Or those that made Frisillian take a swing
At Tyborn in a Legislative String.

Although Impartial Justice hold the Scales,
The Ballance that receives prevayles.

For Law can take a Purse in open Court
Whilst it Condemne's a less delinquent for't.

For Law that make's more knaves then ere it hung,
  Little Considers right or wrong;
But (like Authority) 's soon satisfyd,
  When 'tis to judg on its own side.

  Law is like the Laberinth
With the two form'd Monster in't,
That usd t' eate mans flesh, and devour
Al that it got within its Powr.

Those that in Licencd Knavrys deal
And freely rob the Commonweal
And after make the Laws o' th' Land
A Refuge against Justice stand,
Like thieves that in a Hemplot Ly
Securd against the Huon Cry,

LAW

And make that which they most deser[v]e—
A Halter, for Protection serve.

Paupers are Plaintifs stil, for no man Sues
One that has nothing if hee's cast to loose.

In Law all men are understood
To b' Infants til their Actions are allowd.

There is a mean in things and certaine Lists
Beyond or short of which no Right consists.

Jury-men are never good and true
Until there is a dozen of the Crew.

The same man built the Royal Pallace
In Paris and Moun[t] Faucon gallows,
And afterwards was hangd upon't
For bringing in a wrong account:
He liv'd and might have don so long
But that the fates had spun his thread too strong.

When Rookes on lofty Tuf[ts] of Trees
Do build their Airy Colonies,
If both the owners of a Nest
Leave it ungarded, all the rest
Prepare t' invade with one Consent,
And rob the Naked tenement;
Fal on, and plunder it so fast
Until their worke is Spoyld with hast.
But if the watch, they set to Spy
Th' Approaches of the Enemy,
Discover the Right owner come,
Though ere so far of[f], towards home,
They al make hast to get away,
And leave behinde the —— Prey.

[Law] does not put the Least Restraint
Upon our Freedom, but Maintain't.
Or, if it did, 'tis for our Good,
To give us Freer Latitude:
For wholesom Laws Preserve us free,
By stinting of our Liberty.

LAW

As when a greedy Raven sees
A Sheep, intangl'd by the Fleece,
With hasty Cruelty he flys
T' attack him, and pick out his Eyes:
So do those Vultures use, that keep
Poor Pris'ners fast, like silly Sheep,
As greedily to prey on all,
That in their rav'nous Clutches fall.
For Thorns and Brambles, that came in
To wait upon the Curse for Sin,
And were no part o' th' first Creation,
But for Revenge a new Plantation,
Are yet the fit'st materials
T' enclose the Earth with living Walls:
So Jaylers, that are most accurst,
Are found most fit, in being worst.

                       Lawyers that Deal
In Right, and wrong do never Buy but Sell,
And are sufficiently Supplyd with Both
From Publique Stocks, and those of their own Growth.

The sword of Justice, Legally Compels
All other Arms, to serve for Daggers else,
All sorts of Drubs, and Bastinades and Bruises
To Pass for Real Stabs in Law Reduces:
From whence no Murther is accounted good,
Before the Price, and valews understood,
Of th' wooden Sword and Dagger, or the Gun Stone,
With which the Mortal Feat of Arms was Don.
And if the weapon is not worth a Straw
The Homicide has don no Hurt in Law.

When those that sate for Judges on the Bench
Were False, and Senseles as their Pedlers French,
Had vaulted ore the Bar with so much slight
It was their Luck upon the Bench to light,
More Nice and subtle then those wier drawers
Of Equity, and Justice, Common Lawyers,
And more Impartial then the Judge that Steard
His Jurys by the Compas of his Beard

LAW

And, as to th' Right, or left he turnd the end,
Gave Notice for the Plaintif or Defendent.

The Ins of Court, from their own Claws
Protect the Prisners of the Laws.

For what Court ere allowd of Common-bayle,
In Coats that had been Primd with Grease, or Ale?
Or would Admit the thread-bare, or the Torne,
The Freedom to be Publiquely forsworn?
Or ever minded Affidavit Oaths,
In out-of-fashiond, and Illegall Cloaths?

Like him that let out mony to be Payd
Upon a Day, swore if it were Delayd
And not Dischargd, but half a Day Beyond,
He was Resolvd to Teare, or burn the Bond;
Or he that su'd a man who told his clock,
When falsly, and Erroneously it strook,
And would have brought his Action for a Tryal,
With one, that did but looke upon the Dial,
Or He that Disinherited his Son
For Riding on a Caus-way Pavd with Stone:
To weare his Horses shoos out, when Beside,
There was Plaine Ground, and soft enough to Ride.

For Lawyers keep no Equity at all
To serve their own occasions, but for Sale,
The Real Gryffins of the Common Laws
With Griping Talons on their Claws.

The Statute-Law's their Scripture, and Reports
The Antient Rev'rent Fathers, of their Courts,
Records their Generall Councels, and Decisions
Of Judges on the Bench, Their sole Traditions:
For which, like Catholiques, th' have the greater Awe,
As th' Arbitrary, and un-written Law.
And strive Perpetually, to make the Standard
Of Right, between the Tenent, and the Landlord;
And when two Cases, at a Triall, meet
And, like Indenturs, Jump exact, and fit:

LAW

And all the Poynts, like Chequer-Tallys, Suite,
The Courte Decides the obstinatst Dispute.
There's no Decorum usd, of Time, nor Place,
Nor Quality, nor Person, in the Case:
But both Picquere in Endles Controversy,
Until the one side's forct to yeld to mercy.

How much have our Tribunals been Improvd
Since Clergymen from Courts have been Removd;
And if they had but understood the Law,
Had kept the State and Government in awe.

No Court Allow's Those Partiall Interlopers
Of Law, and Æquity, two Single Paupers,
T' Incounter Hand to Hand at Bars, and Trounce
Each other Gratis, in a Suit, at once;
For one, at one time, and upon Free-cost is
Enough to Play the Knave, and Foole with Justice;
And when the one Side brings Custome in,
And th' other, Lay's out Half the Reconing,
The Dev'l himself wil rather Choose to Play
At Paltry Smal-Game, then sit out (they say);
But when at all, There's nothing to be Got,
The old wife, Law, and Justice, wil not trot.

For he that trust's the Purblind Hostice
Of th' Ins of Court and Chancery, Justice,
Must pay his money down before,
And be misreacond on the Score.
For Justice put's her sword into the Scales,
With which she's sayd to weigh out Tru, and False,
With No Designe, but, like [the] Antique Gaul,
To Get more Money from the Capitoll.

For that which Law, and Equity Miscals
By th' Empty Idle Names of Tru, or False,
Are Nothing else but Maggots blown between
False witnesses, and Falser Jury-men.

Old Laws have not been sufferd to be Pointed,
To Leave th' Interpretation more Disjoynted,

R 2

259

LAW

And yeld a greater Latitude to wrest
On all Emergent Cavil, and Contest.
For all the Sense, the Latin tongue Affords
Consists in the Last Syllables of words,
And, when by Dashes those become in vaine,
How should the Sense the same it was Remaine?
For what supports the Law, or makes it Good
But that it is not to be understood?
And therefore Has been (in its own Defence)
Writ in a Language, that wil Beare No Sense,
And Study'd only in a French Jargone
As Rude and as Insignificant as None.

[Lawyers]

Who never End, but only Prune a Suite,
To make it beare the Greater Store of Fruite!
For Ten times more is Easier to be Gotten
By Interrupting Justice then Promoting.
For Law, by Law, can only be Destroyd
As Statutes by themselvs are Renderd voyd,
Can never be Defeated of its Force
But by some Legal, and Judicial Course
In which the Forms of Law Destroy the Powr,
As Gospell often has been servd before,
Until it has Repeald it self and Run
With Magna Charta Publique Freedom down:
Hence 'tis, of Late, The Fundamental Laws
Were forcd the Ruine of themselvs to Cause,
For while Puntilios only were Asserted
The Government stood Fair to be subverted.

For Breaking of the Laws o' th' Land, at least
Is more then Half, the Publique Interest,
That might as wel have nere been made
As Punctually, by evry man, obeyd;
For then they would but signify al one,
With wisest Governments as if they had been None.
For what, but only Breach of Law, Supports
The Costly Charge, and Dignity of Courts?
That but for Murthers, Frauds, and Stelths,
Would be no Parts of Stats and Common-wealths:

LAW

For how could Justice beare the vast Expence,
If none should dare to give the Law offence?

For Laws are only valid then Reputed
When they can force themselvs to b' executed;
But whe[n] th' are freely broke, and do no Hurt,
They are but Scornd and Antiquated for't.

For 'tis the Constant Fashion of Law Cases
To Put on (under one Disguise) two Faces,
And Put the Client to the Charg, and Trouble
To fine and Pay for understanding double.

Those Judges, who before the Cause is Tryd
Determine which shalbe the Justest side
And Doom like Lightning that Destroys
Before the Hearing of the Noyse.

For those, that do but Rob and steal enough,
Are Punishments and Courts of Justice Proof;
And neede not Feare, nor be concernd a Straw
In all the Idle Bugbears of the Law,
But confidently Rob the Gallows too
As wel as other Suffrers of their Due.

A Reprobate, or Pious Man, bequeths
Their Souls of Course to Heavn at their Deaths,
Because there is no Trique in Law, to Pleade
A faulse conveiance, to molest the Dead,
That wanted Assets, fully to supply,
And Pay the Charges, of the Legacy.

Who can deserve for breaking of the Laws
A greater Penance then an honest Cause?

REBELLION

THE Devil was the first o' th' name,
From whom the race of Rebels came,
Who was the first bold Undertaker
Of bearing Arms against his Maker;
And, though miscarrying in th' Event,
Was never yet known to repent,
Though tumbl'd from the top of bliss
Down to the bottomless Abyss;
A property which from their Prince
The Family owns ever since,
And therefore nere repent the evil
They do, or suffer, like the Devil.

The worst of Rebels never arm
To do their Kings or Country harm;
But draw their Swords to do them good,
As Doctors cure by letting blood.

TREACHERY

THERE's no Integrity, where Faith
Is not obligd, on Paine of Death;
Nor Obligation firm, and Good
That is not seald with mutuall Bloud,
Where both ingagers, can at will
Breake one another on the wheel.

There's no Integrity or trust
Where Intrest do's not make men Just.

Hypocrites with Acted Zeal
Take more then tru Saints with the Real,
That Pray and fast, but to devour
With Greater Greediness and Power.

As Truest Glasses Cheat the Sight
By Representing Left, for Right,
So Right, and wrong, are Counterchang'd
And in each others Places Rang'd.

One Enemy within the wals
Is worth a Troop without as false.

All the Politiques of the Great
Are like the Cunning of a Cheat,
That let's his False Dice freely Run,
And Trust's them to themselves alone;
But never let's a tru one Stir
Without some fingring Trick, or Slur;
And, when the Gamsters doubt his Play,
Conveys his False Dice safe away,
And leaves the Tru ones in the Lurch,
T' indure the Torture of the Search.
May they be Honest when it is too late,
That is undon the only way they hate,
Whose words and Actions are al one
And both together, Past, and don,
And most obliging Favours Civil
As kind indearments of the Devil.

TREACHERY

To Promise only to Betray
Is but to cheat, and loose at Play,
To venture Credit upon Tick
For nothing but to shew a trick.

Chineses have their Publique Schooles to teach
The Libral Arts to cheat and overreach.

Treachery's a Princely Sport
The only Royal Game of Court.

It is in vaine for Cheats to fix
'Mong those, that understand their Trick[s]:
Who therefor Change the Aire, and Stroul,
To Catch the fresh unwary foul.

The Man, that for Profit's brought t' obey
Is only hir'd, on Liking, to betray;
And when he's bid a liberaller Price,
Will not be sluggish in the Work, nor nice.

For those are but Probatione[r]s
That have but once been Perjurers,
And have no[t] don their Exercise
Till Th' have betrayd and Perjured twice,
The Sacrament of Confirmation
To Fix 'em Constant to the Nation.

Wheedleing and Shaming at the best
Is but a kinde of Knavery in Jest.
As Gamsters Practice for their Exercise
The Liberal Arts of Cheating with tru dice.

In the Dark and Secret Passages
That ly between the other world and this,
One mortal Cheat's another of his Right,
As Burglares break houses in the Night,
And, at the wills and Pleasures of theyr mothers,
Transfer their Claimes, before th'are born, to others.

What should I do at Rome? I cannot Ly,
Or if a Book be Bad, Commend and Buy:

TREACHERY

I understand no Mathematique Skill,
Nor can Prædict a Fathers Death, nor will.
Others can beare, what Leachers use to send
New marryd wives, and what the[y] say Commend:
I cannot Steal; nor give the Least Releife,
In Acting of a Robbery, t' a Thiefe:
And therefore Go alone, like one, that's maimd
Of his Right-hand, and for a Cripple Lamd.

Words are but th' outside of the minde
But all the Art is how 'tis lind.

INJUSTICE

TREACHERY and violence
    Are Dutys, binde the conscience,
And such as no Man ought t' omit
When Providence makes way for it.

      Murthers are bewayld and Pittyd
By those by whom they were Committed.

    Ungratefull men do nere forgive
The bad they do, or good receive.

    In little Trades more cheats and Lying
Are used in selling, then in buying;
But in the Great, unjuster dealing
Is used in buying, then in selling.

    For Prejudice condemn's unheard
And still the worst Sense is preferd.

      Many have been forcd to take
A Turn at Tybourn by mistake;
'Tis but an Error of the Court:
The Law is nere th' unjuster for't.

    Men who change Sides have no concerns
For any, but to serve their Turnes.
And that b'ing don; th' have learnd one way
The Readier after to betray.

MODERN WAR

ALL Feates of Armes are now abridgd
   To sieges, or to b'ing besieg'd.
And hee's the Formidablest Soldier
Who fly's (like Crows) the smel of Powder.
To digging up of Sceletons,
To make Brown Georges of the Bones.
It is not wearing Armes of Proofe
Lin'd through with Shirts of Male and Buff
But marching naked in the cold
That makes men valorous and bold;
Nor swords, nor Bullets, nor Bloudshed,
But stealing one anothers Bread
And eating nothing out of mode
But what's in Season Frog, or Toad.
All Blows are at the Belly aimd
Untill 'tis slain outright or maymd;
And one anothers motions watch
Only to ly upon the Catch.
To understand the Time, and Reason
When Toads, and vermine are in Season,
When Frogs come in, and what's the Cause
Why July Spiders make best sause;
As if the wars of Frogs and Mice
Had been of ours but Prophesies:
For greater Crowds are slaine of those
Then upon both sides now of Foes.
No feates of Armes are now in mode
But only living without Food,
Nor weapons handled but for show,
Disease and Famine are the Foe;
And he that against both is Proofe,
Can eate his Bootes and feed on Buff,
Is held impregnable in Armes,
And more, then shotfree made by Charmes.
They do not manage the Contest
By fighting, but by starving best;

MODERN WAR

And hee that's able to fast longest
Is sure in th' end to be the strongest.
He that can dine upon Mundungus,
Is held the valiants[t] man among us
And those the Formidablest Forces
That never mount but eat their Horses
And make 'em serve in th' expedition
For Cavalry and Amunition;
No Helmets now are in Request,
Nor Curacer, nor back, nor Brest;
Nor Armes of Proof accounted good
Because they will not serve for food.

Civil war, like letting-bloud
To voyd the Bad let's out the Good.

Fighting now is out of Mode,
And Stratagem, the only Roade,
Unless in th' out-of Fashion'd wars
Of Barbrous Turkes and Polanders.
They laugh at Fighting in the field
Till one Side Run away, or yeld,
But manage all a Safer way,
Like th' Ancient sword and Buckler play,
And Loyter out a whole Campaine
To forrage only, and Trepan.
All Feats of Armes are now Reduc'd
To Chowsing, or to being Chowsd;
And no Rencounters so Renownd
As those on wals or underground.
They fight not now to overthrow
But Gull, and Circumvent a Fo;
And watch all Smal Advantages,
As if they fought a Game at chess.
And he's approvd the most deserving,
Who longest can hold out at sterving,
Can make best Fricasies of Cats
—— of Frogs and mice and rats,
Potage of vermine, and Rhagoos
Of Trunks and Boxes, and old Shoos;

MODERN WAR

And those, who, like th' Immortal Gods,
Do never eate, have still the Ods.
———— All their warlike Stratagems
Are subtle ferring over Streames,
Or Playing at Bo-peep with Bridges,
Or Crawling under ground at Sieges,
Or swimming over deepest Channels
T' avoyd the Fo, like water Spaniels.

'Tis Strange; That wars, that Lay Pretence
To Piety, and Conscience,
Should more Inhumanly be wag'd
Then those on other Scores ingagd.

What Arms Defensive but a wal
Are Proof against a Canon-Ball
Or strong enough to make Resistance
Unles by keeping [at a] Distance?

COWARDISE

[Cowards]
Like Horses, do Heroique Acts,
Ingage by turning of their Backs,
And use the same Heeles, both for fight
With th' enemy, and persuite, or flight:
So with the same Armes kill and slay
And Rout the Fo and run away.

He that ore-comes himself, and runs
Do's more then he that takes great towns:
If evry man would save but one
No victory would ere be won:
For he that runs may fight again,
Which he can never do that's slain.

Battles but in fancy wag'd
With better Conduct are ingagd
Then bravest fights at Sea or land
Where Fortune has so great a hand.

A Sword Fish fights with greater Art
Because the warrior has no Heart.

Strong Reserves in War are plac't
To bear the Brunt of Danger last,
As Hangmen blind the eies and ty
The Hands of wretches doomd to dy.

He that is all Heart
Is kill'd with the least Prick in any Part,
And, therefore, ougt to have the greater care
In Fight than he, that has a lesser share.

HOPE

FOR greater Numbers have been lost by Hopes,
  Then all the Magazins of Daggers, Ropes:
And other Amunitions of Despaire,
Were ever able to Dispatch, by Feare.

[Fears]
Do better offices to Human Nature
Then Hopes, that only humor us, and Flatter,
That all our Future Happiness Fore-stalls,
And Runs us out of it, before it Falls:
When all our Expectations are alloyd
And thrown away, before they are Injoyd:
While nothing our Fælicity's Indear's
Like that which falls among our Doubts, and Fears,
And in the miserablest of distress,
Improv's Attempts as Desprate, with success.
Succes that owns, and Justifys all Quarrels;
And vindicates Deserts of Hempe, with Lawrells.
Or but miscarry[i]ng in the Bold Attempt
Turnes wreaths of Lawrell back again, to Hemp.

FEARE

FOR Feare, and Fiends are Cussen-Germans
And Partners in the same Determents,
Apparreld in the same Disguise
Of Hornes and Tayles, and Sawcer eies.
Make Fancy Cut of[f] Child[r]ens Heads
Before they're Born, with sudden Dreads,
And more Impossibly, convey
The executed Part away.

   Cowards, like Hot Iron Drencht,
Are hardend more, the more th'are quencht.

THEFT

'TIS Counted Cunning to Retrive
And find out by a Thief a Thiefe;
But nothing is more Sottish, then
To finde out thieves by honest men.

Crimes Punishd, like the weapon Salve
Heal up the wounds and Hurts they gave.

For as the Roman Souldiers once,
When they were Plundering of Towns,
And Robbing of their Churches; found
In one a Little hole i' th' Ground,
Which having greedily unclosd,
To finde out Treasure, they supposd
Was there conceald: out flew a Dampe
That spread Contagion through the Campe,
And suddenly strook many Dead;
From whence, by slow Degrees, it spread
From Place, to Place, til it Possest
All the wide world, from East to west:
So, when Rude Mortals boldly search
For Gain, and Plunder, in the Church,
And Sacrilegiously teare
Her Schismes wider then they were,
A Horrid Plague breaks out, that kills
The wretches first, and after fills
The whole world, like a General Floud
Of Desolation, war and Bloud.

Why should not Piety be made
As wel as Equity, a Trade?
And men get mony by Devotion
As wel as making of a Motion?
B' allowd to Pray upon Conditions
As well as Suiters in Petitions?

THEFT

And in a Congregation Pray
No less then Chanc'ry for Pay?

A Roman Thief was not Affeard
To Scrape the Gold of Jupiter's own Beard;
And either shewd himself, t' have no Beliefe
In Thunder-bolts, or was a Desprate thief.

RELIGION

A GODLY man that has servd out his Time
     In Holiness; may set up any Crime;
As Schollers when th' have taken their Degrees
May set up any Faculty they Please,
Are free t' administer to Soul or Body
Although they never meant it for their Study.

The Greatest Saints and Sinners have been made
Of Proselytes of one anothers Trad[e].

'Tis Hard to understand a Proselyte
Distinctly, from a wholesale Hypocrite,
That one Religion for another trucks:
The money of all Fayths is orthodox
And lofty'st Steeples have Guilt wethercocks.

An Augur Scor'd Imaginary Lines
In Heaven, Proper for his own Designes
T' observe, and Note the Flight of any Bird
That in the Circle of his Scheme Appeared
And by the Computation understand
Th' Event of his Inquiry before hand.
When Egles, Hawks, and Vulturs on their wing[s]
Bore all the Interests and fates of Kings
A Daw, and Raven, and a Monedula
Foretold the Issu of a Suit in Law.

A Teachers Doctrine, and his Proof
Is all his Province, and enough,
But is no more concernd in use
The[n] Shoemakers to weare all shoes.

                          For to do
Is one thing, and to mean is two.

Th' Apostles were but Messengers,
And Angels Letter-Carryers,

RELIGION

But now a Saint's a Secretary,
That open's what they did but carry,
And has a Cipher to reveal
What they brought only under Seal.

Th' Apostate Jews, though zealous Brethren,
That worship'd th' Idols of the Heathen,
Were punishd by Idolaters
Profaner then themselves and worse.

A Convert's but a Fly that turns about,
After his Head's puld of[f], to finde it out.

The Saints, who had Designd to build upon
Th' Imperfect Model, of Old Babilon.
Had taught their Insignificantest Jabb[e]rers,
A Language worse then that of all their Labour[e]rs:
For 'twas confounding Languages Fore-run,
The Fatal Slavery of Babilon.
When Ignorance, and want of understanding,
Was all Reducd to Controversy, and Bandy[i]ng.
And vowd to settle Church, and Commonweal,
Upon Dissenting Principles of Zeale.
When all Pretenders venturd to Proscribe
The Rest, that were not of their Chosen Tribe:
And made 'em guilty Spiritual Bandittys,
Exild from all great Burrough-Towns and Citty[s]:
And Banishd them like Criminals, to Lurke
In Obscure Cottages to do their work.

The Good old Cause, Interpreters believe
To be the serpent, that had tempted Eve,
And taught her to tempt Adam out of Eden,
With godlike Gifts, and Fruit that was forbidden,
And when the Saints, began at first t' adore
Was Titled old, for what it did before
When all her Talent could not understand
But how to break themselvs, and one Command,
And ever since that time, do's still invite
The world to Disobedience with New light.
Whence Saints of all Religions, use t' exclame,
And one anothers Dispensations Damne:

RELIGION

Who once would have Admitted Presbyters,
Upon their Good-behavior, for three years:
But that there could no Common-Baite be found
That to such hard Conditions would be Bound;
By Rapine, Bloud, and Tyranny Profess
New ways, of Suffering for Righteousnes;
And by Revenge, and Insolence Propose
The Evangelique Course, of taking Blows:
For Pardons are Ill Characters of Saints,
As due to those, wee have don Il against.
And do but work, the same Effects; Reprievs
Are wont to do, upon the stubbornst Thieves:
Who apprehend, They have the Greater wrong,
Only because they are but Half-unhung;
And therefore understand the Grace, and Favour,
To be but Binding to the Good Behavior:
Which make's th' Afflicted wretches live in Paine,
Untill th' have don the Injury againe.
Which when an Opportunity falls out,
They never let a Moment slip to do't.
For when the Lashes of a Conscience smart,
Layd on severly by its own Desert,
The Guilty Suffrer thinks it comes from those,
From whom (he knows) He has deservd the Blows:
And still Abhor and hate 'em, more, and more,
The more th' have don them Injury before.
As Huntsmen use to chace the wounded Deare,
But those that have Receivd no Hurt, Forbeare;
For Zealous Men, must be Allowd
The Hot Distempers of their Bloud:
That is not calculated, for the Coole,
And Sober Temper of a Christian Rule;
Enough to make the Rigor of Devotion,
Keep within Compass of Abundant Caution,
But frequently is apt to loose his Credit,
For being Peremptory, and Hot-Headed;
When temper only has Supplyd the Place
Of all their High Prerogativs of Grace:
And that which once past for the word Reveal'd,
Is only now the old Dead Letter Held:

RELIGION

And that which was the Spiritual Light within one,
Reducd to Fancy only and opinion.

    For the best Temperd Saints, are more Stiff-necked
Then all the Hottest-headed of the wicked,
Are Sons so Fierce, and Zealous of the Church,
Some Guess they were begotten in the Porch.
Have got themse[l]vs a General Reputation,
Of welth, and Zeal, and Numbers in the Nation:
By driving Proselyts like Head's of Beasts,
From other Churches, and their Interests:
For what else makes, a Richman's esteemd
So hard, and Difficult to be Redeemd,
But that th' have Mony, to lay down the Prices,
Of all the Dearst Iniquitys, and vices?
And tho the Cause profanely did Propose
To take up Arms, for holy Purposes,
That Scruple Awd th' Erroneous Rabble more
Then all the Right of Just, and Lawfull Powr:
As Post appeare t' have Spurs, and Switches, worse
Then those that gen[t]ly Ride a Startled Horse.

    For Gifted men, in little Benefices,
Use to conform, according to the Prices:
Like him, who lately venturd to Ingross
A Parish Church, and Conventicle House;
Read Common Prayr, and after Preachd it downe,
And hid his Surples underneath his Gown:
Which some Free Consciencd Saints, affirmd hee wore,
And to trepan the Visitation, swore:
Untill in Contemplation of the oath,
And Impious fraud, He was turnd out of both.
For Zealous Saints are but Probationer[s],
That have but once Incurd the Loss of Eares:
But have not don their usuall exercise
Untill they have Betrayd, and Perjurd, twice,
The solemne Sacrament of Confirmation
To fix Perfidiousnes upon the Nation.
Abhord to Read the Common-Prair, as vaine,
And Superstitious, Popish, and Profane:

RELIGION

But Really, because th' have no Occasions,
By Spelling, to Hold-forth their Dispensations:
And th' Ablest of their Brethren, have no shifts,
For Setting off the Meanest, of their Gifts.
As if they were but such Notorious Knaves,
In Nature, as they use to make their Braves;
Before their Extraordinary conversions,
And turning th' Inside outward of the[i]r Persons:
Tho some are Confident, 'Tis but to Raise
Their own cooperating work of Grace:
Whose Gifts are not to be confided in,
Where Nature was so Influencd by Sin.
That never has been known to Quit the least
Puntilio, wholly of her Interest.

For Zeal is only Proper to Imbroyle,
To overturne, Disorder, and to Spoyle,
But has no Temper, Jugment, nor Discretion,
To manage things of Consequence in Reason;
But roote, and Branch, at Random, to demolish
Unsight, unseen; and Cross, or Pile abolish.
For Sober Reason, takes to Complesance,
No less then Pertinacy, t' Ignorance:
And as a Crutch, or wooden Leg, is stiffer
Then one that has its Natrall Joynts, they Differ:
That b'ing in Orders, to Divide the world,
Was after to Divide the Church Impourd:
And gave no Quarter to the Carnall, vaine,
The Naturall, and Morall, or Profane;
But always Prov'd abhominably shy
At Taking Notice of Hypocrisy,
For feare their Hands should slip, and hit upon
These Natural Endowments, of their owne.
As if the Brethren did not mean to win
By fair Means, Heavn, but rather take it in:
And therefore, like the Antique Gyants, Arme
To fall by onslaught, on the Place, and Storme
Had rather venture Force, and violence
Then any other way before, or since:
For all New lights avoyd the Beaten Path

RELIGION

To Heav'n; Good works, and Charity, and Faith.
Whose Piety, and Zeal to send a Martyr,
T' æternity's so great, they give no Quarter:
For were not swords, and Daggers, and Edg-tools
The only means, to save Th' Apostles Soules?

The Turks that have such gentle Tendernesses,
For Brutish Animals, of evry Species:
Are by their false Religion, taught t' have none,
But Naturall Defyance to their own.
Who when th' have payd, the Ransom of a Bird,
Wil perjure, to have Christians Massacerd.
Where Charity, and Cruelty are Drest,
And in their Native Types at once exprest.

Religion once was wrapt-up in Disguise
Of mystique Fables, and Mythologies;
But Modern Nonsense, without Parables,
Pass Muster in Religious Shape, and zeales:
Is like the Indian River-Fish, that's sed
To have a Magot breeding in his head,
And therefore Natrally 's observd, to stem
His constant Directly against the Streame.

No Phrygian Turk durst ever Counterfet
Or Try to Act the Part, of Mahomet,
Assumd his Borrowd Person, in Disguise,
Upon his New Return from Paradice,
With tru, or False Pretences, to maintaine
His Antient Promise, to Come back againe:
When Jews, and Christians, or some counted such,
In evry Age have undertooke as much
That more then twelve Messiases at least,
Have ownd the sacre[d] Function, and Profest:
That 'tis a Miracle, wee have no more,
But Nayler, to set up, upon that Score:
Enough to settle Infamy, and shame,
Upon the Christian Interest, and Name:
But that Fanatiques have been found t' attone,
And blot out all, with what themselvs have don.

RELIGION

For Saints are too transcendent and Sublime
To be suspected, but to own a Crime;
And when 'tis Acted, like a modern Saint
Not ask a Pardon for it, but maintain't.
Impenitence keep's up their Reputation,
As if they never had deservd th' occasion.

The Preachers in the Prologue of a Prayr,
Turn Sins to Gifts, and tell how great they are.
For 'tis the greatest Signe of Gifts, and Graces
To Magnify their Sins, by varying P[h]rases.
And he that dos it, with the Greatest Art
Is held a Man, of Singular Desert.

Men take up Religion, just
As they do other things on trust:
'Tis all one at how hard a Rate
To those who never meane to pay't.

The Church of Rome bende's Heretiques
With Flames of Fire, like Crooked Sticks.
And transubstanciat's them with Tricks
To zealous Fire-new Catholicks.
So Chymists transubstantiate
Base Mettles in the Fire to Plate.

Religion is the Interest of Churches
That sel in other worlds, in this to Purchase.

Good workes are nothing but to give,
And merit only to Relieve.

The Antient Pagans kept their Chequers
Securd in temples from their own Church-breakers
More safe, then Christians can, the Poorman Box,
Tho Double Fortifyd, with Plats and Locks.

Our Blessed Savior never did Discover
To his Disciples, what he was to suffer,
Who therefore strove to Præposses th' Injoyments
In his New Kingdom, of the best Imployments.

ZEAL

NO seard Conscience is so fel
　　As that which has been burnt with zeal;
For Christian Charity's as well
A great Impediment to Zeal
As Zeal a Pestilent Disease
To Christian Charity and Peace.

　　Who did ever know a Saint
That Acted th' Horridst Crime Recant?
Their Priviledg is too sublime
To condescend to own a Crime,
Who Count it a Disparagment
To be but thought to need Repent.

　Hypocrisy will serve as well
To Propagate a Church, as Zeal;
As Persecution and Promotion
Do Equally Advance Devotion:
So Round white Stones wil serve, they say,
As wel as Egs to make hens lay.

CRUELTY

FOR the first Murther that we finde
Was ere Committed by Mankind
By zealous Rage, and Fury, about
Religious worship first fell out;
When fierce Cain having kild his Brother
One fourth of Mankind slew the other.
And ever since an æqual Rate
Of all the world has had that Fate.
For when a Gap was made for Sin
Mad Zeal, and murther first broke in.

CONSCIENCE

FOR wise and Cautious Consciences
Are Free to take what course they please.
Have Plenary Indulgence, to Dispose
At Pleasure of the strictest vows,
And Chaleng Heavn they made 'em to,
To vouch and witness what they do.
And when they prove averse and loath,
Yet for convenience take an Oath;
Not only can dispense, but make it
A greater Sin to keep, then take it;
Can binde and loose all Sorts of Sin,
And only keepe's the keys within;
Has no Superior to Controul,
But what it selfe sets ore the Soule;
And, when it is injoyn'd t' obey,
Is but Confin'd, and keepe's the key;
Can walk invisible, and where,
And when, [and] how it will, appeare;
Can turn it selfe into Disguises
Of all sorts, for all sorts of vices;
Can transubstantiate, Metamorphose,
And Charme whole Heards of Beasts, like Orpheus;
Make woods, and Tenements, and Lands
Obey, and follow it's Commands,
And settle on a New Freehold,
As Marcly-Hill, removd of old;
Make mountaines move with greater force,
Then Faith, to New Proprietors;
And perjure to secure th' Injoyments
Of Publique Charges, and Imployments:
For True, and Faithfull, Good and Just
Are but Preparatives to Trust,
The Guilt, and Ornament of things
And not their Movements, wheels, and Springs.

How many Offices, and Places
Would salve a Conscience in all Cases!

CONSCIENCE

Hence 'twas he raysd his Price so high
That what one Place before would buy
Now all together in a Lump
Would not Come up to his Accompt.
For He Reducd all things to Trade,
And both for right, and wrong was payd.

Conscience is a Damnd Lampooner,
That Feares no Court of Law, nor Honor.

Because a Feeble Limb's Carest,
And more Indulgd then all the Rest;
So frayle and tender Consciences
Be humord to do what the[y] please;
When that, which Go's for weak and Feeble,
Is found the most Incorrigible,
To outdo all the Fiends in Hel
With Rapine, Murther, Bloud and Zeal.

Tender Conscience, Th' half-stervd Snake,
Which those that in their Bosoms take
To cherish, are Rewarded for't
And stung with Gratitude to th' Hart.

FANATIQUES

SAINTS of A Negative Profession
Like Independent Sense, and Reason.
A Mungrell Sect that has its Being
From nothing else, but Disagreeing:
Containes as many Diffrent Sects
As Pillorys Fit Sevrall Necks.

Fanatiques hold the Scripture do's not bar
The Bearing of False witnes, for
A Spiritual Neighbor, but against:
For only that's forbid the Saints.
When some, among 'em, have had cals
To sweare for Brethren, tru, or False
That have been Bred up by the Saints
To sweare, without the least Restraints,
Which when it do's not Reach to Bloud
Weighs nothing with the Brotherhood.

Like other malefactors, only heed
Religions, that the Laws o' th' Land forbid.

[A Brother]
Who strayns so hard upon a Poynt
Untill his Bones are out of Joynt,
And, when his sermons don and Prayr,
Is Rubd down like a Tennis-Player.

Why should not Handicrafts be made
A Church, as wel, as that a Trade?
Are Holders-forth, or Presbyters
The worse for turning Usurers?
Or Was John ere the worst Divine
For Selling Ale, and Cakes, or wine?
Or do's a Cuntry Vicar Preach
False Doctrine, when he turns a Leach?
And makes it equally his Study
T' Administer to Soul, and Body?

FANATIQUES

And keep's his Parishes Glebe Lands
Without Compounding, in his Hands?
And should not shopkeepers as wel
B' allowd to teach and buy and sel?
Or in the Belfrey keep a School,
Without neglecting of one Soul?

   People of such eternal Lungs,
And indefatigable Tongues,
That, though no Motive is so able,
As Creature-comforts on a Table,
T' engage them to put mod'rate stints
Unto their spiritual Gifts, and Hints;
Yet, if the Grace be not begun,
Before the Dinner is laid down,
It will be burnt, and cold agen,
Ere they come half way to Amen.
For Kings as well may lay Embargo
Upon the heav'nly good Ship Argo
As think by Laws to put restraint
Upon the workings of the Saints.

PRELATES

THAT make the Grace of God Create a Prince
But smallest Prælats, Divine Providence,
And all of Th' order Lord's Spiritual call
In meare Distinction from the Temporall,
Altho their Honors are Intaild upon
Their Families, when they themselvs have none:
Would make a King believe, Hee's a Phantastique
Mixt Person, Laique and Ecclesiastique;
And, when they could not Render Prælats Princes,
Made Princes Priests, to serve them for Pretences.

The Roman Emprors, in their Hands at Home
Preservd the Chief Epi[s]copacy of Rome;
And had soe Absolute a Jur[i]sdiction,
Their greatest Lawes were nothing but Rescription:
But when some weake ones gave that Powr the Pope,
The East, and west was lost beyond all Hope.

All Revrend Persons never use to stick
At Marriage, but for an Archbishopprick.

POPERY

THE Pope himself allows a licencd Sinner,
No more for once, then servs to buy her Dinner.

[Priests]
Are by their Lady votaries, with the Best
Of all their Curiositys, carest,
And when th' are searcht for, meet with no Anoyance
But feeding upon Sweet-meats i' th' Conveyance.

The Images of Saints, like Easops Logs,
Are thrown from Heaven down to Govern Frogs.

The Romish Priests, and Turkish Janizarys
Are both Supply'd with Christian Seminarys;
Who have no Lawfull Issue of their own
T' uphold the Legend, or the Alchoron:
Yet, by the Great Conformity between
The Roman-Clergy, and the Musselmen,
Will not Allow their Churches to Consist
Of Mungrels, gotten by a Turk, or Priest:
For Jesuits and Turks Improve the Breed
Of both their Sects, by changing of the Seed.

The Pope, that Lay's his Title, and Pretence,
T' Infallibility, has the Least of Sense:
Is faine t' avoyd a Street, in Rome, for Dread,
Of being turnd t' a whore, and brought to Bed:
By virtu only, of th' Infallible Chair
To get the Church, upon himself, an Heir.

Who first set Townes on Fire For Heretiques
Till Canon-Law th' Inhabitants convicts.

An old Religion, nothing but a Mode,
Far-fet from Hence, and too Deare bought abroad.
Which would have brought the Interlopers in
Too Rich a trade of Slavery and Sin.
That were Resolv'd to turn the Devils Tenants,
And take to Farme of him, a Sinners Penance.

POPERY

To pay down all their Rents upon, their Skins,
To him, and his Joynt Purchacer of Sins.
According to the Custome of the Manner
Which all his Native vassels hold by Tenure
And first Receivd from the Fanatique Jews
That put the Reformation first in use.
For Popery with us was but in Type,
Before the Greatst Impietys grew Ripe
When in th' excess, and Fulnes of Deboshing,
It was Declar'd and Publish'd for Devotion.
Have Fairs and Mercats, of all Sorts of Tradesmen
Fryres, Hermits, Munks, and Seculars, and Beads-men,
The most Deplorable of all those Dunces
That strove t' Import Religion from beyond Seas.
For Roman Pænitents are wont to play
The Guilt of all their Pænances away;
Where He that looses, freely takes the Sins
Upon his own Accompt, of him, that wins,
And is content to lay the Heavyst Sack
Of others consciences, upon his Back.

The Roman Mufty, with his Triple crowne,
Do's both the Earth, and Hell, and Heaven Owne:
Besides th' Imaginary Territory
He lay's his Title to, In Purgatory;
Declares himselfe, an Absolute Free Prince
In his Dominions, only over Sins.
But as for Heav'n (since it Ly's so far
Above him) is but only Titular.
And, like his Cross-Keiys-Badge upon a Taverne,
Has nothing there, to tempt, command or Govern.
Yet when he come's, to take Accompt, and share
The Profit of his Prostituted ware,
He findes his Gaines Increse, by Sin and women,
Above his Richest Titular Dominion.

A Jubile, is but a Spiritual Fair,
T' expose to Sale, all Sorts of Impious ware;
In which his Holynes buy's nothing in,
To stock his Magazins, but Deadly Sin,

POPERY

And Deale's in extraordinary Crimes
That are not vendible at other times;
For Dealing both for Judas, and th' High Priest,
He makes a Plentifuller Trade of Christ.
Can transubstantiate stamps of Lead or Brass
And into gold turn Paltry Beads of Glass.
For all the Horriblest Impieties
Do never fayl to Flock to Jubilies.

That Spiritual Pattern of the Church, Noahs Arck,
In which the Antient world did once Imbark,
Had nere a Helme in't to direct it's way,
Altho bound through an universal Sea:
When all the Modern Church of Rome's Concern
Is nothing else, but in the Helm, and Sterne.

An Antient French Pope chose himself, his Heir,
And made the Nation Conclave to the Chaire:
When all their Anti-Holynesses strove
To stand for Antichrist, the next Remove.

As He, that with Colonna, cuft a Fray;
Was Routed in the fight, and born away:
And eate his Fingers for th' Affront he had
Receivd in Fight, until he dy'd starck-mad.

[The Pope]
By Chymique Transubstantiation turn's
To Crowns of Gold, one Crown of thorns,
And wear's them ore three words, instead
Of ne're a Place to Rest his Head.

When the Jews had kild the Heir,
Priests took Th' Inheritance to share.

There's no Cheat in al the world nor Trick
But has a Twang, and Smack, o' th' Catholique.

What numerous Ly's and Errors did the Days
Of Popery, among the Rabble Raise!

POPERY

As Friers in their Long Capouches
Store up their Privat Close Deboches
And weare them on their Backs behind
As out of Sight as out of minde.

As in the Church of Rome, to go to shrift
Is but to put a Soul on a New shift.

The Greatest Complements are Found most False
As Cardinals that visit Cardinals
Are stript in Querpo, really to know
If they have Armes under their Robes or no,
And al their Counterfet Civility[s]
Are nothing else but [t'] avoyd Surprize,
But in Pretence, to let them understand
They are at Home, and all things there Command.

A Papist
Is but an Ignorant, Implicit Atheist,
That thinks to be Relig[ious] without Piety,
And Eats, instead of worshiping the Deity,
As Woolsy Puld down many a Monastery
To build a Church to Christ and his own Glory.

Jesuits are taught obedience
Before they'r sufferd to Learn Impudence,
And Counterfet a Sheepish Look before
They come to set for wolvs up, and Devour.

Their Leaving of[f] the Habits of the Brothers
And wearing those they Please, of any others;
Their Living out of Covents, Free and Cleare,
From any thing, that's Rigid, and Severe,
Their Arbitrary Intrest, [and] Dominion
Ore other mens Concernments, and their women,
Makes some in taking Orders, not so Nice,
As Possibly they might have been, otherwise.

Some zealous Men in orders more Confirms
Tho Probably th' had been on other tearms.

GLUTTONY

A WRETCH ingendred in his food,
  As French Punayses are in wood,
That ows his Being to his Guts,
As Magots breed in Cheese or Nuts,
Spawnd at the Mouth, as Fishes Breed,
And formd for nothing but to feed.
Had eate his Head out in a Trice,
Like Adam out of Paradice.
More Greedy then the Pox that swallow's
So many Mortals; or the Gallows,
That in a Quarter of an hour
Cart-loads of Sinners can devour.

As thousands are Distroyd by Surfet:
For evry one that's found to sterv yet.
That with their Glutony feed their other Sins,
As Serpents use to cast, and eate their Skins.

TIME

TIME Allow's the shortest measure,
   And Deale's with falsest weights, in Pleasure:
Steale's th' Idle, and it selfe, away,
And is the Greatest Cheate, in Play.

   There are no Vizard-Masks, nor Fans,
To keep Age from a Countenance.

   Time made Truth (like Elnor at Queen Hythe)
Sinke under Ground, for Feare to Spoyle his Syth:
For, thoug[h] at once it mow down Age and Youth,
It turn's Edge, when it ventures upon Truth.

PROSE PAMPHLETS
AND
IMITATIONS

MOLA ASINARIA:

OR,

The Unreasonable and Insupportable

BURTHEN

Now press'd upon

The Shoulders of this groaning NATION:

BY

The headless Head, and unruly Rulers, that usurp upon
the Liberties and Priviledges of the oppressed People.

Held forth in a

REMONSTRANCE

To all those that have yet sound and impartial
Ears to hear, and duly weighed in the Scales of
Equity and Justice.

By *William Prynne*, Bencher of
Lincolns-Inne.

Wherein is demonstrated,
What Slavery the Nation must subject it self
to, by allowing the lawfulness and usurped
Authority of the pretended
LONG PARLIAMENT
Now unlawfully and violently held at WESTMINSTER.

Jusq; datum Sceleri.

Printed at *London*, in the Year MDCLVIX.

MOLA ASINARIA
etc.,

Countrymen:

There is not any thing in the Universe deserves less to be a Member of it, then a self-seeking Man, who unconcern'd in the publick Good, regards onely his private Interest. The World unwillingly contributes to his maintenance; and Nature less abhors a *Vacuum*, then that any place should be filled by a Subject so empty of desert. He is a savage Creature in the midst of civil People, not deserving to be born of others, as not caring to live, but for himself. Nay, it is worthily reputed a kind of civil death, to do nothing else but live: for as long as we have a Country to abide in, we have a duty to tender it. All we have, we have from it; and by consequence owe it all we have. Our Lives and Fortunes are safest, when ventured for the publick Interest; and he is the truest Lover of Law and Liberty, that affects rather to be ruled, then to rule; he the freest Subject, that creates himself a voluntary Slave to his Countries Service. Take from the world this inviolable Law, (that is not writ in brass, but deeply imprinted in loyal hearts) and it shall again turn savage and barbarous. This is a truth so manifest, and not to be dissembled, that never yet was there a Tyrant, but pretended to be a Saviour of the people. Liberty, Conscience, a glorious Nation, *The Good Old Cause*, and such specious Names are made use of: *Nec quisquam alienum servitium et dominationem concupivit, ut non eadem ista vocabula usurparit*[1]. These Machiavilian Tricks, and political Cheats so often put upon the people of our Nation, methinks should have by this time undeceived us with a sad experience of the miseries we have subjected our selves to, by a perpetual itch of reforming, annulling, creating Laws, and framing new Governments to the model of every Grandees ambition; and yet we are againe ready to thrust our Necks into a new yoak of Slavery, rather then any man will engage his private Fortunes, and venture to redeem his Country from Bondage. It is laid to the charge of English-men by

[1] Tacit.

PROSE PAMPHLETS

Forraigners that we are φιλαύτοι, and above all Nations under Heaven pretending to civility, the greatest self-seekers; as regarding much more our own particular, then the general concerns. I must needs say, other Nations would have canonized for Martyrs, and erected Statues after their death to the memory of some of our Compatriots, whom ye have barbarously defaced and mangled yet alive, for no other motive, but their undaunted Zeal. It has been (I know not whether I should say) your misfortune, or my glory, to become a Sufferer for a Legal Vindication of the Liberties of our Kingdom; but yet I never knew what it was to fear, when I perceived my self engaged in so good a cause; not envy nor snarling Pamphlets shall stop the course of my Pen freely running into my Countries defence, which my Profession and Age forbid me to vindicate by the Sword. Let young Men serve it with their strength and arms, let old Men secure it by their heads and counsel: for my part, I desire to live no longer then I can in some sort contribute to so glorious a work. I have of late been snarled at for it by certain licentious Scriblers, that durst not own their names for fear of discovering their Asses ears: however, they are pleased to twitch at the honourable remnant of mine. They thought to have stopt my mouth by their brauling and braying; but I dare yet speak louder; and I hope I shall be heard by all such as have yet sound and impartial ears: but if my cry will not reach you, I fear (dear Country-men) the voyce of blood will speedily interrupt your slumbring security. Those that will be Lawless, finde fault with my Writings, because I vindicate the anciently established Laws of *England*; and tax me of desperate Non-sense, because I will not allow them an unlimited, unlegal, Legislative Power to repeal, annul, alter, and enact what Laws soever they deem best to serve their own turns. They deceitfully cry out *Salus populi suprema lex esto*[1]*!* an Axiome that I no ways deny to be true; but I would desire to be instructed who are to be Judges, of what is expedient for the good of the people? The Author of the forecited Maxime says, *Leges Magistratibus præsunt, ut Magistratus præsunt populo:* And the great Doctor *St. Austin* not doubted to affirm, that those societies where Law and Justice is not, are not Commonwealths or Kingdoms, but *Magna latrocinia*[2], great thefts and trapanning cheats. As for the power

[1] Cicero. [2] De civit Dei.

300

MOLA ASINARIA

of altering Laws, or bringing in new ones, and setting up new Governments, it is allowed by wise men, that all power lawfully exercised upon a Commonwealth, must necessarily be derived either from the appointment of God, who is the supreme Lord of all; or from the consent of the Society it self, that hath the next power to his, of disposing of their own Liberty, as they shall think fit for their good, whose benefit is the end of all Government. Therefore whoever arrogates such power to himself, that cannot produce one of these two Titles, is not a Ruler, but an Invader, or a Tyrant. Now how this pretended Long Parliament, restored by the force of Souldiers, by whose force it had first been dissolved, and was before annulled by the death or murther of King *Charles* the first, that summoned it, he being *Principium, causa, et finis Parliamenti*; after his murther, the house of Lords and Monarchy being abolished, and so many of the ancient Members thrown out, new ones unduly elected, and such horrid thefts, rapes, etc., committed by them upon the people, can lawfully be said the Peoples Representatives, and authorized by them, is the greatest Riddle that ever was propounded to a puzzled State. It was in the year 1649, that I published *a Legal Vindication of the Liberties of* England; in which I demonstrated the nullity of the then-pretended Long Parliament; and lately I set forth a lively pattern of the spurious *Old Cause*, pretended to be revived and vindicated by the fine Pageant or now-sitting Ghost of the long-since departed Long Parliament; neither need I reason farther with reasonable Persons about it: Yet since this Phantastical Hob-gobblin appears still to fright the quiet people, and tempts them (like an evil Spirit) to give themselves to such an unruly Devil; I will here onely hold forth to the view of all good Englishmen, what slavery they must needs subject themselves unto, if they resolve to cast off for ever their lawful Master and Soveraign, and take for new Masters these upstart domineering Tyrants. Let then every honest freeborn Subject of *England*, lay his hand upon his breast, and ask of his own Conscience, whether notwithstanding all former Oaths of Allegiance, Supremacy, Protestation, solemn Leagues and Covenants, etc., he can voluntary submit to, and thereby freely acknowledge, contrary to his former knowledge and the said Oath, etc.

I. That there may be, and now is a lawfully-assembled

Parliament of *England* actually in being, legally continuing after the late Kings death, or lawfully re-assembled without King, Lords, or most of their fellow-Members, consisting onely of a few late Members of the Commons House.

II. That this Parliament re-established by a Military force, and packed together by Power of an Army combining with them, hath just and lawful Authority, and had it before;

1. To arraign, condemn and execute their lawful King himself, with the Peers and Commons of this Realm.

2. To dis-inherit the King's Posterity of the Crown.

3. To extirpate Monarchy, and the whole house of Peers.

4. To violate the Priviledges, Rights, Freedoms, Customs, and alter the Constitution of Parliaments themselves; to change and subvert the ancient Government, Seals, Laws, Writs, Courts and Coyn of the Kingdom.

5. To sell and dispose of all the Lands, Revenues, Jewels, Goods of the Crown, with the Lands of Deans and Chapters, for their own advantages, not for the easing of the people from taxes.

6. To dispose of the Forts, Ships, Forces, Offices of Honour, Power, Trust or Profit, to whom they please.

7. To raise and keep up what Forces, by Land or Sea they please, and impose Taxes, etc., to make what new Acts, Laws and reverse what old ones they think meet.

8. To absolve themselves (by more than a Papal Power) and all the subjects of this Land, from all the aforesaid Oaths, Engagements, Protestations, etc.

9. To permit, settle, or invent what Sect, Heresie, or Religion they please, provided they be not Papacy or Prelacy, and that they allow not blasphemy against the Trinity.

10. I ask now if every freeborn Subject that hath not raised himself an Interest by villany, or an Estate by robbery, or incurred a guilt to the Gallows, for having his hand in blood, had not better venture Life and Fortunes to reduce the true and lawful Heir into a peaceful Possession of his right, then to authorize by his consent a new-fangled Government compacted of Treason, Usurpation, Tyranny, Theft and Murder?

FINIS

TWO
SPEECHES
MADE IN THE
RUMP-PARLIAMENT,

When it was restor'd by the Officers of the Army
in the Year 1659.

*Ut in vita, sic in studiis pulcherrimum, et humanissimum existimo
severitatem comitatemque miscere, ne illa in tristitiam, hæc in
petulantiam excedat.*   Plin. *Ep.* 21. 1. 28.

MR. SPEAKER,

 Though I have always thought, since we last came hither,
that our proper Business is only to sit here, not to vote, unless it
be at second Hand the Resolution of other Mens Debates, and
call them our own; or if we have free Liberty to argue what is
already determined, it is no more than is usually practised at the
Beginning of all Tyrannies, that are wont at first to give Men
a Shadow of Freedom to say what they please, when they have
taken a Course, that they shall do nothing: yet I shall discharge
my Duty to *God* and my *Country*, in speaking my Conscience
freely, while I may, which I believe will not be long. For I
perceive our Dissolution draws nigh, and that we have almost
finish'd our Course, before we have finished the Work, for
which we were pretended to come together, which was, as they
that call'd us hither then told us, *to settle Freedom and Liberty
on the Nation*; but we find by Experience, they meant nothing
less. For how is it possible, we should confer Liberty on others,
when we have it not ourselves? And when we are made Slaves
ourselves, how can they, whom we are pretended to govern, be
free? It is plain enough, that they, who by Force heretofore
drove us out of this House, and now by Force compel us to sit
in it again, do not doubt but they shall easily force us to do what
they please, which is not like to make much for the Liberty of
the People; since that, and the Power, which these Men have
taken upon them, are utterly inconsistent.

But suppose, they should give us leave to act freely, yet how can that be called Liberty, which is imposed upon the People, wholly against their Will and Consent? For with what Forehead can we pretend to the Consent of the People, when we act under the Power of those, who have bereft them of their free Voices; that have so often offered Violence to their Representatives, in whom their Consent was lodged; and so lately turned them out of this House? But though we had the general Consent, and an uncontrouled Authority to establish a free Government; yet how is it possible for the Wit of Man to contrive any thing, that shall agree with so many different and repugnant Spirits and Interests, though we should have no Regard but to those, who believe we are only bound to consider them? Do what we can, that which is a free Government to one Party will be Tyranny to another; and that which some call Liberty, to others will be Slavery; where every slight Faction and trivial Sect calls itself the Public, and would have no Consideration had of any thing, but itself; where every Man can teach us how to govern, but no body knows how to obey. He, that once brought a savage People to civility, and for the difficulty of the Work is said to have charmed Stones, and made them build themselves into a Wall, had such a Kind of Task as we have; for every Stone we are to use, is a Master-builder, and can instruct us to do our Work, and, if we will be ruled by them, to perform Impossibilities. For what is it else to settle any Thing, that shall please those, who can endure nothing that is settled; whom Conscience, that restrains other Men, lets loose to all Licentiousness, and whose Religion persuades them to be obliged to nothing; who, if we should grant all they can propose to us to-Day, would to-Morrow, upon change of Light, renounce it?

But alas! we need not trouble our selves with these Matters; for they are not the Business, for which we are call'd hither, but directly contrary to it; and if we be so vain to think otherwise, and shall but offer to settle any Government, wherein the common Right and Freedom of the Nation may be secured against the licentious Interests of the Army, we shall quickly find ourselves mistaken to our own Cost, and be baffled and hectored, as we have formerly been for the same Reason in this very Place. For no Man can be so ignorant as not to know, that, from the Treaty at the Isle of *Wight* to the last Parliament, there has never any Settlement of the Nation been attempted, wherein Regard has been had to the antient Laws and Rights of the People, but they have presently pronounced it a *Backsliding* from the *good old Cause*, and most barbarously by Violence put an end to it; nor will they ever do otherwise, or suffer any Thing to be established, but the Distractions, which they intend to make their own Freehold, that the Nation may be kept under the Power of the Sword, and that in their own Hands.

By this it is not hard to understand, why this *good old Cause* is of itself *backslided* unto us, who were once chastised for *backsliding* from it; and to what End these Men have returned to lick up their Vomit (like Dogs as the Apostle says) and take us in again, whom they had cast out; which, in plain Terms, is nothing else, but to help them to enslave the Nation in its own Name, though forged and counterfeit; to make the civil Power represented in us, no matter by what Right, depose itself by its own Act; (as they have lately forced their own *Protector* to do, after they had made the same Addresses to him, which they now do to us) to serve them for a Blind, while they undermine the Laws and Liberties of the Nation, and to set a Face of civil Authority upon Tyranny, Fraud, and Violence. And this they did not doubt, but we would dutifully perform, supposing we stood corrected since the last Rebuke they gave us here; and that to avoid a worse, we would be more tractable hereafter: but because they find we are not so forward, as they expected, to dispatch the Work, they now begin to look big and rant, as if, like perfect Slaves, we were to be terrified, and cudgel'd to our Task.

But if we should be so unhappily wicked to conform, and be industrious to follow their Directions; when they come to Particulars, there is nothing, that they propose, that is not full of Contradiction and Impossibility. For they would have us establish a Commonwealth and no Commonwealth, or a monstrous Government with two distinct supreme Powers, neither commanding nor obeying, but at perpetual Defiance, as having contrary Interests; for theirs does as much consist in the Distractions of their Country, as ours in the Peace and Settlement of it. They would have us join Liberty and Slavery together, and settle both on the People; secure Propriety against the Owners, and all Men else but themselves; couple Peace and War, and make them live quietly together; join Religion and Impiety, the Glory of God and Blasphemy; establish a free Equality of Right and Wrong, Law and Violence, Authority and Licence, Confusion and Order. And this is the true State of the work, which we are to carry on, and a faithful Interpretation of all that Canting and Confusion of Language, which they use at the building of this monstrous *Babel*.

For first they would have us frame a Commonwealth, or indeed receive one ready made from them; but they will not promise us to be subject to it themselves, though it be of their own making; no! there is neither Reason nor Conscience in that: besides, it is quite contrary to the Practice of those Saints their Forefathers in the primitive Times, who, our *Saviour* says, used to lay Burthens upon other Men, which themselves would not touch with a Finger. But they will set up another Republic of themselves, like the late other House, with a venerable Senate of new Lords spiritual and temporal, Agitators and Officers, co-ordinate with us, so far forth as they please. Indeed such a Government will come near to the Kingdom of Heaven, and be sure *to suffer Violence*: for these two Powers will be like two Poisons in the Body politic, whence the stronger will presently expell the weaker, and possess itself of all. For what Security can they give us, that they will use more Moderation and Regard to this Government, than they have formerly done to any other of their own erecting? truly none but this, that they will promise nothing, which is not inconsiderable with them, that never fail to break their Words. And yet they expect that no Man should dare to think them other than godly and conscientious Men, of upright Spirits, that will do no wrong and offer no Violence; they would but only have it in their Power to do so, when they please. This is a bold Presumption, (yet no more than they have always had the Confidence to impose upon the World, in their dissolving so many Parliaments, and assaulting so many Governments) that they are Men of greater Wisdom and Integrity than others; that they understand the common good better than others, and are more tender of it, than those, that have the greatest Shares in it, themselves having none, but what they have gotten by the Ruin of their Country, or what is daily picked out of every Man's Pocket by unjust Imposition of Taxes and Excise, all the Pawn, they can give the Commonwealth for their Fidelity; so that, if they should not be better than their Word (which yet they were never known to keep) and overcome the *Devil* and themselves, as easily as they may any civil Restraint, Mens Estates will be a villanous Temptation, where they have nothing to keep them out of Possession, but themselves.

But, perhaps, some may suppose, that now we have voted you *General*, and they have vouchsafed to take Commissions from us, to hold their Commands during our Pleasure, that therefore we do not sit here during theirs.—I am not of that Opinion, but should rather think, that they give Way to us in Things of Formality, that they may take the greater Liberty to oppose us in Matters of real Importance. Will an implicit constructive Acknowledgment bind those, whom solemn Oaths and Vows to Almighty God cannot hold! Will a Parchment Commission given by us, like a Spell, make them lay down those other Commissions (as they call them) their Swords, when we shall judge it convenient for the Safety of the Commonwealth; or hinder them from acting by which they please, as they find it shall make most for their Advantage? Why should their Commissions have a greater Power over them now, than they had heretofore; or keep them from making new *Dispensations of Providence*, and giving us a second *out-going* here, by turning us once more out of Door? Truly it will be a hard Thing for them not to do it, unless we be very careful to unriddle all their *Humiliations*, and be sure to understand what Answer they have agreed upon the *Lord* shall give them, when they seek him, that we may make the Good of the Commonwealth and Reason of State conform accordingly.

But if we should do our Endeavour to be obedient in our Government, and rule under Correction, how can they assure us, where there are so many inferior Councils, and the lowest still, like other Scums, struggling to be uppermost, that they shall not be used themselves by those in the same Manner, as they deal with us? Certainly they have a great deal of Reason to expect it, both from the just Judgement of *Almighty God*, and the natural Consequence of such Courses, which always beget their like. But suppose that Difficulty over, and that they should all agree among themselves; yet where there are so many different and various Interests, beside repugnant Capriches and Whimsies under several Forms, that are first to be reconciled, the Resolutions are like to come so slow unto us, that we shall sit here as the other House did lately, and transact with our fellow Members in the Hangings, who are like to be the only co-ordinate Senate, of equal Authority with us.

Certainly Soldiers are the most unfit Men of all others to be Keepers of Liberties, unless it be to keep them from us; nor is there any Thing so ruinous to the very Being of a Commonwealth as a Militia out of the Command of the civil Magistrate: For as they that have the Possession of the Sword cannot be compelled by it; so is it a strange Vanity to suppose, that they should submit themselves voluntarily to that equal Justice, which all other Men do by Compulsion. It hath been said, that *an unjust Peace is to be prefer'd before a just War*; because the Safety of the People, the End of all Government, is more concerned in the one than the other. If that be true, no doubt a just civil Power is infinitely more fit to be supreme, than an unjust military Power, or indeed than a just; if there were any such Thing in being. But if these Men were the most just and pious Men in the World, as certainly they are not, and as wise and prudent as just, yet imposing a Government by force upon a Nation, so utterly against the Will of the People, that they abhor and detest it, it will be impossible to continue it without extremity of Rigour and Tyranny; beside an unavoidable civil War, which will be most certain frequently to break out, both from the Reluctancy of the People, and the perpetual Occasions they will find in these often Changes of Governours, which must necessarily fall out, where Possession is sufficient Title; and the Will of the Soldiery taking upon it, like the *Devil*, to dispose of the Kingdom, which hitherto they have done with so much Wisdom and Fidelity, that we have seen them set up and pull down three Governments in almost as few Months. For undoubtedly these discreet Tumults and peaceful Seditions, these pious and conscientious Rebellions, and honest and faithful Treacheries will become the only fundamental Constitution of all future Governments, that we can settle; and are the only probable Way to produce that equal Rotation, which our modern Statesmen do so much dream of.

For what else can be expected from Men of their Principles, whom nothing can oblige? that account it a greater Sin to name Faith than to break it, and call Perjury and Perfidiousness *a Dispensation and Work of the Lord*; that pretend to do the same Things by the Spirit of *God*, which other Men are drawn to by the Temptation of the *Devil*; that confine all Providence to their own Concernments, as if *God* had nothing to do with the rest of the World; and are so partial to themselves, or, as they term it in others, given to Selfishness, that they call their own licentious Interests, though purchased with the Ruin of their native Country, or indeed of all the rest of Mankind, *glorious Outgoings of Providence*; that make Religion an Occupation, Godliness a Trade, and Holiness a Commodity; that set up Governments, as the *Jews* saluted *Christ* King, to crucify him the next Day; that counterfeit divine Authority, and forge the Hand of *God* to their own wicked Contrivances; call their own Affairs his Work, and, like *Ahab*'s Prophets, see Visions and bid themselves *go up and prosper*; that pretend to the secret and inscrutable Counsels of *Almighty God*, to give themselves Dispensations for violating his positive Commandments, as if he were best served by being disobeyed; that *break Oaths by Providence*, forswear themselves *to the Glory of God*, and deal falsely and treacherously with Men out of Conscience; enslave the Nation for the Liberty of the People, and pretend to establish Government by destroying the very Being of it, and rendering it contemptible; call all their present Designs and future to fix Governments (if God in his mercy to the Nation do not cut them off sooner) *the good old Cause*. In this, though it be a strange Imposture of Nonsense, they deal most ingenuously; for though the Courses they have taken have been various, to fit all Occasions that served these Purposes, yet the first *Cause* of all their different Effects has always been the same, for which they first engaged, and that is their own Gain and Advantages drawn out of the Distractions of their Country. This is really *the good old Cause*, though it has past disguised under several Titles, and was first sworn to be for Defence of the *King*'s Person, the Protestant

Religion, the Laws of *England*, and Privileges of *Parliament*, of all which it has not left any one in Being: And yet *the good old Cause* is still the same, and ready to swear as much in Defence of Commonwealth and Liberty; and when they are subverted, as certainly they will, serve to set up and pull down any Thing else, as long as there is any Thing to be gotten, and fit as many various and different Pretences, as a Vizard will do several Faces.

This all Men know to be most true, that have had any Acquaintance with their Words, and their Actions, which have ever been so directly contrary, as if all their solemn Vows and Engagements were, like a Witch's Prayer, to be said backward. For there is nothing, that they ever declared against, that they have not out-done themselves; nor any Thing, that they swore to maintain and defend, that they have not utterly destroyed and ruined. And shall we expect better of them now? truly by no means, but rather worse: for as I believe they have formerly done some Things, which they did not intend, till Occasion, that makes Thieves, shewed them the Way; so I am confident, that there is nothing, which they now declare for, which they are not already resolved to subvert, though it be not as yet safe for them openly to own any Thing so odious, and which, in probability, would pull a great Part of the Nation about their Ears. This makes them pretend to take the *Universities* into their Care, which the World knows it is the Business of their Zeal and Covetousness to demolish; and, if they durst do it this Instant, would in the same breath call it *a glorious Work of the Lord*. As for the *Law*, if there be any such Thing left, a Man would guess it may, perhaps, be preserved, because they have not yet absolutely threatened to defend it; they only speak of having it regulated, but that's all one in their Language; but then there's another Thing; they talk of having the Lawyers Fees abated, and no Profession suffered to enrich it self by the Loss and needless Charge of the People; but this makes it plain, they do not mean as they say; or else they forget themselves; for, if they would but keep their Words in this one Thing, we might well forgive them all their Past Perfidiousness, and give them leave to say and swear what they please hereafter.

But shall I tell you the Sum of all, and discover an Arcanum of their Empire, which though as yet they dare not profess, their Meaning is plain enough to be understood; and in due Time they will speak it out, and that is this—That they have conquered the Nation, and so by Right of War may dispose of it how they please. This is the Language of their Actions, which give the truest Account of Men; and we are bound to give the Nation notice of it before it be too late; that the People may know whose Goods they are, and either redeem themselves, or suffer their Ears to be bored through by their new *Jewish* Owners, who have bought them of themselves with their own Money; and, having been their Hirelings by the Day, challenge their Masters Persons and Estates as Part of their Wages. 'Tis a strange kind of Conquest, that is made over those, whom they took Oaths and Pay to defend, yet very like the rest of their Proceedings, and no new Thing among *Heathens* and *Pagans*, as the History of the *Mamertines* in *Sicily*, the *Turks* in *Persia*, and the *Mamalukes* in *Ægypt* can testify, and hath been the Foundation of the greatest Tyrannies, that ever the World knew; but hath seldom been done amongst *Christians*, and never by any before upon their own Country. Nor will these *Holy Men*, though they never so much desire it, ever be able of themselves to bring it to pass, unless we be so wretchedly wicked to assist them, and, while they hold the Nation at a bay, lay on the Yoke for them; for which we shall share nothing, but the Sin and the Curse; and expose ourselves to danger to serve their Lusts, who, when we have done, will not fail to pay us Part of our Desert with Shame and Violence: for so long, and no longer, shall we be allowed not to *backslide* again, until they have in our Names modell'd themselves, by cashiering all those Officers, that are guilty of any Humanity, or the least Regard to civil Government, and filling their Places with such *over-grown Saints*, as are above *God*'s Ordinances, especially that of Government— Then our Work is done; and we shall be declared Sinners against another *new old Cause*, which we never heard of before, nor any Prophet of them all has yet dreamt a Dream of; and not unlikely, when they have won the Game, which they are now playing with the Nation, they will give the Losers leave to tear us, that are their Cards, in Pieces.

To prevent this we have but two Ways, that I can possibly

contrive; and the one is presently to dissolve ourselves, and leave them to do their own Work, and run their own Dangers, before they are in a Condition, to encounter such Difficulties, as they will be sure to find. Or, if we are resolved to sit here, and act according to our own Consciences, not their Dictates, then to pass the Bill with all possible Speed for settling a new Militia in such Hands, as may secure us against their Addresses; that, if it shall happen to be *revealed* to them again, that we are unfit Representatives of their Ambition, Pride, and Avarice, they may not turn us out so easily as they did heretofore; nor make us resign and acquiesce so wretchedly, as they lately did their own *Richard* the second. But you will say, they will never suffer this to be done. I believe they will not if they can help it; but as they do not suffer us to sit here now for our own Sakes, but to serve themselves; so whatever we do, it is more for their Advantage to continue us here awhile, till they have brought their Designs to maturity, than by a too sudden removing of us precipitate and endanger all, by leaving no visible Authority in being, till they are in a Condition to assume it themselves.

In the mean time, if we be not wanting to ourselves, we may do our own Work, and in all probability be beforehand with them; for if any Part of the Nation stir, as it is not to be doubted but some will, if we can but engage the Army against them, we are safe enough; for we do not only rid ourselves of them here, but oppose one Enemy against another; and, while they are contending in Blood and Destruction, we may easily take occasion so to encrease the new Militia, upon Pretence of securing the City and opposing the common Enemy, that, before the Business be determined, we may be strong enough of ourselves to encounter the conquering Party, on which Side soever Victory light. But to make ourselves the more secure, I humbly conceive, we must by all means keep the chief Commands in our own Hands, and trust none with the Charge of a Regiment but Members of this House, or, if such cannot be spared hence, those of the Council of State; and next have a strict Care, that the Forces to be raised may wholly consist of Men obnoxious, that stand or fall with us; or such whose Persuasions in Religion will admit of the least Compliance with any others, and such I suppose to be *fifth Monarchy-Men*, those of the *baptized Churches* and *Quakers*; and if they prove troublesome to us afterwards, as 'tis probable they will, Time and future Emergencies will not fail to present us with Occasions to dispose of them too.

Howsoever a distant uncertain Danger is to be preferred, though it be greater, before that which is present and pressing. The worst that can befal us is but to be turned out again; and I hope we are not so besotted with the itch of Power and Command, that rather than sit out, we will please ourselves with such a Witch's Feast, as they have invited us to. And because they humbly petition us, that we would be pleased to be their most obedient Slaves, and help them to make three Nations so, (for that's the true Meaning of all their Addresses) we should be so vain as to believe ourselves the supreme Authority, when we are but their Parliament-Journeymen, and State Day-Labourers; and are set our Task by them, who, according as they like, or dislike our Work to-day, will continue or turn us out to-morrow. I hope the pleasure of sitting here is not so dear to us, that we should pawn our Souls, Consciences, and Understandings to them for leave to seem a *Parliament*, and deserve the Curses of Posterity, that we may but act the Parts of Statesmen at their pleasure, who in the end will use us no better, than they are wont to do the other Players. For that, or worse, will most certainly be our Reward, for which we must sit here, like Gally-Slaves upon their Banks, and tug at the Oar, while they steer which way they please, and at last, as they are unskilful Pilots, run against some Rock, and sink themselves, and us too.

MR. SPEAKER,

If the Gentleman, that spoke last, had really feared that Danger of Slavery from the Army which he pretends, he durst not have provoked them with that bold Freedom, which he has taken; and therefore 'tis probable he does not believe himself; yet, lest any Man else should, I hold it my Duty to discharge my Conscience too; though I am sure, these great Patrons of Liberty will be so unwilling to allow the same Freedom to others, which they take themselves, that, if they had equal Power to punish it, I should be loath to say the same Things, though with undeniable Truth, of them, with which most falsely and injuriously they accuse the Army.

For there is not any Crime, that they exclaim against, of which their whole Party is not most notoriously guilty; nor any Design to enslave the Nation, that is not wholly their own, and which they now drive on by laying their own Practices to the charge of those, who are the only means under Heaven to keep them from taking effect. And therefore they have the Confidence, not only to charge the Army, with that Perjury and breach of Faith, which themselves committed here (of which the Soldiers are innocent, unless the Guilt of some of their chief Commanders, Members of this House, could infect all the rest) but exclaim against them before *God* and the World, as if they intended to introduce that, which, they confess, none can do but themselves, that is Tyranny; and which, were but the Army removed, would immediately fall of itself into their Hands; though these good Patriots should but sit still, and not use their *Christian* Endeavours to bring it about, which they have so long waited for an Opportunity to do. For Tyranny and Servitude are not so easily laid on the Neck of a Nation by plain downright Force, unless that Force be foreign and receive its Recruits from abroad, as the *Turk* does; or, not to travel so far for an Example, as you do by the *Scots* and *Irish* at this instant. The more certain way to make a Nation enslave itself is performed by politic Impostures, and State Cheats, zealous Pretences to *public* good, the *Glory of God*, and *Increase of Trade*, under a Face of free Government. These are Nets into which the People are easily drawn, and rather than fail will catch themselves; and by these, backed by wrested Law, and tortured Scripture, must domestic Tyranny be upheld, and not by Force only: For as, when the Sea breaks over its Bounds, and overflows the Land, those Dams and Banks, that were made to keep it out, do afterward serve to keep it in: so, when Tyranny and Usurpation break in upon common Right and Freedom, the Laws of *God* and the Land are abused to support that, which they were intended to oppose.

This hath been the Course, which these Men have taken, and this, were the Army now disposed of, would immediately lay the heaviest Bondage upon the Nation, that ever People groan'd under. For can there be a greater Tyranny than a Government unlimited as theirs is? an Authority unbounded by the Laws of *God* or Man, where all Things are laid waste to the Will of the Rulers, and they without so much Tye or Obligation as a vain transitory Oath; where the Estates, Persons, Consciences, and Lives of Men are merely at their disposing, who can not only act what Injustice or Cruelty they list, but when they have done, make it lawful; that may murder whom they please with the Sword of Justice, and rob legally; depopulate the Land by the Constitution of the Government, and sell the free People by their own Laws. All this and more they may do, and when they have done, enact it; and nothing can hinder them, but their own Will and Pleasure, which, in probability, will not be nice, where the Wages of Iniquity is left to themselves, and they may freely share the Spoils of the Land, by *Privilege of Parliament*, as they did heretofore.

Certainly that Tyranny hath the Advantage of all other, that has Religion, Law, and Liberty among the Instruments of Servitude, as this hath; that hath a greater Power in temporal Affairs than the *Turk*, and in spiritual than the *Pope*; that is, Head of Churches not yet in Being, and Judge of more Faiths than all the *general Councils* ever were; that can damn and save, and bind and loose in this World, in despight of the next; make what it will holy or prophane, true or false, *Scripture* or *Apocrypha*, and no Man dare to question its Infallibility. So that if the Army would have them, as the Gentleman says, establish Contradictions, they are the only fit Men in the World for such a Work; for nothing is impossible to them, who are confined to nothing; that can not only vote, but swear Contradictions, as they have often done, and made others do so too, or pay them for it. For certainly these are the most prime Engineers of Oaths, that ever the World knew, (though they are too modest to put it upon others) and have approved themselves the ablest Swearers, that ever made Perjury an *Expedient*. I have heard it was a Custom amongst the *Jews*, when any Man made a Vow to Almighty *God*, which afterward he found inconvenient to be kept, he might be by any three other *Jews* absolved of it; but every one of these, as if he were three *Jews*, can absolve himself.

315

Thus vast is the Latitude of their Power; and yet you hear what Complaints they make, as if their Authority were hidebound: but if we consider the Persons, into whose Hands this overgrown Monster is intrusted, the Danger that hangs over all our Heads will appear to be so much the greater, by how much they are the unfittest Men in the whole World for such a Trust. For you cannot but know, that these, or the greatest Part of them, are the very same Persons, that for their approved Liberty of Conscience, and Unguiltiness of Faith, Honesty, or Shame, passed two several Probations by *Oliver Cromwel*; the Dregs and Sediment of the *long-Parliament*, that have been made instrumental to all his contrived *Providences*, until they grew so odious to all Men, that he found their Infamy did him more hurt, than their Diligence good; and that the last and best Advantage he could make of them was to turn them out of Doors; which signal Piece of Justice he had no sooner done, with the general Applause of three Nations, but he made that the first Step of his Ascent to the Throne, as if he had a confest Title to that Power, which he had so justly rescued from the common Enemies of the Nation; nor did the People then oppose him, to whom they believed they owed their Deliverance. And yet out of these did he afterwards pick a third Scum, who served him in their Callings, as Ministers of that Government, which since upon change of Light they call Tyranny, and in due Time have voted down, with Hopes to be taken again into Employment under a worse; where with double Diligence they may expiate the Mischief they have done their Country, by doing greater, and deserve a new Trust for their great Experience in serving all Occasions, and saving their Tide in all Turns of State.

But, if we look a little further backwards, and call to mind what their Actions were, when they last swayed this mighty Power, we may the easier guess what they are like to do hereafter. And truly the most faithful Histories of their renowned Deeds contain little else but Things of this Nature—That first of all they made diligent Inquiry after all ways of raising Money by fleaing of the People, that had ever been used here, or by foreign Tyrannies; these they introduced for the good of the Nation, and confirmed with so much Care, that since they have proved to be the only Things they settled, and are like to continue their Memory to the Curses of Posterity—That, after they had destroyed *Religion*, they pulled down Churches, (as being then of no Use) and rased the noblest Structures in the Land, to sell the Materials; cut down Woods, and demolished public Monuments with more than *Goth* and *Vandal* Outrage, in which they were so greedy, that they spoiled more than they devoured—That they imbezzled the Jewels, and sold the Lands and Goods of the *Crown*, and cheated one another and the Public of the Money—That they advanced Fools and Ideots to Places of Judicature, for their good Affections to the Government, that is, their own Preferment, which they could never have had under any other; and also for their assured Diligence, to do injustice upon all Occasions according to Directions—That upon single Perjuries suborned by themselves they condemned Men unheard, and sold their Estates without suffering them to speak for themselves—That they broke Articles of War, and took away Mens Lives and Estates, to whom they had given Conditions—That they propagated the Gospel by turning learned Ministers out of their Livings, and in their Places appointing seven or eight Mechanics errant, Vagrants and Rogues by the Statute to straggle about the Country, and compass the Land, as the *Devil* does, to spread such Doctrines, as they should judge orthodox to their Occasions, and render the Word of *God* and preaching contemptible; while themselves and their Creatures shared the Profits of so many Churches, forcing the poor Ministers with their Wives and Children to beg—That to keep up a Reputation of *Godliness* (notwithstanding all these pious Works,) and to stop the Mouths of the *Saints*, (who would else cry out, they had done nothing for *King Jesus*, but all for themselves) they used to make severe Laws against swearing, drinking, and *prophane walking*, unprofitable Sins, that did yield them nothing, that there might be the less Notice taken of the Impunity, or rather Encouragement they gave to blasphemy, Murder, Sacrilege, Perjury, Bribery, Oppression, and all manner of Cheats and Robberies of the Commonwealth; by acting of which themselves, or dispensing with them in others, they got more Money then ever *Pope* did. And yet, notwithstanding all these Ways of Gain, they turned bankrupt with the poor Soldiers, and made those dreadful Tyrants take 17d. in the Pound for the Price of their Blood, by a lewd Cheat forcing those to double their Debentures and buy Land, that wanted Money, or lose all—By this odious Fraud many have greatly enriched themselves, by robbing those, who had so often ventured their Lives to save them from the Gallows. All this, and much more, you cannot but know to be most true, which drew so great an hatred of *God* and Man upon them, that, when some of the Army were made use of to dissolve them, never was *Parliament* chosen with greater Acclamations of all Men, than they were turned out; and if the free Voices of the People, in whom they had then placed the supreme Power, may justify the Action, never was *Parliament* more lawfully dissolved.

But you will say, 'tis probable, that having seen the Wickedness and Danger of these Courses, and suffered that, which is much to them, to be laid by and reduced to a private Condition, they will amend their Lives, and beware how they do the like hereafter. Truly no; for, beside the perpetual Nature of Wickedness, which is always to grow worse, we find, that the Grace of Repentance and Amendment seldom falls to many Sinners together, and never to any one Hypocrite, much less to such a Number. And I rather believe, we shall find that true here, which our *Saviour* says upon such another Occasion.—*That when the Evil Spirit is cast out, and returns to get in again, he brings with him seven other worse than himself, and the last State of that Man is worse than the first.* For they have suffered nothing, that will not rather encourage than deter them, Time being all they have lost, which they will endeavour to redeem; and 'tis like they have not so misspent their late Leisure, but that they will come forth *Eruditiores ad nocendum*, better studied in Mischief, and taught to be more cautious, till they have rendered themselves secure. Beside this, they are like to return with the fiercer Appetite for this Restraint, like Beasts that prey eagerest, when they are hungry. 'Tis said, *nullus superbus aliquando servit nisi dominandi spe*, and then, if they are such Slaves to the Army as they say, why do they endure it? unless, as those that pay for their Places are wont to make the most of them; so they intend to have that Slavery with interest out of the People, which they are fain to purchase with their own. But they would have the World believe, they are forced to sit here against their Wills; when I will undertake that, rather than leave these dear Benches, they shall vote and swear to Blanks, address Petitions and Advices to the very Redcoats, and, if they had any such Design, as they pretend, to enslave their Country, offer their Service, humbly sue for the Trust, and beg for the Honour *to carry on the Work*, rather than part with that mock Power, which they would seem to make so contemptible. And how can we then expect, they should ever put an end of themselves to this *Parliament*? Believe it, they have not the Hearts to do it; and the longer they sit, the more unwilling they will be to rise. They talk'd of a Year; but when that's expired, they will not want Pretences to put it off to a further Time, as the *Turks* do *Mahomet*'s Coming; and rather than fail, make Disturbances abroad to continue themselves secure here; which if they can but do against Force, they are in for Term of Life, and perhaps their Heirs after them; for out they will not, but by Force, that's certain. 'Tis true, it is the worst Way, but yet it is the last, which is the chief thing they look after: for though they were sure to be turned out to-morrow, they would not lose so much Time to go out of themselves to-day. And yet they are as like to dissolve, as limit themselves, and will as soon put an End, as Bounds to their arbitrary Power. Those free and mercurial Consciences of theirs will never be confined within any certain Lists. 'Tis a hard Matter to force Nature, but more difficult to make her force herself. Did ever Lion, that broke loose, return of himself again into the Grate? or is it probable that they, who have broke through all Laws to assume an unlimited Power, will make new ones to deprive themselves of it? But suppose, they were willing to do it, and did really intend it, how is it possible for them to bind themselves, when the same Power, that binds, can also loose? Can a Man be bound in a Bond to himself, and lose any Thing by the Forfeiture? Or pass a Deed to intrust himself with a Power, which he cannot alter at Pleasure? All the Laws, that they can make, and all the Laws of the Land too, will be, like their Wills and Testaments, revokable, while they sit here, and never valid till after their Departure; nor is it possible for them to settle any Government, that will be, like a natural Body, firm and compact, but rather, like Puppet-Work, fastened with Screws, to be taken to pieces again at Pleasure.

As for the Design of settling a new Militia, if there were nothing else, this is sufficient to make it appear, who are they, that endeavour to enslave their Country: for what other possible Account can be given, why so heavy a Burthen should be laid upon the Nation, to raise a Force only against itself; for what other Enemy can they pretend to have, unless it be the Army, which has been their Guard for so many Years against all Dangers? But what are the People like to suffer under so great a Power, that are already so opprest merely by their own Permission? All the Hope they have is, that they can hardly suffer more than they do in this one Thing: for what can Tyranny do worse, than reduce them into the Condition of the damned, and make their own Consciences testify against them for that, which is now Crime enough, their Estates? Or what greater Slavery can Men endure, than to be compelled to swear what they have, when no Man can justly say he hath any Thing, as soon as it is known? Is this the way to secure *Propriety and Liberty of Conscience*, which these Men take upon them so confidently to vindicate, by imposing that, which must of necessity oppress the one, or violate the other? Is this the Way of having regard to *tender Consciences* (for which so many Professions have been made) to contrive Engines, that shall catch only such as will not forswear themselves, and let such as will go free? Is not the Nation perjured enough already; or are not the public Debts great enough without this aggravation? But perhaps they believe this is the readiest way to pay them. I do confess, if this Militia were once settled, the Army and Fleet were instantly paid all their Arrears, I mean all they are ever like to have, and well if they come off so (for no doubt some will be found guilty of some Feats of Arms formerly done in this Place, which will easily be explained to be within the Exceptions of Indemnity) and yet the Nation shall not save a Peny by it. It will be a pretty handsome Reserve (and therefore it is still deferred.) When there is no more to be racked out of the People upon any other Pretence, then the Arrears will not fail to do the Feat, and serve to continue the Year within the Compass of four Months, and make it yield three Harvests; until we reckon our Taxes no more by the Year, but the Year by our Taxes, as the primitive *Christians* did under the *Heathens* by the *Roman* Indiction. But they are much troubled at the *Councils of Officers* of the Army, but never consider, when every Member of the *Council of State* is Colonel of a Regiment, what difference there will be between that Council and a Council of Officers—Whether the Sword will then be in the Hands of the civil or military Power will be a hard Question to determine; and yet the Nation is like to pay dear for it, and be in a worse Condition than now it is: for after a while you will be forced to raise another new Militia, to get the Power out of their Hands, who will never part with it upon other Terms; and I do wish, that those future *Rotations* as they call them, may prove to be no more Charge and Disturbance to the Nation, than such as have been lately made by the present Officers.

And now, Sir, I believe it is no hard Matter for any indifferent Men to judge, who are most like to enslave their Country, they or the Soldiers; whether those Men, whose insatiable Avarice devours like the Grave, and still gapes, like Hell, for more; whose Ambition and Itch to handle the public Affairs would force them upon any Danger, that extends but to Soul and Conscience, or the just Curses of the People; that would act under *Jack Straw* or *James Naylor*, rather than sit out, and condemn Men to Death for committing high Treason against them; that would renounce *Christ*, be circumcised, and serve the *Turk*, rather than live out of Command and Authority, or live under the Laws of *God* or Man—Whether such Men, I say, are not more like to enslave their Country than those who are content with what will hardly satisfy Nature; that pawn their Lives for that little, that will keep them honest, though poor and miserable; that are contented (at least quiet) with less than the Laws of *God* require of them: for we do not find that they are commanded in *Scripture* to be contented with no Pay, as they have been of late for some Years, and yet have not been known to mutiny, or offer Violence to any Man. As for that Violence, which they are charged to have done to several Governments, the chief Authors of those Atchievements were Members of this House, and here learned the way of it, which the inferior Officers and the rest of the Army are so far from being guilty of, that they did no more than their Duty, which consists in obeying, not arguing, the Commands of their Superiors, without making themselves supreme Judges of State Affairs, which do not at all belong to them. This was all they did heretofore, and all that they are like to do hereafter, only oppose Tyranny, when they are commanded. And is it possible, that these Men should have any Design to enslave others, that have suffered themselves to be made such Slaves, as instead of receiving their just Arrears, to be sent away to starve in the remotest Parts of the Earth, as a great Part of the Army have been; to be shipped away for *France*, *Flanders*, *Sweden*, and *Jamaica*, just at the framing of new Tyrannies, which they were like to disturb, if they had been suffered to stay at Home; that have patiently endured to see so many of their Officers cashiered, without any Thing laid to their Charge, or being heard to speak for themselves? And yet they are accused for enslaving those, from whom they have suffered all this, and charged with those Designs, which they only keep from taking Effect, with such transcendent Confidence and obstinate Hypocrisy, as if their Accusers intended to blot out all Notions of Right and Wrong, and Truth and Falshood out of the World. This is the only Reason, why they are made so great a Grievance to their Country by those Men, who do not only owe their Wealth and Greatness, but their very Lives to their Protection. For by them have they been secured to sit here, to brood Riches, to share the Fruits of other Mens Blood and Danger, and talk themselves great; and by them are they at this Instant protected from the Outrage of the People, which would inevitably fall upon them, were they left to themselves. And yet they desire nothing more than the Destruction of their Preservers, and to put Arms into other Hands, to whom they owe less, and who less understand them; and consequently would be never serviceable to their Purposes. But if that were once done, they would not only assume, but own, and justify that, which they now exclaim against, before *God*, and the World.

What would follow afterwards it is not hard to foresee: for as there is no Government, that they can settle, were the Army removed, that would not immediately be thrown off by the People; so if they can but raise a Force of their own to secure themselves, they will never settle any at all, but make themselves supreme Lords of this vast unlimited Power, that, like a *Terra incognita*, cannot be determined how far it extends, nor will it ever be by them. This they will execute most righteously, no doubt, under these serene Princes, their *invisible Highnesses*, the Keepers of the *invisible Liberties*, that like the *Persian Magi* never appear, but keep State and their no-Charge in some enchanted Castle nobody knows where, nor can tell how many they are. And yet, to give them their due, they are the most benign and gracious Sovereigns to their Ministers of State in the whole World: for they will give them absolute Power to do what they please, how unjust or inhuman soever, and never admit of any Appeals, nor call them to account for any thing, but freely let them enjoy such a large Dominion, as the *fifth-Monarchy Saints* propose to themselves under King *Jesus*, whom they would now compel, whether he will or no, to take the *Devil* at his Word, and accept of all the Kingdoms of the Earth, and the Glory of them, which he refused so long ago, merely that they might create themselves his *Popes* or Vicars upon Earth, and rule according to his, that is, their own will. And just such a Prerogative will these Men enjoy under their magical liege-Lords as long, if no outward Force disturb them, as they can continue united, which, were their common Dangers removed, will be but a short Time, where there are so many supreme Powers, and so many that would be; who believing they have equal Right, as well as Itch, to it, will not fail to keep up perpetual Faction, and spread Sedition, which that just Hatred of the People will be always ready to assist—By this means (as all Tyrannies of many have ever been short-lived) so will this quickly fall into other Hands, and from many to one, and from one to many again; until between these different Usurpations, that pull several ways, the whole Nation will in the end be sawed in Pieces. All the Hopes we shall have of Liberty will be only this—That the Stock of the *Commonwealth* will not be long able to bear the Charges of its own Slavery; and so Tyranny itself, as well as all other Trades, must in the end be forced to break. In the mean Time we shall not have so much as a settled Slavery, but be forced to change our Masters, as *Christian* Bond-slaves are in *Turky*, as they shall please to dispose of us; and be conveyed from Government to Government, as Rogues are from Constable to Constable, still to be whipt and punished according to Law, as they will outface us, until we come to the Place where we were born, *a just and lawful Authority*.

A
SPEECH
MADE AT THE
ROTA

Among the excellent Orders of that glorious Senate of *Rome* one was, that any Senator having a Right to speak to every Business in Debate, might instead of giving his Sentence to the present Question (if he had no mind to declare himself) propose any Thing else, that was in his Judgment *e Republica*, of Concernment to the Commonwealth. This Custom I humbly desire may be received into this ingenious Assembly, and that I may have the Honour to be the first Man that shall put it in Practice. For I perceive, we have not only heard all, and more than all, that can be said to the Purpose concerning *over-Balance and Propriety*, but like those that are out of their Way, the further we go the further we are from our End; and I doubt, in Conclusion, shall come to discover, that there is no such Thing at present in the *English* Nation, as either the one, or the other—Besides, Sir, as all *Rotations* and Wheelings cause a kind of Giddiness in the Brain; so if we provide not some wholesome Diversion for those that we have so often heard of, it will not be in the Power of this sober and considerate Coffee to keep us in our Wits. Although if it be *the black Broth* which the *Lacedemonians* us'd, as some learned Authors are of Opinion, I grant it hath a sovereign Operation to strengthen politic Notions, especially such as concern *Republics*, and is the same which *Lycurgus* himself drank, when he form'd his Commonwealth; and among other excellent Constitutions, hit upon that excellent Law, that enjoins Women *to wear Slits in their Petticoats*, and Boys *to steal Bread and Butter*, as *Plutarch* writes in his Life; and I could wish Mr. *Harrington* may be desired by this Assembly to introduce it into his *Oceana*—But this is not that, which I purpose to propose at this Time, but something that does more immediately concern the present Government, which as yet we live under, for whose Service I suppose these Meetings are peculiarly intended—And that is, whether the late Name of

324

A SPEECH AT THE ROTA

Rump be significant, proper, and adequate to the present *Parliament*. I doubt not, but at first Sight it will appear to most Men to be nothing less; but if you please to trust me with your Patience for a few Minutes, I dare undertake to make it appear, not only out of all Antiquity and the Consent of all Ages, but the Testimony of Nature herself, that it is not only the most proper, apt, and significant, but the most honourable Denomination, that could by the Wit of Man be given unto it.

The learned *Eben Ezra* and *Manasseh Ben Israel* do write, that there is in the Rump of Man a certain Bone, which they call the Bone *Luz*; this, they say, is of so immortal and incomprehensible a Nature, that at the Resurrection out of it all the rest of the Bones and Members shall sprout, just as a Plant does out of a Kernel: and is there any thing that can bear a nearer Resemblance to this Rump Bone than the present *Parliament*, that has been so many Years dead and rotten under Ground to any Man's thinking, that the Ghosts of some of the Members thereof have transmigrated into other *Parliaments*, and some into those Parts from whence there is no Redemption, should nevertheless at two several and respective Resurrections start up, like the Dragon's Teeth that were sown, into living, natural, and carnal Members? And hence it is, I suppose, that Physicians and Anatomists call this Bone *Os Sacrum*, or the holy Bone.

The *Ægyptians* in their Hieroglyphics decyphered a Prince by a Bee: now a Bee, you know, does carry not only his Militia or Defence, but his whole politic Interest in his Tail; for when he has lost his Sting he is presently banished that well order'd Government, as an unprofitable Member and a Drone.

The *Greeks* call Rule or Empire βασιλεία, as the Etymologists tell us, because it is βάσις τοῦ λαοῦ, the Base or Fundament of the People: for as the Rump or Bum in the natural Body is called the Fundament, because it is the Foundation on which all the rest of the Members depend; so is the State and Government in the Body politic.

The Philosophers say, that a Man is a Tree inverted, and that his Head is the Root, by which he takes in his Nourishment, and his Arms and Legs the Branches—If that be true, it must follow that his Rump is the Head.

PROSE PAMPHLETS

It is a Custom of the *Eastern* Kings to vail their Faces from public View, only to avoid prostituting the Majesty of their Persons to common Eyes; and what is that more than the universal Custom of all Nations and Ages hath always carefully observed to the Rump? And therefore, when the *Philistines* resolved to put the highest indignity upon *David*'s Embassadors, they could not think of a way more ignominious than to cut their Garments above their Buttocks, and by that means to render those reverend Parts cheap and despicable in the Eyes of the Rabble.

Some are of Opinion, that Honour is seated in that Part only, chiefly at least: for it is observed, that a small Kick on that Part does more hurt and wound Honour, than a cut on the Head or Face, or a Stab or Shot of a Pistol on any other Part of the Body. And hence it is, that in all Combats all the rest of the Members are ready to expose themselves to any Danger to screen the Breech; as if the whole outward Man were but a Life-Guard to that Part: and he, that by turning his Back, exposes that to Danger, is ever after branded with the ignominious Name of a Coward.

The ancient Heroes were wont to wear Horse-Tails in their Helmets, as our young Gallants do Ostrich Tails in their Hats; from whence we may infer, that it hath been the Consent of all Ages, that the Head can receive no greater Ornament than that which is conferred on it by the Tail. And in all funeral Pomps and public Shews, he that hath the longest Tail to his Robe is understood to be the most honourable Person; and, therefore, when *Oliver Cromwel* was to be installed, his Robe had a Tail of six Yards long, which was born up by six young Noblemen, merely in Honour to that Part, in Contemplation whereof the Charge was bestowed; for all the other Parts bore a nearer Proportion to the Body.

Is not the Chair the most honourable Part of the Parliament? Then that which sits in it must of necessity be the most honourable Part of the Speaker. It is an Axiom in Philosophy *levia sursum*, *gravia deorsum*, and can any thing imaginable be more *grave* than so venerable a Senate? And hence, I suppose, the Wisdom of our Ancestors called it the *lower-House*, in relation to the Place it held in the Government. All Birds in the Air, and Fishes in the Sea guide themselves with their Tails, from the Leviathan to the Sprat; and the most famous of our modern Philosophers hath of late made a Discovery, *that Leviathan and Republic are all one.*

The greatest Honour, that can be given to Man, is either to go before, or sit above others—In sitting the whole Honour is conferred on the Breech; and in going before, the Breech is more immediately waited upon than any other Part, and therefore receives the greater Respect—And from all this I doubt not but by this Time it plainly appears, that the *Rump*, as I said before, is not only the most honourable, but most apt and proper Name, that can be given to those, whose only Business is to sit.

TWO
LETTERS,
One from *John Audland a* QUAKER,
TO
WILLIAM PRYNNE.
The Other,
WILLIAM PRYNNES
ANSWER,

By the AUTHOR *of*

HUDIBRAS.

LONDON,
Printed for *Jonathan Edwin* at the *Three Roses* in
Ludgate Street. 1672.

JOHN AUDLAND'S
LETTER
To
WILLIAM PRYNNE.

William Prynne,

Thou perpetual Scribe, Pharise, and Hypocrite, born to the destruction of *Paper*, and most unchristian effusion of *Ink*, thou Ægyptian Task-master of the Press, and unmerciful destroyer of *Goosequils*, that dost plunder and strip thy poor kindred naked to the skin, to maintain thy self in a Tyrannycal and Arbitrary Way of Scribling against thy Brethren, even the *Independants* and *Quakers*, over whom thou settest up thy self as an unrighteous Judge, for a Righteous Judge hath an *Ear* for both *Parties*, and thou hast *none* for *either*. Verily *William* thou dost evil, and against the light within thee, to accuse thy Brethren of that, whereof thou art more guilty thy self; for though they break an Act of Parliament, yet thou didst worse, when thou wouldst have made one thy self, after thou hadst engaged thy Faith unto the House, that thou wouldst never lift up thy Heel against them more: Truly thou shewest thy self in this no better then a *Jew*, in throwing the first stone at them, unless thou wert innocent thy Self, and all thy Fundamental, Municipal, Common, Natural Law, will not serve to prove thee other, who hast been judged by the Laws of the Land, as a Pharise, to weare a *Phylactery* in publick, and hast had thine Ears bored through according to the *Mosaical* Law: And I fear thy pretended Conversion to Christianity, is but in order to something else, even as the *Mahometans* (they say) will not admit a Jew to turn Turk, unless he first become a Christian. And that is the reason why thou art so cruel (like a Renegado) to those of thine own Sect, yea even unto those in whose quarrel thou hast lost Leather, for as one of thy Ears was cut off for *Presbytery*, even so was the other for *Independancy*. But now I speak of thine Eares, give me leave to ask thee one question. I have heard that those who have lost their Legs, do somtimes

331

nevertheless feel pains in their Toes; and I would fain know, whether toward change of weather thou dost not feel a kind of itching and tingling in those defunct *Parings* of thine, especially when *Presbytery* and Governement are like to peep out again. For what else does thy rayling against the Bishops (as well as us) hold forth? but that thou art the very same *Will. Prynne* Utter Barrister, that didst heretofore publish against them so many ridiculous Hatcases, and Bandboxes, in which thy works are alwaies bound up, and are to be sold on the Southside of *Pauls*-Church-yard, where thy Stationers live. Among those I have seen thy Title pages pasted like Mountebanks Bills, in which thou dost alwayes write *Reformation, Law, Religion,* and *Fundamental* in *Capital Letters*, even as those *Quacks* doe *Pox* and *Running* of the *Reins*, and both to the same purpose, namely to deceive the Reader, and vapour of more then thou art able to perform. But oh the verbosity of thy writings! *Solomon* saith in many words there is folly, and thou hast prov'd it true: For thou writest perpetually in the Language of a *Conveyance*, and dost not indite, but draw; and when thou shalt answer for every idle word, all the Bills and Answers in *Chancery* will rise up in judgment against thee. For thou usest so many impertinent Tautologies, that thy Reader can never understand what thou meanest, unless he should take the paines to draw Breviates of thy senceless repetitions which is insufferable and not to be endured by a Free-born *English* man. And this serves thee to the same purpose that *Hems* and *Hahs* do thy guifted Ghostly Fathers, that is to lose time, and put off thy Commodity, namely Wast-Paper, whereof thou endeavourest to obtain the *Monopoly*, and thereby undo hundreds of Families that live by writing lewd and profane Playes. For when thou has ingrost the whole Commodity of Wast-Paper into thine own hands, their Works will be left upon theirs; and in this thou takest a more wise and rationall Course, then thou didst heretofore in writing Indentures against them. For thou knowest not how to write in any other strain, and therefore to let thee see how easy it is to attain unto thy gifts, I will now speake unto thee a few words in thine own way. Dost thou not remember *William Prynne*, when the long Parliament according to the antient, known, fundamentall, established Custome, Practice, Usage, Example, of all Rebels, Traytors, Cades, Tylers, Straws, set open the Prisons, Goales,

JOHN AUDLAND'S LETTER

Dungeons, Cages, and tooke the Prisoners, Felons, Malefactors, Jayl-birds into their Protection, Patronage, Safeguard, Tuition, and among others, thy self *William Prynne* aforesaid, with thy Brethren, Companions, Copemates, Associates, *Burton, Bastwick, Lilborn, Poe,* &c. How the Saints, Brethren, godly, wel-affected, rod[e] out to meet thee, with the Sisters, Helpers, Damsels, Hand-maids, behind them, on the tayl of the Beast, stuck with Antechristian, Superstitious, Idolatrous, *Rosemary* and *Bays* to celebrate, welcome and congratulate thy Remitter! How they dawb'd, dashed, defiled and polluted thee the said *William Prynne,* with Durt, puddle, greetings, Salutation[s], that thou didst look more like unto a Pimp, Pander, Bawd newly Carted, than an Utter-Barrister Triumphant, and with how durty and filthy a grace, fashion and demeanure, thou didst bow, stoop, and lowt to thine Idolaters, the Rabble, rout, crowd on both sides of the street, or streets, who made an Idol of the *Rings* of thine *Ears,* even as the *Jews* did of their *Ear-rings.* This verely *William* is thy perfect Stile, and right manner of expression, in which thou art the freer of thy windy Stuff, because thou comest easily by it, for thou doest but turn over thy Concordances, and the Indexes of thy Books, and wheresoever thou findest any thing of *Quake, Tremble* and *Shake,* from the motion of the Heavens to the wagging of a Dogs tayl, thou applyest it right or wrong unto *Us,* and that it may seem to be to some purpose, thou dost always print it in CAPITAL LETTERS, because such were heretofore, to very good Purpose, imprinted on thy cheeks by the Ministration of that Son of *Belial,* the *Executioner.* But I cannot understand how thou or thy Rabble of Saints could answer the Churches for committing the abominable Sin of *Bays* and *Rosemaryness* which they had before and have since so often condemned, for if it be Idolatrous and Superstitious (as they have determined) to sticke those Creatures in the windores of Steeple-houses, much more must it be on their own Vessels. All that they have (in mine opinion) to say for themselves, is that they serv'd thee up (like a *Westphalia Ham*) with *Bays,* as thou art a Pagan Poet, according to the profane Custome of thy fore Fathers the Heathen, though he that has the patience to read thy vile untunable Dittys, will rather take thee for an *Irish* Ratcatcher that is said to Rhim[e] Vermen to Death, then the *English Prudentius* or *Robert Wisdom* Junior, as some of thine

333

own Tribe stile thee, according to the Flesh: for thou dost abuse Scripture most unconscionably against it's own express command, in casting holy things into Doggerel, which is worse and more abominable then unto Dogs, and this thou performest so dully that some of the *Vertuoso's* have been puzled to find out the reason of it, till they were informed that when thou writest, thou dost use always to set a Deaths head on the *Desk* before thee, as one *Campanella*, a Popish Frier, is said to have done the Pictures of those to whom he intended to address his writings, and found it most certain upon several experiments, that the person to the Resemblance of whose Countenance he could nearest force and screw his own, was always most pleas'd with his writings: And this they are confident is the natural reason why thy compositions are so flat and dul, that they will hardly hold till the Ink is dry, and when they are printed, not one of an hundred will endure the stitching, but turn to such homly uses as they are most fit and proper for. Truly *William*, if I were your friend I should advise you to leave this freak of the Deaths head, lest the young Gentlemen of the House surprise you again (as you know they once did at Midnight) and make you drink healths-Sickness in it again on your bare Marrow-bones. But I wonder in what part of the world thy Readers live, if there are any such Creatures in nature; verily they ought to have their shoulders grow above their heads, like *John Mandevile's* People in *Afrique*, for there is more of labour and drudgery, than understanding required, and they ought to have a large measure of *Patience*, *Long-suffering* and *Ignorance*, that can endure to read one Page of thine: For as in the *North*, the more durty and foul the High-wayes are, the larger measure they allow to their Miles; even so dost thou to thy tedious dull Impertinencyes, in so much that some are of opinion that thy Readers ought to be Dieted like Running-Nags, before they can be in breath to read thy long-winded Periods, which none but such as thy self will submit to, for if few words do best with the Wise, none of those will ever endure to have any thing to do with thee. And yet I have heard that thou dost not a little glory that thy works have past through all sorts of times, (but only those wherein they were refuted by the Hand of thy old *Antagonist* the Hangman) without dispute or question. It is very true indeed, they are utterly incapable of confutation, as some places are rendered impregnable by their barren Rockey Scituations, or by being fortifi'd with Mudwals and Ditches. He that should venture to Encounter thee at thy own Weapon, might be said to Revive the old way of fighting with Sandbags, the true Types of thy dry disjoynted Stuff, and beside must of necessity cite so many several sorts of Wares, from *Plums* and *Sugar*, to *Mundungus* and *Rats bane*, with which thy works are always bound up, that his writings will be charged with Quotations as full and dul as thine own. But since so many *Chandlers* and *Habberdashers* of smal wares, have undertaken to confute thee, and proceeded so far therein already, it were an act of great imprudence to take the taske out of their hands who are best able to go through with it. And therefore I shall leave it to them to determine, whether thou hast substantially and solidly prov'd the *Quakers* to be Jesuitical Romish Capouchin Frogs, with maskes on their faces put on by the *Jesuits* and puld off by thee, as thou dost confidently undertake to perform in thy Title Page. Truly *William* I do confess those *Jesuits* are dangerous fellows, thou hadst best looke about thee and have a care, for it is verily believ'd by many knowing Persons, that they have always set thee on work no less than the *Independants*: and have receiv'd a better return from thy *Horse-like* drudgery, though thou hast no more wit to perceive then a Foole has to know by what hand it is set on work. And if they bewitched the *Quakers* (as thou dost confidently affirm) it is most certain they have drawn thee into that feat too. For if it be true, as some carnal Learned Men aver, that Witches fetch the materials of their Medicines, from Gibbets and Pilleries, the Parings of thine ears have been among their Ingredients, and thou art guilty thereof.

But I fear I begin to be like thee, that is tedious to no purpose, for I do not expect that any thing can do good upon thee, who hast been so often incorrigible to the Laws, for as the strength of two men in their wits is not sufficient to hold down and quiet one Madman, even so art thou proof against all reason and light, and therefore I will cast away no more upon thee, but leaving thee to thine own Darkness, with the old saying, bid thee twice Goodnight.

John Audland.

THE
ANSWER
OF
William Prynne

John Audland,

Thou Quaking Quack, Jesuitical Romish Franciscan Frog,
See my *Quaker unmasked*, pag. I. 13. Thou that art the Devils
dicebox which he SHAKES, Rattles, wags, to gull, cheat,
delude, and seduce the intoxicated giddy-headed, *English Nation.*
Thou that art sick of thy Church, and hast catch'd thy Religion
like a Palsey, Epilepsy, Ague, and art taken with Tertian,
Quartan, Quotidian cold fits, at thy Super[sti]tious, Idolatrous,
Jesuitical Meetings, Assemblies, Conventicles. See my *Healths
Sickness*, p. 150. The *Northern blast*, pa. 90. *The Pope crossing
the Cudgels*, p. 297. Whereas thou saist I have no Eares, &c.
therein thou shewest that thou hast no Light, Reason, understanding, For as a house is judged to be a house in Law as long
as any part thereof is standing, and a light piece of Gold is good
and lawful English Coyn, currant with allowance, although it
be clip'd, filed, washed, or worn; even so are my *Eares*, legal,
warrantable, and sufficient *Eares*, and good in Law, however
they have been clip'd, par'd, crop'd, circumcised, and I have a
better Title to the Remainders then thou hast to thine, for they
have been twice adjudged to me by the Laws of the Land, which
thine never were. For those parcels, scraps, shreds, that I was
deprived of, did but confirm my Right to those that are (see my
own Abridgement at large, *pag.* 29. *Lisle upon Gerrard, pa.* 26.
The Legality of Treason, in two parts, *S.G.* upon both, *pag.* 666.)
left, for *exceptio firmat legem in casibus non exceptis.*

This shews that the light within thee, of which thou dost
vapour, brag, vaunt, and extol thy self so much, is but a kind of
dusky Owl-light, a trembling, twinkling, stincking snuff, which
thou carriest in thy Paunch, Guts, Bowels, as an Ox, Bull or
Cow doth Tallow to make Candles of, or the Cattle of *Lin-*

colnshire do the Fewel of the Countrey, and thou knowest who it was that looked over *Lincoln*, and cryed, *All's mine*, as he will in time do over ye *Quakers*, Frogs, Vipers, See my *Hidden works of darkness*, p. 400. *A Looking glass for a blind guide*, p. 79. *Fryers a Fry of Frogs*, p. 200. &c.

Whereas thou sayst, urgest and objectest, that I would have made an *Act of Parliament*, therein thou art mistaken, deceived and deluded, for I would rather have marred, spoyled and perverted one according to the sense, judgment and opinion of the House (and *ejus est interpretari cujus est condere*, see *Bracton*) by putting in, adding and incerting some thing or things of my own invention, wit, contrivance, that had not passed their Votes, and putting out, eracing, and expunging other things, which had, which cannot be said, held, or judged to be a breach of Law, because it was before it was made one, and if it had been so, yet it would have proved no great crime, fault, offence, for exchange (thou knowest) is no robbery. See *The foot out of the snare*, pag. 53. *Prynnes Principles*, p. 200. which is more then you can say, produce, or alledge for your selves, who are a generation, Spawn, Litter of Vipers, Frogs, Serpents, so obstinate, peremptory, incorrigible, that you break the Act of Parliament, at the same time that it is put in Execution against you, like unto a Cut purse that picks a Pocket when he is going to be hang'd, for you croud, thrust and intrude your selves into Prisons by shoales, that you may in defyance of Law, Government, Authority, meet more then five together, although it be in the Goale. See my *Sword of Christian Magistracy suppressed*, p. 550. *The Sectary dissected*, p. 82.

Whereas thou saist, I write in the stile, form, language of a *Conveyance*, therein I do according to my Profession, Calling, Vocation, and if thou hadst done so too, thou hadst been but a Mechanick still, and hadst not ordain'd thy self a Hedge-Sir *John* of an Orderless Order and unruly rule, the Original, Rise, or beginning whereof, is as uncertain as the Head or Heads of *Nile*, or the hatching of Woodcocks, for no body can tell from whence it came, (See *Truth Triumphing*, pag. 79. *The Jesuite a Jebusite*, p. 904.) a Church, or rather Chappel indeed, that is built upon a *Quaking Bog* (mark that) or flat quick sand, without superior or inferior in it, like the Knights of King *Arthurs* (See the

Seaven Champions of Christendome) Round Table, or the Serpent *Amphisbœna* (of which, see *Pliny*) that has a head at both ends.

Mahomet the false Prophet of the Turks, was the first Prophet, Patriarch, Founder of the *Quakers*. For he had trembling trances, and frantick fits of the *Falling sickness*, in which he had Revelations, dreams, Visions whisper'd into his ear by a Dove Pidgeon or Widgeon, that he had instructed and taught, used to pick seeds out of his ear or ears; which seeds, are the seeds of your Church as well as his, for they produce the very same fruits, effects, workings in both, and both equally hope to be saved by him. And hence it is, that all your wishes, longings, desires are in the Turks overrunning of Christendome; for as both they and you account Fooles, Ideots, Madmen, Saints; you do not doubt but to pass easily for such with them, for your great abilities in those gifts. And therefore as your Brethren the aforesaid Turkish *Mahometan Fanaticks*, devote, destine, damne, themselves to destruction, meerly to tire, weary, make work for, and put a stop to the Christians in their Wars: and fill up Ditches, grafts, trenches with their bodies, carcases, outward men for their fellow Musselmen to march over; even so ye also think to weary out the Officers of Justice, with your numberless numbers, and render your selves as hard to be cast out as Legion the Devil incorporate did, of whom ye are a Type. See *The Stationers Beacon fired*, pag. 1000. *The Sectary in Sippets*, pa. 202.

By all which, it appears that ye have a Turk as well as a Pope in your bellies, and that ye delight in Persecution, in affliction, Tribulation, as some old extravagant fantastick fornicators, find a pleasure in being whip'd, and out of these sores ingender one another, by æquivocal generation, as Flyes blow Maggots, which afterwards becom Flys and blow others. See my *Romes Masterpiece*, p. 808. *Settle brain for a Sectary*, p. 9. *A siringe for a sore sinner*, p. 78.

That you are Jesuitical, Romish, Franciscan Frogs, Witches, Sorcerers, appears in that ye meet to quake, tremble, quiver, and converse with your Spirits, Imps, Familiars; and that ye came from *Rome* out of the North, from whence evil and destruction cometh, as I have proved, cleared, demonstrated, and evinced in my *Quaker Unmask'd*, p. 84. *Lights Darkness*, p. 26.

WILLIAM PRYNNE'S ANSWER

For as the Needle in the Marriners Compass *Trembles* (mark that) and points to the *North*, even so do ye, ye trembling, Quivering, Shivering *Quakers*. And as Witches are most frequent in the *North*, and the colder a Climate is, the apter are the Inhabitants thereof (see my *first answer to thy self*) to quake, &c. It follows that *Quakers* and Witches are of the growth of the same place, and both of the same Nature, quality, and condition; For as Witches swim upon the water like light scum, even so are *Quakers*, the scum of the earth, that shake themselves like water-dogs when they come out of a Pond (see my *Popish Royal Favorite*, p. 800. *Sweet sips of Soul-savingness*, p. 53). Lastly, as Witches liquor their staves, and fly through the Air; even so do *Quakers* liquor their throats with inchanted Potions, and gape to suck in the air that it may fly through them, and blow the light within them; (see *Emmot and Gilpin*, pa. 7. *Aldermanbury bottle opened*, p. 20.) at their Exorcisms rather than Exercises of Devotion. Whereas thou saist I was branded, burnt or Stigmatiz'd in the Cheeks, 'tis true, I was so, nor am I at all asham'd of, sorry for, or abashed thereat, but rather set a greater value on my self therefore, as I believe I have very good reason, cause, consideration to do, for I was only us'd like a sealed measure, burnt, branded for being true. See my *Verses* written on this occasion in the *Tower* of *London*, *in hæc verba*.

> *Of this Opinion* William Prynn *was the*
> Sixt[h] *day of* March, *six hundred thirty three*.

Nor was it improper, unfit, or unbecoming a man of my Profession, cloath, vocation, that is, to measure equal Law, right, Justice between man and man. See *Truth Triumphing*, p. 10. *The Pricking Provender of Prelacy*, p. 907.

As for the Jesuites, who thou saist made use of the scraps of my Ears, to bewitch the Quakers, &c. If they did so, it was no fault of mine, nor am I bound to answer for it; for when the aforesaid parings, scraps, shreds were sever'd from my freehold, they were no longer mine, nor am I to be accountable for the evil administration of them, when they were out of my power, charge, tuition. But if they had been in my own possession, and the Jesuits had stollen them to bewitch the *Quakers* to listen to their enchantments: It is not Just that I should answer for their Ears and my own too. See *Speculum Insect*. p. 95. *The frantick Franciscan*, p. 700. *A hole pick'd in the Popes coat*, p. 30. Whereas thou saist the *Brethren, Godly, &c. rode out with the sisters, helpers, &c.* I do confess, thank, acknowledge their loving kindness therein; And if they did evil in sticking *Rosemary* and *Bayes* upon their Vessels, bodyes, outward Folkes, as thou saist against the doctrine and discipline of the *Presbyterian* Church: It is no more then the Members, Tooles, Limbs of the Devil and thy Synagogue did to the Patriarch, Patron, and Founder of their Order *James Nayler*, whom they exalted above his brethren upon an Ass, and ran bare before both, against the Fundamental, known, establish'd Rule, Canon, Constitution, of their disorderly Order. See *The Buckle of the Canonical Girdle turn'd behind*, p. 63. *The Quaker Quash'd*, p. 4.

Whereas thou saist my works are bound up in Hatcases, &c. If thou wouldst but buy one of those, and put thy hat therein, it would operate upon, and instill into thy Noddle, sconce, Logger head, more sense, reason, understanding; and teach thee better manners then to keep it on before a Court of Justice: by which thou dost but shew, declare, demonstrate, that thou hast a Crack, Flaw, soft place in thy Scull; and in that respect art very careful to keep it warm, least thy sickly brains (if thou hast any) should take cold. And as for those Chandlers and Haberdashers of small wares &c. which thou saist have undertaken to oppose, answer, confute me:

Verily they will find it a harder task then they are aware of, for I have already written, Printed, published, 160 odd Works, Books, Labours; and before they have done with those, do not doubt to have as many more in a readiness, and to find imployment, work, business, enough for them all; as long as Church and State can furnish, store, supply me with subject matter. Provided I may have process enough to carry on the work; and can but procure, induce, engage our *Presbyterian* brethren the *Nonconformists* to help, aid and assist me, which (it being so much for their own advantage, interest, concernment, and they having at present nothing else to do) I do not doubt to obtain.

Will. Prynne.

AN
OCCASIONAL REFLECTION
ON
Dr. CHARLTON's feeling a Dog's Pulse at Gresham-College. By R. B. Esq.

TO LYNDAMORE.

Do you observe, *Lyndamore*, that domestic animal, the Vassal and menial Servant of Man, on whom he waits like a Lacquey by Day, and watches like a Constable by Night, how quiet and unconcerned it stands whilst the industrious and accurate *Dr. Charlton* with his judicious Finger examines the arterial Pulsation of its left Foreleg; a civil Office, wherein both Doctor and Dog, Physician and Patient with equal Industry contest, who shall contribute most to the experimental Improvement of this learned and illustrious Society—Little doth the innocent Creature know, and as little seems to care to know, whether the ingenious Dr. doth it out of a sedulous Regard of his Patient's Health, or his own proper Emolument; 'tis enough to him that he does his Duty; and in that may teach us, to resign ourselves wholly to advance the Interests and Utility of this renowned and royal Assembly.

Do you observe how generously he exhibits his Leg; and though a Dog's Leg, in the Language of the Vulgar, signifies a thing worth nothing; yet even that may teach us, that there's nothing so contemptible, but may, if rightly applied to, contribute something to the public Good of Mankind, and Commonwealth of Learning.

But if a Dog be a Logician, as the learned hold, and in his sagacious Persuits does use to make Syllogisms, we could not have made a better Choice than of this Animal, to *persue* and *chase* this experiment through all its Operations, till we have *run* it down to Demonstration.

Nor is the diligent and solert Dr. less proper for this Administration, as having so natural a Propensity to this Kind of venenous Operations, that it is not long since (as you well remember) when the King of *Macassar*'s Poison was sent hither, the Dr. was so impatient to try the Experiment solitary, that, rather than attend the Pleasure of the *Royal-Society*, he adventured (though at the Price of their Displeasure) to invade it by Surreption and Involation, and secretly deprived the *Hint-Keeper* of it; for which he received, I will not say whether condign Punishment, or severe Castigation, from the learned and honourable *President*, in a grave and weighty Oration pronounced by his Lordship before this celebrious and renowned Assembly.

Truly, *Lyndamore*, I am of Opinion, that a Dog is much more proper for this Experiment, than that vigorous and vivid Animal commonly called a Cat: For a Cat, you know, is said to have nine Lives, that is eight in Reversion and one in Possession; and it is a Matter of no mean Difficulty exactly to trace and observe, how many of these the lethal Force of this destructive Medicament will reach; and therefore you may have taken Notice on a Creature of that Species, although but a weak and feeble Kitten, the venemous Quality proved so innocuous, that the secure little Beast laid it self down to sleep in the hollow Concave of that Emblem of our Jurisdiction over the Lives and Limbs of Dogs and Cats, the Mace; and in that Posture, as if it had triumphed over its mortal Enemy, and all our Hostilities, was born before the most excellent and accomplished *Lord President*.

You may also, *Lyndamore*, observe the Strength of Judgment, and Ingenuity of the acute and profound Dr. in the topical Application of the mortiferous Unguent to that Part of the Dog's Neck, that is situate nearest to his Brain and consequently to lesion, and furthest out of the Reach of that natural Chirurgery, as I may call it, of his Tongue; that nothing may obstruct the free Passage of this pernicious Composition, but give it full Scope to exert its Efficacy in the several and respective Organs of the passive Animal.

You may remember, *Lyndamore*, what the subtle and judicious *Sorbier* says of a worthy Member of this Society—That 'tis a Work of Admiration to behold a Person bred up in Courts and Camps, and at this present employed in the most weighty Affairs

ON FEELING A DOG'S PULSE

of the State, to appear in Mechanical Querpo in *St. James*'s Park, and managing the *Sidrophelian* Tube, to muster the Life-guard of *Jupiter*, and to take an Account of the Spots in his Belt: So we may say, it is no less wonderful to behold this exquisite and solert Dr. whose Province lies in the Cabinet of fair Ladies, and whose daily Employments are to sollicit the tender Arteries of their Ivory Wrists; that he, I say, should nevertheless condescend to animadvert the languishing Diastole of an expiring Mungrel.

From this, *Lyndamore*, we may learn, that as in general Nature there is neither higher nor lower, but *Zenith* and *Nadir* are equally on a Plane, as well as the *Poles*; so we may receive Matter of Instruction from Objects of the meanest and most contemptible Quality, as well as from Things of higher and more sublime Condition; even as the most industrious and elegant *Mr. Hook*, in his Microscopical Observations, has most inge-niously and wittily made it appear, that there is no difference, in point of Design and Project, between the most ambitious and aspiring Politician of the World, and of our Times especially, and that most importune and vexatious Insect, commonly called a Louse.

POLITICAL OBSERVATIONS
AND
REFLECTIONS

THE

LOYAL SATYRIST,

OR,

HUDIBRAS

IN

PROSE.

Written by an unknown Hand in the
time of the late Rebellion. But never
till now published.

Si Cato reddatur, Cæsareanus erit.

LONDON,

Printed for *Jos. Hindmarsh* at the Sign of the **Black Bull**
near the Royal Exchange in *Cornhill.* 1682.

MERCURIUS MENIPPEUS

Mercurius Menippeus:

OR, THE

LOYAL SATYRIST

[Memoirs of the Years 1649 and 50]

Since the Liberty of the Subject, and Free-quarter; since New Lights, and Selling Malignants by an inch of Candle, the World hath produced *Mercuries* as fast as *Darby-House* spawn'd Committees, or Committees started Delinquents. For why do *Westminster-Abbey* Lubbers sit so long, but onely to have their Pictures drawn? But yet no Ink could represent them black enough. The fittest Emblem of the Parliament House, is a Turky-Pie, the Heads without will inform you what Birds are within.

But alas, poor Infants! We must be whipt, and yet not have leave to cry: Kiss the Rod that scourged you. Women in some Countries never love their Husbands till they be well beaten by them; and certainly our REFORMERS would have us as good natur'd as their Spaniels. And indeed, to what purpose is Hue and Crie sent after a Troop of Horse? 'Twere ridiculous for a Constable to charge the Peace upon *Cromwel*, or make privy search into *Lental*'s Exchequer, especially since the Kingdom was reformed into a *Lacedæmonian* State. For when *Lilburn* was *Lycurgus*, Plundering must needs be Statutable. What other Laws can we expect from him and *Newgate*? Felony already is a Crime onely in some silly Wretches, who are punish'd for it; but Parricides are still above the reach of Justice. While two Armies murther, and imprison, an honest man may be *Burleigh'd* for beating up a Drum. As if in a Country of *Cannibals*, a poor innocent Cutler should be hanged for grinding a Stilletto. Pillories are more cruel than Scaffolds, or perhaps *Prin*'s Ears were larger than my Lord of *Canterburie*'s Head.

But Lord! to what an height were May-Poles grown? And could they be reformed without Sequestration and Excize? Nay, the Primitive Zeal had almost melted the Bells, and made them ring backwards for themselves. A Psalm of Mercy is even denied the Chimes, and masculine *Tom* of *Lincoln* must be gelded into a Roaring *Meg*. Roundheads and Atheists hate Superstition, onely CROMWEL and the DEVIL are afraid of Crosses.

'Tis well Churches survived thus long; for since my Lord *Brook*'s Groom and Coach man propagated the Gospel, Christians were born in Stables onely. So *Job* came to be a Saint, but upon a Dunghil. And why may not a sanctified Whipster be a Heaven-driver, as well as *Brereton* and *Harvey* Bishops? Who would have thought that Snaphaunches and Baskethilts were of Apostolick Institution? or that Buff and Feather were *Jure Divino*? *Croyden* and *Fulham* are not inhabited, but haunted; nor do they lodge Inmates, but Apparitions and Goblins. Thus have Christian Churches been converted into *Turkish* Mosques, and Abbies have been made Nests for Rooks and Daws. The Devil is an Enemy to all Hierarchy, and therefore Holy-days must be abolished, and so farewel Saints and Angels. All renounce *Whitsontide*, and yet boast the Holy Ghost. *Simon* and *Jude* are vanquished by *Lilly* and *Booker*, and *Michael* is subdued by another Devil. *Time*'s Sith was turned into a Saw, nor was he bald enough to be a perfect Roundhead. But an Execution must have some Reprieve. All stickle for their *Powder-Treason*: The Prentices rescue *Shrove-Tuesday*, and the Sisters must be indulged a *Valentine*. What need any other Observations? They can feast themselves without a *Christmas*, and starve others without a *Lent*.

Well then, adieu *Fridays* and wellcome Monthly Fasts; adieu Idolaters, and wellcome New Moons. This still Sow hath devoured more than all the Bishops Hospitality. Their Idol-Humiliation, like *Bell*, consumes all, and yet eats nothing. But all this is merciful. Their too much Fasting hath made them Cannibals. They can say Grace over Mummy, and give Thanks for my lord of *Strafford*. As if they had abstained onely, as Beasts tied up, that they might devour poor Martyrs more greedily, savagely. Nay they eat up one another. Both the *Hothams*, like two Thieves, wait upon their crucified *Bishop*. The Parliament, like *Sejanus*, is destruction both to their Friends and Enemies. My Lord *Brook*'s New Light at last blinded him: He was first made a Mole, and then earth'd: A fit end for the

MERCURIUS MENIPPEUS

Underminers of a State! *Lucas* and *Lisle* were both revenged, since the Vice-Admiral and *Rainsborough* were levelled. For as he was regenerate, so he died twice. 'Tis thought his Sea-sickness purged the better half away: The Haddocks had as good a Breakfast as the Worms. *Crassus* built a Sepulchre to his deceased Lamprey: And what was all this Funeral Pomp dedicated to, but an Otter? To be Mourners at the Death of a Water-Rat, is a vanity beyond being Maudlin Drunk. Why all these ridiculous Attendants? A single Sculler is good enough to carry a Dog to *Wapping*. The numerous wild Gang is exceeded every Execution day. We see a fuller Appearance at *Newgate*. The Worthy was but two Wheels above an ordinary Villain and differed onely in the blackness of his Soul, and his Wardrobe.

And most of the Heroes are such twisted pieces, one knows not from which part of the *Centaur* to name them. Whom their *Alchoran* writes Prophets, others think Impostors. The Devil will still be Black, though the *Indians* paint him White. All their Patrons die, like *John Huss*, both Hereticks and Saints; nor can we discern, whether 'tis a Martyr or a Witch that burns. My Lord *Say*'s Sanctity is somewhat like his Son *Nat*——'s Valour. The Jewel hath too much of *Bristol* in it. The Dog in the *Tower*, though proof against Lions, is no *Daniel*. O what a godly thing is the Sign of the Hand Bible! What a devout company of Saints are *Rebecca*, her Book, her Pattens and her Stool? For all must together: Nor would you think her going to Church, but removing House. I wonder she is never apprehended for carrying Burthens upon the *Sabbath day*. Well, this Coif and Cross cloth, this Blew Apron'd Saint is as much in the Church as the Parson's Hour-Glass, the Hassocks, or the People that are buried there. Nor will she tire with a single Hearing, but trudge from *Tantlin*'s to *Tellin*'s, and hold out killing of a Brace or two, and all long Courses. Thus are they carried from Ordinance to Ordinance, like Beggars from one Church to another, that they may ply at both places.

And what are their *Levites* but their *Friars Mendicant* for both the Houses? Not a Sunday since the Combustion past without a Brief. How oft have they picked our Pockets with the Relief of *Ireland*? This Knack has been as beneficial as

351

their Plundering. As much hath been gotten by a *Good your Worship*, as by a *Stand and Deliver*. We could never get out of the Church without a Composition: The Parson's Application was certainly directed to our Purse: Every Motive strained our Pockets, and the last Use was an Use of Sequestration. See how the Pulpit-Duellist fights with *Bellarmine*, how he sweats and toyls, plays out all his Weapons, and (you may be sure) hath got the better; but after with an Address to the Spectators to throw him some money.

Well, Who's for *Aldermanbury*? You would think a Phœnix preached there, but that Birds will flock after an Owl as fast. And a Football in cold Weather is as much followed as *Calamy* by all his rampant Dog-day Zealots. But 'tis worth the Crouding to hear the Baboon Expound, like the Ape taught to play on the Cittern. You would think the Church as well as Religion were invers'd, and the Anticks, which were used to be without, were removed into the Pulpit. Yet these Apish Tricks must be the motions of the Spirit, his Whimsie-Meagrim must be an Ectasie, and Dr. *G.* his Palsey make him the Father of the Sanctified Shakers. Thus among *Turks*, Dizziness is a Divine Trance; Changlings and Ideots are the chiefest Saints; and 'tis the greatest sign of Revelation, to be out of ones Wits.

Instead of a dumb Shew, enter the Sermon Dawbers. O what a gracious sight is a Silver Ink-horn! How blessed a Gift is it to write Short-hand! What necessary Implements for a Saint are Cotton, Wool and Blotting-Paper? These Dablers turn the Church into a Scrivener's Shop. A Country Fellow last Term mistook it for the *Six-Clerks-Office*. The Parson looks like an Offender upon the Scaffold, and they penning his Confession, or a Spirit conjured up by their uncouth Characters. By his Cloak you would take him for the Prologue to a Play; but his Sermon, by the length of it should be a Tailor's Bill, and what treats it of, but such Buckram, Fustian Stuff? What a desperate Green-sickness is the Land fallen into, thus to doat on Coals, and Dirt, and such Rubbish Divinity? Must the *French* Cook our Sermons too? And are Frogs, Fungos and Toad stools the chiefest Dish in a Spiritual Collation? Strange *Israelites*! that cannot distinguish betwixt Mildew, and Manna. Certainly in the brightest Sunshine of the Gospel, Clouds are the best Guides, and Woodcocks are the onely Birds of Paradise. I wonder how the ignorant *Rabbies* should differ so much, since most of their Libraries consist onely of a *Concordance*. The Wisemens Star doubtless was an *Ignis Fatuus* in a Church yard, and it was some such *Will o' th' Wisp* steered prophetical *Saltmarsh*, when riding Post to Heaven he lost his way in a Forest. Indeed their rare Gifts have one property of the Spirit, to be Invisible, and so much of Revelation, as not to be understood; like the Musick of the Spheres, which never was heard.

But Cyphers may make an Assembly, though no Number: And what can we expect from an A B C Synod, but a Catechism? *Mount Sion* hath at last brought forth a Mouse, though it was long enough in Spawning to have been an Elephant. They have Reformation *Pauls* work, and O may they have the Scaffold for their Pains! For what have they given us for Lawn-sleeves but Sackcloth and Misery? Instead of Liturgies they have brought upon us all those Afflictions, we there prayed against. The Church, while beautiful, was the *Whore of Babylon*. Their Zeal was never hot enough, till it had scorched them into *Blackamores*. Too much fair Weather, forsooth, had almost starved us. Seven years purging would kill an *Hercules*. To be always snuffing, must at last put out the Light. And what can be pure enough with them, that dare Article the Creed, and attempt to Reform the Apostles? These will shrive the whole *Bible*, and have interpreted *Our Father*, *etc.* so long backwards that they have made some believe 'twas Conjuring. The Synod was the Parliaments Spiritual Block-house, and the Prolocutor was the Speaker's Echo. All the Divines, like Priests of old, were inspired from Vaults, and the Lower House.

Oh! How sweetly did the Syren-Representative sing at first! How quickly it brought forth destruction, and proved a Monster! *Nero* was pretty tolerable for five years, and this Butter-print Parliament was Gold in the Morning, and Lead at Night. For what have our precious States done, but cured and smothered little Diseases with the Plague? They have redressed the *Counter*, and by all their Reformations, made the Kingdom at last truly to want a Reformation. But Vengeance overtook them, and by spinning backward they have made Ropes for their own Necks. Silly Conjurers! who have raised a Devil, and now cannot lay him. The Lease of your Dominion is out. Face about! Now the Fiend must be Master. Thus shall Anarchy revenge the King, and Conventicles punish the Synods Sacrilege. Lice and Frogs plague the *Egyptians* for the injured *Israelites*.

Who would have thought that there should have been a Reformation beyond Root and Branch? Or that there should be such antipathy between a Spider and a Toad? Souldiers are omnipotent in Uncreating and Destruction. This *April* (they say) shall dissolve a Triennial Parliament, adjourn Eternity, and put an end to Perpetuity. *Cromwel* hath Wolves enough to silence the *Speaker*, and make *Lental* a dumb Dog. Alas, poor *Directory*! Thou must give up the Ghost too, the Spirit must the way of all Flesh. Now Law it self must be arraigned, and the new Judges to Execution. What a fine humour would it be to see *Wild Burleigh'd* by a Drum and Souldiers? And *Rolls* Coach it up *Holborn* instead of *Fleetstreet*? O! That they may have their Coifs all turned into Night-caps, and instead of old Women become proper Men. Since the Members Regent were in durance, the Two Houses look like the Representations of *Ludgate* and *Newgate*. What need the distinction of Upper and Lower? *Cromwel* will serve both for King of Hell, and Prince of the Air. *Warwick* for all his juggling, may perhaps suffer Shipwrack. *Xerxes* was a Leveller, he fettered the Sea; and why may not these put the *Admiral* in Chains? *Prin*'s Head must after his Ears, and the *Speaker*'s Bags will ere long prove him a *Judas*. My Lord *Say*'s white Powder is no longer silent and innocent, but must submit to *Cromwel*'s black. *Pembroke* may be Visited, and *Manchester* Universitied: One is not Fool, and the other is not Fool enough to be secure. And indeed these are Saints in comparison of *Cromwel*'s Life guard. *Hammond* is a Christian, compared with *Rolf*. The Head-quarters make *Newgate* a *Sanctum Sanctorum*: The Souldiers are not good enough for Gibbets, in their Reformation the Gallows is under Persecution, and *Tiburn* suffers Martyrdom. Not one of *Peters* his 1500 Saints, but may with St. *Francis*, give place to the Devil. If these propagate the Gospel, it must be as the Painter finished his Picture by defacing it, when the Sponge did the Work of his Pencil. To hope for Reformation from Levellers, is to gape for the Miracle of *Andromeda*, and to expect beauty from a Negro. *Agitators* are as good Physick for a sick Church or State, as Chips of the Gallows are for the Ague. There is not a Souldier but changes his Religion as often as his Shirt, that being sooner lousie than his Linnen. They void their Principles at every Sermon, nor do they go to Church, but to Stool. And well may they part with them so easily, since their Religion is no better than toasted Cheese, every man is his own Cook, each Trooper, like a Knight of *Malta*, is both Priest and Souldier. Revelations are so common, that the Spirit is become a meer *Familiar*. You may be of all Religions, but the *Protestant*, as the *Pagans* worship all Gods but the true one. As if that Uniformity did not become the Church as well as Confusion; and the Surplice were not as handsom as the Beggars Coat. *Rossiter* is a *Jew* extraordinarily *circumcised*, Root and Branch. *Martin*'s Paradise is the same with *Mahomet*'s, his Heaven is onely in a *Seraglio*. *Cromwel* may pass for a Pope *Joan*, or a Whore of *Babylon*, and differs onely thus much from a *Papist*: they torment themselves, he other Folks. He believes in Merits so far, that he thinks he shall be saved by Villanies, and go to Heaven, like *Hercules* and *Theseus* because he hath been in Hell. Indeed all of them are Religious Mimmicks, devout Vizards, and if Sanctity be Snot or the Pox, and seated in the Nose; they are as perfectly God's Apes, as the Devil is. These zealous Pyramids always point at Heaven, as Fire, though in Hell, mounts upwards.

> And thus we see who first began
> This Monster *Reformation*;
> A *Set* of vile amphibious *Creatures*,
> Of diff'rent Shapes and diff'rent Natures.
> For 'ere that *civil Broils* broke out,
> *Religion* spawn'd a numerous Rout
> Of Vermin, that from Putrefaction
> Deriv'd their first and sole *Extraction*;
> Who now like *Toads* against wet Weather,
> Gender and croak, and sprawl together.

But they are Angels, onely that they may be Devils. A *Jew* cannot be a *Turk*, till he be a *Christian*. They put on Religion to murther the King, as that damn'd *Monk* poisoned the *Emperour* with the *Eucharist*. They bring in Reformation, as the old Poets did their Gods, to conclude their Tragedy more easily.

POLITICAL OBSERVATIONS

Bloudy Conspiracies are always shrouded under Leagues. When
a Massacre is intended, they Chime all in to *Sicilian Vespers*.
When they cry out *the Church! the Church!* they mean our
Grave. What degrees of Misery are flung upon us! After a
Parliament comes an Army: Rods are turned into Scorpions.
We have all these years been almost ridden to death by a Night-
mare, and now must be tormented with Devils. Had we waked in
time, we might have dismounted that Load: But nothing now
under a Miracle can dispossess us of these Legions. These *Turks*
shall enjoy the *Holy Land*, while we poor *Jews* sojourn at home,
and live Strangers in our own Countrey. They level others,
but advance themselves. Angels descend, but 'tis the Devil's
Posture to be raised up. All, who have kept their Innocency,
must be stript; whilest these Buff-Sinners flant it in Beast-Skins.

> These *Saints* in *Masquerade* would have us
> Sit quietly whilst they enslave us:
> And what is worse, by *Lies* and *Cants*,
> Would trick us to believe 'em *Saints*;
> And tho' by *Fines* and *Sequestration*,
> They've pillag'd and destroy'd the *Nation*,
> Yet still they bawl for *Reformation*.

But *Cromwel* wants neither Wardrobe nor Armour: His
Face wears natural Buff, and his Skin may furnish him with a
rusty Coat of Mail. You would think he had been christened
in a Lime-pit, and tanned alive, but that his Countenance still
continues Mangy. We cry out against Superstition, and yet
worship a piece of Wainscot, and idolize an unblanched Almond.
Certainly 'tis no humane Visage, but the Emblem of a Man-
drake, one scarce handsom enough to have been the Progeny
of *Hecuba*, had she whelp'd him when she was a Bitch. His Soul
too is as his Body; for who can expect a Jewel in the head of a
Toad? Yet this Basilisk would King it, and a Brewer's Horse
must be a Lion.

> In *Cromwel Art* and *Nature* strive,
> Which should the ugliest Thing contrive;
> First Nature forms an ill-shap'd Lump,
> And Art, to shew how good Wits *jump*,

MERCURIUS MENIPPEUS

> Adds to his *monstrous Shape* and *Size*
> All Sorts and Kinds of *Villanies*;
> So that he was by *Art* and *Nature*
> An *ugly*, *vile* and *monstrous Creature*.

I wonder how Sir *Samuel Luke* and he should clash, for they are both Cubs of the same ugly Litter. This Urchin is as ill Carved as that Goblin Painted. The Grandam Bear sure had blistered her Tongue, and so left him unlicked. He looks like a Snail with his House upon his back, or the Spirit of the *Militia* with a Natural Snapsack, and may serve both for Tinker, and Budget too. Nature intended him to play at Bowls, and therefore clapt a Bias upon him. His mother longed for Pumpions. He was begotten in a Cupping-glass, and engendered in a Tod of Hay. Some Earthquake hath disordered the Symmetry of the Microcosm: Sunk one Mountain, and put up another. One would think a Mole had crept into his Carcase before 'tis laid in the Church-yard, and rooted in it. He looks like the visible type of *Æneas* boulstring up his Father, or some Beggar-Woman endorsed with her whole Litter, and with child behind. You may take him for *Anti-Christopher* with the Devil at his back. O that Knot-grass should purge the Kingdom! We must be ridden by a Camel, and reformed by the Sign of the Dolphin. You would think that he were levelled sufficiently: But *Harvey* will have him lower yet, and down with the Wall, though it be built with a Buttress.

> Sir *Samuel*, whose very sight wou'd
> Entitle him Mirrour of Knighthood,
> Was one of those who first march'd out
> To raise a *Regimental Rout*.
> Have you not seen an old *Baboon*,
> From Chain broke loose leap up and down,
> Such was our Champion's antick Zeal
> For *Parliament* and *Commonweal*.

But *Harvey* is not so much for levelling the Men, as *Martin* the Women. Look to your *Jane Shores* you *Lumbard-street* men. He brings no Maiden-Troop: This is no Eunuch General. The Stallion is of so prodigious an Itch, you would think he had been gotten of *Lot*'s Wife, after she was turned into a Pillar of Salt. He is the Bane of *Guiacum*, and the Despair of Syringes.

357

POLITICAL OBSERVATIONS

So excellent gifted for a Conventicle, that he will edifie you out of *Cornelius* his Tub. Are the Godly Ones like Sacrifices, never accepted till they are burnt? Is there no way to destroy the Whore of *Babylon* but by a Town-Bull? Strange, that none of the *Luthers* can Reform without Nuns! Dr. *Burgess*, forsooth, must have his *Hagar*. And *Peters* cannot propagate the Gospel without Marrowbones, without the help of Lamb-stones, and the Butcher's Wife.

> *Harvey*, that sneaking, senceless *Elf*,
> Would *level* all Men but himself;
> And there's that *Stallion Martin*, who
> *Levels* both *Men* and *Women* too.
> *Burgess* and *Peters* Day by Day,
> For Marrow-bones, and Lamb-stones pray.
> A very hopeful *Reformation*,
> When such as these must *Rule* the *Nation*.

Martin is not so great a Sinner against one Commandment, but my Lord of *Pembroke* will out-throw him half a Bar at another. One you would take for *Aretine*'s Pictures moralized, the other for the Covenant incarnate. *Martin* for a *Knight of the Burning Pestle*, and *Pembroke* for a *Knight of the Post*. This *Hercules* instead of a Worthy, is nothing but an adverb of Swearing. He swallows the Covenant as easily as an ordinary *Dam-me*. This Landskip, this Map of Nobility differs as much from a true *Brittain* as a *Mountgomery* Beacon from a Star, or a *Welch* Leek from Saint *David*. Yet rather than not be famous for somewhat, he will murther the Universities, like that Villain, who burnt *Diana*'s Temple to get himself a name. This is the Second Part of *Manchester* to the same Tune, *Kimbolton* of the Second Edition. One made the Kingdom a Lord *Brooks*, and the other a roasted Pig. He carries a dull foggy Ignorance about him, would blind the Kingdom, though it were an *Argus*, and is more unlucky in an University than Monkies in a Glass-shop. He would make an excellent Chancellour for the *Mews*, or were *Oxford* turned into a Kennel of Hounds, and the *Sheldons* and *Hammonds*, *Motleys* and *Jowlers*. His own House is an Academy for Hawks and Spaniels, and an Hospital for many Cures, Glanders, and the Fashions. This *Nero* keeps a Wilderness at home, and is so much given to his brutish Society, that you would take him for *Nebuchadnezzar* turned Beast. *Olds-worth* is his Crony, because his four-legged Animal. For what are *Michael* and his Lordship, but a blind Man and his Dog? And any kind of Creatures would make as good Subjects as such Earls. Some Dogs scorn *Cromwel*'s health, and will not eat, but for King *Charles*. Though Parrots may be taught Allegiance, and Crows have been storied Royalists and Linguists too, the blind Whelp hath not docility enough to know his Master. Yet shall he be the Peoples Idol too, and a reprobate *Welch* Goat one of the Elect, though he is not so much a Christian as the Thorn at *Glastenbury*.

> *Pembroke*'s a *Covenanting Lord*,
> That ne'er with God or Man kept word,
> One Day he'd sware he'd serve the *King*,
> The next was quite another *Thing*;
> Still changing with the *Wind* and *Tide*,
> That he might keep the stronger *Side*.
> His *Hawks* and *Hounds* were all his Care,
> For them he made his daily Prayer,
> And scarce would lose a hunting Season,
> Even for the sake of darling *Treason*.
> Had you but heard what Thunderclaps
> Broke out of his and *Oldsworth*'s Chaps,
> Of Oaths and horrid Execration,
> Oft with, but oftner without Passion,
> You'd think these *Senators* were sent
> From HELL, to sit in *Parliament*.

But why may not my Lord Billet in Heaven, as well as *Will. Lilly* and *Booker*, and take *Bedlam* for a Paradise rather than make a Saint of the Man in the Moon? Indeed for these that change Religion every Year, the fittest Gospel is an *Almanack*. But who would take these Star-gazers for the *Wise men*? Well, Wise men they must be; but the Question is, Whether of *Greece* or of *Gotham*? O the Infallibility of *Erra Pater*, *Lilly*! The Wizard, perhaps, might do much at Hotcockles, and ghess well at Blindman's Buff. But I durst undertake to pose him with a Riddle, and stand his Intelligence in a Dog in a Wheel. An over-turned Salt is a surer Prophet. The Sieve and Shears are Oracles to him. A whining Pig sees farther into a Storm. Rats will prognosticate the Ruine of a Kingdom with more certainty. And as for Palmestry, a Gypsie, or *Derrick* may be his Tutor. The Wittal is cuckolded over and over, and yet the *Oedipus* is blind. Like the old Witch, who, being consulted to discover a Thief, could not smell out who had shit at her own door. Indeed he is excellent at foretelling things past, and calculates the *Deputie*'s Nativity after he is beheaded. And then by starting a Prophesie, he excites the credulous Vulgar to fulfil it. Thus can he antedate *Cromwel*'s swift Malice, depose the King five years before hand, and instruct *Rolf* how to be damned. Impious Villains! to make the Spheres like the Associated Counties, and the Heavenly Houses so many Lower Houses, fix a guilt upon the Stars, and persuade the Planets are Rebels. As if there were a Sequestration-Star, or any Constellation looked like a Committee. Away with your Bulls and Bears! should we be subject to their Influence, each Constellation would make a Man a Beast, every Planet a wandering *Jew*. What fit Instruments are Astrologers for Rebels! Heaven as well as *Pauls* is made a Stable. Their Prophesies are, like Pictures, commendable, because they look every way. They are calculated for every Meridian, and are as much truth to the *Turk* as the *States*. They are all born under *Gemini*, every Prediction is a Twin. Oracles must still speak double: Sure the Devil is always drunk, or treats with his Foot, or the Serpent must have his Tongue cleft too. *Lilly* has christen'd himself an Ape of Hell: *Merlinus Anglicus* is nothing, but an *English Devil*. He might ken all *Phænomenas* upon Earth better, would he for prey, like the Kite, descend. What are all our New Lights, but so many prodigious Meteors, exalted perhaps from Dunghils, admired a while for Stars, and are found onely slime and Gelly? *Cromwel*'s Nose is a Comet in grain, and the Grand *Eclipse*, certainly is no *Common-Council*.

> *Booker* and *Lilly* with their Lies,
> Are hir'd to blind the Peoples Eyes,
> And cast a mist before their Reason,
> That they Might not distinguish *Treason*.
> The Stars all o're the *Firmament*,
> Are call'd to vouch their black Intent,
> And to denounce the speedy Doom
> Of the whole Race of Kings to come.

MERCURIUS MENIPPEUS

If the *Londoners* by this time have not enough of *Parliament*, may they still fight with Images, and adore a Representative; still quarrel with Superstition, and worship the Host of Heaven. They will perceive at last what kind of Physick is Reformation, and being drunk once a Moneth. Sure all the Women in the City are with Child by *Martin*, and so longed for Levellers. For were Altars Plea enough to offer up the Bishops? Must *Abel* still suffer for his Sacrifice? Sure his *Holiness* was the Pope, and Justice on *Prin*'s Ears a piece of *Auricular Confession*. Their *Deputy*, forsooth, hath made away their Churches, and was executed like the poor Ass for drinking up the Town Moon. Proceed, proceed, my fine Reformers! So may your *Conduit-Knight* vanquish his *Idol-Grove*: So may the *George* on Horseback subdue the *Green Dragon*, and after all their Victorious Gambols, both Man and Horse become Reformers Laureat. But what have you got for your *No Plum-Pottage*? Nay, what hath all your Plate got, but Ironsides? Examine all your Pressures that contain Pluralities of Monopolies. Patents for Rags are not so rank, as Excise for Turds. The Dunghil is sweeter than the Jakes and *Atkins*. Since the offended Souldiers were your Masters, the *Livery-men* walk as if they ran the Gauntlet. Now the City is turned Delinquent, what doth the *Lord Mayor* but ride the Horse? And what are the *Aldermen* but ordinary *Red-coats*? Thus the Parliament, like the *Spaniards* fatal Room, instead of Treasure hath coined Destruction and Invasion. Like silly Mariners, you have adored that *Pharos* for a Star, and so split your Selves on your Security.

> And will you *Londoners* be still
> Cuckolds and Rebels 'cause you will;
> What have you for your Wealth and Pains
> But broken Bones and knock'd-out Brains?
> You see this blessed *Reformation*,
> At last must end in *Desolation*;
> And that to take you Man by Man,
> You're ten times worse than you began.

But the States have redeemed all by their Treaty: Yet that was but a Death-bed Repentance, they laid down their Commission just before they were to be cashiered. The *Turks* imprisoned their Emperour or King: *Turks* are Reformers, or Reformers *Turks*. But CHARLES must suffer more than one single Person can inflict: Levellers heat the Fire seven times hotter. No Mercy, no Act of Oblivion; they can admit of any thing from Hell but *Lethe*. These *Medes* and *Persians* are unalterable; *Daniel* must to the Lion's Den, *Hurst-Castle*. What can succeed the Dungeon but Execution? What can a King expect but Death, who is already buried alive? The next Enlargment translates him out of the World. *Cæsar*'s Tragedy is best presented in the *Senate*. *Westminster* (alas!) is the ready way to the Tombs.

> But now the fatal Period's come,
> *Charles* must prepare for *Martyrdom*:
> These Levellers know no Remourse,
> But he must murder'd be in Course;
> And to exalt the Crime the more,
> This must be done at his own Door.

Cromwel must triumph with the Axe before him, though that, as of old, should properly be directed to the Conquerour. *Lilly* can prognosticate no fair Weather till the Sun set Red. The Queen must submit to Mother *Shipton*, and CHARLES be murthered to fulfil old Prophecies. Thus still Rebellion is the Sin of Witchcraft. The King can never please them, till he looks, as in his Coin (their Idol) beheaded; and nothing can be too dear an Offering for their *Molock* Reformation. They build up Scaffolds (the Devil's Altars) and sacrifice Men for pure innocent Ones. They cry out against Idolatry, and yet are *Cannibals* in Superstition. As the Covenant was sealed from the *Bishops* Veins, so Levelling must be ratified by the *Bloud Royal*. The *Presbyter*, of the two, proved the gentler Thief, and differed from the Independent, as a Tinker from his more Savage Trull: One stripped and bound the King, that the other might cut his Throat. One silenced the Bells of his Nativity, and the other made them ring out for his Funeral. Both are guilty of his Bloud, onely this *Pilate* would wash his hands. Presbytery made him an Anchorite, and Independency a Martyr. This kills CHARLES, and that the King. To prepare the Axe, is little better than to give the Blow.

MERCURIUS MENIPPEUS

The *Presbyter* and *Independent*
Had in their Turns been both ascendant;
And tho' the latter got the Saddle,
The former did him first disable;
From whence upon the whole we note,
One bound him, t' other cut his Throat;
And 'tis in Law almost the Same,
To lend the Sword as kill the *Man*.

Now we see what 'tis to be made a GLORIOUS KING by
Rebels; what the Devil's Landskip means, when it promises all
the Kingdoms of the Earth. In the Trial, as at the General
Doomsday, all appear naked. Now there is none disguised,
but by *Gray*, or the Hangman. Henceforth take heed of Vizards,
though never so holy. Murthers are committed in Masquerade.
But yet all their Slaughters are Expiations, and their Hands are
the whiter for being washed in Bloud. They must be thought
Isaacks for offering up their *Abraham*. None are marked for
true *Israelites*, but those that have the Bloud of their *Moses*
on their Doors. Thus they can sin, and yet preserve their
Saintships. As *Mahomet*'s Paradise is both a Brothelhouse and
a Nunnery; his Virgins whore it, and yet continue *Vestals*;
are Heavenly Bawds, and yet may lead Apes in Hell. We perceive at last, why Plays went down; to wit, that Murthers
might be acted in earnest. Stages must submit to Scaffolds, and
personated Tragedies to real Ones. Mock-shews of Cruelty
are but poor Feasts to their flesh'd Appetites. Leeches will
suck no Pictures. They hate all Images and Fables, but must
murther the King in sincerity and truth. No need of heightning
Revels; these *Herods* can behead without the allurements of a
Dance. These Tragedians have out-vied Invention, and acted
what Monsters in their most monstrous wishes could hardly
reach. The Head and Members have but one Neck; our compendious *Caligula's* have dispatch'd not onely the King, but the
Kingdom too, at a Blow.

A thousand *Ages* yet to come,
Shall mourn, great *Charles*, thy *Martyrdom*;
And if the Muse can ought foretel,
Thy Sons shall crush this Crocodile.

POLITICAL OBSERVATIONS

Oh! may I live to hail that Day,
And sing loud Pœans in the way;
When their *Return* shall free this *Nation*,
From future Fears of *Usurpation*.

'Tis the Thiefs best play to kill the Judge; and great Robberies
are seldom committed without Bloud. Or else what Wolves,
but would have tended such a *Romulus*? Such an *Elias*, what
ominous Ravens but would have fed? A Prince! whose goodness might rather fear Idolatry than Injury; deserved rather
to be prayed to, than condemned, made a Saint, than murthered.
A Prince! whose Merits were so far above all Flatteries, that
the oiliest Courtier was as scandalous as *Peters*; and *Encomiums*
defam'd as much, as that *Rabshekah* of *No more Addresses*. His
Sight, his Wisdom was at first eclipsed, but the Cloud only
made his Influence prove Lightning, and whom he could not
illuminate, at last he scared into a Belief. But yet he still shewed
more of the Dove than the Serpent, and 'twas the want of Gall,
that made him lose his Head. When Wasps and Hornets usurp
the Hive, the Royal Bee suffers, because without a Sting. They
turned Wolves because the Lion was a Lamb. All his Tyranny
was not to slay, but have his Throat cut. And he now must
bleed for not bleeding seven years before. Tumults forced him
hence, and the last Tumult murthered him.

Thus, thus he dies, a Prince whose Innocence had taught
Poison Allegiance, made Pistols Royalists, and kept *Rolf* from
being curs'd. A Prince for whom *Hotham* was a Martyr, *Brown*
a Prisoner, and *Shimei Prin* undertook a Vindication. *Hammond*
at last becomes a Captive to his Charge. The good Apostle
converts his Gaoler. He disarms the Rebels even with his
Fetters, and like the hand of Providence, is then most powerful,
when it is thought most weak. He subdues, as if the Castle
were not his Prison, but his Fort. 'Tis a question whether he
was more miraculous for curing Disloyalty or the Evil. *Hammond*'s blindness was as desperate, as the *Womans*. He dispos-
sesses so fast, *Cromwel* can scarce find Devils enough to bait
the Exorcist. Let the Vipers but kiss his hand, and they are
Innocent. Had *Bradshaw* that condemn'd him, been longer on
the Bench, or single, that *Dagon* too had fallen before the Captive
Ark. But oh! At the Scaffold he engrosses Miracles. There he

Christens by wholesale. That one Blow slew more Rebels than all these seven years. Our *Sampson*, though shaved both Hair and Head away, killed more *Philistins* at his Death, than all his Life time. Now they would swear Fealty to his Trunk, and Homage to a dipt Handkerchief. They adore his very Ghost, and will atone their Rebellion by being Subjects, now there is no King. And who cannot continue Loyal to such a King that dies for the Sins and Safety of his People? Who would refuse to be his Subjects, who is their Martyr? He acted a Christian better than most Divines can describe one; and bled Doctrines freelier than they can speak them. He shewed Graces the Schoolmen scarce ever heard of. We might edifie more from the Scaffold in one Hour, than from the Pulpit in an Age. His Passion was greater than all Queen *Maries* days, and he suffered more than the whole *Book of Martyrs*.

> If *murd'ring Kings* be *meritorious*,
> And the right Way to make 'em *Glorious*;
> To shew the utmost they could do,
> They murder King and *Kingdom* too;
> And as they say good Deeds are best
> That are more secret than the rest,
> That they in no respect might err,
> They mask the *Executioner*;
> But some give this a diff'rent Turn,
> And argue with Revenge and Scorn,
> That these immortal *Rogues in grain*
> Murder'd the King purely for Gain;
> That they might seize on his Dominions,
> And parcel it among their Minions.
> Others there are pretend to know,
> That Reprobate that gave the Blow,
> Had neither Modesty nor Grace,
> Altho' he hid his Villain's face.
> I rather think the Case lay here,
> He was afraid some *Cavalier*
> Might know him, and be so uncivil,
> To send him headlong to the *Devil*.

THE END

THE
CASE
OF
KING CHARLES I.
TRULY STATED,
AGAINST
JOHN COOK, MASTER OF GRAY's INN.

PREFACE To The READER.

The Publisher of this following Discourse has thought fit to oblige the World with a Piece of Curiosity: it was penn'd about forty years since by the ingenious and celebrated Author of Hudibras. *The Libel, which he answers, was the Labour of one* John Cook, *Barrister of* Gray's Inn, *formerly a great pains-taker in the Mysteries of Rebellion. To give you the original of it,* 'twas a studied Invective against the Person of King Charles I. before the High Court of Justice (so called) of infamous memory; but upon the non-pleading of the Royal Martyr, 'twas afterwards metamorphos'd into a Pamphlet, with the specious Title of King Charles's Case; *or an Appeal to all rational Men concerning his Tryal. How rational this Appeal was, may be easily discover'd from those numerous Fallacies and notorious Falshoods which our Author has detected in him, not only as to what concerns plain matter of fact, but also in the Pamphleteer's pretended way of reasoning, false Logick, and worse Law. I shall not enter into the merits of the Cause; for I suppose the more rational part of Mankind is abundantly satisfied in the Innocency of that Great Man as to any thing that was laid to his charge; and upon that account indeed there would have been little occasion at this time of day to produce so great an Advocate for his Memory, but that there is risen amongst us a new Race of the old Republican Stamp, who have reviv'd the Quarrel, and copied out the obsolete and almost forgotten Scandal of our Libeller, and made it their own. The Author of* Ludlow's

366

KING CHARLES'S CASE

Letter may be reckon'd amongst the first of these, one that always sat up for a Patron of Faction, and a Promoter of the Good Old Cause, *but shew'd himself most in that famous year, when he was one of the Tribunes of the People. I should not have made such a Digression upon this worthy Patriot, but that I find him to intrude amongst his Friends Mr.* Milton *and our* Libeller, *and seems to be the very copy of their Malice at least, tho not their Wit; and for that reason I must confess he seems to be least pointed at by our Answerer. I shall say no more of him at present, but pass him by with the same Contempt as the Government has wisely done; 'tis but unseasonable quarrelling with a Man that is arm'd with so much dirt, you'll be sure of that if you have nothing else.*

I need not trouble the Reader with any Harangue upon our Author or his Book; I suppose he is no stranger to the honester and more learned part of the Kingdom; and as for the rest, 'twas their best security they were not known by him. I shall only add, that it was Mr. Butler's *design to Print the Discourse himself, had not Death prevented him; and since it has fell into the Editor's hands, 'tis but a piece of Justice to his Memory to let the World make their Advantage of it.*

POLITICAL OBSERVATIONS

THE
CASE
OF
KING CHARLES I.
TRULY STATED

Mr. Cook,

Having lately seen a Book of yours, which you are pleased to call, *King CHARLES's Case, or an Appeal to all Rational Men concerning his Tryal*, I was much invited to read it, by the Ingenuity promised in your Title. For having heard you stile your self Sollicitor-General for the King's Dread Sovereign, and your own Honourable Client, the People; I was much taken with your Impartiality, that not only exempts all rational Men from being your Clients in this Case, in making them, by your Appeal, your Judges: For no Man, you know, can be Judge in his own Case, but acknowledge your High Court, from which you appeal to all Rational Men to consist of no such: But indeed I had not read many Lines before I found mine own Error, as well as yours, and your Proceedings nothing agreeable to the plain Dealing I expected from you; for you presently fall to insult upon the Unhappiness of your undeserved Adversary, and that with so little Moderation, as if you strove to make it a Question whether his incomparable Patience, or your own ungoverned Passion, should be the greater Wonder of Men, preposterously concluding him Guilty, before with one Syllable you had proved him so: A strange Way of doing Justice! Which you endeavour to make good by a strange insolent Railing, and more insolent Proceeding to the secret Council of Almighty God, from whence you presume to give Sentence on him; a Boldness no less impious than unjust in you, were it true, since we can never know it to be so.

But indeed it is hard to say, whether you have shewn more Malice, or Vanity, in this notable Declaration of yours; for he that considers the Affectation and fantastic Lightness of your

Language, (such as *Ireland*, a *Land of Ire*; *Bite-Sheep for Bishops*, and other such ingenious Elegancies of Quibble) must needs confess it an Oratory more becoming a Fool in a Play, or *Peters* before the Rabble, than the Patron of his Sovereign's Sovereign, or the Gravity of that Court, which you say, right wisely, shall be admired at the Day of Judgment. And therefore you do ill to accuse him of reading *Johnson*'s and *Shakespear*'s Plays, which, it seems, you have more been in your self to much worse Purpose, else you had never hit so right upon the very Dialect of their railing Advocates, in which (believe me) you have really out-acted all that they could fancy of passionate and ridiculous Outrage.

For certainly, Sir, I am so charitable to believe it was your Passion that imposed upon your Understanding; else, as a Gentleman, you could have never descended to such Peasantry of Language, especially against such a Person, to whom (had he never been your Prince) no Law enjoins (whatsoever his Offences were) the Punishment of Ribaldry. And, for the Laws of God, they absolutely condemn it; of which I wonder you, that pretend so much to be of his Council, should be either so ignorant, or forgetful.

Calamity is the Visitation of God, and (as Preachers tell us) a Favour he does to those he loves; where-ever it falls, it is the Work of his Hand, and should become our Pity, not our Insolence. This the antient Heathen knew, who, believing Thunder came from the Arm of God, reverenced the very Trees it lighted on.

But your Passion hath not only misled you against Civility, and Christian Charity, but common Sense also; else you would never have driven your Chariot of Reason (as you call it) so far out of the Road, that you forgot whither you are going, and run over every Thing that stands in your Way; I mean, your unusual Way of Argument, not only against Reason, but your self, as you do at the first Sally; for after your Fit of Raving is over, you bestow much Pains to prove it one of the Fundamentals of Law, that the King is not above the Law, but the Law above the King. And this you deraign, as you call it, so far, that at length you say, the King hath not, by Law, so much Power, as a Justice of Peace, to commit any Man to Prison; which you would never have done, if you had considered from whom the Justice derives his Power, or in whose Name his Warrants run; else you may as well say, a Man may give that which he hath not; or prove the Moon hath more Light than the Sun, because he cannot shine by Night as the Moon doth. But you needed not have strained so hard, for this will serve you to no Purpose, but to prove that which was never denied by the King himself; for if you had not a much worse Memory than Men of your Condition should have, you could not so soon have forgotten, that immediately after the reading of that Charge, the King demanded of your high Court, by what Law they could sit to judge him (as offering to submit if they could produce any) but then Silence, or Interruption, were thought the best Ways of confessing there was no such Thing; and when he undertook to shew them both Law and Reason too, why they could not do it, the righteous President told him plainly, he must have neither Law nor Reason; which was certainly (as you have it very finely) the most comprehensive, impartial, and glorious Piece of Justice that ever was played on the Theatre of *England*; for what could any Court do more than rather condemn itself, than injure Truth.

But you had better have left this whole Business of the Law out of your Appeal to all rational Men, who can make no use of it, but against yourself: For if the Law be above the King, much more is it above the Subject. And if it be so heinous a Crime in a King to endeavour to set himself above Law, it is much more heinous for Subjects to set themselves above King and Law both. Thus, like right Mountebanks, you are fain to wound and poison your selves to cheat others, who cannot but wonder at the Confidence of your Imposture, that are not ashamed to magnify the Power of the Law, while you violate it, and confess you set your selves really above the Law, to condemn the King but for intending it.

And indeed Intentions and Designs are the most considerable Part, both of your Accusations and Proofs, some of which you are fain to fetch a great Way off, as far as his Coronation Oath, which you next say, he, or the Archbishops, by his Order, emasculated, and left out very material Words, (which the People shall chuse). Which is false; for these Words, were not left out, but rendered with more Sense, (which the Commonalty have) and, if you consider what they relate to, (Customs,) you will find you cannot, without open Injury, interpret. *Elegerit* (in the *Latin* Oath) shall chuse, not hath chosen; for if you will have *Consuetudines quas vulgus elegerit*, to mean Customs, which are to be not only Use, which must be often repeated before it become a Custom, but Choice, which necessarily precedes Use.

But suppose it were as you would have it, I cannot see with what Reason you can presume it to be a Design to subvert the Laws, since you know he had sworn to defend them before, in the first Article of the Oath, from which I wonder how you can suppose, that so wise a Prince (as you acknowledge him to be) could be so irrational to believe himself absolute by this Omission. But you are not without further Contradiction yet, for if he were so perfidious a Violater of Oaths, as you would have the World believe, what Reason had he to be conscientious of taking them? Certainly he hath little Cause to be nice what Oaths he takes, that hath no Regard what Oaths he breaks.

Nor can I possibly understand your other Construction of his Refusal to take the Oath, as his Predecessors had done, which you will have a Design to refuse his Assent to such good Laws, rather than bad Ones, as the Parliament should tender; for besides the absurd Conceits, that he must still like the bad better than the good, if you consider what you say afterwards, the charitable Sense will appear, by your own Words, to be the truest; for you confess he gave not his Assent to any bad one, else you had not been fain, for want of such, to accuse him of a few good ones, as you do there; which of these is most probable, let every rational Creature judge.

Your next Argument to prove the King's Design to destroy the Law, is thus ordered: Those Knights that were by an old Statute to attend at the King's Coronation, being promised by his Proclamation (in regard of the Infection then spread thro' the Kingdom) a Dispensation for their Absence, were after fined at the Council Table; no doubt by the Procurement of some of your own Tribe, where they pleading the Proclamation for their Indemnity, were answered, that the Law of the Land was above any Proclamation: Your Conclusion is therefore, the King had a Design to subvert the Laws: Sure there is no Man in his Wits, but would conclude the contrary; such Arguments as these are much like the Ropes that *Oeneus* twisted only for Asses to devour.

But if this should fail, you know you were provided with another, not less substantial, and that is, his Alteration of the Judges Commissions, who heretofore had their Places granted to them during their good Behaviour, but he made them but during Pleasure. Of this you make a sad Business of a very imaginary evil Consequence; but if you had considered before, what you say presently after, that the King, and not the Judges, is to be accountable for the Injustice and Oppression of the Government, &c. you would have found it very just that he should use his Pleasure in their Dismission, as well as Choice; for Men of your Profession, that have lived long enough to be Judges, are not such Punies in Cunning, to play their Feats of Iniquity above-board; and if they may sit 'till they can be proved to have mis-behaved themselves: The Prince that is to give an Account for all, may sooner know he is abused, than how to help himself.

All the Inconveniency which you can fancy possible to ensue it, is only to such bad Judges as buy their Places; of whose Condition and Loss you are very sensible, as if they had too hard a Bargain of Injustice, and Believe they may have Reason enough to give unjust Judgment, rather than lose their Places and their Money too, if they shall receive such Intimation from the King. But you forgot yourself, when you put this in your Appeal to all rational Men; for they will tell you this was a bold Affront done to your high Court of Justice; for if it were potential Tyranny (as you will have it) in the King, to have but a Design to indure the Judges to give Sentence against the Law, which you say brings the People the next Step to Slavery: What is it in those who presume to give Sentence themselves, not only contrary to Law, but the declared Opinion of all the Judges, and those of their chusing too? And, I beseech you, whither by your own Doctrine, does this bring the People that submit to it? Certainly, if you that can accuse the King of this, had been a *Jew* heretofore, you would not only have stoned your Fellows, but your Saviour too.

KING CHARLES'S CASE

But if all your Arguments should miscarry, you have a Reserve left that does (as you say) irrefragably prove the Design; what's that? He is restless to destroy Parliaments, or make them useless. Believe me, this is right *Ignotum per Ignotius*, excellent Consequence to prove his Design by his Desires; you should have proved his Desires first, if you would prove his Thoughts by his Thoughts, for certainly if ever he designed it, he desired it first. You had better have concluded plainly he did it, because he designed it, for that is all in one Sense: But if I might be but half so bold with your Designs, I should, with more Reason, guess you have one to make us believe your familiar Acquaintance with the secret Councels of God, which you so often pretended to, else certainly he has given the Desires of Men so private a Lodging, that, without his own Discovery, which you can give us no Account of, you have no other Way to know them. You'd do well, and if I may advise you, you shall give over this unlucky Thing called Reason, and betake yourself wholly to Revelations.

How these Arguments might prevail with your high Court of Justice I cannot tell; but, in my Opinion, they had little Reason to thank you for this last, for while you make the King a Traytor, and prove his meer Desire to destroy the Parliament, or make it useless, on Purpose to subvert the Laws, you do but tell them what they are that have already done it; and the People, what a deal of Law they are to expect hereafter. All you can justly, in your own Sense, accuse the King of, is but Discontinuance, or untimely Dissolution of Parliaments, which I wonder with what Sense you can interpret a Design to destroy the Parliaments, since all the World knows he parted with his Power to dissolve the Parliament too. But see how doubly unjust you are; you accuse him for not calling Parliaments so often as he was bound to do by the Law, once a Year, (as you say) or oftner, but never consider how that is impossible to be done without dissolving them as often; for doing which, notwithstanding, with so much Clamour, you condemn him. Thus you charge him with Inconsistencies, and may with much more Reason accuse him for calling of Parliaments, because if he had not called them, he could never have dissolved them, which is very like your Way of Argument.

But much better than you commonly use; for your next, to remove an Objection out of your Way, is thus managed: The King, and not the Judges and evil Councellors, ought to be accountable for the Male-Administrations, Injustices, and Oppressions of the Parliament. Your Reasons are, because he made such wicked and corrupt Judges: Were they not his own Creatures? And ought not every Man to be accountable for the Work of his own Hands? Believe me, this were something, if you could prove he made them wicked, as well as Judges. But if this Plea hold, you have argued well for your honourable Clients, the People; for if they made the King, as you say they did, you have cleared him of all such horrid Crimes, Murders, and Massacres, which you take so much Pains, to no Purpose, to accuse him of; and, like a right Man of Law, have undone your Clients, upon whose Score you set them. Your next Business will be to prove God guilty of the Sins of wicked Men, for they are his Creatures, and the Work of his own Hands, I take it. But this is your perpetual Method of doing him Right, to make him sole Author and Owner of all his ill-ordered, or unhappy Actions, and not allow him a Share in any good Deed, or act of Grace.

And these are the Fundamentals of the Charge, only Suppositions of Intentions and Designs, which how far you have proved just, or profitable, let any Man but yourself judge. The Course you take afterwards, is much worse, in my Opinion, for you make your own Grounds, and either not prove them at all, or, which is worse, prove them upon their own Bottom, as when you take upon you to state the Ground of your Wars, and prove the King to be the Cause of it, you do it thus:

The King (you say) set up his Standard of War for the Advancement and Upholding of his Personal Interest, Power and pretended Prerogative, against the public Interest of common Right, Peace and Safety. How do you prove this? Because he fought for the Militia, for a Power to call and dissolve Parliaments, a negative Voice, to make Judges, confer Honours, grant Pardons, make Corporations, inhance, or debase Money, and avoid his own Grants. These you call his Personal Interest, Power and Prerogative, which, you say, he fought for: Now, put the Position and Proof together, and see what Sense it will make; truly none but this: That he made War for his Prerogative, because he fought for his Prerogative: Is not this fine Logick! But suppose it were Sense, how do you prove he fought for his Prerogative? To this you have not one Word to say; and why then should we rather take your Word than the King's, who protested he took Arms in Defence of the Protestant Religion, the Liberty of the Subject, the Privileges of Parliament, and Laws of *England*? Certainly there is no Man in his Wits, but would rather believe his Words, than your Arguments, if he does but consider that the most improbable Part of all (he protested to fight for the Defence of the Privileges of Parliament) is found, by Experience, to be no Paradox: How true the rest is, Time will instruct you. But yet I cannot see, why we should not rather believe them, than the Pretences of the Parliament, which were more to fight in Defence of his Person, and their own Privileges, which, how they have performed, your self can tell. But all this while you mistake your own Question, which was not the Right of the Cause, but the Cause, or, as you have it, the Occasion of the War; and if you had a Purpose to know that Actions had been the only Guide of your Enquiry; for Intentions and Words are uncertain, and if they make no Assaults in private Quarrels, I know not why they should in public; and therefore, since we can never agree about the Truth of more remote Causes, 'tis most just for us to place the Cause of the War, where we find the first Breach of the Peace. Now, that the King was cleared of this, all indifferent Men, who had the Unhappiness to be acquainted with the Method of their own Undoing, can very well testify. And if the Parliament should deny it, their own Votes would contradict them, as well as their Actions; for when they first raised Horse and Arms, they pretended to do so, because it appeared, the King, seduced by wicked Council, intended to make War against the Parliament; whereby they confess he had not then done it, and they had so little Ground to make it appear he ever would, that they were fain to usurp the Right of his Cause, to justify their own; and, they say, took Arms for the Defence of the King; which, if we grant, it must follow, they first made War against him, for no Body else ever did, against whom they could possibly defend him; nor did their Actions, in offering the first Violence, less declare who began the War, when having an Army ready to invade him, before he set up his Standard, they both followed and set upon him, as they did at *Edge-Hill*. Go as far as you can, you will still find the *Scots* (whose Quarrel the Parliament took up at the second Hand, as well as they followed their Examples) were the first Beginners of all.

This being granted, how the King could afterwards do less than he did, I cannot understand: *First*, he was by the Law of Nature (which you say is Legislative, and hath a suspensive Power over all human Laws) to defend himself. *Secondly*, by his Coronation Oath, which he took to keep the Peace. And how could he do that, but by his raising Power to suppress those who had already broken it? *Thirdly*, By the Laws of the Land, which you say, trusted him with the Power of the Sword. And how could he preserve that Trust, if he had sate still, and suffered others, not only to take it from him, but to use it against him?

But it is most probable that he never intended it, else he was very unwise to let them be before hand with him, in seizing upon his Castles, Magazines, and Ships; for which there can be no Reason imagined, but that he was loth to give them any Occasion (in securing them) to suspect he did but intend a War. And by all this, I doubt not but it appears plain enough to all rational Men, that he was so far from being the Cause of the War, that he rather fell into it by avoiding it; and that he avoided it so long, 'till he was fain to take Arms at so great a Disadvantage, as he had almost as good have sat still and suffered. And in this you have used the King with the same Justice the Christians received from *Nero*, who having set *Rome* on fire himself, a Sacrifice to his own wicked Genius, laid the Odium of it on the Christians, and put them to Death for it.

But this Way you found too fair and open for your Purpose, and therefore declined it; for having proved his Intentions by his Desires, and his Actions by his Intentions, you attempt a more preposterous Way yet to prove both, by what might have been his Intentions: And to this Purpose you have the Confidence, in spight of Sense, to make Contingencies the final Cause of Things, and impolitic, accidental, possible Inconveniencies, which all the Wit of Man can never avoid, the intended Reasons of State. As when you will have the King fight for the Militia, only to command the Purse of the People; for a Power to make Judges, only to wrest the Laws; to grant Pardons, that public-spirited Men, as you call them, may be made away, and the Murderers pardoned, &c. All which being Creatures of your own Fancy and Malice, and no Part of his Quarrel, you are so far from proving what he fought for, that when you have strained your Ability, all you can say is but this, in your own Sense, that he fought for Power to do that which he never would do when it was in his Power. But if you take this Liberty, I can't but think how you would bestir yourself, if you could but get your God, as you have done your King, before such an impartial high Court of Justice as this! How would you charge him with his Misgovernment in Nature, for which, by the very same Logic, you may prove he made us all Slaves, in causing the Weaker to hold his Life at the Pleasure of the Stronger; that he set up a Sun to dazzle our Eyes, that we might not see, and to kindle Fevers in our Veins; made Fire to burn us, Water to drown us, and Air to poison us, and then demand Justice against him; all which you may easily do, now you have the Trick on't, for the very same Reason will serve again, and with much more Probability; for it is easier to prove that Men have been burnt, and drowned, and died of the Plague, than to make it appear the King ever used your finer Device to remove public-spirited Men; or can you, without extreme Injustice, suppose he ever would? For 'tis so much as very well known, he highly favoured and advanced his greatest Opposers, for such you mean, I know, whom he found Owners of any eminent Desert, as he did the Earl of *Strafford*, and the Attorney-General *Noy*, and for other honest Men, as you will have them, whom Frenzy, or Sedition, set against him, by your own Confession; he did not suffer those black Stars, very strange ones, to slit their Noses, and crop their Ears.

But now I think of these honest public-spirited Men, certainly some of them have not so good an Opinion of the Honesty of your public Proceedings, but they would willingly venture, not only their Ears again, if they had them, but their Heads too, in Defiance of your most comprehensive Piece of Justice, whose Cause, while you take upon you to plead against their Consent, as you have done your honourable Clients, the People, you deserve in Reason to be thrown over the Bar, by your own Party; for you but confess your own Injustice, while you acknowledge the public Honesty of those that most oppose it.

How solid, or pertinent, those Arguments of yours have been, let any Man, that is sober, judge: But you are resolved, right or wrong, they shall pass; to let us know how easily he that has the Unhappiness to be judged by his Enemies is found guilty of any thing they please to lay to his Charge; and therefore satisfied with your own Evidence, you proceed to Sentence, and condemn the King with much Formality, by the fundamental Laws of this Kingdom, by the general Law of all Nations, and the unanimous Consent of all rational Men in the World, for imploying the Power of the Sword to the Destruction of the People, with which they intrusted him for their own Protection. How you got the Consent of rational Men to this Sentence, I cannot imagine; for 'tis most certain, by your own Confession, that he never employed the Sword, but against those who first fought to deprive him of it; and by that very Act declared they did not trust him, and consequently absolved him both from the Obligation that he had to protect them, and the Possibility too: For no Man can defend another longer than he defends himself; so that if you will have your Sentence to be just, you must confess it to be Nonsense; for you must not only prove, that those who fought against him, were the People that trusted him, not those who fought for him, but the lesser, or less considerable Part of the People, the People, as you have the Confidence to call your honourable Clients, being not the twentieth Part of the very Rabble; which if you can do, you are much wiser than *Solomon*: For it is easier to divide a Child in two Parts, than to make one of those two Parts a whole Child; and if you have the trick on't you shall be next allowed to prove, that take four out of six, there remains six. Nor is there more Justice, or Reason, in the Sentence, than in the Course you take to uphold it; for while you deny the old Maxim or Law, That the King can do no Wrong, you maintain a new one much worse, that he may suffer any; and having limited his Power to act only according to Law, expose him to suffer, not only without, but against Law. Truly it is hard Measure, but, rather than fail of your

Purpose, you will make as bold with Scripture as you have done with Reason, if it stand in your Way; as you do when you interpret that Place of the Apostle, *Where no Law is, there is no Transgression*, to mean, where there is neither Law of God, nor Nature, nor positive Law: I wonder where that is; certainly you had better undertake to find out a Plantation for *Archimedes* his Engines to move the Earth, than but fancy where that can be, which you must do before you can make this Scripture to be understood to your Purpose; and I cannot but smile, to think how hard a Task that will be for such a strong Fancy as yours, that cannot conceive what your self affirm; for when you deny it possible to suppose two supreme Powers in one Nation, you forget that you had acknowledged much more before; for you confess the King to be Supreme, when you say, very elegantly, he made head against the Parliament, who acknowledged him to be Head thereof, and yet you say the Parliament is the supreme Authority of the Nation. Thus you affirm that really to be, which you think is impossible to imagine.

But such lucky Contradictions of your self, as well as Sense, are as familiar with you as Railing; for besides the many before-mentioned, and your common Incongruities of Speech, as far from Construction as the Purpose, there are others which, for your Encouragement, ought not to be omitted; and when you would prove the King the most abominable Tyrant that ever People suffered under, yet you say he was beloved of some, and feared abroad: His Judges you compared to the Saints sitting in Judgment at the last Day; and yet, by your own Doctrine, they are more like Bears and Wolves, in sitting by a Commission of Force; Their High-Court is a Royal Palace of the Principles of Freedom; and yet, 'till the People voluntarily submit to a Government, which they never did to that, they were but Slaves. The Parliament (you say) petitioned the King, as good Subjects; and yet, immediately after, you make them his Lords, and himself Servant; so they give him the Honour of his own Royal Assent, and yet they often petitioned him for it. His Tryal you call most impartial, and yet cannot deny all his Judges to be Parties, and his profest Enemies. But you hit pretty right, when you say he caused more Protestant Blood to be shed than ever was spilt either by *Rome*, Heathen, or Antichristian; for grant that partly to be true, and confess as much Protestant Blood as ever was spilt by the Heathen *Romans*, unless they could kill Protestants eight hundred Years before there were any in the World: which eloquent Piece of Nonsense we must impute to your Ignorance in Chronology, or Confusion of Notion, which you please. Nor are those Riddles of Contradiction only in your Words, but in the whole Course of your Proceedings; for you never do the King any Right, but where you do him the greatest Wrong; and are there only rational, where you are most inhuman; as in your additional Accusations, since his Death. For there you undertake to prove something, and give your Reasons (such as they are) to make it appear, which were fair Play, if you do not take an Advantage too unreasonable, to argue with the Dead. But your other Impeachments consist only of Generals, prove nothing, or Intentions, which can never be proved, or your own forced Constructions of Actions, or what might have been Actions, but never were; all which you only aggravate with Impertinency and foul Language, but never undertake to prove; and if we should grant all you would say, and suppose you said it in Sense, or Order, it would serve you to no Purpose, unless you have, by Proof, or Argument, applied it to him, which you never went about to do.

But if this were the worst, you might be borne with, as a Thing more becoming the Contempt, than the Anger of Men; but who can preserve any Patience, that does but think upon that Prodigy of your Injustice, as well as Inhumanity, to accuse the King after his Death, of what you were ashamed to charge him with when alive? For what you say concerning the death of King *James*, you will become the Scorn of your own Party; for they never used it farther than they found it of Advantage to some Design they had in hand; as when they would move the King to grant their Propositions, they made it serve for an Argument to him; if he would sign, he should still be their *Gracious King*, if not, *he killed his Father*. But when they found he would not be convinced with such Logic, they laid it utterly aside; for (without doubt) they had not lost an Advantage, so useful as they might have made it in the Charge, had they not known it would have cost them more Impudence to maintain, than they should need to use in proceeding without it; but let us consider your Student's Might, with which you first say you are satisfied, and yet after have it as a Riddle. First, he was observed to hate the Duke, but instantly, upon the Death of King *James*, took him into his special Grace and Favour, of which you conceive this Art must be the Cause. Believe me, your Conjecture is contrary to all Experience, and the common Manner of Princes, who use to love the Treason, but hate the Traytor; and if he had been so politic a Tyrant, as you would describe him, he would never believe his Life safe, nor his Kingdom his own, while any Man lived (much less his Enemy whom such a King would never trust) of whose Gift and Secrecy he held them both; nor is it likely that he, who would not spare the Life of his Father to gain a Kingdom, should spare the Life of his Enemy to secure it. As for his dissolving the Parliament, I believe not only all wise Men, but all that ever heard of this will acquit him; whether he did it to avoid the Duke's Impeachment, you cannot prove; but if you could, you must consider that, in such Cases, Princes may as well protect their Favourites from Injury as Justice, since no Innocence can serve them, if they lie as open to the Question, as they do to the Envy of Men.

But for the better Satisfaction of those you appeal to, I shall add this: It is most certain, that this Humour of Innovation began to stir in the first Parliament of this King, and grew to an Itch in the Commons for the Alteration of Government; to which End, they first resolved to pull down the chief Instrument thereof, the Duke of *Buckingham*: But having then no *Scotch* Army, nor Act of Continuance, to assure their Sitting, all the Wit of Malice could never invent a more politic Course, than to impeach him, and put this Article, true or false, into this Charge; for thus they were not only sure of the Affections of the People, who, out of the common Fate of Favourites, generally hated the Duke, and are always pleased with the Ruin of their Superiors, but secured from the King's Interposition, whom they believed, by this Means, bound up from protecting the Duke, tho' he knew his Innocency, lest the Envy and Fury of all should fall upon himself: But the King who understood their Meaning, and knew this was but in order to their farther Attempts, which always begin with such Sacrifices, suddenly dissolved the Parliament, and, by his Wisdom and Policy, kept that Calamity sixteen Years after from the People, which the very same Courses and Fate of these unhappy Times, have since brought upon them. But you have taken more Pains to prove him Guilty, since his Death, of the Rebellion in *Ireland*, altho' with as little Reason, or Ingenuity; only you deal fairly in the Beginning, and tell us what to expect from you, when you say, as a Ground of all your Proofs, "If you meet a Man running down Stairs with a bloody Sword in his Hand, and find a Man stabbed in the Chamber, though you did not see this Man run into the Body by that Man which you met, yet if you were of the Jury, you durst not but find him Guilty of the Murther." I hope not, before you knew whether the Man killed were sent by the King to fetch the Man you met, for then you may say it must be in his own Defence. Truly you are a subtle Enquirer, but let us hear some of the clear Proofs. First, *He durst never deny it absolutely*; besides the notorious Falshood of that, it is most senseless to imagine, that he who had Wickedness enough to commit so horrid an Act, should have the innocent Modesty not to deny it, when he durst not own it. He sent Thanks to *Muskerry* and *Plunket*, by *Ormond*, which you are confident his Height of Spirit would never have done, if he had not been as guilty as themselves; and may not *Ormond* that carried the Thanks, be, by the same Reason, as well proved guilty as the King! What's next, "If he had not been guilty, he would have made a thousand Declarations, and have sent to all Princes in the World for Assistance against such Hell-Hounds and Blood-Hounds," &c. That was impossible to be done, without sending to the Pope, and then you would have proved it clearly indeed. But the Copy of his Commission to the *Irish* Rebels, is in the Hands of the Parliament. 'Tis most certain they never believed it themselves, else it had not been omitted in the Charge. But now for an Argument to the Purpose. After the *Irish* were proclaimed Traytors and Rebels by the King, their General Council made an Oath to bear true and faithful Allegiance to King *Charles*, and by all means to maintain his royal Prerogative, against the *Puritans* in the Parliament of *England*; which they would never have done, unless he had commanded, or consented to the Rebellion. But observe then what will follow. After the two Houses at *Westminster* were proclaimed Rebels and Traytors by the King, they made a solemn Covenant to defend his Royal

Person, Rights and Dignities, against all Opposers whatsoever, and therefore by the same Reason he did command or consent to the War raised by the Parliament against himself. "But did they not say they had his Commission, and call themselves the King and Queen's Armies? But then, you forgot who they were that said so, Hell-Hounds and Blood-Hounds, Fiends, and Fire-Brands, and Bloody Devils, not to be named without Fire and Brimstone; do you think such are not to be believed (especially when they speak for their own Advantage) rather than the People of God, the faithful of the Land at *Westminster*, who likewise, when they raised Forces, said, they did it for the King and Parliament? Can any Man in his Wits deny but the King is to be believed before either of these?" And yet you cannot be persuaded, but his Offer to go in Person to suppress the Rebellion, was a Design to return at the Head of 20, or 30000 Rebels, to have destroyed this Nation. That's very strange! but first, how shall we believe what you say before, to shew your Breeding? Never was Bear so unwillingly brought to the Stake, as he to declare against the Rebels, if he offered to adventure his Person to suppress them. When you have made this agree in Sense, let us know how you can suppose the same Person, the wisest King in Christendom, and yet so foolish, to study his own Destruction; for who could suffer so much in the Ruin of this Nation as himself? For his hindering the Earl of *Leicester*'s going into *Ireland*, he had much more Reason to do so than the Parliament had to hinder him; and therefore you may as well conclude them guilty, as him, of the Rebellion.

That he sold, or exchanged, for Arms and Ammunition, the Cloth and Provisions sent by the Parliament to the Protestants in *Ireland*, you must either accuse the Parliament, which seized upon his Arms first, and used them against him, or prove them above the Law of Nature, which, I believe, you had rather do, that commands every Man to defend himself. But the Rebels in *Ireland* gave Letters of Mart for taking the Parliament's Ships, but freed the King's, as their very good Friends. I see you are not such a Wizard at Designs as you pretend to be; for if this be the deepest Reach of your Subtilty, had you been a Senator in *Rome*, when *Hannibal* invaded *Italy*, and burnt all the Country, but that of the *Roman* Dictator, you would have spared no longer to prove him Confederate with the Enemy. But I fear I may seem as vain as your self in repeating your Impertinencies. There is one Argument that might have served instead of all, to convince you of Wickedness and Folly in this Business, and that is the Silence of the Charge, which, by your own Rule, ought to be taken *pro confesso*, there was never any such Thing.

I will not trouble my self nor any Body with your *French* Legend, as being too inconsiderable to deserve any serious Notice, built only upon Relations and Hear-says, and proved with your own Conjectures; which, how far we are to credit, from a Man of so much Biass and Mistakes, any of those you appeal to shall determine; to whom I shall say but this, that you do but acknowledge the Injustice of the Sentence, while you strive to make it good with such Additions; for if you had not believed it very bad, you would never have taken so much Pains to mend it: And, I hope, your high Court will punish you for it, whose Reputation your officious Indiscretion hath much impaired to no Purpose: For tho' we should grant all your Additions to be true, as you would have it, it does not at all justify the King's Death, since he did not die in Relation to any Thing there objected; and all you can possibly aim at by this pitiful Argument, is but to prove him Guilty, because he was punished; for you can never prove him punished because he was Guilty.

For your Epilogue, I have so much Charity to believe it, being of a different Thread of Language, none of your own; but either penned for you by your musty *Peters*, or else you writ Short-Hand very well to copy after the Speech of his Tongue. However you came by it, sure I am, it could come from no body else; and having said so, I hope I shall need say no more; for I shall be loath to commit the Sin of repeating any of it. But since 'tis a Frippery of common Places of Pulpit Railing, ill put together, that pretend only to Passion, I am content you should use them your self, and be allowed to say any thing with as little Regard, as if you wore your Privilege: Yet lest you should grow so conceited as to believe yourself, I will take *Solomon*'s Advice, and answer you not in your own Way of

Railing, or Falshood, but in doing some Right to Truth, and the Memory of the Dead, which you have equally injured.

That he was a Prince of incomparable Virtues his very Enemies cannot deny, (only they were not for their Purpose) and those so unblemished with any personal Vice, that they were fain to abuse the Security of his Innocence, both to accuse and ruin him. His Moderation (which he preserved equal in the Extremity of both Fortunes) they made a common Disguise for their contrary Impalations, as they had occasion to mis-call it, either an Easiness to be misled by others, or Obstinacy to rule by his own Will. This Temper of his was so admirable, that neither the highest of Temptations, Adorations and Flattery, nor the lowest of Misery, Injuries, the Insolency of Fools, could move him. His Constancy to his own Virtues was no mean Cause of his Undoing; for if he had not stated the Principles of Government upon unalterable Right, but could have shifted his Sails to catch the popular Air when it grew high (as his Enemies did) they had never undone him with empty Pretendings to what he really meant. His Wisdom and Knowledge were of so noble a Capacity, that nothing lay so much out of his Reach, as the profound Wickedness of his Enemies, which his own Goodness would never give him leave to suspect, nor his Experience Power to discover; for they managed the whole Course of his Ruin, as they did the last Act of it, in Disguise; else so great a Wit as his had never been circumvented by the Treachery and Cheat, rather than Policy, of ignorant Persons. All he wanted of a King was, he knew not how to dissemble, unless concealing his own Perfections were so; in which he only deceived his People, who knew not his great Abilities, 'till their Sins were punished with the Loss of him. In his Death, he not only out-did the high Resolution of the antient *Romans*, but the humble Patience of the Primitive Martyrs; so far from the Manner of Tyrants, who use to wish all the World their Funeral Pile, that he employed the Cares of his last Thoughts about the Safety of his very Enemies, and died not only consulting, but praying for the Preservation of those whom he knew resolved to have none, but what was built upon their own Destruction.

All this, and much more, the Justice of Posterity (when

POLITICAL OBSERVATIONS

Faction and Concernment are removed) will acknowledge to be more true of him, than any of those Slanders you (or the mad Wickedness of this Age) have thrown upon his Memory, which shall then, like Dung cast at the Roots of Trees, but make his Name more flourishing and glorious; when all these Monuments of Infamy you have raised, shall become the Trophies of his Virtue, and your own Shame. In the mean Time, as your own Conscience, or the Expectation of Divine Vengeance, shall call upon you, you will see what you have done, and find there is no Murther so horrid, as that which is committed with the Sword of Justice; nor any Injustice so notorious, as that which takes Advantage, both of the first Silence of the Living, and that of the Dead. In this last, you have been very sinful, and, in accusing the Dead, have not behaved yourself so like a Saint at the Day of Judgment, as the Devil, whose Office is to be Solicitor General in such Cases. I will not judge you, lest I should do worse, imitate you. But certainly you will find it the worst Kind of Witchcraft, to raise the Devil by sacrificing to your own Malice, especially to so bad a Purpose as you have done, that you might invade the Judgment-Seat of Christ, and usurp his Jurisdiction before his Coming, which you have presumed to do with more Rudeness than *Hacket* used, and less Formality, in not sending your Fore-runner to proclaim (in a Turnip-Cart) your coming to Judgment. But the worst of all is, you seem to glory in your Sins, and assert the Martyrdom of your Wickedness; for having supposed a Possibility you may fall by the Hands of Violence, you arm yourself with a forced Resolution, which you may be confident you will never have need of: for you have no Reason to think any Man can believe you have deserved a violent Death; no, you have deserved rather to live; long, so long, till you see yourself become the Controversy of wild Beasts, and be fain to prove our Scare-Crow. Unless you shall think it just, that as you have been condemned out of your own Mouth, so you should fall by your own Hand. Indeed there was not a Hang-man bad enough for *Judas*, but himself; and when you shall think fit to do yourself so much Right, you shall be your own Sooth-sayer, and fall by the Hand of a *Raviliac*, to whom, with more Likeness, compare yourself, than to *Henry* IV. for you are no King. What *Raviliac* was is very well known; what you are, I leave to your own Conscience.

386

OBSERVATIONS
UPON THE
LONG PARLIAMENT
Of
CHARLES the First

After the *King* in the *long Parliament* had past the Act of
Continuance, he was forced in a few Months to prorogue and
dissolve himself from them, who never left, until they had
adjourned him to another World. For the Members of the
House of Commons are but a kind of Botchers and Members of
decaying Governments, which they sometimes dress and turn;
but have nothing to do with those that are firm and substantial.
They meet to reform the Miscarriages of others; but are commonly prorogued and dissolved for their own, when the Remedies grow worse than the Diseases. For Moderation among
so many Men where no one has more Power than another, was
never heard of in the World; and therefore, as they know no
Mean, they naturally run into all Manner of Extremities.
They meet like a Consultation of Physicians, where every
Man's Business is to apply to his own Advantages, and not to
consider the present Condition of the miserable Patient: and
therefore let the Countries choose whom they please, they admit
of none, but such as they find most fit for their own Purposes.
And although this be practised every Day, it is incredible, what
great Sums of Money some will lay down, only to be but half
returned, and admitted to stand to the Favour, rather than the
Justice of the House; where commonly those, who have been
at the greatest Charges, lose all for want of insuring their Adventures, and rightly placing some more Money amongst the
most powerful of their Judges. Hence it is, that Elections are
now become Purchases; and the more infirm the Government
grows, the higher the Rates rise, quite contrary to the Actions,
as they call them, of *Holland*, that every Day advance with the
Recovery of the State, and fall again with the Relapses of it.
By this means, although the only End and Purpose of their

first Institution was to preserve the Liberties of the People, yet they take the Freedom of their Voices, in which their Liberty chiefly consists, from them; and are not satisfied with making Money of that Power with which they intrusted them, and imposing a Belief upon them that they have it still, when they have sold it and forced them to pay for it, but will undertake to choose for them, or rather against them, whom they please; that if a new Member should be demanded, what Country or Corporation he serves for, he can make no true Answer, but that he serves for the House—That in time every particular Member, that shall hereafter sit, can represent no less than the whole Nation, and consequently become Masters of it, and serve for the King also.

They are furnished with all the Tricks, that have grown up with the Practice of the Law for so many hundred Years; and whosoever is but qualified with Impudence enough to back his Ignorance, and enable him to become a small Orator, he presently expects his retaining or retiring Fee, and, till he has received it, is implacable; but as soon as he has it, like a regenerate Man, his Eyes are opened presently, and he puts off the old Man, and has new Thoughts and Opinions, and Judgments, as if he had lived before in Error and Darkness all his Life time. Of these there are not more at a time than a Dozen, or twenty at the most; who govern all the rest of the House by combining together, and seconding one another, and studying every Man his Part. By which Arts they can easily prevail upon the greater Number of the House, who only come as Spectators, not to act, but look on, and cry up, or down all that they see others do, whom they have chosen for their Proxies. And as these Grandees, as they call them, are taken off with Bribes or Preferment, others start up in their Rooms, and keep the Party on foot; who, if there was nothing to be gotten by it, would give it over of themselves. But when this kind of Juggling is rendered the readiest Way to Advancement, and that nothing is more common than to see those, who have done their Exercises best in those liberal Arts in the House of Commons, to be always promoted to that of the Lords, there will never want Proficients, and those of the worst Men; while Princes reward those best who serve them worst, and trust none with the greatest Charges of the Nation, but only such as have forced their Way by opposing the Interest of both King and People; that can give no Security for their Faith and Integrity, but the Perfidiousness of those Courses which they took before to put themselves into a Capacity of Preferment.—And this, indeed, has for some Years been reputed the Test of Men's Parts and Abilities, by which they only can deserve to be either trusted or employed, as if Treachery were like the Small-Pox, which every Man is to expect one time or other, and those who have had it are free for ever after.

All they get by retrenching the King's Prerogative commonly lasts no longer than the Sessions; and only proves an Advantage to the Judges and great Officers in the Law, who for Preferment restore it back again to the right Owner. They abominate to pay the King's Debts, lest it should prove a leading Case to the Payment of their own; which they cannot endure to think upon, and therefore dread nothing (next a dissolution) so much as a Prorogation of three Terms, the only Way the King has to reduce them with *Judgment*, *Outlawries*, and *Executions*. For many of them serve only, not to redress, but continue the Grievances of their Creditors, or those of others who will pay them for the Loan of their Protections, and give their pretended Masters Wages to serve them, and follow their Business, against all *Mayors*, *Sheriffs*, *Bailifs*, &c. for forty Days before, and forty after, which are worse than two Lents to their hungry Creditors. They are so greedy of Power and Authority, that they are never satisfied with cutting out of new Work for themselves; but cannot abide to finish any Thing, lest they should chance to want something to do, that is, to sit and shew their Parts upon, until the Bugbear Prorogation comes; and then all they have done is undone, and themselves also.

When any of them dies, he who is able to produce most Ale and bad Wine is in the fairest Way to succeed him; out of the Dregs of which the new Member (like Aquavitæ and Brandy) is commonly extracted. He is made, like an Insect, by equivocal Generation, and produced out of Dung and the Flyblows of the Rabble, whose Votes, right or wrong, are sufficient to enable him to vote in the same Way, with as little Under-standing and Judgment, as they used in the Choice of him, though he be a Senator *infra Ætatem*.

POLITICAL OBSERVATIONS

The Lawyers among them are a People they have no Kindness for; and although they have for many Years endeavoured to redress the Grievances of their Trade, yet they could never bring it to pass without making greater, as they have always persuaded them; and by that means still keep their Ground, and spoil all they do by wilful Miswording of their Acts, which they afterwards discover, and render all they do, how well soever intended, unuseful to the Purposes it was designed for, without a new Act of Explanation.

The longer they sit, they are inevitably the worse; and all the Experience they get never tends to any other Purpose. For their caballing is the same Thing exactly with packing of Cards; by which means they can deal and play into one another's Hands, and cheat the more plain and dull Part of the House, who want Wit and Skill to perceive their Tricks—And of these there be many Sorts; some for designing, and some for acting only according to Instructions; in which they observe the Method of Bowlers, of whom some are best at leading, some at seconding, and some at laying a Bowl in the Way, and some at striking away the Jack. These Cabals are commonly prepared at Taverns, where they meet as Players do at a Rehearsal, to find how perfect every Man is at his Part. In these Meetings they are always supplied with abundance of Lyes for all their Occasions, but when they come to Tryal, are always found (like the Virtuoso's Experiments) to fall short in the Proof, and do most Hurt to their Undertakers; for as they are founded upon Hearsays (the Bastards and Sons of the People) they never light upon the true Fathers, who commonly disown them, and lay them upon others, when they come to be questioned for them. By this means they seldom do any great Hurt to those, with whom they are most angry: for as soon as the Delinquent knows who are his greatest Persecutors or most dangerous Enemies, nothing is more vendible than those Animosities, as perhaps undertaken for no other Purpose. For they do not believe themselves obliged to that Strictness of Justice as other inferior Courts do, who are more tyed up with Oaths, and Rules in their Proceedings, and fear of Punishment by loss of their Places, if they should be discovered. For though Conscience be said to be a thousand Witnesses, they are all *Knights of the Post*, when they are to testify on their own Side, I mean in this World, in which they are not so competent Witnesses as in the next.

The King sends for them to advise with him about the hard Affairs of the Nation, that is, how to raise Money; and they advise him to let it alone, till they are in the Humour, and in the mean time by letting them do what they please, endeavour to bring them to that good Humour, and suffer them to redress him, as the likeliest Way, until he is forced to redress them by letting loose the Laws upon them, as much the better Way. They give the King Money just as the Bankers used to lend it him; and make him pay so much in the hundred for it, the more his Occasions require it, in ready Prerogative down upon the Nail: and make him stay long enough for it, as all those are wont, who pay for any Thing before they have it. They preserve and improve their own Interests most by complaining of that, which makes most for it, that is, the extravagant Expences of the Crown, which consequently reduce it to Wants; and the supplying of those is the only Thing that renders them considerable, though the Crown is forced to pawn all its own Jewels to them for mere Brokage and Forbearance: For they are but a kind of Scriveners that put out the Nations Money, of which they have the disposing, for all Sorts of their own Advantages, but nothing less than that of the Public. They seek all Occasions (as if they had not too many offered them) to pick Quarrels with the Government, as Hectors do with Chowses, until the Business is compounded, and then they are made Friends and reconciled for ever after, and are well paid for doing that, which in all good and wise Governments they would be punished and hanged for. This is one of the most barbarous Knaveries in the World, though but a just Judgment upon those unhappy Princes, who bring themselves into a Condition to be so wretchedly baffled by their Subjects, to be forced to pay Fines to them for their Miscarriages, and the ill Management of their own Affairs; and sue out their Pardons of those very Persons, whom the Laws of the Land deny all Pardon to, and afterwards trust and employ them; as if Sale Faith were not, like all Things else that are made for Sale, slight and adulterate.

They are never useful but to the best Princes, who best know how to manage them; nor necessary to the People, but in the

Government of the weakest. For when all Things are brought into Disorder, they usually restore them with greater, as Agues are cured by being turned into Fevers: for no Physic will work upon the Body Politic, but only such as is fit for Beasts to take, and Mountebanks or Farriers to give. And yet for all this they are so necessary an Evil, that the Nation does as little know how to subsist without them; as to endure the Inconveniences, which they suffer by them.

BENEFICIAL REFLECTIONS
UPON
MILFORD-HAVEN

The Security of *England* consisting most particularly in the Circumvallation of her Ocean-Walls, it must needs be dangerous to leave a Gap open for a Navy of a thousand Sail to enter at, without so much as a Parapet, or a Battery furnished with Artillery, to oppose the landing of an Enemy. If it was held necessary by our former Princes of *England* to employ their Care in fortifying the *Cinque-Ports*, it is not less needful to put the famous Haven of *Milford* in the county of *Pembroke* in *Wales*, in an equal Posture of Defence with the rest. Such is the Situation thereof, that being directly opposite to *Ireland*, and within six or seven Hours Sail of it, that Enemy, that would invade it, and were wind-driven on the *British* Coast, would find safe Harbourage in *Milford*, without Danger or Opposition, until the Wind served for his Design.

Should an Attempt be made upon *England* by that Port, the Attempter, by landing there, would receive these ensuing Benefits—First, a safe Harbour from the Violence of all Winds, as being secured from the Cliffs; Secondly, a Conveniency for disembarking, being no considerable Forces could be suddenly assembled to dispute it; Thirdly, a Country abundant in Provision, to supply the Wants of an Army; Fourthly, the Distance of two hundred Miles it is from the City of *London*, and four-score from *England*, would afford an Enemy Liberty, either to fortify it for his own Use, or sufficient Time in his March to encrease his Army with the Natives, which Benefits the most prudent King *Henry* the seventh made perfect use of, to his Exaltation to the Crown.

To frustrate an Enemy of these Advantages, *Nature* hath afforded us Instruction, by her Bounty with human Art to perfectionate the rest. At the very Mouth of the Haven there is a Peninsula, extending it self a pretty Way into it. This hath Ground sufficient to erect a Fort upon; and will require but

393

small Fortification, to make it strong. The Neck of it landward being narrow, it may with no great Charge be cut, and so separated from the main Land. The one Side inward is a Precipice, and inaccessible; seaward it is somewhat oblique, but by Labour of a few Hands may be made as inaccessible, as the other. The Point encroaching upon the Mouth of the Haven hath as much even Ground, level with High-Water Mark, as will serve to make a large Battery. Within this Peninsula is an Islet at a convenient Distance, at whose Foot, on both Sides, Batteries may be erected, to the Offence of Intruders. At a proportionable Distance from this lies another Island, about the same Magnitude, corresponding with the opposite Shore, where Batteries also may be made to the like Advantage. The Peninsula, or Promontory, and the two Islands lye in a triangular Figure, and that Distance the one from the other, and from the opposite Shore, that no Ship can pass by them into the River, but must inevitably be subject to the Shot, either of the Shores, or the Islands.

The Islands need no Fortification, *Nature* having made them impregnable through their Precipices. All the Charge necessary for their Completion will be only the Erection of Batteries, and a small Lodging, with a *Corps de Gard*, for a few Soldiers and Gunners. The greatest Cost and Labour will be the making of two Demi-bastions or a Hornwork, for the Defence of the Peninsula toward the Land Side. On the opposite Shore may be built a small Redoubt, as the Conveniency of the Place will afford.

Before the late Troubles three Pirates entered into this Haven, landed two Pieces of Artillery upon the Shore; under whose Protection, and that of two of their Ships, the third took the Benefit to be careen'd, and continued there for fifteen Days, in spite of all the Strength and Endeavour, the whole County could make to expel them. Having finished their Work at their Leisure, they quitted the River, and landed in some of the adjacent Islands, where they furnished themselves with as many Muttons and other Provisions as served their Turn, and sailed away without the least Prejudice received.

If so few Ships were able to commit so evident Insolences without Controul, let us consider, what might be acted by a

394

MILFORD-HAVEN

whole Navy landing there to the Detriment of the Country, which by fortifying of the Haven might undoubtedly be prevented; otherwise an hostile Fleet entering there, may easily seize the Haven and fortify it, plunder and burn all the Towns and Villages in the Country, and retire at their Pleasure, before any Shipping could be sent from the *Thames* or the *Downes* to encounter them, three several Winds being requisite to sail with into those Parts from the east of *England*.

A deplorable Inconvenience through the Defect of Fortification to this Haven happened in the time of the late Trouble. His Majesty's Forces being superior in the Field in that Country, the adverse Strength confined within the Walls of *Pembroke*, one *Swanley* Captain of the *Swallow-Frigate*, in the Enemy's Service, entered the Haven, who joining his marine Forces to those of *Pembroke*, they unitedly took the Field; and finding the *Royalists* careless, as contemning their weak Number, fought them in the plain Field, and routed them; through which Misfortune the *Royalists* were beaten quite out of the Country, and shortly after out of all *Wales*, through the Benefit of that Victory; when, had the contrary happened, *Wales* had continued a firm footing for his Majesties Army, and an advantageous Retreat, upon all sinister Events.

Now we have discovered the Inconveniencies *Milford* Haven is subject to, for the want of small Fortification, we shall manifest the Advantages the Town and Haven of *Tenby* and the Island of *Caldee* afford. The Town, standing upon a Plot of high Land, with a small Castle at the Extremity of it towards the Sea, may be made as impregnable to the Landside, as it is inaccessible on the Seaside, being a very high Rock and a most formidable Precipice, if at the narrow Juncture of it toward the Land (it being there not an hundred Paces broad) it were separated from it. That Side, which flanks on the Sea and Haven, needs no Art to fortify it, *Nature* having supplied that with the Inaccessibility of the Precipice. The opposite Side landward is oblique, and, with no great Cost or Labour, might be made as inscalable as the other. The Kay, though but little, is capable to receive Ships of great Burthen, and secure from all Winds, except that of the north-east. Those Ships, which cannot arrive thither to receive Shelter upon Occasion of Distress, shall receive it between *Caldee* and the Land, where there is good Anchorage, and Security from all Winds. This Place lies so conveniently for the Discovery of all Ships, that shall sail between it and the Lands End of *England* into the River of *Severne*, that no Ship in the Day time, can pass unken'd; and those, that harbour there, can easily interrupt all the Commerce of foreign Parts with *Bristol*, *Glocester*, *Chepstow*, and all the rest of the Towns within the *Severne*; so that the Consequence of this Place will not be inconsiderable, did the Realm (which *God* forbid) fall again into a Relapse of Disobedience.

APPENDIX

DRAFT OF BUTLER'S LETTER TO HIS SISTER ON THE EDUCATION OF HER SON

Deare Sister,

I have read your letter, that you sent to my wife In which you Desire my Advice about breeding of your Son, and although I have considerd much and long of it, and not only conferd with my Cussen Kemish, but severall others of my Friends about it I know not what to say to you. For not knowing the Naturall Parts and Inclination of the youth I know as little what to Propose to you in it, For if he doth not naturally take a Delight in his Books, it wilbe in vain to think by any other meanes to Prevayl upon him to do it. And therefore All I can say to you concerning that, is to Put him to some Grammar School among which there is no great Difference that I could ever observe especially to those who have not extraordinary Inclinations of their owne Tempers to it. Where with little Industry they may easily attaine to so much as will serve them in their ordinary Occasions of Busnes, which is the Common Rate of all Mens Educations, and sometimes more Prosperous to themselves then it proves to those who indeavor to go further. As for your breeding him to the Law, whether he be fit for it or not: Is much more difficult to Determine. For as in all that Profession, there are many hunderds that make no Advantage at all; for one that dos, So there is nothing certaine but th' expence and Danger, where youth being left to it self without so much as a Tutor Or Governor, shall meet with so many that make it their Trade and Busnes to Corrupt, and if they have any thing undo them. This I have seen in a Friend of mine an Eminent Lawyer of the Temple, who bred up 3 or 4 Sons in his own Profession, and under his own eie, and yet could not with all his Care Possibly preserve them from being utterly ruind by the ill Company that perpetually lay in wayt for them.

But if you have a mind to send him to any Schoole in this Towne I need not tell you how careful your Sister wilbe to her Power of him, nor shall I be wanting in any thing that is in mine. But the lease of the House where we live, being neare expiring, wee shall be necessitated to Remove, I suppose the next Quarter, where wee shall indevor to finde better conveniences for him then this Place can afford.

TENTATIVE LINES ON VARIOUS SUBJECTS

Wit and Folly

And when his wit has leakd it's moysture
Is empty as a Gaping Oyster.

And might as wel for prophets pas
As Livies Calf or Balams Ass.

In Plays, the last Act's but the Fag
And therefore may b' allowd to flag.

That do's but Dictate and Compile
At charge of nothing but the stile,
Which al that chance to light upon
May freely chaleng as their own.

This sayd— Another of the Crew
Stood up, and sayd —This is to shew
How easy things that are above
Or under Reason are to Prove,
And how far wit upon the Stretch
In things that are not fixt; wil reach,
That may be wrested any way,
But never Renderd at a Stay;
Or if they are, unfix mens Braines,
And seldom prove worth half the Paines:
For Demonstrations rarely Rise
T' outweigh mere Probabilities,
And, though most Certaine, yet th' are such
In matters that import not much,
Are like Mecha[n]iques, Tru in small
Designes, but greater, not at all:
For who would give a Straw to know
The Reason one and one make two?
But Probables, that nere Conclude,
Are of a Nobler Latitude.

For Subtlety and Politiques
Alloy great valours when they mix.

       Fooles in Judging
Are Faine to swallow many a Gudgin.
And Cheat themselves with Tricks as False
As Gamsters Dice, or Juglers Bals.

But, if she takes to virtuosing
To Dabling, Scribling and Composing,
Shee's more insufferable yet
And gives no Quarter with her wit;
On both sides Moote's upon all Cases
With Love and Honor Common Places;
Runs down the Stars, and has the Ods
At Reprimands of all the Gods,
And Rants, as if they were no more
But Statues stil as heretofore
And, like their Images, but Logs
Thrown down from Heav'n to govern Frogs;
And is a Dreadfuller Earestretcher
The[n] the Ablest Conventicle Teacher;
But, if she takes to sing or fiddle,
Her vertus center in the middle,

APPENDIX

The Sphere to which al virtu tends,
And leaves to vice ——— Ends;
Does all her Feates by mode and fashion
And Clips false Coyn of Affectation;
At selling Bargaines, far exceeds
The Signe of the three Logger heads,
And cry's down al that is not wit
With Fire and Flame as Juglers spit.

As if his Tongue had got the Bit,
And Ran away with all his wit.

Like Races, where the longest winde
Leave's all the Shorter-breathd behind
And strive's to make his Rams-horns blow
With Noyses alone, down Jericho.

Dilemmas of Polemique wits
When if one misse, the other hit's.

Pride

As when Dogs set up their Tayles in Pride
Th' expose those Parts that Nature meant to hide.

Learning

When most men have so hard a task, to shun
Their being by themselvs imposd upon.

An able Judge may have a Heavy head
As Gold and Silver's tryd with Tests of Lead.

Who, like a Skilful Rhetorician,
Knew how to order his Transition
So Cunningly, the Quickest Sense
Could nere unriddle his Pretence,
Nor what he went about Discover,
Untill the whole Design was over.

For Truth and Falshood, like a Gun, that's shot
Make æquall Noyses, tho they hit, or Not:
And some still growe the worse, the more they Reade
As Elks (they say) Go Backwards, when they feed.

The New Divice of Fiddle strings, to Rayse
Above the Mean, or Tenor-Part; the Base:
For when two Strings are straind t' an unison
(A greater and a less) and stil straind on
(Both æqually) the greater wilbe found,
B'ing straind before, to have the Higher sound.

APPENDIX

A wondrous Hard Invention to unriddle
The Natrall Reason of, upon the Fiddle,
Which Gallileo shew'd himself an Ass
To take no Notice of, but overpas.

So those that by the Oracle had been
Infallibly Declard the wisest Men,
Were but affected Humorists and Drols,
That might have past as wel for Errant Fooles,
That held it wisdom freely to commit
All sorts of madnes, when the Magot Bit.
Which some were faine to counterfet and Act,
T' avoyd the Law, that favours the Distract;
And one of them, made statutes, that concern
The Regulating al that Teach, or Learne.
Did not omit Proviso's for their Play,
But put it, in a Legislative way,
That nobody could play at Trap, or Ball,
Unless it were allowd Juridicall,
With Peremptory Injunctions, and Commands
About the Managment of Clokes, and Bands,
Mad[e] Rules to spit, and after tread it out
More Regular then ever had been taught,
Made Politique Provisos, to Put off
Their Breaking winde with sneeres, or a Coffe;
That Tully (had he lived then) had abstained
To rub his face so often with his Hand.

For those that valew things too cheap, or Deare,
More then the Standard of the world wil Beare:
Mistake Th' Intrinsique Rate, and put their Talents,
And Inclinations, only in the Ballance:
And those, to whom the Hardest things are cleare,
Will make the Plaine as Difficult appeare;
When all the Antients fancyd of the Trick
Was but a Stoiques Earthen Candle-stick,
That to some Pædants of his Tribe was Sold,
And Purchacd for its weight in Ready Gold.

So he, that sainted Queen Elizabeth
So many Scores of yeares, before her Death,
And cald her *Diva*, Th' Antients nere allowd
To any Prince, till Dead, and made a God.
And, tho the Learnedst of our Antiquarys,
Let such a Blemish on her Commentarys.

The sturdy Gaul bore Cæsar, like a Sack,
H' had Loaded Prisner ore his Horses Back,
A Greater Captive then the Roman Foe,
Who had been taken Prisner, by a Crow.

APPENDIX

Extravagances wil not Pass in Nature
On those that live so many Ages After,
Tho all the world indeavors to excuse
The most Prodigious Custome of their use,
Like Boys, and Girles Implicitly held best
To Gather in their Spices, in the East.
Or that Blind Moor that smelling to a Clod
Led on the Caravan upon the Road,
As one that is of Classical Esteeme
Relates the Story, and the Rest from him.
If any have so feeble a Beliefe
To credit such a monstrous Narrative.

For men that are in Greatest want of Sense
Have all and more supplyd by confidence;
And, as some Printers have (among the Popish)
Been Hangd for Printing truer then their Copies,
It is a Dangrous thing, for those that write
All sorts of Truths, to bee too much i' th' Right.

Like him that usd to stand al Day and night
Congeald into a Posture bolt upright,
A Deep occult Philosopher and Scribe,
The Lutum Sapientiae of his Tribe.

For those that take most Pains to under[stan]d,
Like great Estates Run furthest behind hand,
Retaine the measure, which at School they took,
When only for the words, they read a book.
And all their freest thoughts, can never leave
What Custome first Ingagd 'em to receive;
Who still the more, they Toyle in Books and Drudge,
Are found the more untowardly to Judge,
Resolve i' th' Dark of Matters ere so Hard,
Like Jury men of Fire, and Light debard:
That many a Learned Metaphysique Clarke
Has been bred-up, Like Singing Birds, i' th' Dark.

Chaldeans brag th' have been Astrologers,
Before the Moon, so many Thousand years:
But could not Cast their own Nativitys,
For want of her, without so many Lyes;
Yet those, that can Put down Astrologers
And outly those five thousand Falkoners,
And Huntsmen, which the Macedonian youth
Allowd his Tutor, only to write Truth,
The Learnd wil pas for tru, and Current all,
If th' Authors have but Past for Classical.

APPENDIX

That crack their brains to find out by what trade
The fabrick of the world at first was made;
Who drew the model of it, and what sect
Produc'd the philosophick architect;
Or whether chance, necessity, or matter
Contriv'd the whole establishment of nature;
That all the antique poets were not mad
And crackt enough to do it half so bad,
Until the deep and learneder Wiseacres
Philosophers became the undertakers,
Who more stupendiously perform'd the fact,
And prov'd themselves more exquisitely crackt;
That when the moon's at full a Madman's dreams
Are sob'rer than their wisest theorems.

Make one man's teeth grow in another's chops,
And brew, with ginger, beere, instead of hops;
Make silk of canvace, and Virginia grasses,
And grind on flakes of ice new burning glasses;
Make prawns and crawfish, and all shellfish else
With sympathetick powder of their shells;
Make chips of Elm produce the largest trees
And sowing saw-dust furnish nurseries.

For sentences have greater latitude
To quibble in, than single words, allowd,
The new rhetorick figure clinch and pun,
To make two diff'rent senses pass for one,
The dear delight of reverend men, whose wit
Is grown no further back than childhood yet,
And therefore may b' allow'd to play its wild
Vagaries in its journey down to child,
To jumble contradictions, and make good
And bad in the same subject understood,
Force wet and dry t' ingage, and hot and cold
Like nature in another Chaos hold,
A more ingenious and absurd device
Then grinding burning-glasses upon ice,
Which th' Irish prophet us'd so long ago
To light a fire, and burn great heaps of snow,
And ought to pass for modish, since the French
Have not outgrown Carwichet yet and clench,
But use to make the rime and equivoc
The sole ingredients of a witty Book;
And if they can by chance but make the fadge,
Believe th' have gotten ground of all the age,
And laugh at all the ignorant liefhebbers,
And witless virtuosos of their neighbours.

APPENDIX

For those that treat of —— are wont
To write down all that authours say upon't,
But have no further prospect in their thoughts
Of reason and invention then their notes;
And when they have been laid by and forgot,
Admire their parts anew, and put it out:
As he that wrote a sturdy musick book,
And never knew a note but those he took,
Discover'd nations to be brave or base
By their pronouncing I's and O's, and A's,
Determin'd poetry only by the feet,
No matter for the fancy, sense, and wit,
Came over to instruct the English nation,
And was not only paid with admiration,
But for his pains had all he would but ask for,
As Merchants Sell glass-beads at Madagascar,
And th' Indian-company for paultry trinkets
Bring over Orient pearles, and pretious ingots.

Whence writers of the later times produc'd
A list of all the Authors names they us'd,
That alphabetically trac'd begun
With Appian, and reach'd to Xenophon;
And tho' they never read one syllable
Of any one, their names prevail as well
To make them pass the publick test instead
Of learned men profound and deeply read.

And like their Books in Librarys, their Braines
Are always tyd up, where they were in Chains:
For Scholle[r]s have no way to make a Thesis
Hold-out, untill th' have taken it to Pieces,
And when they would Determine False, or Tru;
'Tis but because Some other things are so.
And all their Art to make obscure things good
Depends on nothing but similitude.
A vanity that's not the least Ingredient
In th' Hotch-potch composition of a Pedant.

T' invent's a faculty that's given
By th' absolute free grace of heaven;
Which nature keeps in her disposing;
And all the arts of virtuosing
By industry can ne're attain to
By any human non obstante.

Whence some have found out, how a Separate Ghost
In Furious Stormes, and Hurricans, is Tost.
Know what they use to Drink, and what they Eate
And what they suffer in the Cold, or Heate.

APPENDIX

That use to write Stupendious Narrative[s]
Of all th' Adventures of their After-Lives;
Know what makes Form, and Matter stick together
As Boys weights with Sope, and Scraps of Leather,
Or two Stones ground with æqual Superficies
Are Difficultly to be Drawn to Pieces:
All which Demonstrated by D.E.F.
Among the Learned never miss Belief.

                      Learning and devotion
Adord when both were lesse then nothing
Had Colleges and Monasterys
Erected for their Seminaries,
But Scornd as soon as understood,
For Better's a Curst Fo to good,
And owe their Present maintenance
To former Ages of Ignorance.

  In Sciences have Just enough
To talk impertinently of.
Like Virtuosos and Industrious
The more their Aimes Appear Preposterous.

  Men are not Dumb, for want of Tongues, but Eares;
For nature lets none Speak, before he Heares:
To make them learne Good Manners, at th' expence
Of such a wonderful Convenience.
For Those that take (against her will) a Course
T' extend their Latitudes, grow worse, and worse,
A Crime as great, as to Remove the Bounds
That have been set to th' Property of Grounds.

Arts and Sciences

  Some Arts, and Sciences, are only Tooles
Which Students do their Busnes with, in Schools,
Although Great men have sayd, 'Tis more Abstruse
And Hard to understand 'em, then their use.
For, though they were Intended but in Order
To better things, few ever venture Further;
But as all Good Designs are so accurst,
The best intended often Prove the worst.
So what was meant t' Improve the world, quite Cross
Has turnd to its Calamity and loss.
For Scholers are but Jorny men to Nature
That shews them al their Tricks to Imitate her;
Though some mistake the Reason she Proposes
And make her Imitate their Virtuoso's;
Is both the Best, or worst way of Instructing
As men mistake or understand her Doctrine.

APPENDIX

The French that Read anatomy-Lecturs
Upon the Lineaments of Pictures;
And by the Mussles of the Face,
Can tell what Thoughts the Dumbe thing has;
Could nere unrridle, by his Blinkes,
The Crafty Subtleties he thinke's.

Draw Models of th' Invisible Mountain
That all Philosophy do's Contain,
Of which the Sons of Art make Landskips
And Copy out their unseen Transcripts.

As water thrown on sayles of ships
Serv Mariners for Spurs, and whips,
And, by opposing of their Course,
Do's make them sayl with greater force.

Was like those Virtuosos, that Condole
Their want of Breeding in a Publique School,
Where they, by Robbing Orchards, might have Got
The Cabal of Designe, Surprise, and Plot,
The Arts of Keeping Counsel with their Fellows
In time t' have gone forth Doctors at the Gallows;
Such Moral Laws of Judgment, wit, and Art
As good as those Tiberius made to fart
No doubt, are wondrous like t' improve Mankind
If th' are but halfe so wholsom, as the winde.

For Raritys in Art Mechanicall
Are most admird, when they are don in smal,
As th' Indians have Birds as smal as Bees
The[y] count their Greatest Curiosities.

That count it Art, to understand the Nomen
Cneus, or Gaius, of an antique Roman.

                    The Courtly Science
Of Application, and Complyance
Changd in the Cradle of the Arts
Like Soules, and Bodys by DesCartes,
Imployd the best Artificers
To Labour in their Trades, some years,
And, when h' had Learnd their Arts, deducted
And Stopt their Pay for b'ing Instructed,
And what he understood amiss
Past for their own Defaults, not his.
Made Rules and Fables to abstract
And Ad to evry matt'r of Fact,
As if the Art of Horsman-ship
Lay only in the Spur and whip.

APPENDIX

A Man of Eloquence and Stile,
He usd to polish much and File,
But had no further aime, then clothing
In Phrase Polite, and easy-Nothing,
Like Dressing Babies Spruce and Fine,
Although Deformd in ev'ry Line;
Espousd all Controversy of Course,
And understood for bett'r or worse.

And when he Playd his Tricks would stoop
As low as Tumblers through a Hoop,
Would make his Application Humbler
Then a Two-legd, or a Four-legd Tumbler,
As Mastive's on their Bellys Creepe
To get a Bul upon the Hip,
With all submission and Address
Approach his High-and-Mightines,
Until th' are got within his Guards
And then they fasten their Petards.

The greatest Part of Learning's only meant
For Curiosity, and Ornament;
And therefor most Pretending Virtuosos
Like Indians bore their Lips and Flat their Noses,
When 'tis their Artificial want of wit,
That Spoyls their work, instead of mending it.

He that would Pass for Learnd and Polite
Must never Speak a vulgar word or write.

For Arts and Sciences were over-don
Before in Schools they came to be ful-grown,
And since their Best Designes have been no more
But to Retrench what was too much before,
Or else that Pædant was a Ninni hammer
That wrote two thousand Books of th' Art of Grammer.

For there are more Anomalies in Reason
Then in a Schoolboys Difficultest Lesson,
That will not be obedient to Rules,
Nor own the Jurisdiction of the Schooles.

What but Powder of its own
Can give a Luster to a Stone?

For what's an Anchor but a Hook
With which the Greatest Ship is took?

Hieroglyphiques Th' Idiom
And Language of the Deaf and Dumbe.

APPENDIX

Pædants

An Elephant['s] Proboscis is a Paw
That serv's him, to lay hold, and Pul, and draw.

For when the Comment Creeps into the Texts
No Critique such a Desprat Flaw Corrects.

An Amorous Pædant at the same Time whips
And makes Adresses to the School Boys hipes
And when the Poor Delinquent cannot Pearce
Apply[s] his services to Madam ———
And, haveing had his Solace for a while,
Waytes till his Happy Stars againe shall smile.

Are unconcernd in Insides of their Books
As some unsight unseen buy Pigs in Pokes
And German Authors usd to set a Price
Upon their works, according to the Size.

When all his Study is t' appeare at once
To Idiots Learnd, and to the Learnd a Dunce.

That most unnaturally forcd their Brain
In all they undertake against the Grain,
As Carts draw Horses down the Steepest Hils
Tho with their Natral Legs tyd up their wheels.

For evry Language has an Idiom,
That's only Graceful when it is at Home.
Yet Pædants falsly think, it never Pleases
So fully, as in Forraine Modes, and Dresses.

The many Inconveniences they Run,
Between their Tutors folly, and their own:
Has been the Cause, That greater Stores of Fooles
Have not been Changd i' th' Cradle then the Schools.
That Breed up youth to expiate the Curse,
Prepostrously, by making of it worse;
Take Paines to Reconcyle those Languages
That first had been Divided, for its Ease.

For Jesuites are the Regularest Pædants
Bred, all their Lives, like Schoolboys, in Obedience
And Dare not own a word of Truth, or Reason
Unles it be Prescribd 'em for a Lesson.

Some use to write a Treatise in a Letter
With half a Reame of Paper in't and Better,
Enough to Fill the Largest Pacquet-male[s]
That ere were sent to th' Jesuits-Generals.

APPENDIX

Northern Pædagogues
Are brought to their Perfection, by the Lugs,
As Large as Hounds to Keep their Hearing Close
From Hindring, and Diverting of the Nose.

Virtuoso

That think unjustly to deny
A Traveller his Right to Ly,
Or Virtuosos Free Command
Things how they please to understand.

As silly as b' a weathercock
To think to finde out what's a Clock.

As Antient Statues without Arms or Noses
Are Reverencd for their Age by virtuosos.

Whence some believe Ægyptian Hieroglyphyques
Are all that's left of Natural Specifiques;
When evry Letter Signifyd the Nature
Of Beasts, and Birds, and Fishes in the water;
Which made the Antients Celebrate an Owl
For th' only Proper Philosophique Foul.

Of time take measure with a string
And make it measure any thing.

As modern Painters take it for a Glory
To steal a Posture, or a Limb in Story,
And use it as an Argument they Come
Nearest to some Old Greek they stele it from.

Who, by the smutty Coullers or the Fair,
Can only Judge how New or old they are;
Whence some, by being smokd like hams of Bacon,
For Antique Masters Hands have been mistaken
By those who have no Notion of the lines,
The only Rule to Judge of tru Designes.

Antiquity

And when there is no Natral Difference
Betwene the Antique and the modern Sense
Admire the Excellencies of the one,
And as Implicitly Cry th' other down;
[Ap]prove of nothing til 'tis out of Date,
[As] Drownd Men use to Swim, when 'tis too late.

410

APPENDIX

An Antiquary's better Pleasd with viewing
A Prospect of some venerable Ruine
Then if it stood as firm and undefacd
As if it had not bee[n] s' antiquely raisd.

For tho the Critiques, finde no Flaws of Sense
In all the writings, of the Antients,
Or if they did; Nere offerd to correct
A Plain, and most Notorious Defect.
But chargd it all upon the Ignorance,
And careles Errors of Librarians,
Yet in their works, th' are found, as Plentifull
As modern Authors, of mistake, and Bull.
Who take no Notice, where an Over-sight is,
Like him that cald th' Athenians Quirites:
Or he that gave Atrides Methridate
Some thousand yeares before it's first Receipt.
Were fain t' erect a Chancery of Figures,
To Over-Rule the Peevish Critiques Rigors,
That when the Learnd, were Guilty of a Flaw,
Against the Sense, and Letter, of the Law,
Th' Offender, by the known Rules of the Court
Might be Relievd, and stand ackwitted For't.
Which since has been allowd of, for a Trick
In æquity, and held for Rhetorique.

For had the Antients had the luck to know
Our way of Binding Books that's Practicd now,
The world had never lost so many Pieces
Of Celebrated Authors as it misses.

History

The Saxons rooted al Religion out
And afterward became the most Devout.

The Barbarous Goth, and savage Hun
Could by no Human Power be won
T' indure Civility, and Artes
Til th' had destroyd 'em in al Parts.

So Paul the second was no sooner made
Christ Vicar, from a Merchant by his trade,
But he convicted those of Heresy
That did but Name an university.

Like the French Hercules, and as strong
In all the Labours of the Tongue.

411

APPENDIX

As Socrates stood Day, and Night
In one Stiff Posture Bolt upright.

That for their goodly length and Space
Are of the true Arcadian Race.

Like Alexanders Steward Demophon,
Scorchd in the Shade, and Frozen in the Sun.

The antient Greeks, kept constantly their Guards
To save, from Storms of Hayle, their viniards;
And when the least Suspected Cloud Appeard,
T' avert the Tempest, sacrificd a Bird.

King Harry the eighth had many a Mistress
And yet there's no News of their Names in Historys.

As he that made his Queen to ride
Naked through Coventry astryde.

Like Chinese Ladys where the Fair and comely
Are faine to pay the Portions of the Homely.

Th' Americans had no wit, and less Beard,
When to the first Discovrers, th' Appeard.

In Spain the greatest Ladys that Ly in
Are fancyd with Rich Presents by their kin,
And for their Paines in serving of the State
Are Payd in Duckatoons and Lumps of Plate:
So are their Ladys, when they are let Bloud,
As if They had spent it, for their Cuntry's good.

The Antient Romans tooke great Care
  To match, and Size, and pair
Their Varlets, as we do a Coach horse or a mare;
  And were as Curious to see,
Their Statures and their Cullers just agree,
To fit the Black and brown and Sorrel haire
  And Critically Size
Their Beards, their Noses, and their eies.

As Probable as that of Guicciardine,
Who at Bolognia write they sprung a Mine
So great, and high, That those that were within
By those without, might Perfectly be seene;
And yet the wal fell in the same Place
It stood before, and so dos, to our Days;
Which makes some doubt how much a smoke of Powder
Should be transparant to the Comon Souldier.

APPENDIX

Absurdities

A Man of Stile, and Eloquence
Although as far from wit and Sense
As He that made a house deliver
A long Oration to a River.

As if the Devil to make Proof
He's a clean Beast, should shew his Cloven-hoof.

As Just as 'twas for Burning Paules
To build it with excise on Coales.

Made an Empty Noyse with words
As Fencers stamp upon the Boards,
To Daunt the Enemy with th' Sound
But go's for nothing on the Ground.

Mistake the Meanes for th' Ends of Life,
And like the Prussian eate a knife.

Swift as two Taylors Run a Race
At sewing twenty Score of Lace.

A Trible
More silly then a Statesman Quibble.

As Curiously as Paper wasts in Print
When evry Page has weight, and measure In't.

And when th' have cald them by another Name
Perswade themselves th' are Really the Same.

As Brisk and Frolique in a Smoking-shop
As Swallows are upon a Chimnys-top.

As Horses when th' are Spurd and prickd
But kick again, for being kickd.

All Cattle use, the shorter
Their Commons are, to feed the Heartier.

Custome

Custom, that Fatal Epidemique Ach
Which all mankinde of one another Catch
As in the Alphabet; No Letters
Take place of one another, as their Better[s]
But only use and Custome makes th' As
Of all their Equall Followers take Place.
For nothing is so Infamous, and Shameful
But may be vindicated by Example.

APPENDIX

Opinion

Opinions held by Custome and Prescription
As Legally as Reason and Conviction:
As Greatest Nonsense serv's for Tearms of Art
The Mysterys of Science to Impart;
When, if th' had been agreed on, Hum, and Buz
Had don the Feat as wel, or Mumpsimus:
For Sense has less to do, with Tearms of Arts
Then Spades with Diamonds, or Clubs with Hearts.

For as a Noose, the more 'tis Puld
Is wont to take the Faster hold,
So his Opinions allwayes far'd,
The more th' were Hammerd, grew more hard:
For confidence is nere so strong
As when 'tis Certainst in the wrong

Folly

Those that have to do with Fooles
Must turn themselves t' as very owles.

Sober Folly is the worst
Of all Sorts, and the most Accurst.

An Idiot is but an Almes at Court
The King bestows on those that aske him for't.

For Idiots (Anatomists Maintaine)
Have no Commerce, between the Heart and Braine.

For no exact and true Proposition Pleases
The Ignorant, like Pretty uglinesses,
That serv's to set an Edge on Fancy with
As vineger and Sowr Fruit do's the teeth.

No wonder Ignorance is Counted Holy,
Credulity it self's the Nurse of Folly,
Or (as some say) a medcine to anoynt
And Ease the Torment of a Gouty Joynt,
When most mens memorys are found so Dul
They cannot think on Death without a Scul.

A Mad man Seldom forfets al his wits
Without some Intervals Between their Fits.

Eternal talking's but an overheat
O' th' Brain, as some put rume in Parrot's meat.

APPENDIX

Nonsense

As By-blows having Right to more then one
Presumptive father, Legally have none.

For those that undertake to Teach, have less
Then other men of that which they Profess;
For commonly the greatest Folly's wont
To be Cast up, and Placd to their account;
And all the Freaks and madnes of a noddy
Ascribd to nothing but th' excess of Study;
As 'tis the Constant Nature of Excess
In any thing to turn to a Diseas;
As Monsters seldom have been found to Neede
A Natural Limb, but Frequently t' exceed.

Truth

For Truth in Morals and Mythologies
With its own weapons Passes upon Lys.

What more Prodigious wonder can appeare
Then Naked Truth would to a Princes Eare,
Whose Interests and wills b'ing inconsistents
Th' are by their Ministers kept at a Distance?
For Truth and Princes are Antagonists,
That only meet t' incounter in the lists,
And both are sayd t' have made Confederacies
With wine and women ———— Allies:
For Truth has always been a Friend to wine
And Kings with women Natrally Combine.

Reason is but the ———— way to Truth,
Which seldom has been understood in Youth,
That think they have a greater Latitude
Ore Tru and False then Travellers allowd,
That Fancy Things are not to be Receivd
Because th' are Tru, but as they are Believd.

Physique

There was a Doctor, That with Sturdy Paines,
And many years vexation of his Braines:
Believ'd H' had found-out, (As they call their Guesses,)
An Universall Cure, for all Diseases;
And now Durst challenge Death to do it's worst,
And Meet him at more woepons, if it durst,

APPENDIX

Then ever Charletan, upon a wall,
Did Post him up, to Play a Prize with all.
And Rout him Easily, at all the Ills,
With which the Coward clogs the weekly Bills:
This b'ing Resolvd, He now began to count
To what his Fees, would in a yeare Amount:
And found 'em Rise (each Malady b'ing ceast
One with another) rather with the Least
Then Over-Rated, To a Sum more vast,
Then all the Publique Thieverys could wast.
Some times He thought of Building Hospitalls
And setting-up his Name, upon the wals,
Where those of all Professions, that had livd
By Physique formerly, might be, Relievd.
But then he Guest; That would but make them worse,
And hinder some to take a Better Course.
For those Endowments allways are Possest,
By none but those, that have deservd the[m] Least;
And therefore Rather Pitcht on Colledges
Where Lazy Drones might Study Sleep and Ease
And Dunces, that are Fit for nothing else
Might loose their time, Industriously in Cels;
But then He cald to minde, there are such Store
Of those Already, that to Set up more,
Where Greater Numbers Freely might Retreat,
And take Degrees, to Loyter, sleep, and Eate;
The Church, and State, in Time, might want Supplys
Of Able Men to be Imployd, and Rise,
And forcd to take in, tho against their Hearts,
Men of Indiffrent Honesty and Parts.
  One Afternoone, His wife unsatisfyd
With what her Share amounted, to Divide;
Who had endowd her, with some slight Disease,
To buy her Pins, and Trinquets, with her Fees:
After a Feind and Counterfet Caress
Of False, and Artificial Tendernes,
She thought, at last to whedle, and Trepan
Of some Maladies the Good old Man,
And told him in a Childs Affected Tone,
She must have more Diseases of her own;
For those she had already would not bring
The Money in; as tru as any thing.
And therefore some small Gruntling must to adjust
The Sum, b' allowd, Indeed, my Deare, it must,
Altho my only Naming of a Sum
Has made thee look a little Tiny-Grum;
For when but two are Buryd in a week,
It is not like that many should be sick.
And when Diseases happen to fall short

APPENDIX

I am not like to fare the Better for't.
What Times were Those! Had wee but had it then
When evry week eight Thou[sa]nd Dyd, or Ten!
And when we shal againe have such a Season,
I see but little Hopes, we have, in Reason:
And therefor, as I sayd, some Paultry Aile
Must be Allowd for what is like to Fail.

    Quoth he! That Mad Extravagance, The Pique
Of which your Sex Perpetuall is Sick,
That Longs for what, was never meant, for Food:
And Loath's as much the wholsom, and the Good:
I finde is Proof against the Greatest Pow'r
Of Medcine, though my universall Cure:
Is still unsatisfid in some Defects
And Faylings, of our Better Temperd Sex.
And Still, The Expectation of Fruition
Determines in as Vaine, and Idle wishing.
Have I not Freely given thee the Meazles,
With one as Rich and Hopeful a Disease else?
Only to buy thee Pins, and to Defray
The Charg of Trinkets, to be Thrown away?
That b'ing cast-up, have been found-out to cleare
(All Charges Born) Two Thousand Pounds a year.
And is not that Eno[u]gh to beare Expences
Of little Trifles and Impertinences?
At this Rate Nothing's Able to hold out
Untill, at last, thou Hast my Pox, and Gout.

    I thought (Quoth She) you had not been so Nice
Of Little Beggerly Infirmities.
At least if you consider who it was
That made your Credit first and medcine Pass,
When all the Dose of Ginger bread and Manna
And Isinglas, were but a Pen'north ana,
Or who it was, First supplyd your Tub
With Jorny-work, and brought in many a Job,
Helped you to Patient-makers, of the Trade
That trusted you to take off all they made,
Who payd your Rent? the Apothecary's Bribe?
H' allows of Course to all that but Prescribe?
That did not only Furnish the Disease,
But had you Freely Payd your Bills, and Fees:
When all your Busness was to talke of Symptomes,
Tho but of Th' Itch, and Meazles, or the Grincomes.

    'Tis tru Quoth he, this Little Shifting Course,
We have been forcd to take t' avoyd a worse:
And thou hast not been wanting for thy Part
In all a woman's wit can do or Art,
Nor must we wholly give it over, yet
Whatever 'tis our luck to loose, or Get.

APPENDIX

It has by others frequently been don
And wilbe so againe, when we are Gone,
Which make's me Confident, The safest Shift
And Easiest way to bee brought about is Thrift.
Thou knowst the Charges of my House and Table
Must needs grow more, and more, considerable,
And much must be, in Projects that begin,
Layd out at first for Drawing vouchers in.
For when 'tis Nothing, but Discourse and Talke,
Wee ought as much for all things else Defalke:
And much in Reason is to be allowd
For making New Designes (beforehand) good.
Besides the vast Expences for Materialls,
Of Dead Mens Bones embalmd before their Burials:
Proportionable Hogs-heads of May-Dew,
That are not Like to be Supplyd b' a Few.
With Competent Allowance of the mixture,
Of th' universal Spirit, The Elixer.
And Sevrall Inches of the Long-streit-Line,
To which such wonders Natrallists Assigne;
With equal Doses of th' ossacrum-Luz,
Th' Immortall Redeviver of the Jews.
And Central Fire, that Persecutes the Species,
Of Plants, and Minerals to the Superficies:
With Astral Spirits, and Intelligences,
All Probable to multiply Expences.
With other strange Ingredients never known,
And therefore Like to go the better down.

But if our Medcine do but finde Success
We shal not want for what supplys wee Please,
For all Inventions Difficult and Hard
Do seldom Miss a competent Reward.
But if it should unluckyly miscary,
Wee shal not want at least things Necessary.
For tho we commonly set-up so soon,
T'is Hard to Get in Practice, or be known:
Until w' have long applyd t' Apothecarys,
Nurse-keepers, Coffy-houses, Ordinarys,
All Sorts of Greatmens Laquais, and valets,
Only to Bayt our Hooks, and Spread our Nets;
Are sometimes forcd to Practice in Compliance
To others Humors, Things below the Science;
Have Tricks to set Diseases Back, and Aches
To Nicks of Idler times, Like Finger-watches,
And Prorogations to give Present Ease,
T' Adjorn, But not Recover a Disease,
With other curious Arts enough to live
In such Deare times, but not Grow Rich and thrive,

APPENDIX

Like that Physitian, who to get his fees,
Kept Store of Cats, to furnish him with Fleas;
That, when they bit the Ladys, Did him service,
To Pass for Sharpnes of the Bloud, and Scurvies:
Or He that held mens inward Fabrique lay
To Justify Anatomy, one way,
And that Mankind was made to none effect
But only for a Surgeon to Dissect.

As He that came up then, to fetch down whores
To fill the Cuntry's Magazins with Stores
And fill his empty, and exhausted stocks
With fresh Recruits for Botches, and the Pox.
And, when th' Infected Chare-women had don't,
He curd their Manges on his own account
And sent them up to follow their occasions
And bring down New Recruits the next vacations.

For when Physitians were from Rome expeld
All sickly People, their Diseases heald
With eating Cole-worts only, simply taken,
Without the least Ingredient of Bacon.

When Health is at it's Height, 'Tis Naturall
It should Decline Immediately, and fall.

So Rings made of the Bones of Hippocamps,
Are Amulets against the Rage of Cramps.

He that would Cure a wound, must have a Care,
To keep it close, from taking of the Aire.

The least and most Innocuous of Diseases,
Is Desprater, the Nobler Part, it ceases.

Has more wounds then the Man, i' th' Almanack
Run through by all the Signs i' th' Zodiack.

When evry Spot, produces but the Name,
And Nothing else, of Plants, that are the same:
And Fruit-trees have as great a Difference,
In their Productions, to the Dullest Sense.
Whence 'tis so hard to meet with an Ingredient
That to our own Præscriptions, wilbe obedient.

For when a Plant Degenerat's t' a weed,
They freely Pass, in one another Stead,
An Antient Composition, and a Fresh,
Have æquall virtue, over a Disease:
That 'tis Impossible, t' administer,
To th' Itch, and Mange, with safety, and not Erre.
Beside the Dangerous Gibberish of Pædants
To learn the Bumbast-Names, of all Ingredients,

APPENDIX

That No Man is permitted to be Sick,
But must be Cur'd, in Latin, or in Greek,
For No Men love so Naturally to Dabble,
As those that Pass for Learnedish, and Able.
That can put down (in fustian) th' Ablest Brushers
Of hinder Parts, Inculcaters, and ushers.
So he that knew a Tayler, by his Stale,
Because with shreds, H' had stopt the urinalle.

And tho He understands no Medcines Name
He Know's them all by Sight, and Common fame.
And has so great opinion, of their Skill,
That he Dares trust 'em, to Destroy, or kill.

For those that Do no Hurt, at least, secure
Their Patients, from the Desperatst Fit, the Cure.

The Patient give's the Doctor, Half th' A[d]vice
That He Return's, and for his Fee, Apply's.
When he Informe's him, of the first Accesse
And Symptomatique Freakes, of the Disease,
And Lay's out nothing, but as weake Reflexions
Upon the Sickmans Tru, or False Directions,
But oft exchanges for some other Course
When he Perceiv's himself grow worse, and worse.

Who ever was a more frequented Doctor
Then th' Antient Trig? or late Inceptor Lockier?
Created out of nothing, but their own
And all the Rabble's mandate, of the Town.
And did their Exercices, with Chimeras
Not much below the Sorbonists vesperys,
That Post their Theses, on their Colledg-wals
With great mens Pictures, t' own 'em, tru or false.

A very visitant's an Operator,
That strives with Flams to Practice upon Nature,
Tells what a Friend of [his] had strangly sufferd
In that Distemper, but was now Recoverd,
Untill the Leech must be calld in, to Try
Th' experiment, and virtu, of a Ly,
Mean while the wretched Patient is set back
And Desperater Infirmity o' th' Quack.

For most Liefhebbers usuall Relapse
Upon the News of other Men's Escapes.
Especially, if the Medcines operation
Have but a Hint, of Supererrogation
Which, when it is cunningly Designd, and layd
Bring's in a great Advantage, to the Trade.
And those, that Practice it, Have found it yeilds
More Patients, then Padua, or More-fields.

APPENDIX

That never Dub a Doctor, till he has
Givn Caution, not to Practice on the Place.

As wounds in the left Leg, tho ere so slight,
Are Harder Cur'd, then Greater in the Right.

Nature

And as in Animals the smell
Is plac'd by Nature Sentinell
Upon the Mouth; To pass, or stay,
All Aliments that go that way.

As Pliny's Partridges are sayd to Tread
Another Covey flying 'ore its Head.

So Beares (some write) are whelpd with Staring eies
As large as when they are at their largest cize,
Altho at first no bigger then a Rat,
Until they have been lickd up to their Height.

Thunder the sole Artillery of Nature
Is Fird with Cold, and chargd with Ice, and water.
Thunder is Natures Demy-Canon-Piece
Dischargd by a Cold Antiperistasis.
It is in vain, and Ignorant to force
What Nature do's beyond her Constant Course,
That, when she's Idly over-chargd, Recoyles,
And all that's meant T' impose upon her, Spoyles.
The sea itself throws up the Beech and sand,
To Keep it from Incroaching on the Land,
And th' Amplest River's never wont to Rise
Above the Level, where it's fountaine Lys.
The smallest Parcel[s] of the universe
To all the Rest o' th' world are Forrainers,
To Human Nature and Mankind within
The Species only Hardly are of kin.
And what the one half's naturally for,
All others as Impetuously abhor.

For all the Ruggedst and most Desperat
Of Storms at Sea, are in a narrow strait.

A single Thumb can equal strength command
To all the Fellow-fingers, of the Hand.

So lions hunt conducted by Jackalls
And little fishes steare the vastest whales.

As men with little fishes, use to Bayt
Their Hooks, and Lines to tempt and catch the great.

APPENDIX

Birds have but one Lid, to preserve their sight
From taking Hurt, when upon trees they light.

As in the Middle of a River, Tides
Run Counter, to the Current of both Sides,
Against the Streames of Chanels, take their Course,
Where Th' are encounterd with the greater Force.

The Sun drinks up the Bottom of the Seas
Before the Top, because it is more Fresh:
From whence it is the upper Superficies
Is only usd to prey on ships by Fishes.

Great Rivers th[r]ough as spacious Lakes wil Flow
And never mix their waters, as they go.

Tides do but Change the Natrall Al[t]itudes
And Constant Elevation of the Fluds.

As Gold and Silver's in the Basest Mine,
But 'tis not worth the Charges to Refine.

As Thistles satisfy an Ass
And serve for Sallets to his Grass,
Whose Rude, and undiscerning Pallate
Is fit enough, for such a Sallet.

As by Antipathy Eagyptian Rats
When ere they meet, destroy and Strangle Cats.

London's serv'd with Fire by water
That both together serve all Nature.

As sure as Tumbling of the sheets
The Death of men in mortal fits.

As violent windes when th' are most fleet
In Motion, are affirmd to sit.

As Natural as 'tis for Sots
T' Admire Phantastique Idiots.

Begotten by an Excrement
And born to give ease and Vent.

There is no Doubt of things that are Perpetual
And in a Constant Course of Nature Settle.

So all the Backs of Fishes are by Nature
Dyd of the Native Culler of the water,
But all their Bellys, like the Airy Light
Of the upper Superficies, perfect white.

APPENDIX

Chymistry

What wil not Pass for the Philosophers Stone?
An Art that has no Language of it's own?
But is all Canting: a Confounded mixture
Of all things else, as Quintessence, Elixer,
A Spirit, and a water, and will Passe
For any other Thing, it never was.

Magique

The Irish never Pray a Cow or Horse,
But Spit upon it Constantly of Course,
To Keep it safe and sound against the Harms
Of witches Conjurations and their Charms.

For if the Devill Publiquely were known
His Deeds of Darkness never could be don:
And therefore 's Forc't to manage out of Sight,
His Hidden Principality of Night.
Whom evry Small Magician would Disarme,
And send upon his Errands, with a Charme;
And when his witches, are but ceizd upon,
He gives them over, to be Hangd for None.
And, tho H' was bid to get behinde by Christ,
Is chargd T' Avant before, b' an Exorcist;
That Bayts his Hook with Witches to Beguile,
And take 'em for his Croney-Imps a while,
That when the Time's expird, the false Deceiver
May take 'em in his vassellage for ever.

The Antients usd to Draw th' Eumenides,
Th' Infernal Furys, in a Fœmall Dress.

The Devill who was Hidden in a Barne,
And Thrash'd unmercifully in the Corne:
Durst take no Notice of the Blows, for Feare,
Of being worse usd, if H' had been taken there.

For Fooles are but Familiars to themselves;
That serve the Cunning-men Instead of Elves:
And all their Magicall Contrivances,
Impose upon themselves, with greater ease.
With Drams of Opiats, and Narcotique Doses,
Intoxicate Besotted virtuosos,
Make Nets for Sub[t]le vermine in the Aire
Invisible as Snakes in vineger;

That use, to fetch, and carry, all Diseases,
And Spot Infected Bodys like Punaises;
Preserve 'em Ready Bottled-up in Glasses,
For all occasions, and Designes, and Places.
And vent in Blasts of Poysond winde,
Their Share of Mischief to Mankinde.

Make Charms t' Inable Irish Ratcatchers
T' Inchant and Poyson vermine with, in verse.

And these are th' original Traditions
Of th' Antient Incantations of Magitians
And all their Magicall Infatuations
But upstart Heresys, and Innovations.

As Learnd as those Great Doctors of the Chair
Among those Academiques of the Aire,
That Offerd to Dispute with Cardans Father
In Metaphysiques of the upper Æther;
From whence he grew a Deep Philosopher
As well as Mad man, and Astrologer,
And by their Nearer N[e]ighborhood, with the moor
Knew better, how those Mystique feats are don.

Astrology

How Planets in Conjunction, evry minute,
Are Chopt, and Changd, yet Do their Busnes in it:
While those, that since the worlds Originall
Have been unfixt, yet never Could forestall.
As 'tis Impertinent for cheats to fix
Among the understanders of their Tricks
But rather strive, To change the Aire, and stroule
To catch the Ignorant, and unwary foule:
Whence 'tis the Stars, that dwel in th' upper Æthers,
Have all their Intrests, only in the Neather:
And as their Influences are sayd by some
To give us, what they never had at home
So all their other operations, tend
To as Ridiculous, and vaine an End:
For there's no other work of Nature else
But æqually th' Events of things foretels.
As Monsters, that for nothing were Designd,
With Omens, and Prædictions stock Mankind:
And greatest Empires steard their Interests
With Flights of Birds, and Garbages of Beasts,

APPENDIX

Or He that Future Earth-quakes Could foretell
By Feeling Mud, i' th' Bottom of a wel,
As true as Conjuring with Virgils verse,
T' unriddle all mens fates, and Characters:
For all the Stars Conjunctions, and Ecclipses
Prædict but Picking-Pockets, worse then Gypsies.

The Sun, and Moon, in Heaven, at so vast
A Geometrique Distance, have been Plact
That all their Different Dimensions, Here
Do of a seeming Magnitude, appeare.
Some make the Sun to th' under-Earth draw neare
So many Scores of his Diameter,
But cannot tell, If th' Antients Days, and Houres,
Were of a lesse, or Greater Length, the[n] ours:
But have no more Ground, then Astrologers,
Have for their worms, and magots of the Stars.
But have less Sense, for all they undertake
Then all their Frenzys in the Zodiack.

And if the Heavns be but one Constellation,
As all to Any, have the same Relation,
(Except those Few Erroneous Vagabonds,
With which, The Earth, as falsly Corresponds)
The whole to all the Rest may Freely clame
An æquall Property, beside th[e] Name.

The Best Astrologers are always made
Of Crackt Mechaniques, of some other Trade.
And when the Planets are Designd to Erre,
How much more must the Dul Astrologer?
When those, He is to be directed by,
Are Namd from Fraud, Imposture, and a ly?
And have their most Erroneous Santrings made,
The Principles, and Basis of a Trade.
For Tradesmen, and Mechaniques are the Primest
And Best of all Astrologers and Chymists.

Only the Devil is, yourselves aver,
The most Profound, and Deep Astrologer:
With whom no other, ever durst compare,
For, as hee's Prince, and Sultan of the Aire:
Without whose Licence, and Commission had,
No Influences dare Presume to Trade,
For 'tis but Labour thrown away, T' Incline
Unless he give them, Special Quarentine:
And Hee, who Perfectst understands their use,
Do's æqually know where to Pick, and choose,
Then whether you Apply yourselvs to him:
This way, or any else; 'tis but a whim.

For whores, and Hectors, when th' are Past
Their Labour, and grown Old and Cast,
Turn Naturally, as the Imps
To other Harlots, Bawds, and Pimps.

As those that buy a Salmon-draught
Pay for the Fish, before 'tis Caught.

Suppose a Figure Calculated,
The Geniture exactly stated:
Another of the Self-same Person
With æqual care, and Animadversion
By way of Horary-Inspection,
Th' Effect, of this, or that Erection
Must be the very same; or else
The one, or both must need[s] be False.

Or He that snapt the Guards of Jupiter,
And listed them to serve the Emperor.
When all the sevral ways of virtuosing
Are but a formal Sort, of Dry Deboshing:
Which made the A[n]tients Celebrat an Owle
As th' only Proper Philosophique Foul.

For witches are no sooner taken
By their Treacherous Imps [forsaken],
And when by Law, th' are ceasd upon
Are only Hangd for being None.
As Empson with the sivs he wrought,
Could never finde his Fortune out.

One Night the Sun far more obscures,
Then all th' Ecclipses He Endure's.

All Poynts of Heaven, are at Noone,
As soon as Entred by the Sun.

A Prophet has no need of Being wise
When all his Art, in Dreams, and visions Ly's.

And like a Second sighted Scot
Could foresee, all the Heavens Plot.

Did not Menippus mounted in the Moon,
Discover all, that upon Earth was don?
Or shee at th' Entrance of th' Ecclyps, foreshow
The Macedonians Kings overthrow?
And did not only make the Dire Portent
But was the Real Cause of the Event.
For th' Antient Romans, only by their Cuninge
In our Profession, stoutly overrunne him.
And if wee can th' Ecclyps it self foretell
Why should wee not th' Event of it, as well?

APPENDIX

Love

Love's but a Running of the Fancy,
A Clap of fond extravagancy,
That, if it be not stop'd in time,
Break's out in Botches of vile Rhime:
And when 'tis with Love-powder laden,
And prim'd and Cock'd by miss or Madam,
The smallest Sparkle of an eie
Give's fire to his Artilery.

Th' Arabian Goat Inragd and Furious turns
When any other Beast has touchd his Horns.

Some Love with Orenges, Boon Christians,
And some with Lemon-Pils and Citrons.

Loves Arrows are but shot at Rovers,
Though all they hit they turn to Lovers,
And all the Desprate Consequents
Depend upon as Blinde events,
As Gamsters, when they play a Set
With greatest Cunning at Piquet,
Put out with Caution, and take in
They know not what, unsight-unseen.
So Fairest Gamsters at the Banes
Take paines, and Plod to win by chance,
And study how to Draw a Prize
With greatest Skil at Lotteries.

Like Bucephalus Brutish Honor
Would have none mount but the Right owner.

As Ladys, not to see nor heare
A Play, frequent the Theater,
But to be seen, and tempt some Squire
At a feigned Passion to take fire.

When by the swelling of the Girdle
The Lover findes his Soyl fertile.

Welth is all these, she that has that
Is any thing she would be at:
Wit, Bewty, honor, virtu, vice
Are always valu'd by the price;
For what are lips, and eies, and Teeth
Which Bewty fights and Conquers with,
But Rubys, pearles and Diamonds,
With which a Philter Love Compounds?
Or what is Hair but threads of gold
That Lovers Hearts in fetters hold?

APPENDIX

Your eies are not two Pretious Stones
Nor twinkling Stars but radiant Suns,
That Dazle those that looke upon yee
And Scorch all other Ladys tawny.
Your Shining Hair of the same Fleece is
With that of Hev'nly Berenices;
Your Lips no Rubys, but the Staine
Of th' Hev'nly Dragons bloud in graine:
Your Teeth not Pearles but whiter far
Then those of th' heav'nly Dog-star.

One who was still as warme with Love
As a Dutch-vrister keeps her Stove,
And weares in winter time between her thighs
To keep her Dyke from freezing with Ice,
But always fayld to hit his mark
Unless it were in Whetstones Park,
Where Lovers Arrows oft Rebound
And those that shoot at Random wound.

As Irish Lovers use to make Adress
By Darting Rushes at their Mistresses,
That do more Execution then the Darts
And Bows and Arrows us'd to Conquer hearts.

As Ladys of the Greatest Quality
Make Love themselves to those of less degree.

For Love, that is both man and Beast,
Is equally with Both possest,
And like a Pythagorean Soul,
Run's through al Sort[s] of fish and Foul,
Retaine's a Smack of evry one
He shews his mighty Powr upon;
And when so ere hee's mad and fond
Has something of the vagabond.

That in the Game of Ladys Hearts
Know how to pack and Marke the Carts.

What ere the Devil shee do's ayl
This Bearers Spouse looke's very Pale,
And, by the Culler of her Cheekes,
Eate's cheese of Chalk and bread of Bricks.
[I] know y' have Store of Remedies
[For] maladys much worse then this;
Then, pre'thee, looke among thy bookes
[F]or something that wil Cure her lookes,
[For] hee's asham'd to have it sed
[He] has not had her Maydenhead;
Though, to Confess the truth to you
(Who are my friend), it is too true;

APPENDIX

For he is no such sturdy Porter
T' indure a Woman made of Morter;
For, if h' had venturd to have —— her,
[He'd] be no Husband, but a Doctor;
And he is loath to have his ——
To save his Purse turn Emperique.
Then, Prethee, thinke upon his Case,
And give him something for her face;
For while it looke's so like a Clout
[It] will still be lent and wedding out.

His face on which appeard no bristles
But gentle as the Down of Thistles;
But as those Thistles weare the softest down
To hide their Prickles til th' are grown,
So did that softnes do Lovs Darts
Until it surprizd and piercd their tender hearts.

That Bewty Nature give's to flowrs
And sweetnes too is Dul to yours,
And that bright Luster which she paints
On Eastern Stones, grows dim and faints,
More glorious then those she limnes
On Tayles of Birds and Eastern Jems.

That Relique must be most Divine
That's kept in such a bewteous shrine.

Marriage

The —— spawn of Love and Feare
That Haunt, and Hag the Marryd Paire
And make them both Ride one another
With Fits of th' Incubus, and Mother.

Devour by Great, and little Friends,
Like Candles burning at both ends,
The Insolence of Great Relations,
And Petulance of mean, and Base ones.

[Who] Would have hang t' have been possest
Would do as much to be Releast.

                    That with worldly Goods
Indow each other, Claps, and Nodes,
Until his Horns become the Theams
Of Western-pug-wit on the Temes,
The Everlasting Subject matter,
Of Repartees, upon the water.

APPENDIX

Whence Lovers who had often been slighted
For b'ing Adventurers, unknighted,
As soone as once they have been Dubd
Or else more honorably Tubd:
Their Names in Blazon vamp'd with Sirs
Have now the Damzels, and their Spurs.

Make marriages a Greater Sin
Without Degrees then those within;
No wonder then th' are no more ty'd
To Articles on either side,
But rather use their Freedom more,
And own it, then they Durst before:
For those who take but one at once
All others for the Time Renounce,
And that's sufficient to perform
Engagements only made for Form,
And, if at Certaine times th' are free,
'Tis at their Choyce when they shalbe.

Who Henpeck none to that Degree
As Grave men in Authority,
And still the more th' are great and Rich
The more they Hug, the Dear Caprich.

For whores of Hectors get the Pox
As Pullets have been clapd by Rooks.

Turn's her gentle Soft Compliance
To Endless Quarrels and Defyance.

That would not sel his Liberty
His ease and Quietness to Buy.

Marryd a Crossgraind Lady, more Ill Naturd
Then Malice (in the Letany) and Hatred.

A man that like a By-blow, and his mother,
Were æqually ashamed of one another.

Especially, so great a Son o' th' Church,
Th' h' was thought to be begotten in the Porch.

Women

So Homer stole his wars of Troy, and Greece,
In Ægypt, from a Spinster Poetesse.

A Lady with Top-gallant Fowr
And Busk behind her and before,
Relict of all those virtuosos
Disceasd of French Stoccades in Nose,

APPENDIX

Or all those Hospitaler-knight[s]
Disceasd of wounds in single fights.

Make Nature operate out of Season
Or women to submit to Reason.

As easy as a Lady Buxome
Dos make a Cully of a Coxcomb.

Lust

Had got a Grant for al the Bodys
Of Gossips, Gammers, Dames, and Goodies,
And by Abolishing the Notion
Of Chastity, Prevent Deboshing.

Who[se] Forehead spread as Lazy and Full
As his wh' was Got and Horn'd b' a Bull.

That do their work in Hugger mugger
As Cautiously as Pædants Bugger.

And Swathd together by a Surgeon
As Feeble as a kick of Sturgeon.

As Common as it is for Misses
To Pass with Revrend men for Neeces.

The Jews that by their Laws allow
An ox to Thrash as well as Plow.

Honor

How many Sinners Dissolute, and Common,
By Cuntry Squires made Honest Gentlewomen?
And won, and wedded out of Puddle-Dock
To Eldest Sons and Heirs of Antient Stock.
When Having in the Quality of Neeces
Servd out the best of all their time, for Misses.
By uncles, or Imaginary Cusses
Have been put off to worshipfullest Houses.
B' Adopted Uncles, have been past for Spouses
To Worshipfull, or Honorable Houses.

That's puft up with his own conceipt, and swels
With vanity, and Pride, and nothing else,
Like empty Bladders, i' th' Pneumatique Engine,
Blown up with nothing; but their own extension;

APPENDIX

Whose Titles, like French Noble Mens Degres
Are but distinguisht by their Gallowses,
Where those that on Most Numerous Pillers stand
Take Place of Monsiers of the Greatst Command,
And he['s] the Richest Person, that is full
Of most work for his stallion-Horse or Bull.
When he that by the Crop, lets out t' his Tenants,
His Land, and ovens, has the greatst convenience.

As one Descended of the Empereres
Of th' East; In Rome, sold lately all Th' Arriers
And Tittles in Remainder, of the Honors
The Turk usurp's still, from the Legall owners.

For t' hang ones self is counted No Disgrace,
But to be hangd, by others, vile, and Base.

And when the Sottish Ignorant extold him,
Found Human Nature was too weak to hold him.
For Puft-up Greatness has a Speciall Care
Before its Haughty Selfe, of standing Bare:
Is his own Betters, and not Proudly sufferd
Among Inferior Persons to bee Coverd,
But like an Usher, is obligd to stand
Before himself with awful hat in Hand
And by his own Respect, t' himself, invite
His lesser Visitants to do him Right.
Least others freely should Presume to do,
The same things, in his Pers'nal Presence too.
But by his own Example take occasion,
To Imitate his ways of Application.
For Haughty Greatnes must not stoop so low
As those that only serve to make it so:
Must turn it's careless Back to all Inferiors
And proudly look before upon Superiors.

Approchd with Distant aw and Reverence
As terrible as Plague, or Pestilence,
But no man Introducd without a fine
Untill h' has wayted out his Quarentine.
For Saints noe other votaries Receive
Untill th' have watchd and wayted out their Eave.
And Lay for't most Religiously, before
They can be freely Admitted to Adore;
And when they are, An Insolent vouchsafe
Is all the Favour they can hope to have.

So the Great Cham proclame to the Grand Signor
When he has din'd free leave to go to Dinner.

Put of[f] His Hat, and Bowd, and made Addresses,
And Boun Professes, to his Footmans Sneezes.

432

APPENDIX

Grew Proud, tho of the wretchedst Priviledge,
To Ride to execution on a sledge,
To shew his Rank, while those of less Deserts,
Are only alowd to be conveyd in Carts:
Tho he Disparagd, and Contemnd them for't,
As born t' an æquall Penance through the Durt,
While He was Drawn more Easily, and Cleane,
To shew the Diffrence of the great, and meane.

The World

As Diamonds of Ordinary weight,
For evry Caract, beare a Certaine Rate,
But, when they once outgrow the Common Size,
The least Addition multiplys the Price.

'Tis easier to Counterfet a Stone
Of any Dy, then Diamonds of None.

As 'tis more gallant to command
Then to be able to know how,
So 'tis to Censure then to know,
And to Controll then understand.
For knowledge is a thing below,
And 'tis more noble to appeare
Above it, without Charge or Paines
Or the Dul Industry of Braines,
Then earne it at a Rate so deare:
For as all People would be rich,
But Fortune only ha's the Power
Or Industry to appoint which,
And makes some Poore
Only t' advance the other more,
Soe all men would be wise and know,
Though Nature only orders who
Shalbe and shal ne're be so.

Devour's his Fortune in a Trice
And eates himself like Adam out of Paradice.

The Magique of Mens Native Soyles
Though 'ere so Homely, stil Prevailes
To make them rather Settle there
Then —— better any where.
And 'ere they dy would faine Return
To be buryd, where th' were Born.

APPENDIX

When that which Order's all the matter
Is th' High and mighty Powr of Nature;
Nature the Universal Sovraine
And Custom her Colleague, that Govern.

He that's Drunkest
Is in the Fairest way of Conquest.

The world for other Sins was drownd
Before the use of wine was found,
When Fishes that by Drinking Live
Were only worthy a Reprive.

The smooth fac'd youth freed from his Tutors care
Loves Dogs and horses and the Chirgeon Aire,
Prone to debauch, but obstinate t' advice,
Regardles how his time and money flys.

Our Sighs and Feares give no relief
To them at al but our own grief.

So when the unwise are Powr shun
Into the Contrary they run.

And as in Ships of war we do not State
Their greatnes from their Burden or their Rate,
Nor as in Merchantmen count by their Tuns
But by the men she carrys and the Guns,
So he, that would know her Proportion just,
Must reckon by her mischief and her Lust.

Vulgarity

That went to Heaven in a slip
As Seamen swing from ship to ship,
And might have been for just desert
Raysd from the Dongeon to the Cart,
And after Risen step by step,
Untill he fetched a higher leap,
And swung to New worlds by the Neck,
As sea men do from Deck to Deck.

Morality

A man may be a foole with sense
As well as mad with Patience.

Punishment[s] do not grow less
But rather by Delays increase;
For all they by Forbearance gain
Do's only aggravate the Pain.

APPENDIX

A Man that swell Pride and Fat,
Like the Scotch Minister of State.

Who when they are Intrap't and Caught
Are but possest of what they sought;
And if they like the Artifice
They need not quarrell at the Price.
The Spider do's not seek the Fly,
But leave's him, of himself t' apply,
Nor do's the Trap pursue the Mice,
But freely they themselves surprise.

Avarice

As Poorest Beggers are the Best
And those the wretchedst that want lest.

And those who venture to climb high
In th' Air, for want of Aire dy,
As men on Tenarif are se'd
For want of Aire to fall down dead.

To whom no Honey combe nor Sugar
Was ere so sweet as filthy Lucre.

To nothing tru in no Condition
But filthy Lucre and Ambition,
And, like a Greedy Cormorant,
Devouring but increast his want;
Knew all the Secret ways t' amasse,
And drove more Trades with Publique Cash
Then all the Scribes and Publicans
In Princes Customs and Divans.
So greedy and Insatiable
He layd on Right and wrong a Gabel.

Fortune

Our Fortunes now are such, Remorse
Can never mend but make it worse,
And 'tis Below the worst of Fooling
To think to Help it by Condoling,
To spend our little Time and thoughts
In Quarreling and finding Faults:
For None are wretcheder undon
Then those Condemnd to wayl and mone.

APPENDIX

Wealth

Why should not wit as wel as wealth
Be raysd by Forgery and Stealth?

Vice

One who had no Leisure
Between his Bus'nes, and his Pleasure
To think of any thing but what
To th' one, or th' other did relate.
—— Could carry on his Load
Like Mules that travel in a Road
And understand which way to take
As well asleep as broad awake.

A Prodigal nere fayles to hate
Those who have purchacd his Estate,
Although at ere so great a Rate;
Is safer trusted with untold
Cabals and Secrets, then with Gold.

Begotten as great Princes wed
By Proxy in his Fathers stead.

One that was Peevisher and testier
Then Botches when they Rage and fester;
Revenge, and Mischief, and Despight
Were both his Bus'nes, and Delight.

Though Squemish in her Outward woman
As Lewd, and Rampant as Dol Common.

Poetry

This may be don by those that shall come after,
But no Age wil indure its own Satyr.

There has been such a glut of Plays of late
The Plenty of them ha's brought down the Rate.

Prologue

If I could hope you would not tell agen,
Fayr Ladys and most worthy Gentlemen,
I've something to say t' yee; but am afeard
I should, by some within, be overheard:
In brief 'tis only this, wee have within
Two Poets such as yet were never seen:

APPENDIX

One is a writer, and of great Renown,
But by an envious Faction now kept down,
And yet in this new Play he has thought [fit]
To entertaine a Partner of his wit,
One that did never write, yet understands
How to put of[f] what Ly's on th' others hands,
And now th' are setting up with a Joynt ――――
To deal for what you at the Dores have payd,
Like Indian Merchants, that, for Beads and Trinkets,
Make rich Returnes of Orient Pearls and Ingots.
I wish they may do so; but how so ere
We are secur'd, and run no hazzard here:
They have insur'd us against al mishap,
You shalbe pleasd, and cry it up, and clap.
W' have let 'em but our house, the Cloaths, and paines,
And have no venture in their loss, or gaines.
Then, whether you do Cry it up, or down,
The gaine or loss is sure to be their own.

A man may be a Poet that nere writ,
As some that cannot read set up for wit;
Critiques no doubt, that might impartial seeme,
If good and bad were but alike to them.
But they, out of a Bravery of minde,
Are always to the weaker side inclin'd,
As Courts of Justice use: else right and wrong
Would not be able to hold out so long.
And such a Court are some of you that sit
By your half-Crown-Commissions in the Pit.
To Judg, according as your Talents are,
Between the King and Prisner at the Barre.
But, as some Judges, whether wrong or right,
Are found, in hanging men, to take Delight,
A Poets ruine gives you more content
Then Fals of Great men in the Government,
Though you gaine nothing by 't: For seldome comes
A Better (say's the Proverb) in their Roomes.
For Poetry, like other Heresies,
By being persecuted multiply's,
And, the more wickedly some authors write,
Others to write worse are encouragd by't.
Thus, whether you do cry Plays up or downe,
The Thing is found in th' end to be al one,
And the best way is to let both alone;
For, should they leave the Trade, they would get more
Then ere they did by dealing in't before:
For some are made by being crackd, as wel
As Birds are hatchd by breaking of the Shel.

APPENDIX

He has observd there's but one certaine way
To please you al, in writing of a Play,
And that's by Scribling such a Paultry one
Of Purpose as you'r surest to cry down:
For then you have your wishes to the height
And al you're wont to hope from those that write;
Which is uncharitable and severe
To those that have so hard a Province here.
For what in England can a Poet hope,
Though one of late beyond Sea is turnd Pope,
In spight of Robert Wisdom, and some feare
The rest o' th' Tribe wil fare the worst for 't here.

As Birds and Beast[s] of Rapine heretofore
Had their Heads payd for at the Churches Dore,
So Poets have at ours: and if you were
As Just in al your other Censures here,
You were brave Judges, for to steal and prey
On Others wits is now to write a Play,
That's like a Cuckolds Child, no man can gather
By any Feature of it who's the father,
But, as in China when a Child is born
The Man lies in for't in the womans turne,
So when a woman do's but write a Play
Some male-wit fathers it and ha's a day:
Hence 'tis that while such Numbers strive to write,
So few among them honestly come by't.
For few bring any thing here of their own,
But, like a Case in Law by Counsel drawn,
Put in, and out, b' advice before it pas,
Til 'tis another thing from what it was,
Or else 'tis stollen out of Pedlers French
That is French wit: while you upon the bench
Allow it and beleive the Author made it,
Because he did not tel you where he had it.
Those rob the State of wit, and have undon yee,
Like those that have to do with publique money,
That, in their bottomless and hel-like purses,
Store up the Peoples money and their Curses.

He do's not write to gaine Applaus or Fame
And therefore that way cannot miss his Ayme.

Has taken of[f] the Quibble and the Rimes
To make it fit the fashion of the Times.

For, as a Durty Pond is aptest
For Launching of an Anabaptist,
So Durty Fopprys are most fit
For those of Durty braines, and wit.

APPENDIX

For Poets are more rayld at then the Gods
Or Stars by Lovers when they fal at ods.

That swel and looke as Big, as if th' had payd
An Empire for each Comedy they made,
As once a Learned Critique but to own
An old Song, swore he freely would have don.

Plato, thinking to exile
All Poets from his Sancho's Isle,
Unwittingly expeld himself
His own Poetique Commonwelth,
With all his Sect of Followers,
Mere Poets, only bating verse.

Government

The Sun ecclips'd in water best appeares,
So should the fall of Kings be seen in Teares.

What has this Government don more
Then what the other did Before?
When State, Religion, and the Laws,
Have all espousd the Good old Cause.
The selfsame Ministers imployd,
That were before on th' other side:
And all that has been Past, and don
Is but the same Continud on.

Raysd to preferment in the State
Like False Scale, for want of weight.

Mighty monarchs, are exprest
In visions by some horned Beast.

A Government so silly and perverse
Is only fit to be destroyd by Beasts.

For what can hold, when truth, and kings
And wine, and women Rout all things?
'Tis Desperate to trust th' Advice
And Pardond Faith of Enemies,
Who use t' accompt the Grace and Favor
But binding to the good Behavior:
For there's no Livery, no Ceasin,
Nor Fines in alienating Treason,
Nor Bonds, but merely at Discretion
One Minute to secure Possession,
Who thinke they have the greatest wrong
Because they are but half-unhung

439

And only listed for the Gallows
Against the next mischance that Follows;
Which they believe has rather earnd
Revenge, then Fayth to be returnd;
And those that have venturd and came of[f]
Long most to make a Second Proof.

    False Designes require more Care
In Management then Just and fair.

    As Princes Favorite, when th' are Boys,
For all his Faults by Proxy pays,
So in Miscarriages of State,
The Favorite is sure to pay't.

    When once a Princes wil meetes with restraint
His Pow'r is then esteem'd but his Complaint.

    That meet not to consult, but Snap
And th' Adverse Interest intrap
To snatch all small Advantages
As if they Playd a Game at Ches.

    More subtle at unriddling Cabals
Then Foxes are in Æsop's Fables
At over-reaching other Beast[s]
And Jugling with their Interests.

    Nothing sinks so soon as Empires
Upheld by Feeble Crazy Tempers.

    Bees are Governd in a Monarchy,
But 'tis some more noble Femal Bee;
For Femals never grow Effeminate
As men Prove often, and subvert a State:
For as they take to Men, and men to them
It is the safest in the worst extreame.

    The Gracchi were most Resolute and stout
Who only by their Mother had been taught.

    And though he livd a Beast and Sot
That still his word, and Faith forgot:
And nere was, till he came to Dy,
In Perfect minde and Memory;
To make his will, in which He gave
Profusely, what He could not save:
As first his Soul to his Creator,
But nere Considerd the maine Matter;
Whether 'twere Just He should Receive
A thing he did not give, but Leave,
Which He so Carelessly Had Kept,
The Devill hardly would accept.

APPENDIX

As those, who by the Law o' th' Land,
Are Sentencd to be burnt i' th' Hand:
Give thanks upon their Bended knees,
For Having th' honor of th' Imprese.

That have more Politique Intrigues
In Poynts, and Knots, and Periwigs,
Then Statesmen have in breaking Leagues.

Law

For how can a Lawyer though 'ere so infirm
Have Leasure to dy in the midst of a Tearm?

That poore Rogues fate and thine are one,
Who being ready to bee hangd
Behold's the worke himself had don,
The Hemp he has so often bangd;
And when hee's dead wil hang in th' a[i]re
As sure as Mahomet's Sepulcher.

Laws to their Executions Prefer
At best but th' Executioner.

For when a Nation is a Slave,
What Crowns of Monarchs can be safe?
And still the less we wast our Right
W' Injoy the greater Freedom by't.

For Constant Right's The Tru streit Line
To which such wonders some Assigne,
For Forfeiture in Law, or Reputation
Is Irrevocable as Privation,
From which it is as much Impossible
To be Redeemd, as Souls that are in Hel.

As, in Utopia, Judges Hands
Are burnt for taking Bribes, with Brands,
To give the Court, and Hangman Reall
Security under Hand, and Seal.

That use t' ingage Both Houses, in Contest
Against the Nations Publique Interest;
Trot up, and Down, the Hall, to meet, and Heard,
And cast up what Course next is to be steard.
Make Publique Tests to Sweare to, ex Officio
With many [a] subtle Politique Proviso,
T' establish Perjurers, that can forsweare,
And Honest Men, that cannot do 't, cashiere;

APPENDIX

All urgent Busnes of the House Abridge
To nothinge else but breach of Priviledg.
Admit the Important, and the Necessary
No nearer minding then Præliminary
And vote the Sessions, more Compendious
To be against the Orders of the House.

Th' expences of Dividing what th' had gaind
Had Run the Publique money behind Hand,
That Rapine, Sacriledge, and Providence,
Could not Supply th' extravagant Expence;
Nor turning all the Churches of the Nation
Into one singular Impropriation:
Nor Sale, nor Sequestration, could suffice;
Nor Decimation, forfiture, Excise,
Nor Selling Scots, by th' Head, our Pretious Brethren,
To stock Plantations, 'mong the Indian Heathen.
That Prayd, and taught, and Fasted to Devour
With more Insatiate Greediness, and Powr,
And Run through all the Difficultst Affairs
Upon th' Account of Zeal, and Fasts, and Prayers,
And by their owne self-seeking of the Lord
Gave Revelations as Designs concurd,
Destroyd Religion by Humiliations
And strove to sow, and Sprinkle down three Nations.

For Laws and Money are the same,
And from the selfsame Derivation Came.

As Daughters pass for Sons, in Legal Authors
But not all Sons Indiffrently for Daughters.

As in Sealing writings, He allone
That take's the seal off, 's held to Put it on.

Are held of Bums the bravest fellows,
The Hangmans Life-guard at the Gallows,
Without whose Ayd, the Populace
Would hang him up, in his own Place.

As equal Jurys use to Hang one Half
Of Criminals, and th' other moeity save.

As sinners in the Church of Rome do trust
To be savd by the Suffrings of the Just.

A Pirat do's more mischief of himself
Then all together Storm, and Rock and shelf.

When He, whose Present Turn it is to Read,
Do's both their Talents, and their Bodys, feede,
Expounds upon all Diffrent Sorts of Meates,
And on, at least, five Hundred Dishes treates,

APPENDIX

Resolv's the Case in Law, the Poynt, and Reason,
Of ven'son, Fish, and Foul, that are in Season:
And with a most Judicious Tast, Defines,
And states the Cases, of all Sorts of wines:
And all his welcome Hearers Edifys
With Hammes of Bacon, Tongues, and Red-Dear-Pies.

Treachery

A Man as Virtuous and Good
As ever in a Galley Rowd.

Discover Secrets but in whispers
For th' Easy Credulous to Disperse.

Whose words and Deeds are Counterfet
And like a Printers letters set,
Are not to be interpreted
Unles by being Backward read.

As Hangmen aske Delinquent Mercy
And truss 'em up with wondrous Curtsy.

No Jew ever had more Care
To do his Busnes neat and fair
And not like Judas, who betrayd
So like a Bungler, and Delayd
But was more Civil in his way
And never let his Master stay.

Like Rookes that use to drive subtle Trade
By taking all the Odses that are Layd,
And who so ever hap's to have the Best
Are sure to win, or save themselvs at Least.

But strive's t' assert a Supererrogation
Of Inhumanity, and Profanation,
Disdains to tread in any Beaten Path
Of Vulgar Treachery, and Breach of Faith,
But findes new ways, as some have don of Lechery
The Sponsors and the Collarys of Treachery,
Take's naturally to all Expedients
Of the great work, to ruine Government;
For those that have been hangd, and Cut in Quarters
For Treachery are but the Devils Martyrs,
Had servd in all Perfidiousnes, between
The Legal years of Sixty and Sixteen.

APPENDIX

Injustice

Was falser then the Mercury
He trust's to, in his hollow Dy.
There was no Gouty Politique
Of which he could [not] streit be sick
And wel again with equal Speed
As with his Bus'nes best agreed.

Look'd as Politique and shrewd as
His antique Predecessor Judas,
For those that make, no more keep Oaths
Then Taylors make and weare al Cloaths.

War

For what but Risings was the Stubborn war
Between the Clans of York and Lancaster?

He thought no Stratagem so warlike
As ceazing Danger by the Forelock,
Nor any martial Disingagments
So honorable as Detachments.
He knew the force of woman Conduct
By h[i]s Cuntry woman bold Queen Bonduc,
And what H' had found himself by proof
And therefore Soldierlike drew of[f]
Surprizd him in his new Redout
Without a Sentinel or Scout.

Glory gaind by fighting's little
Unless it be in Stealing Vittle.

Hope

That use to magnify in Microscopes
All that concern's their Losses, or their Hopes.

That some times Pass for greater, sometimes lesser,
According as they happen to take Measure.

Feare

Feare keepes all other Passions out
As Lesser Pains decline the Gout.
There neede's no other Conjurer
To Raise all Sorts of Fiends, but Feare,
That give the Enemy no quarter
When 'tis upon it's last Departure.

APPENDIX

Courage

Mens Courage is not Limited, between
The Periods, of Sixty and Sixteen;
In which The yonge, are Entred in the List,
And when th' have servd so many years, Dismist:
The only Trade that men begin so yongue,
To serve a Prentiship, that lasts so longe.

Life may be boldly taken from Superiors,
But never Given, but to mean Inferiors.

Some warlike Nations have Receipts for Courage,
By seasoning, with Gunpowder, their Porrige,
That Renderd Cowards Bold, as if th' had layd
The Devill, in the Pummel of a Blade.
That in the Fortresses, upon their Backs
Instead of Belts weare mighty Zodiacks,
In which they Paltry little Cutlaus ty
Like th' Antique Cabales in a Needles eie;
That out of Politiques, make Choyce of those
As Proprest Engines to Encounter Fo's,
That, if their Courage should (by Chance) miscarry
Against too Confident an Adversary,
Th' excuse of all the Feat of Armes ly
I' th' feeble weapons Imbecility.

Religion

As Confounding Languages Forerun
The Fall and slavery of Babilon,
So Canting brought the thorow-Reformation
T' inslave and over-run the English Nation.

All this is Right—but 'tis a Fiction
To pass the Trick upon Conviction,
Or put it on th' Accompt of Conscience
Or opend eies,—a Flam, and Nonsense:
'Tis Temper make's a Renegado,
To which Conviction's but a Shadow.

Their Perilous Designes upon
Hierusalem and Babilon,
Which, being faythfully expounded,
Meant only Cavalliere and Roundhead,
Two Names the Rabble understood
Both went by in the word of God.

APPENDIX

T' assume the Cause like th' old Croysado,
And weare it only for a Shadow,
Set up above all Ordinances,
But only those of Dreames, and Traunses,
As if the Powr of Godlines
Were but a Lunatique Disease,
And all New-lights but meare Effects
Of th' Incubus, and Apoplex.

Despise the Common-Prayer, as vaine
And Superstitius, and Profane,
Because they meet with no Occasions
To shew by reading Dispensations,
And ablest Saint[s] can make no shifts
To hold forth, the meanest of their gifts.

What was once but mere pretence
Is now made good by Providence.

All Miracles of Furthest Places ceast,
And wonders of the Revealation-Beast:
Whose Feats, that had so long, and oft appeard,
The Joy, and Admiration of the Heard:
And had a Magique Influence to win,
And whistle all the Long-ear'd Rabble in.
Had been so many yeares, in Publique shown
That now they were grown out of Date, and known.
And brought to a Generall Nauseous lothing,
Men would not see, not heare of them for nothing:
The Heavy'st Blockheads Scornd, and over-reacht,
Th' Impertinent Designes, they Prayd and Preac[h]t.
All Characters of either Good, or evill,
That walkd in utter Darknes, like the Devill:
Or usd to lurke in one anothers shapes,
Broke out in Murthers, Thieverys, and Rapes:
And that which had before been understood,
For Good, Prov'd Bad, but seldom Bad the Good.

As Evill Spirits, have been, in Adust,
Black Choler, sayd, to find a Tempting Gust
(From whence their own Familiar-Imps, like Leaches
Are Nursd, and Suckled, at the Teats of witches)
So crazd Phanatiques make The Just, and Good,
Take Pleasure in their Bishops-footed Bloud:
And from their Foul unwholsom Constitutions,
Derive their Spiritual Graces, and Infusions.

A Mungrel-Breed of Men, as Cross, and Aukerd,
As those that were Producd, by Stones cast Backward:
Or Evangelique Myrmidons, turnd Saints,
From Busy, and Pragmatique swarms of Ants:

That strive to cheat their Publique Interests,
As Rookes to Pilfer one anothers Nests.

So Oliver, when he had sought the Lord,
But was affeard to give him back his word,
Had Dund his Privy Counsellers to Dun him,
To take the Crown, and Royalty upon him.
Had Forgd him selfe an Answer, and Subornd,
His Pack of Seers, what should be Returnd:
But durst not undertake it, for his Eares,
And upstart Saints, as wel as Cavalliers.

'Tis now the most Impertinent, and vaine,
Of all the Hopes we once had, to Complaine.
And no less Mad, to Dream awake of Force,
As long as all the British world Concur's:
When those we freely Made, the supreme Powrs,
The English Nation, have Disposd of ours
Impossible, by us, to be Restord;
By Acting Politiquely, above Boord,
But by the craftier Intrieges of State,
T' Impose, and Juggle, and Insinuate:
The Devils Dark Georgiques, which some write,
He Practices, to sow his Tares by Night
Heapes-up, and Spreads his Dong, on Barren Soyles,
To bring up Plenteous weeds of New Turmoyles:
To make us, undertake, to Prog, and Tamper:
Between the Hall below, and Painted Chamber:
For who but we alone, are Fit, and Able,
To Manage so Mysterious a Cabal?
Have Gifts, and Dispensations Necessary,
Such wonderful out-goingses to Carry?
Wee who have been bred-up, and Edifyd
To steare Designes of Providence, and Guide:
Have Powr to Rais them, for the Causes service,
Supplys of Mony, Able men, and Purveyse;
It is but only shifting of the Scene
For th' Antient Actors, to come in agen:
The Plot, Designe, and Actors, are the same
Persue the self-same Argument, and aime:
When all the Church Preferments in the Nation,
Are but one Generall Impropriation.
Which tho w' Indeavor to Inlarge, and Stretch
Wil never, to our Hopes, and Projects reach:
Altho w' have Bred-up all our Ablest Pupils
In all the Curiositys of Scruples:
To know why Horrid Crimes are swallod easy
And little Faylings Difficult, and Queasy:
The sevrall Methods of Improving Scismes,
Upon the Least, and Slightest Criticisms:

447

APPENDIX

As those that could not beare with Bays, and Rings
Made nothing of the Heads, and Bloud of Kings.
'Twil serve to make our Former Doctrine good,
The Covenant can never be withstood:
Nor any Powr on Earth prevayl against
The soveraine Right, and Intrest of the Saints;
Who Human Nature æqually Improve,
By vice below, as wel, as Grace above:
And carry all their Actions, closer then
The Good or Bad of other Pious Men.
For when Religion's settled in a state
'Tis nothing, but a Church Incorporate,
In which, both Saints, and Sinners are inrould,
And all their Gifts by æqual Charter Hold:
A spiritual Rabble, where the Bad, and Good,
Are undistinguisht Priviledge allowd;
And when 'tis Renderd Uniforme, is made,
And Regulated only like a Trade;
Designd for Natural, and Carnal Ends,
And not Religious unity of Friends:
So all our zealous taking Parts, and Siding
At first grew out of Nothing, but Dividing:
And all our Prizes, Playd at Fasts, and Prayer,
And Holding-forth, but New Designs, to share;
When Saltmarsh, Sedgwick, Arrowsmith, and Jenkins
Had Jealous Eies of one anothers Sinkings
And evry Pretious, and Enlightend Brother,
Suspected th' over-Earnings of another:
'Twas only sharing of our Dividends
That first of all, Divided Saints, and Friends
Untill they turnd to Sects, that had their Being
From mutual Jealousy, and Disagreeing.
Did nothing but from others Lights Dissent,
As stubbornly as Laws and Government.

When all their Saints, for virtu, and Religion,
Might have been Chaplains to the Devil Legion:
And when the Independent Disciplin
Had turnd us out, and brought their own tribe in:
The Good old Cause became another thing,
To make their Patriarch Oliver a King:
Which those that had been most Imployd upon,
Obstructed all, that others would have don;
Provd Brethren of a Negative Profession,
With Independent Consciences, and Reason.
Tho No men else Free wil so much Disown,
And what th' are most Devoted to, Cry down:
Had rather suffer all the Despratst Ills,
Then to be Debard the wretchedst of their will:

APPENDIX

And when wee by th' Immutable Decres
Of Providence, can Sentence whom we Please,
They gave themselvs, a voluntary warrant,
Of æqual Powr, to execute before hand:
Enabled both the one, and th' other Saint
Like Æacus, in Hell, and Rhadamant;
As both a Judge to Destiny, and Sherife
T' Arraine, Condemn, and hang-up or Reprieve:
That servd for Partys, witnesses, and Jurys,
And Executioners to all the Furys.
And scornd as much In Spirituals t' obey,
As in Profane Ingagements, but for Pay.
Were wont the Christian Faith t' adulterate,
With Jewish Principles of Church and State,
And cobbled a Religion up, that's neither,
The New, nor Old, but forgd of both together,
Made Peacefull Precepts o' th' New testament,
For Rapine, Bloud, and war, as Pertinent
As Orthodox, and Apostolique Hold
As all the Desolations of the old
For since both æqually wee, Scripture name,
In all things else they ought to be the same.

A Levits Concubine, that Nation stood
In more Distruction, Massacres, and Bloud
Then Greece, and Troy did either give, or take,
In ten yeares time, for Bewteous Hellens sake:
And, if they were so lavish of their Bloud,
Why should the Saints less Freedom be allowd?
Especi[a]lly that have so great a Stake,
Deposited for what they undertake?

Which makes some other Zealots, to Proscribe
And worry all, that are not of their Tribe:
Omit no time t' Increase, and Propagate
The mutual correspondences, of Hate:
For no wars else, of Turks, and Renegados,
Were ever so Inhuman, as Croysados.
That Breaking Ground Accompt as th' only Course,
Of taking in the Gates of Heavn, by Force:
Or working in a Strong fortification,
The very same with working-out Salvation;
And therefore spends his Longs, and melts his Greace,
In Picking Quarrels with the Publique Peace:
And where there was no kinde of Government,
About Absurd Dividing it Dissent;
For no seard Conscience ever was so fell
As that, which has been burnt with zeal.
At conventicle Dutys, do's but say
His more then Houres Canonique, and not Pray.

Who censure, and condemne the Papist[s] for't,
Because they do the same thing, but more short;
That Bear's up Confidently, by mere force
Of Ignorance, against his Governors,
Indures no Power on Earth to be supreme,
As Empty Boates sayl best against the Streame.
For Nonsense being neither False nor true,
A little wit to any thing, may Screw!
Tell all the sottish Tales of Former Clergies
And lay 'em only to the Moderns Charges
That make the Independent-Church Metropolis,
Of all their Simoniacall Monopolys:
And forcd the Brethren to conforme to one,
That in their Hearts, and Principles had none.
But like the Antient Sanctum of the Jews,
Held nothing else, but Lumber, and old shoos!
And since Christ, when he was to be betrayd,
Appeard Impatient of his b'ing Delayd
He is more civil, when it lights in's way,
And has a Special care he should not stay.

For as the Turkish Sultan makes his Farms,
To beare him Mighty Crops of Men at Armes:
And evry Cuntry Messuage, and Timar,
Instead of Beasts to breed him Men of war.
So where the Brethren Are Impourd, They turn
To Bloud, and Massacres, the whole Concern:
And make all Cuntrys serve for Nurserys,
To furnish Desolation, with Supplys:
And tender Consciences, are always found
Of such Recruits, to bee the Richest Grounde.

For the Religion, when it wages war
It go's against its Native Character,
Yet nothing has a greater Powr to further
Their out-ward men, then Sacriledg and murther.

And as their Interests agree, or Differ,
Make evry man a Saint, or unbeliever.

That leave the Church, their Hives, like Swarms of Bees,
To build in Rotten Holes, or Hollow Trees.

Zeal

Proselyts are stil most Real
And busy with their smattring zeal,
Like other Thievs, that Before Christmas Steal
To keep the Holy Feast with Greater Zeal.

APPENDIX

Cruelty

Who Taunted with a Silly Flurt
Buryd alive an Army for't.

Conscience

The Tongue of Conscience is no slander,
For, though it call a great Commander
Pultron and Coward to his face,
He nere considers what he says.

Prelates

Who since they Could not make a Priest a Prince,
Have made them Convertible ever since;
And, by Inferring a supposd mixt Person,
Maintain the proud sophistical Conversion,
By which all Truth and Reason 's Sacrifict
To th' Arbitrary Intrest of a Priest.

Popery

As Proper as Figleaves did Suite
With Eating of Forbidden Fruite.

The Catholique Religion, for the Souls Good,
Make's no Distinction between Truth, and Falshood
And as they use to falsify a Blow
'Tis all their Art to pass upon the Fo.

Infallible as the Pope made Henry th' Eighth
Defender of his Signory of Faith,
Who in a few months Provd a brave Defendant
And did his uttermost [to make] an End on't.

As Naturally as a Jesuite
To th' Gallows turn's a Zealous Proselyte.

As Fewest Popes, and Cardinals, and Priests
Of al Saints else, are in the Churches Lists:
And more Consecrated women, then
The Rubrique can Produce of Sainted men.

For Pasquil and Morphorius are the Sum
Of all th' Apostles modern Acts in Rome.

APPENDIX

As Barbers in the Church of Rome Degrade
Or shave a Priest int' Orders by his Trade.

As Papists cannot Pray to Saints, unless
Th' are Prompted to it by their Images,
Forget th' are in the Number of Mankinde
Unless th' are by a Deads head put in minde.

Trade

Ships are the Only Caravan
That Trades upon the Ocean,
And travels through the wildernes
And Barren Deserts of the Seas
Without the Feare of Beasts of Prey
Or wilder Arabs in their way;
And the wooden Dromedary
The Merchant and his Cargo Carry.

For trade has wonderful Effects
T' Improve the Factory of Sects,
For which Dutch Brethren, in Japan,
Renounce the Name of Christian:
Turn Musselmans again in Afrique
To Propagate the Faith of Traffique.

As Holland Merchants when the States in Peace
Do finde their Actions constantly increase;
But English Banians, that Deal with Sects,
In Doubtful Times improve their Lewd Effects.

Friendship

Those whom Conscious Crimes indeare
Are Friends ingagd by Hate and Feare;
Are but united with the Cement
Of Fellow-Sufferers Agreement.

Infancy

The wit of Children that begins too soon
Before th' outgrow their Infancy, is gone.

For words are Fitter for a Child to learn
Then Matters of a weightier Concern.

APPENDIX

The only Cloaths, that Embryos weare in th' womb
But leave them off, when in the world they come,
And Put on others which the Midwife trims
To fit the Fashion of their Tender Limbs.

Musique

Musique is Bewty to the Eare,
That charm's the Soules of all that Heare;
Attracts Devotion, with its Aire, and words;
To string its Beads upon its Charming Cords....
Can se[w] Devotion to an Aire
And set a Saraband t' a Prayer.

Stinke

A Stink that's able
To cure th' Infection of a Stable
And Prove as great an Antidote
Against the Horse-pox as a Goate.

A Goat, the Antient say, is never
Without an everlasting Feaver.

Raysd like a mighty Lord in Mary-land
Where he that stinks most, has the greatest Command.

Sidrophel

Imploy your old Malitious Arts
To undermine all Mens Deserts,
And, like a Pauper, question those
Who you believe have most to loose,
Discover Counterfets and Fooles
By your own Practices and Rules,
Fall foul on all that's good, or Rare,
To gaine a Base Informers share,
And lewdly intitle others to
What you your self are wont to do,
Although it yeald you in Returne,
Nothing but Infamy, and Scorne.
Provoke the Enemy by whom
Y' have been Subdu'd, and overcome

And by the Law's, and Right of war
Have forfited t' your Conqueror
All Right and Title you had once
T' your Inward, and Outward Dunce.
You take a Right Course to reclame
The world from Infamy and Shame:
For Slander e're so foul, or true,
Turnes Honor when it comes from you,
And though no Flesh can 'scape the wrong
Of your unworm'd, Impetuous Tongue,
That still stand's ready to attack
Th' unknown, and known behinde his Back
(As Cutpurses nere minde what Sum
Nor who it is they take it from)
You never slip the least occasion
T' invade the Instant Reputation:
As Heraulds in a wolf or Beare
Make Tongue, and Nayles one Culler weare,
So you, whose valour's to defame,
Make Slander, and Revenge the same;
And, as when haughty Sathan fell
From Heaven, to the Pit of Hell,
He made it his first worke t' intice
Mankind to fall from Paradise:
So 'tis your Aime to bring all down
To that lewd Infamy of your own;
An Envoy to negociate in
Transactions of Decrepit Sin,
In Baudery a Heretique
And Pimp to those, that whip and Lick,
Has vented many a Strange opinion
As if the Dev'l himself were in him.

Unclassified verses

Iris, on the Banks of Thames,
Her Eies bedewd with Teares,
To Chloris sayd, Reserve your Flames,
For Men are Flatterers.
They'l sweare and tell you, it may bee,
They Passionately Love,
But after ten days Absence—see
What Traiters they wil Prove.

VARIOUS READINGS OF, AND ADDITIONS TO, *HUDIBRAS*

That had the greatest orator
Of all the Greekes, who heretofore
Did fill his Mouth with Peeble-stones
To learn the better to pronounce,
But known his Harder Rhetorique,
He would have usd no other trick.

I. i. p. 6, l. 23.

Our Style from War to Love wee turn,
And tell how Hudibras did burn
In Amorous Flames, what wofull Distres
He was Reducd to by his Mistres,
What Misery and Griping Paine
He sufferd from her Coy Disdain.

II. i. *beginning*.

He thought it now the fittest moment,
The Lady's Am'rous Pangs to Foment,
The Hopefulst Criticall Occasion
To Pass upon her with his Passion,
The likelyst Planetary Crisis
For Stratagems and Love-Surprises.
Who ever was a Homelier Lover
Then Hercules th' Heroique Lover Drover?
Yet, when he wood at Quarter staf,
What Ladys Purtenance was safe?
For Sympathetique Blows as wel
No doubt may wound as Powder heal.

II. i. p. 112, l. 32.

God dos not put those strict Restraints
Upon his Favourites the Saints,
As on his slaves the Reprobates
The Drudges he abhor's and hates;
No[r] do's he look for that Attendance
From Privy Chamber Independents,
As from the Presbyterian Rout,
That wayte like Sentinels without.

II. ii. p. 134, l. 36.

Whether the Ganza's, or a Scarab,
Or Mahomets Hors, by birth an Arab,
Did beare him up, or that he flew
With bladders of Attracted Dew,
Since Authors mention to the moon
Men only those four ways have gone.

II. iii. p. 158, l. 37.

455

APPENDIX

As Campanella, when he writ,
Striv'd to look like his Readers wit:
So Sidrophel stil striv'd to looke
As wise as those to whom he spoke,
And oft would shake his Pensive head,
To stir his wit up, when 'twas dead;
As Clerks their Ink bottles do shake,
To make it shine more bright and black.

II. iii. p. 165, l. 27.

With Cowitch meazled like a Leper
And smutch'd i' th' Nose with Guinny Pepper,
With Drink and dewtry cast in Trances,
And all the madst extravagances;
Dismounted into slough[s] and Ditches
By Fiends and Spirits raysd by witches,
And Conjurd into Raving fits,
Like one that's outed of his wits.

III. i. p. 205, l. 33.

Imploy's mee out, upon Perpetuall Jobs
Of Gimcracks, and Fantastique Jigambobs;
Or grinding Glasses in a Punctuall Minute
For Mysterys which they Believe are in it.
That keep me in insufferable Feares,
And everlasting Danger of my Eares;
When Guiltlesser Delinquents have been Scurgd,
And Hempe, in Docks, on wooden Anvils forgd.
That have not had such Diabolique Hanks,
Upon the Easy Rabble, of all Ranks
Nor ere Injoy that Fatall Influence
To sway their understandings, and their sense.

III. i. p. 206, l. 5.

That think their Talents most adroit
For any Mystical exployt;
To deal in Love, and News, and weather
And thievs, and Matches, altogether.

III. i. p. 206, l. 38.

The Dev'll had granted him a Lease
Of 's Life, for secret Services,
Which Hee made ore in Trust to mee;
A[nd] I, t' appeare a Just Trustee;
Found out a Flaw in 't, which I knew
Would make [him], when I pleasd, Renew:
And therefore when the Time drew nigh;
I put his Bill in Equity,

And Bid the Devill take his Course;
But he who knew that Medcine worse,
Then the Disease, Let fall his Suite,
And Fled to Hell, t' avoyd Dispute.
But yet, conceiving himself wrongd,
And knowing what t' his place belongd,
That, tho he Could not touch a life,
Could Plague with Botches, and a wife:
He sent me that Mysterious Fob,
As he had don before to Job:
And gave th' ungratefull wretch Commission,
To use me in this sad Condition.
To pay m' in kinde for all my Sins,
As whips are made of Horses Skins.

III. i. p. 207, l. 13.

When all his Suite is but a mart;
For if he win the Lady's Heart,
Upon the Marrige-day is payd,
Or Hour of Death the Bet he layd;
And all the Rest of bett'r or worse
Is but a Looser out of Purse.

III. i. p. 212, l. 15.

With Rhime, and begging Presents prove
To make Returns of Hearts and Love,
As Indians, for Glass beads and Trinkets
Exchange rich Stones, and Pearls, and Ingots.
For there's no Mystery nor Trade
But in the Art of Love is made.

III. i. p. 223, l. 17.

As in Dreames, The Hands and Feet
Are not so vigorous, and Fleet;
But when th' ingage to strike or run,
They both fall slow, and faintly on:
So did the Renegado Knight,
Perform his waking Dream of Fight.

III. i. p. 226, l. 18.

And Ingeneres the Best Divines
And Sou[n]dest Doctrine, Drawing Lines;
Or taking forts and Sconces in
The safest way to Conquer Sin;
And make military Discipline
Reveald to be by Right Divine;
Or Men of war to overcome
The Flesh and Devill with a Drum.

457

APPENDIX

Else what can Engines and Edgd tools
Pretend to do with saving souls?

III. i. p. 235, l. 5.

The Persian Magi, who were Brothers
To those that got 'em on their Mothers,
And held unqualifyd t' enjoy
That Dignity any other way,
With all Submission had giv'n place
To this unmixt and purer Race;
So we and they became of kin
Wh' are both our Sons and Brethren.

III. ii. p. 239, l. 21.

As Politique as if one eie
Upon the other were a Spy,
(And Jealous as if both his eares
Had Eavesdropt what each other Heares)
And to trepan the one to think
The other Blinde both strove to blink.

III. ii. p. 248, l. 29.

As if the Changling had been truckd
In Clouts by witches, whom he suckd
The Magique from, to turn himself
To any Figure like an Elf.

III. ii. p. 249, l. 3.

For as, at th' ends of Games, 'tis Lawful
Before the next to Cut and shuffle,
He understood all Common Places
Of Treachry and their Intricases;
The Doctrine and the Discipline
Of all Cheats, moral and Divine;
The Price of Principles, and Rates
Of Shifting them at Turns of States,
And always valewd them the more
The oftner th' had been Sold before,
For he believd Perfidiousnes
Was, like the Smal Pox, a Disease,
Which no man's Temper's free against,
But first or last the Bloud attaints;
And only those are Treason Proof,
Wh' have had it once and are come off.

III. ii. p. 249, l. 25.

Still the Ignoranter they provd,
Became the Stiffer to be movd;
For Fooles are Stubborner t' obey
As coynes are harden'd by th' Allay.

III. ii. p. 251, l. 35.

APPENDIX

Was this the Mystery we meant
In th' Holy League and Covenant,
To take it like Tobacco then,
Only to be blown out agen?
To Hold up one hand for a Brother,
And Pick a Pocket with the other?
That all the Bus'nes of the Cause
Was but to tickle Eares with Straws,
And Pick the Purse of John a Nokes,
That did but Scratch it, like Squire Cok[es].

III. ii. p. 252, l. 23.

'Tis true, we are in some Confusion
For want of Zeal, and Resolution.
When Haughty Prentises Rebeld,
And beat their Masters in the Field,
And after venturd to reduce
The Guards at Whit-Hall, and the Mues,
But, fayling in the Interprise,
Took in the City, in a Trice;
And kept it with a Strong Recruite,
And Fresh Supplys of Horse and Foot,
Till Gallant Hughson, with a Handfull
Of Men at Armes, resolvd and Manfull,
Drew up, where th' Enemy made Head,
And shot an Aple woman Dead,
Put th' Haughty Enemy, in Spight
Of all their Confidence, to flight,
And took the Town, with th' only slaughter
Of his great Rivall a Translator.

III. ii. p. 252, l. 31.

Till finding th' Hangman like to bord,
Our Vessels grappl'd to his yard,
T' avoid the danger tack'd about,
And turn'd our vile Commanders out,
To put in others in their steads,
Of stouter hearts, and wiser heads,
Who quickly got the weather-gage,
And then came boldly up t' engage,
Maintain'd couragiously the fight,
And put the Enemy to flight.

III. ii. p. 266, l. 25.

To keep out Surplices and Rings,
Was fitter for your wit then Kings;
Or cast the Quakers out and Ranters
For out-reforming Covenanters;

459

APPENDIX

Or banish Rosemary and Bays,
And Pyes on Christ-tide holidays,
Fitter for Talents of your rate,
Then botching of a Church or State.

III. ii. p. 269, l. 23.

Those whose Intrest lies between
His keeping-out, or bringing-in,
Mean nothing but to make a Mouth,
And take th' Advantages, of both,
Like Rookes, who drive a Subtle Trade,
By taking all the Oddses layd.
Which Side so ever has the best
Are sure to win, or save at least:
So they have no Design to bring
But Cunningly hedg in the King
And that secur'd, which side th' event
Takes Part with th' are Indifferent.

III. ii. p. 269, l. 35.

When the Scots had march'd to Wor'ster
What Presbyterian ever durst stir?

III. ii. p. 271, l. 37.

The Burning of the Rump

Nor were our Powr, and Interests abroad,
Contemptible, if Rightly understood;
Who, next the Catholiques themselves, are Best
Of all, secur'd with Forraine Interest.
In France are Backd, with zealous Huguenots,
And in the Northern Parts, our Brethren Scots:
In Holland have their Diffrent Churches Prayers
With Salves only to their Trade Affaires;
Have lately much obligd the Piemonteses,
By owning of them in their greatst Distresses:
Were Fellow-suffrers in their Persecution,
And Payd our æquall Shares, of Contribution;
Are in a Strickt Alliance, with the Suisse,
And league with theirs, and our Metropolis:
That from a Paultry Town is Come
By our Assistance to Contest with Rome.

A Speaker with a Mace before it,
Cut by an Artist in a Carret,
With many a Tatterd Talisman
For Bradshaw, Ireton, Scot, and Vane:
Next Statu's, they have shown much Art in,
For Tichborn, Munson, Downs, and Martin;

APPENDIX

With Lambert, Desbrow, and the Rest,
In Proper Charecters exprest:
All which, with Rumps, are on a Flame,
And our Approaching Fate Proclame.
More Ominous then Comets Tayles,
To all our Junto's and Cabals.

Made Images in Bung-hole-clay
For Peters, Clement, Scroop and Say;
Another Bore the Name and Stile
(Though but a Calf's) of Fines, and Lile.
A Goat's with Squibs and Crack[er]s farting,
For Representing Harry Martin.

Through all the Flaming Kennel Course us,
To shoot the Fiery Gulph, like Curtius,
As if the Fortune of the State,
Depended wholy on our fate:
For what do's all their Fury mean else
By sacrificing Rumps in Kennels?
By Burning Fundaments, and Hanches,
But to supplant us Roots, and Branches?
To Burn the most Refin'd of Christians
With Postique Botches like Philistians?
To make our Patriots Ridiculous,
Scorch'd in the Touts, like Chaucers Nicholas,
And Sacrifice our Hinder Quarters,
More like to Heretiques then Martyrs,
To Blow us up, worse then the Plot;
To charge their Morter-piece, For Shot
With th' House of Lords, and Fire the Hall
Instead of a Granado ball?

And now stand ready with Granados
Of Squibs and Crackers, to invade us;
And ev'ry Jornyman and Prentice,
With Rumps in Kenels represent us;
And now are Damning us, and Drinking
Strong Ale and Curses to our Sinking.

III. ii. p. 278, l. 17.

For none but Jesuits are allowd here,
To Propagate the Faith with Powder;
For what can serve their Pu[r]pose fitter,
To Prove their Church Derivd from Peeter?
Who sow it like the seminarys
Their Brother-Saints, of Cape Saint-Mary[s]
Who Plant it, and as Sturdily
Believe 'twil grow and multiply.

III. ii. p. 279, l. 20.

461

APPENDIX

The Roots of all Trees are the Head,
By which they are maintaynd and Fed;
And therefore all their Tops and Branches
Are but their Rumps, and Arms, and Hanches.
Were not the Fundamental Laws
The Rump, and Fundament o' th' Cause?
The Cause which we have vowd t' intayl
And settle on our Heires Male;
And therefore Rump's a name most fit
For those whose Busnes is to sit.
A Peacocks Tayl's more Rich and Gaudy
Then all the Feathers of the Body.

III. ii. p. 280, l. 18.

Nor is this News to us, or more,
Then what we might expect before:
For when when we had been renderd once
The Subject Matter, of Lampoones,
The Argument of Storys, Libells,
News, Quæres, Politiques, and Quibbles:
In which which we have been sayd, and sung,
And Clinch'd and Pund upon, so long,
'Twas no Hard matter, to forecast
How long our Government would last:
For when our Folly had renderd us,
And all all we did, Ridiculous,
Men have obeyd, as much in Jeast
As we have usd our Intrest;
And when a State becomes a Farce,
There needs No Prophesy of Stars
Nor long-tay[l]d Comet, to Presage
Implicit Changes to the Age:
The smallest Conventicle-Prophet
Might Dream awake the Ruine of it;
For nothing can Destroy a Nation,
So soone, as Fooles in Consultation.

III. ii. p. 281, l. 25.

Before the Bluster of whose Huff
All Hats as in a Storm flew of[f],
Whose Legislative Nods gave Law,
And Frowns kept Multitudes in Awe.
Enact and ordaine with a looke,
And with as free a Breath revoke,
Adord and bowd to by the Great,
Down to the Footman, and Valet;
More prayd to then the Crowns of Hats
With knees bent to, then Chappel-mats;
Approach'd like Plague and Pestilence
With Distant awe and reverence.

APPENDIX

Had more bent knees then Alters-Floures
And Prayers then Canonique Houres,
More trusted to, then all the Creeds,
And prayd to, then a Friers Beades.

III. ii. p. 281, l. 29.

A Man, s' Impartiall in his Calling
That Right or wrong to him was all one;
Was never known to bee s' unjust
As when H' was Bribd, to Break his Trust;
So Just, That He who Bribd him first
Was never known to have the worst;
But, when they strove to give him most,
The Despratest Case was never lost.

III. iii. p. 298, l. 15.

Hudibras's Visit to the Lawyer

To this Brave Man the Knight Repaires
For Counsell in his Law-Affaires,
And though the Sage were not at Home
Were Led into an Inward Roome
And told, He should have Speed Advice,
To wait upon 'em, in a Trice,
Meane while the Clerke flew out in Hast,
And lockd the Dore upon them fast:
And left the Knight, and Squire, once more,
In Durance Closer then before.
    The Lawyer was that morning gone,
Some Miles off, to a Market-Town:
Where He was wont to Ply for Fees,
And Regulate Enormities
To vend his Trumpery-Opinions
With Turnips, Cabbages and Inions
And in the Market put to Sale,
Recognisence, and comon Bale.
But when his Clerk had found him out
And told him what he came about
How Long his two New Clients had
For his Advise, or Justice stayd
Three Howrs at least; to give him Handsel
To execute the Laws, or Cancel.
Why then, Quoth hee, 'tis ten to one,
The Birds before this Time, are Flown.
Flown! Quoth the Clerk, Th' are Fast enough,
I'l warrant 'em from Getting of[f]

463

APPENDIX

I have 'em under Lock and Key
Too well Securd to Run away.
That's Right, Quoth he, But wil the Gaines
W' are like to have, outwey the Paines?
Th' are such, as neare as I could Guess
That seldom faile to Pay their Fees;
True Virtuosos, and Lief-hebbers
Of Suits in Law, among their Neibours
That bleed wel, though the Dotterels
Are faine to Spare in all things els.
They are the Liklier, Quoth Bracton,
To bring us man' a Sleevles Action.
Then let us Trudge away a Pace
To ceaze 'em for our wefts and St[r]ays
As fast as Jockies Post to breake,
Or Padders to preserve a Neck:
Where let us leave 'em, while we tell
What new Exployts the Knight befell.

 Clapd-up, before hand, for their Fees,
The Knight, and Squire, in Little-ease,
Some Howrs had lay'n; and did not know,
How many more they were to do.
When wearyd with their Tedious Stay
The Knight to Pass the time away,
And Squire ingagd in Fierce Dispute
To Pass their Judgments on the Suite
And what they came to understand
Resolvd between 'em before hand
But wagd with mortal Heat to Squabble
As ignorance is apt to dabble
For none are fiercer in Contest
Then those that understand it least.
Just as both Partys were Preparing
To break the Peace and good abearing
They Heard a knocking at the Gate
That stopd the Desperat Debate
And forcd them both to wave th' Assault
And by consent to make a Halt.

 Soon as the Lawyer was at home
He sent his Clerke t' approch the Roome
Where he had shut them in the Pound
Like Beasts, for breaking int' his Ground
T' excuse his Masters great Occasions
Of Privat Busnes, and the Nations:
And let them know what Great Affairs
He had neglected, to do theirs.
What Clients he had wav'd and Fees
To serve them, and their Busneses.

III. iii. p. 299, l. 20.

APPENDIX

Additions to Hudibras

The Knight, upon a Turne of state,
Is care-ful not to come too late;
But, by betraying his own side
In timely Season, save's his Tide;
Leave's Cause and Covnant in the Lurch,
And set's up for the King, and Church.
Turnes true, and faythful, though against
His Conscience, and is highly advanc'd.

His Mantle buttond down before,
And ore the shoulders cast he wore.
It had been Red, but was turn'd white
With Revrend Age, as well it might;
For it the Civill war between
The Red Rose and the white had seen,
And in the Culler of the Cloth
Retain'd some Tincture yet of both.

NOTES

The Elephant in the Moon [1676?] *is printed from* The Genuine Remains.

In Thyer's MS. we find the following lines under the title *Verses wrote under the Same Sheets with the Elephant in the Moon:*

> Was not our Countryman, the Great Manage....
> (See p. 182, ll. 11–18.)

> The World has less necessity of Truth
> To find so many Work, as Falshood doth;
> For Truth has seldom been improv'd by Art,
> That rather studys Falshood to assert.

> Who like our Virtuoso Sidrophel
> That in a publick Tax is said t' appeal....
> (See p. 177, ll. 5–6.)

> Like Pliny's Partridges affirmd to tread
> Another Covy flying ore its head.

> Our making Ptolemy a Math'matician
> A King of Ægypt only by 's Profession.

> Our taking Ptolemy to be a King
> Of Ægypt, when the World had no such thing;
> Unless they made him such that use to go
> Between King Ptolemy and Spirit Po.

> Nor registring of greater Lyes
> Then all those Huntsmen cou'd devise
> And Falc'ners, which the Grecian youth
> Allow'd his Tutor, to write Truth.

N.B. *These four verses seem design'd at first by the Author to have been inserted after Line 218, but afterwards rejected, as one wou'd guess by a line being drawn through them.*

> The World's occasions cannot be supplyd....
> (See p. 185, ll. 23 sqq.)

> The greatest Lyars are observ'd t' appear
> Most credulous of all, they chance to hear;
> And tho' they ne're speak Truth themselves, they know,
> Are confident all other Lyars do.

> A Mouse, whose martial valour had so long-
> Ago been try'd, and by old Homer sung,
> And purchas'd him more overlasting glory
> Than all his Grecian, and Trojan story;
> Though he appears unequal matcht, I grant,
> In bulk and stature by the elephant,

Yet frequently has been observ'd in battle
To have reduc'd the proud and haughty cattle,
When having boldly entered the redoubt,
And storm'd the dreadful outwork of his snout,
The little vermin, like an errant-knight,
Has slain the huge gigantic beast in fight.

p. 5, l. 99.   See Butler's MS. fol. 68 r:

The old Arcadians that could trace
Their Pedigrees from Race to race
Before the Moon, were once reputed
Of all the Grecians the most Stupid,
Whom nothing in the world could bring
To Civil life, but Fiddleing.

p. 6, l. 123. unparalel'd,.   l. 140. were of.   l. 152. stor'd..
p. 7, l. 183. War,.
p. 11, l. 316. won't.   l. 332. see..
p. 13, l. 407. solit'ary.

The Elephant in the Moon—In long verse. *Printed from* The Genuine
Remains.

See Thyer's note (1, 26): *After the Author had finished this Story in short Verse,
he took it in his Head to attempt it in long. That this was compos'd after the other
is manifest from its being wrote opposite to it upon a vacant Part of the same
Paper; and though in most Places the Poet has done little more than fill up the
Verse with an additional Foot, preserving the same Thought and Rhime, yet, as
it is a singular Instance in its Way, and has besides many considerable Additions
and Variations, which tend to illustrate and explain the preceding Poem, it may
be looked upon not only as a Curiosity in its Kind, but as a new Production of the
Author's.*

p. 17, l. 9. accurate, as.   ll. 17 sqq. See Butler's MS. fol. 120 r:

When th' Antients only took her for a Piese
Of Red Hot Irn, as big as Peloponese,
And after them; The German Rabby Kep[ler]
Was the first Man, that undertook to People [her,]
Though at his own charg, with Inhabitants,
With Sub- and Privolvans, and Elephants,
Which cost him more, the virtuous say
Then Ruind al the Family to Pay.

p. 18, l. 35. who for.   l. 61. Privolans.
p. 19, l. 96. season their.
p. 20, ll. 125–126. See Thyer's note (1, 34): *These two Verses are inserted
instead of the following in the other Copy in short Measure.*

And in the Register of Fame,
Had entered his long-living Name.

NOTES

The Poet *had added the two following Lines in this Character, but afterwards cross'd them out.*

> And first found out the building *Pauls*
> And paving *London* with Sea-Coals.

p. 21, l. 171. Care..   l. 185. Pains..

p. 22, ll. 217–218. See Appendix, p. 404, ll. 22–23.

p. 24, ll. 298–299. See p. 166, ll. 1–6.

p. 25, l. 335. Monkey's.   l. 336. practise.

p. 26, l. 352. salving.   l. 384. Appearences.

p. 27, ll. 411 sqq. See Butler's MS. fol. 15 v:

> For Truth is to[o] Reservd and Chast
> By all the Town to be imbract,
> A Sullen Anchorite that dwels
> In Private Holes, and obscure Cels,
> Disdains assemblys, and Defys
> All Publique mixt Societies.
> Her Busnes is to live Retyrd
> And not to Ramble to b' admird
> Nor ventures Publiquely abroad
> But in Disguise for mankinds good.

p. 28, l. 449. specia.

Satyr upon the Royal Society. *Printed from* The Genuine Remains.

The title has been added by me. Thyer, giving this fragment in a note, says (1, 53): Butler *formed a Design of writing another Satire upon the* Royal Society, *part of which I find amongst his Papers fairly and correctly transcribed. Whether he ever finished it, or the Remainder of it be lost, is uncertain: The Fragment, however, that is preserved may not improperly be added in this place, as in some sort explanatory of the preceding Poem.*

p. 31, l. 15. went?.   l. 16. meant!.

p. 32, ll. 49 sqq. See Butler's MS. fol. 100 r:

> Springs on the Inside of the Earth Do run
> Directly upward, but on th' outside Down.

Satyr upon the weakness and misery of Man. *Printed from* The Genuine Remains.

p. 34, l. 1. Compare with the following lines in Butler's MS. fol. 80 r:

> Who would believe this wicked earth
> Should be a Nursery for Heaven,
> Where Nature only brings us forth
> At best to be found guilty and forgiven,
> And all wee can expect to do
> Will not pay half the Debt we ow.
> And yet as if that were   ·
> Too much for those eternal Powres
> [Our] great and mighty Creditors,
> Wee desperately dare

NOTES

[Not o]nly slight those Dutys they injoyn
But pay them Driblets in adulterat Coyne
And, for a little vaine excess, destroy
    So great a Mas of solid Joy.

        Let Merit sterve!
For to confer on those that do deserve
    Is not to give but pay,
The Thankes and obligations thrown away;
But he, that give's where there is no desert
    Shows the free Bounty of his Heart,
And settles all the thankes upon himself
Without allowing hungry merit halfe:
For he that gives to one that can pretend
    Cashiere's and pay's of[f] an old friend;
    But he, that give's where nothing's due,
    Finde's out and purchase's a New.

As Beast's are hunted for their Furs
So for their virtues good men fare the worse;
    For ev'ry Artificial Cheate
    Do's thrive by making fayrer shows
    Then that it do's but Counterfet.
Al Dress is but a meare Disguise
Put on to hide us from the world's dul eies;
    Al our fine cloaths
    Are but the remedys of our Defect
    With which our Nakedness is Deckt;
    And yet a greater glory boast
As if Mankind had gain'd by being lost.

        The world thinks nere the worse
Of what is purchas'd by the basest Course,
    But rather like's it as a Cheat
    That's wittily performd and neat;
    For what men cannot justly gaine
Believe's they ought by Roguerys [t'] obteine.

No Jesuit ever tooke in hand
To plant a Church on barren Land,
Nor ever thought it worth his while
A Swead or Russ to reconcile;
    For where there is no store of wealth
Soules are not worth the Charges of their health.

Spaine on America had two Designes:
    To change the gospel for their mines;
    For, had the Mexicans been poore,
No Spanyard had twice landed on their shore.

NOTES

It was the Gold th' injoyd,
For which so many Millions were destroyd
And so much Catholique Religion Planted
Which, if th' had wanted gold, they stil had wanted.

p. 35, ll. 43 sqq. See Butler's MS. fol. 134 v:

Mungrels of all Specieses, take the least
To th' Nature of the Generouser Beast;
And the[re]fore Mules are never heard, to Neigh,
But rather take to th' Parent-Asse, and Bray.

p. 37, l. 119. Heav'n.

p. 38, l. 168. See Thyer's note (1, 65): *Though this Satyr seems fairly transcribed for the Press; yet on a Vacancy in the Sheet opposite to this Line, I find the following Verses, which probably were intended to be added, but as they were not regularly inserted, I chuse rather to give them by way of Note.*

For Men n'er digg'd so deep into
The Bowels of the Earth below,
For Mettals that are found to dwell
Near Neighbour to the Pit of Hell,
And have a magic Pow'r to sway
The greedy Souls of Men that Way;
But with their Bodies have been fain
To fill those Trenches up again;
When bloody Battles have been fought
For sharing that, which they took out.
For Wealth is all Things, that conduce
To Man's Destruction, or his Use;
A Standard both to buy and sell
All things from Heaven down to Hell.

p. 39, l. 205. nice,. l. 213. subtler. ll. 223 sqq. See Butler's MS. fol. 110 v:

Things that are either Difficult or vaine
Are like Abortives that have more of Paine
Then lusty vigorous Births, are wont to finde:
And so 'tis in the Labours of the minde.

Satyr upon the licentious age of Charles the 2d.....*Printed from* The Genuine Remains.

p. 41, l. 38. Hell..

p. 42, l. 78. 'against. l. 80. Nature spite. Laws debauch;.

p. 43, l. 123. hold.

p. 44, l. 190. that those.

Satyr upon Gaming. *Printed from* The Genuine Remains.

p. 46, l. 23. tutelar.

p. 47, l. 39. Condition,. ll. 53–54. See Butler's MS. fol. 131 v:

As Indians with a Scarcrow-man of Straw
Use to encounter Lions, Hand to Paw.

473

NOTES

Satyr upon our ridiculous imitation of the French. *Printed from* The Genuine Remains.

In Thyer's MS. we find the following passage under the title *Verses wrote on the same sheet with the Satyr against our affected Imitations of the French:*

> No sort of Beasts from richer grounds remov'd
> To poorer Pastures, ever were improv'd;
> And, therefore, all our generouser Breeds
> Of Mastif-Dogs, and Spaniels, Hounds, and Steeds
> In France convey'd degenerate to worse
> Then Jades, to draw in Carts, and mungrel-Currs.
> Only young Squires, and Knights, and Gentlemen,
> Laquais, Valets, and Pimps, and now and then
> A Statesman, Taylors, Barbers, Riding-masters
> Are Beasts that use to fatten in their Pastures;
> And those, that breed up Youth to frisk and dance,
> Improve by b'ing translated into France;
> Gallantry-Brokers, Fidlers, Botchers, Pages,
> And skilful Operators in Pottages;
> When nothing's found to thrive of English growth,
> But sottish Pedants, and untutor'd youth,
> That undertake to new-instruct the Saplings
> Secur'd from Pop'ry by their Father's Chaplains;
> Who from our famous Academies fly
> Translated to a snipt Academy.

Besides these, there are on the same sheet a good many other verses, but very unconnected, and seemingly of little Consequence.

p. 49, ll. 11–12. See Butler's MS. fol. 43 v:

> Those that catch Munkys use to Lay
> Gloves, Shoos and Stockings in their way;
> Then shew them how 'tis to be don;
> The Drills themselves wil put them on.

Satyr upon Drunkenness. *Printed from* The Genuine Remains.
p. 55, l. 100. Vignerons..

Satyr upon Marriage. *Printed from* The Genuine Remains.
See in Thyer's MS. *Verses wrote upon the same sheet with the Satyr on Marriage:*

> When Continence and Chastity in Rome....
>
> > (See p. 217, ll. 13–20.)

(These eight lines seem to have been intended by the Author to be inserted after this Line:

> By whom (good Men) or how they were begot.)

> So necessary then were all th' Acquests....
>
> > (See p. 217, ll. 21–38.)

474

NOTES

(*These eighteen lines seem by the place they are writ on the Paper and by the Sense, to have been intended to be inserted after this line:*

Return'd 'em to their Husbands back agen.)

The following Verses seem to be writ on this Sheet, without any visible connection with any part of the Satyr, only because they relate to the Subject of Marriage.

The Dutch (of course) lay Matrimony by....
(See p. 218, ll. 1–8.)

The Roman Empire, that was built upon
Revenge for wrong to injur'd Virtue done,
Was after by a common Harlot sav'd
From being everlastingly inslav'd.

Mean time the wretched Implement that marrys,
Like th' antient Emp'ror Antonine in Arras,
Is hang'd up in effigy all his life,
To share i' th' ignominy of his Wife.

Birds hatch the Eggs they use to sit upon....
(See p. 218, ll. 9–16.)

For Widows but raise up horns to th' dead
As th' antient Jews did Issue in their stead.

The antient Greeks, the Oracle profest....
(See p. 218, ll. 17–22.)

For Matrimony's but a bargain made....
(See p. 218, ll. 23–28.)

The following Lines are added at the End of this Satyr, but at a different time, as appears by the Handwriting and Ink; and do not seem to connect with it:

Adam, who was but accessary to 's Wife....
(See p. 211, ll. 1–24.)

There are more naked baudy pictures made
Of chaste Lucretia, with her Bilbo-Blade,
Than all the famous Lady Courtesans
In Classic history, or in Romance.

Sick of a fatal Pleurisy, a Bride....
(See p. 217, ll. 11–12.)

When universal Ladies unconfin'd
Were real Feme-coverts to all Mankind.

As Jupiter's reported to beget
Transform'd t' a Bull, an antient King of Crete.
His Queen is said t' have us'd him like his Mother,
Transform'd t' a Cow, and horn'd him with another.

For those that strive to match themselves below
Their Quality, are fain to court and woo;
As all Superiors are oblig'd t' address,
And make their Applications to the less.

475

NOTES

p. 56, l. 36.   Plate..

p. 57, l. 65.   Callus's.

p. 58, ll. 87–88.   See Butler's MS. fol. 134 r:

> For if Adul[t]ery's honorable confest
> Incontinence is worshipful, at least.

Upon Critics who judge of modern Plays precisely by the Rules of the Antients. [1677?] *Printed from Butler's MS.* The title was added by Thyer when he published this composition in *The Genuine Remains.*

p. 60, l. 6.   Vandlal? *Thyer prints* Ostrogoth and Vandal?

ll. 27–30. *Alt. reading:*

> No Pudding shalbe sufferd to be witty
> Unless it be, to terrify, or Pitty;
> Nor Regular Lutero be Allowd
> To Rore, and Spit fire, but in the Dorique Mode.

p. 61, l. 45. *Alt. reading:*

> And serve for nothing but t' insnare the weake.

Satyr upon Plagiaries. *Printed from* The Genuine Remains.

See Thyer's note (I, 168): *It is not improbable but that* Butler, *in this Satyr, or sneering Apology for the* Plagiary, *obliquely hints at Sir* John Denham, *whom he had directly attack'd in a preceding Poem—The Charge of Plagiarism in borrowing the* Sophy, *and buying the* Cooper's Hill, *coincides with, and confirms this Supposition; and I am the rather inclined to think so by many satirical Flings of the same Nature against this Gentleman, which I find in our Poet's poetical Common-place.*

Butler *was not pleased with the two first Lines of this Composition as appears by his altering them in the Margin, thus:*

> Why should the world be so averse
> To every small-wit Privateer?

And indeed the Alteration is much for the better; but as it would not connect grammatically with what follows, I did not think proper to adopt it.

p. 63, ll. 19–20.   See Butler's MS. fol. 77 v:

> As Poysonous Peaches from the East removd
> In Italy to wholsom Fruit improvd.

p. 65, ll. 87 sqq.   See Butler's MS. fol. 50 v:

> And Virgil found the stone among
> The Filth of Ennius his Dong,
> As one of our Gold finders Rakes
> For Spoones, and Mony in a Jakes.

l. 99.   See Thyer's note (I, 172): *Our Author here lashes the Vanity of those Writers, who affected to lard their Works with a Variety of learned Quotations, and prefac'd their Books with pompous Syllabus authorum. He has explain'd*

NOTES

his Meaning by a few lines scribbled in the Margin, which, though not correct enough to be admitted into the Text, may yet be allow'd as a Sort of Comment:

> When no Man writ so small a Book,
> But nam'd where this or that he took;
> Run through the Alphabet of Names,
> From whom he made his chiefest Claims;
> And wheresoever he begun
> He ended still with Zenophon.

Ending with Zenophon *alludes to their alphabetical Catalogues of Authors, which must of course end with Z.*

p. 67, l. 184. in,.

Satyr upon the Imperfection and Abuse of human Learning— Part 1st. *Printed from Butler's MS.* The title was added by Thyer when he published this composition in *The Genuine Remains.*

See Thyer's note (I, 202): *In the large General Dictionary, or* Bayle's *enlarg'd by Mr* Bernard, Birch, *and* Lockman, *we are told by the learned Editors, under the Article* Hudibras, *that they were personally inform'd by the late Mr* Longueville—*That amongst the genuine Remains of* Butler, *which were in his Hands, there was a Poem intitled,* The History of Learning—*To the same Purpose is the following Passage cited from the* Poetical Register, *Vol.* II, *p. 21—*"*In Justice to the Public it is thought proper to declare, that all the Manuscripts, Mr* Butler *left behind him, are now in the Custody of Mr* Longueville (*among which is one intitled,* The History of Learning, *written after the manner of* Hudibras) *and that not one Line of those Poems lately publish'd under his Name is genuine.*"

As these Authorities must have given the World reason to expect in this Work a Poem of this sort, it becomes necessary for me to inform the Public—that Butler *did meditate a pretty long Satyr upon the Imperfection and Abuse of human Learning, but that he only finished this first Part of it, though he has left very considerable and interesting Fragments of the Remainder, some of which I shall subjoin.*

The Poet's Plan seems to have consisted of two Parts; the first, which he has executed, is to expose the Defects of human Learning, from the wrong Methods of Education, from the natural Imperfection of the human Mind, and from that Over-eagerness of Men to know things above the Reach of human Capacity— The second, as far as one can judge by the Remains, and intended Parts of it, was to have exemplified what he has asserted first, and ridiculed and satyriz'd the different Branches of human Learning, in characterizing the Philosopher, Critic, Orator, &c.

Mr Longueville *might be led by this, into the Mistake of calling this Work a* History of Learning; *or perhaps it might arise from* Butler's *having in one Plan, which he afterwards alter'd begun with these two Lines,*

> The History of Learning is so lame,
> That few can tell, from whence at first it came.

What has been said will, I flatter myself, be a sufficient Apology for the printing an imperfect Work, if the many good Things to be met with in it, does not make one unnecessary.—However, for this reason I did not think fit to place it amongst his other Satyrs, which are perfect in their different ways.

p. 68, l. 4. Constracted. l. 10. *Thyer prints* Body and.

NOTES

p. 69, l. 46. the.   ll. 57-60. *Alt. reading:*

> For where there are most Languages, No sense
> To Entertaine them al, wil beare, th' expence,
> Are Scaffolds raysd to build a wo[r]ke upon,
> But never after, to be taken down.

l. 64. Character. l. 68. *Thyer prints* in his own. ll. 75 sqq. *Alt. reading:*

> When Testy Pedants use their Plyant age
> To Constant sights of Impotence and Rage
> And make the Busnes of their Education
> A Spectacle of Peevishnes and Passion:
> For little Tyrants are the most Severe
> And worse then Great ones use to domineer.

p. 70, l. 82. fits..   ll. 91 sqq. *Alt. reading:*

>   Sense.
> Nature herself ly's Fallow half the yeare,
> To Render th' other Half, the Fruitfuller;
> And what the Pregnant Spring, and Summer store's
> The Lazy winter Squander's, and Devours:
> So He that over-stock's his Natural Parts,
> Will Sterve th' Acquird, of Sciences, and Arts.
> And if he do's not take a Special Care
> Run's out of Both before he is Aware.
> As 'tis a Harder Province to Maintaine
> An Acquisition, then it was to Gaine.
> Besides, what more Impaires their tender Age,
> Then Constant Sights, of Impotence and Rage?
> To have the Busnes of their Education
> Turnd to an Odious Spectacle of Passion
> And set them Tyranizing in their Empires,
> Enough to Spoyl the Admirablest Tempers.

ll. 107 sqq. *Alt. reading:*

>   Ruine.
> So He that Publishd, and gave out a List,
> Of all his Famous Works were to consist:
> But utterly forgot it, when H' had don,
> And layd by all, H' ingagd to write upon.
> Which Poets are more Guilty of, then those
> That are not tyd so strictly up, to Prose.
> For those that are ty'd up to any thing
> Are wont to take, the Liberaller Swing,
> As Virgil, in 's Georgiques, for that Reason,
> Sowd Cumming seed, so long before it's Season,
> Made Mountaines Tops, the Dear Delight of Hogs,
> That use to take their Quarter up in Bogs.
> And yong Ascanius, (Right or wrong) become
> So Long Before 'twas built, The Hopes of Rome.

l. 110. beyond,.   l. 111. *Thyer reads* The bravest.

NOTES

p. **71**, ll. 123 sqq. *Alt. reading:*

allowd.

> For all Mistakes and Errors of the wise
> Are Naturally of the Largest Cize.

The following lines are written in the margin:

> Though Adams Knowledg was too dearly bought
> It was his want of it betrayd him to't
> For, had his eies been Able but to see
> Before he tasted the forbidden tree,
> He never with the loss of Paradise
> Had purchacd it at such a Desprat Price.

ll. 131 sqq. *Alt. reading:*

> For Knowledge never bore so high a valew,
> As when 'twas Low, Contemptible, and Shallow:
> For when the Goth, and Vandal, had by Burning
> The Antient Librarys, destroyd all Learning,
> The Barbarouser Schoolmen, to Restore
> The Ruine, made it greater, then before,
> Reducd it all to Quarrel, and Contest,
> Where the most Peremptory get the Best;
> And, tho Intended only for the Souls-good,
> Serv's rather for Imposture, Fraud, and Falshood,
> And therefore is the Mode of Playing Prizes
> In Academies for their Exercises.

l. 132. *Thyer prints* As when 'twas low.   l. 133. Academy.
l. 136. Fasces..   l. 138. it..   l. 145. wit:.   l. 150. fort:.
l. 152. *Alt. reading:*

> But the one Half's for use the other show.

p. **72**, ll. 161–4. *Alt. reading:*

> As a French great mans Library, by th' whole is
> So much an ell for Quarto's, and for Folios;
> It is no matter what they treat upon:
> They were but meant for garniture alone.

l. 175. *Alt. reading:* Collects all.   l. 178. *Thyer reads* they quote.
l. 185. *Thyer prints* by so mean.   l. 189. *Thyer prints* And He's.

Fragments of an intended 2d Part... *Printed from Butler's MS.* Published for the first time by Thyer.

p. **73**, l. 1. Whose Talents.   ll. 11 sqq. *Alt. reading:*

sphere.

> Know how the Representatives of Sense
> With th' Intellect do hold Intelligence
> And how those Subtle Spirits that attend
> The memory, are in a Trice convend.

l. 14. then.   l. 24. *Alt. reading:* Establishment of Nature.

NOTES

p. 73, ll. 29 sqq. *Alt. reading:*

> Pisse.
> May undertake to move the Earth as soon
> Without a Place to Plant their Engines on.
> Things so Stupendous; Nature has Deny'd
> The wit of Mankind ever should Decyde.

l. 29. Payd.   l. 30. *Thyer prints* antient.

p. 74, l. 50. with Sandals.

p. 75, l. 77. And, Polemiques.   ll. 79 sq. *Alt. reading:*

> For if there's Nothing once to be understood,
> How came they first, to make that Nothing, good?

l. 99. Stoiques.

p. 76, ll. 123 sqq. *Alt. reading:*

> Sense;
> That, whether 'tis their luck to mis or hit,
> They do no hurt to one anothers wit;
> Like that Italian Mercenary Skirmis,
> That had but one man kild in both the Armies,
> And he with mere unweldines, and Fat
> Sunk underneath the Burden of his weight.

l. 123. th' wont.   ll. 125 sq. *Alt. reading:*

> Foe.
> But with Impertinent Distinctions, force
> The most Familiar Reason, from it's Course:

ll. 141 sqq. *Alt. reading:*

> So some Polemiques, use to Draw their Swords,
> Against the Language only, and the words:
> But lay the Merits of the Cause aside,
> By those, that understand 'em to be try'd.
> Advance Couragiously, by Force of Arms,
> To storme the works of one another's Tearms;
> Fall Foul on some extravagant Expression,
> But nere attempt the main Designe and Reason;
> Talk on, and leave no Roome for Contradiction
> The only Certaine Method of Conviction:
> And when they use to Rayle before they write,
> Like Hectors, do but strip before they fight:
> As other Brothers of the Blade are wont
> With Ranting Language to begin th' Affront.
> While some more Civilly approach the Lists,
> With Praises of their own Antagonists:
> And magnify the Fo, th' Intend to out brave,
> And beare themselves away, the Spoyles they Gave

For when those great Endowments are put down,
They are but new Additions to their own.
And those that understand the Question least,
Are still most Formidable in Contest.

. . . .

With Illustrations Render more Obscure,
And Prove, by vindicating, but untruer:
Unriddle Subtleties by way more Subtle,
Like Commentators upon Aristotle,
Until by over-nice Distinguishing,
Th' have chang'd the sceane of all t' another thing.

p. **77,** l. 160. *Alt. reading:* Curious Gudgeon.   l. 161. over-understing.
   ll. 164 sqq. *Alt. reading:*

                                   none.

As Lyers with long use of telling Tales,
Forget at Length if they are Tru, or False:
So those that Plod on any thing too long
Know Nothing, when th'are in the Right or wrong.
For what are all their Demonstrations else
But to the Higher Powrs of Sense Appeals?
Sense; that they undervalew and Contemne
As if it lay below their wits, and them.
That spend their Time, and Braines, to understand
Things that the Laws of Nature Contraband
And proudly think t' unriddle evry Cause
That Nature uses, by their own by-Laws,
When if th' had but aggreed on it, Hum and Buz
Had don the Feat as well, or Mumsimus.

l. 178. *Alt. reading:*

As Greatness, Insolence, and Ignorance.

ll. 183 sqq. *Alt. reading:*

                                   lyes:
And, therefor, 'tis not strange it should abuse
What Nature Purposd for the noblest use:
For That Great Dunce (The world) the more it knows,
The more Debauch'd, and wickeder, it grow's;
Is but more Ignorant, and Foolisher,
The more it strives to turn Philosopher.
For all Mens Nat'ral Tempers are not Fit
For Truth, and Ingenuity, and wit;
And Knowledge Fair and Honestly acquird
More Painful then th' Adulterate and Inspird,
Where men have leave t' assume with Greater Ease,
Then Drudgery, and Study, what they Please;

NOTES

And as they Grow more Rich by Publique Thieft
(The Shortest, and the Easiest way to Thrift)
Appeare more Able men, and fit for trust,
Then if th' had ventur'd to be tru and Just.
Hence 'tis, The world Perpetually takes Part
Against the true, and Genuine ways of Art,
But studys all Impostures to Advance,
As Fitter for its Native Ignorance,
That Joyn'd with Greatnes, is so much concernd
T' Abet an Idiot-Quack against the Learn'd;
And justify their sottishest Pretences,
How False so ever in their own Defences:
That when their Ignorance Puts knowledge down,
It may b' a Meanes to Justify their own,
And make 'em Pass for Men of sounder Parts
Then those, that have th' Impediment of Arts;
That Henceforth no great Person may for want
Of Letters be Reputed Ignorant,
And what all former Ages held for Good
For worst of all may now be understood,
The only Practicable way to level
And take away al Feuds of Good and Evil;
To Reconcile the Antique Prejudice
Between the Clans of virtue, and of vice,
When Nothing's left to make a Difference
Between the High, and Low, but Insolence,
The only Moral Thorough-Reformation
To fit the late Religion of the Nation.*
Nor Has the world usd truth and knowledg Rougher
Then from themselves they have been forcd to suffer:
For there's no Idle vanity, an Author
Takes up on Tick, or Pilfers from another,
But other Virtuosos of his Rate
In Wit, and Judgment, strive to Imitate
And Propagate the Epidemique Ach
Which all the Rest of one another catch.

* Here is added in the margin and mark'd as if intended to be inserted:

For wise, and Just, and Honest means no More
Then Sot, and Fool, and Knave, did heretofore,
But has not half the Countenance and Grace,
That evry Impudent Impostor has.
For Fools not only use to make men Laugh
But serve, instead of Foyles, to set them of[f]:
For evry Idiot takes Delight to see
Some other Creature have less wit then He;
And therefor Great men keep 'em and Delight
T' have Dwarfs, as wel in wit, and sense, as height;
But no man can endure with Patience
To see another Have more wit and sense.

p. 78, ll. 197 sqq. *Alt. reading:*

> Impart.
> Enables Sick Men, in their Desperatst Ills,
> In Perfect Minde, and memory to make wills,
> Supplys all Seminarys, with Recruites
> Of Endles Controversys, and Disputes,
> Make's Men of Sylly Names exchange a letter
> To make it Nonsense, and twis pass the better.
> For Learned Nonsense has a Deeper Sound
> Then Easy Sense, and go's for more Profound.
> Besides, It do's not only make men Laugh etc....

l. 201. *Thyer prints* For all our Authors now compile....
Alt. reading:

> Whence all our Learned Authors now Compile
> At charge of Nothing but the words, and Style.
> And all the virtuosos, of the Learnd
> Believe themselvs in nothing else concernd,
> Retaine the Measures, which at School they tooke
> When only for the words, they Read a Book.
> As if the Sense, lay only in the Style,
> Tho all the Rest, were ere so Lewd and vile;
> When all the Prodigies of Eloquence
> Had never ore Mankinde, that Influence,
> That in some Ages, altogether grew
> And after were extinguisht in a Few.
> And tho they had no Language, but their own
> Have all Succeeding Eloquence outdon.
> Were so Admird by Roman Politicians,
> They usd to Haunt the Schools of Rhetoricians,
> To heare the Greater Magistrate of th' School
> Give Sentence in his Haughty Chair-Curule;
> And those, who Mighty Nations over-came,
> Were faine to say their Lessons, and Declame.

l. 211. *Thyer prints* only in.   l. 212. *Thyer prints:*

> And in their Stiles the Wit of greatest Clerks.

ll. 223 sqq. *Alt. reading:*

> declame:
> When all their Modish People had a Trick
> As ours do now speak French, to smatter Greek,
> And Ladys in their Pleasures usd t' affect
> Th' Injoyment, in the Proper Dialect.

p. 79, l. 233. Another copy begins:

> An Orator enchanted with the Twang
> Of his own Trillos, takes Delight t' Harangue....

NOTES

and goes on:

> As if Harangue were meant, and Eloquence
> For nothing, but to outface Truth and Sense:
> For all the Flourishes of Oratory
> Serve only to Imbellish a False Story,
> A Garniture and Artificial Sauce
> For seasoning a false Insipid Cause.
> Their Tropes and Topiques are but sev'ral Cases
> Of Drawers, that hold only words and Phrases:
> As Scudry with his Richest jewels, set
> And Inlayd a Poetique Cabinet,
> But when H' had furnisht it with all his wit
> Had nothing left to be layd up in it.

p. 79, l. 243. *Thyer prints:*

> For if the Language will but bear the test.

ll. 251 sq. *Alt. reading:*

>   excuses.
> Is always jealous of its own designs
> And, e're 'tis charged, compounds with words, and fines.

p. 80, l. 265. *Thyer prints* The Pedants.

Thus in another copy:

> A Pædagogue is one that has been broke
> T' an Artificial shuffle of the Book
> And Pædantry is but a kind of Pique
> Of which Prepostrous Apetites fal sick.
> For Pædants are but a Mungrel Breed etc....

Alt. reading:

>   [Pedants]
> Are but a kinde of banc-rupts, that by Driving
> Too great a Trade, Run out instead of thriving;
> Who valew Mans Ability and Parts,
> Not by their Skil and Judgment in the Arts,
> But for the Paines and Labour they have spent
> To be Industrious, tho Impertinent.
> For al a Pedants art lys in his Tearms,
> As conjurers and witches in their Charms.
>
> .   .   .   .
>
> That use t' observe the greatest complaisance
> To th' outward form of things and circumstance
> Resolve the difficult'st of all book-cases
> Only by proper or improper phrases;
> Affect a nasty mien and out of pride
> Neglect themselves, and all the world besides;
> As if it were an argument of virtue
> And judgment to be slovenly and dirty;

NOTES

> From whence 'tis evident the greatest fools
> Have not been chang'd i' th' cradle, but in schools,
> And Stationers, that only deal in books,
> Are found to be the greatest knaves and rooks.

p. 80, l. 274. Nursery and Folly.   l. 280. Distort.   l. 282. th.
l. 293. Compare with p. 165.   ll. 301 sqq. *Alt. reading:*

> So he that had the most Laborious been
> Of all the Age he liv'd and Flourishd in,
> And with the Paines he took, Reducd his Body,
> And Brain to nothing, with Perpetual Study.

p. 81, l. 312. vowel.   l. 316. Arts..

PINDARIC ODES

Upon an hypocritical Nonconformist. *Printed from* The Genuine Remains.

p. 85, l. 2. barbarous; or.   l. 9. Procounc'd.   l. 23. adore..

p. 86, l. 39. Heav'n.   l. 52. Foundations..   l. 59. Heav'n.

p. 91, l. 226. hold.

Upon modern Critics. *Printed from* The Genuine Remains.

To the happy Memory of the most Renown'd Du-Val. *Printed from* The Genuine Remains.

p. 97, l. 5. *Ed.* 1671 *reads* settlement.   l. 16. *Ed.* 1671 *reads* no gold at all.

p. 98, l. 39. gentee.   l. 44. See Thyer's note (1, 148): *Whoever will take the Pains to compare this Stanza with the Satyr upon our Imitation of the French, will be convinced, that they are the Production of the same Muse. However, to give an undeniable Proof of it, I shall add a few Lines scribbled by* Butler *in the Margin of that Satyr; a thing very usual with him.*

> To make a Scruple when they dine
> *On out-of fashion Meat and Wine;*
> Conform their Palates to the Mode,
> And relish that, and not the Food;
> And rather than transgress the Rule,
> Eat Kitchen-stuff, and stinking Fowl;
> For that, which we call stinking here,
> Is but piquant and haut-gout there;
> And still the more th' are gull'd and cheated,
> Believe they are the better treated.

l. 50. *Ed.* 1671 *reads* out-of-fashion'd.

p. 99, l. 74. Wit,.   l. 75. Arts..   l. 85. *Ed.* 1671 *reads* From the.

p. 100, l. 95. *Ed.* 1671 *reads* Made them.   l. 109. *Ed.* 1671 *reads* The Excise.   l. 114. *Ed.* 1671 *reads* That oft.   l. 119. *Ed.* 1671 *reads* win. l. 122. *Ed.* 1671 *reads* To a.

p. 101, l. 129. *Ed.* 1671 *reads* valiant Thief.   l. 136. *Ed* 1671 *reads* the undaunted waggonners.   l. 137. *Ed.* 1671 *reads* higlers.   l. 149. *Ed.* 1671

NOTES

reads the inchanted. l. 159. *Ed.* 1671 *reads* lock. l. 161. *Ed.* 1671 *reads* and ponderous chains.

p. **102**, l. 163. *Ed.* 1671 *reads* Prisoners hearts. ll. 194 sqq. *Ed.* 1671 *reads:*

> They life itself began to hate;
> And all the world besides disdain
> Made loud appeals and moans....

p. **103**, l. 119. *Ed.* 1671 *reads* swell'd in sighs.

BALLADS

A Ballad. As close as a Goose.... [1657?] *Printed from Butler's MS.* Published for the first time by Thyer as *A Ballad upon the Parliament which deliberated about making Oliver King.*

p. **107**, l. 3. *Thyer prints* the Royal. l. 30. serve for.

p. **108**, l. 33. trya.

A Ballad. Draw neare, good People.... [1657?] *Printed from Butler's MS.* Published for the first time by Thyer under the title of *A Ballard, as 'tis conjectured, upon O. Cromwell.*

See Thyer's note (I, 193): *To this humorous Ballad* Butler *had prefixed this Title*—The Privileges of Pimping—*but afterwards cross'd it out, for which reason I have not inserted it; and only mention it, as a Circumstance, which may amuse such, as are curious in hunting out the Explication of Niceties of this Sort. It does not appear to bear any Sense consistent with the Subject; but some other Critic may perhaps find one; or at least please himself with thinking so.*

p. **109**, l. 15. *Thyer prints* at Bart'lmy Fare. l. 23. *Thyer prints* On which.

p. **110**, l. 44. *Thyer prints* Gapes to.

p. **111**, l. 72. *Thyer prints* loud did rumble. ll. 73 sq. See Thyer's note (I, 199): *This whimsical Liberty our Author takes, of transposing the Words for the sake of a Rhime, though at the Expence of the Sense, is a new kind of poetic Licence; and 'tis merry enough to observe, that he literally does, what he jokingly charges upon other Poets in another Place*...Hudibras II, i, 29. l. 84. *Thyer prints* and Roof. l. 86. *Thyer prints* out o' th' Top.

p. **112**, l. 115. A eke.

MOCK ENCOMIUMS

To the Honourable Edward Howard, Esq.; Upon his incomparable Poem of the British Princes. *Printed from* The Genuine Remains.

See Thyer's note (I, 104): *Most of the celebrated Wits in* Charles *the Second's Reign, addrest this Gentleman, in a bantering Way, upon the Poem called the* British Princes, *and among the rest* Butler. *What he wrote upon this Occasion was inserted in* Dryden's Miscellanies, *under the Name of* Mr Waller, *and upon that Authority, Mr* Fenton *has introduced it into his Edition of* Waller's *Works. That this Piece is not* Waller's *must be evident to every distinguishing Reader; and that it is* Butler's *is no less clear, not only from the* Manner, *but also by its being found among his other Manuscripts accompanied by the* Palinodie *which follows it; but to make the Matter still more demonstrable, I must add, that I find several of the Lines and Thoughts in his common-place Collection.*

NOTES

We read in Butler's MS.:

> Had Homer flourishd in this Age, or Maro,
> He would have wishd himself with hardned Pharo;
> And as he, when the Greekes in Counsel sit,
> Make's them all very nimble of their feet,
> So do your Epithites, although by chance,
> Jump properly with ev'ry Circumstance,
> As Naturally as a Bagpipe Drone
> Stands equally in tune with evry tone.
> How justly then do you the world defy!
> To shew you such a piece of Poetry!
> For, if it should presume to write like you,
> All wise men in it would defy it too.
> Your Busnes is to govern and Command,
> And make your Pleasure for your reason stand,
> Give words a new construction and new Sense
> Beyond all, but your own Intelligence:
> For why should he, whose wit is absolute,
> Admit of Contradiction or Dispute?
> These are the Noble Causes that bring forth
> Envy, the Bad Companion of all worth,
> Such Heights as no wit ever could have nick'd
> But only his that stript a Naked Pict.
>
> Unles y' have sent in a Particular
> Of all your wit, how could we choose but err?
> No Grazier e're bid money for a Beast,
> Till he had felt him in the Flanke at least.
> Were you not known to be Infallible,
> Some would be apt to judge you very Dul,
> Who, when a Jury of good men and true
> Have found the Bill against your workes and you,
> (By your own self approvd) wil not submit
> And crave a Pardon for your Guilty wit,
> Except against them after Judgment past,
> When by your Poet Peres you have been cast,
> Arraigne your Tryall when it is to[o] Late,
> Like Malefactors that grow Desperate.
> In this you are insufferable, and Madder
> Then Thieves that use to huff upon the Ladder.
> Whose wit by Nobody was e're admir'd
> But only those that are subornd and hir'd.
> For such y' are forc'd to maintaine of your own
> To cry your great Parts up and others down,
> Like vouchers, as you please, to prayse or rayle
> For Contribution Meat, and wine, and Ale.

**A Palinodie to the Honourable Edward Howard, Esq.; upon his
incomparable British Princes.** *Printed from* The Genuine Remains.

NOTES

A Panegyric upon Sir John Denham's Recovery from his Madness. [1667?] *Printed from* The Genuine Remains.

In Butler's MS. we find also the following lines written in the same vein against Sir John:

> If all great wits have some allay
> Of Madnes, as the Learned say,
> How great is your Prodigious wit,
> That has so large a Dose of it!
>
> No Pædantry nor Quibling all the while,
> Nor hot Disputes about Jargon and Stile;
> No wit araign'd and by false witnes cast
> Nor Sense discoverd where 'twas never plac'd;
> No wit Cryd up or down in the wrong place,
> Nor any thing found out, that never was;
> No alteration thought on, nor Repair,
> Nor Structure now designd unles in th' aire.
>
> And those rare Poems you in Poland writ
> To th' Elevation of that Cuntrys wit
> Make the Dogs Bark, and frighted Children run
> To see your Naked Armes tan'd in the sun.
> Tel how you lost your wits, where ere you come,
> Call evry woman Bes, and yourself Tom.
> Beg Bacon in a Tragical base tone.
> And drink in a great Horn like Prester John.
> All this your Predecessors were sworn to,
> And by your order you are bound to do.
> More then to own yourself a Patriot,
> And in a National Councel sit and vote.
> Who is't that could have you on the hip,
> And bring you back to your Fresh Straw and whip?
>
> Setting the Hare's head of your skil in th' Arts
> 'Gainst the Goosgiblets of your other Parts,
> They'r found so equal in comparing,
> There's nere a Barrel better Herring,
> And b'ing all adjusted with your Muse
> Agree so well there's not a —— to choose.
>
> Who do's renew
> Not only youth but childhood too:
> For he that breeds new wit may wel be stil'd,
> After Decays and madnes, twice a Child,
> And, as he got it, so let it pack
> Under the Devils belly, and ore his back,
> And gave no Quarter when it did ingage
> Without regard of Person, Sex or Age.

488

NOTES

TRANSLATIONS

Satyr on Rhyme. [1667?] *Printed from* The Genuine Remains. Thyer published it under the misleading title of *Satyrical Epistle to a bad Poet*. The learned editor did not see that this is an excellent translation of Boileau's *Second Satire*, addressed, not to a Bad Poet, but to Molière himself.

Cydippe her Answer to Acontius. [1679?] *Printed from* Ovid's Epistles. Translated By Several Hands. The third Edition. London...1683.

p. **128**, l. 5. I vain In deck.

p. **130**, l. 103. hast.

MISCELLANEOUS PIECES

Repartees between Cat and Puss at a Caterwalling In the Modern Heroic Way. *Printed from* The Genuine Remains.

p. **136**, l. 34. an *omitted*.

Upon Philip Nye's Thanksgiving Beard. *Printed from* The Genuine Remains.

In Butler's MS. we find the following lines on the same subject:

> This Rev'rend Brother, like a Goate,
> Dos weare a Tayl upon his throate,
> The fringe and Tassell of a Face,
> That give's it a becoming grace,
> But set in such a Curious frame,
> As if 'twere wrought in Filograin;
> And Cut so eav'n, as if 't had been
> Drawn with a Pen upon his Chinne.
> No Topiary Hedge of Quickset
> Was ere so neatly cut, or thickset;
> That made beholders more admire,
> Then China Plate that's made of wire.
> *But being wrought so regular
> In ev'ry Part and evry haire,

*   *Alt. reading in the longer measure:*

> But bing Designd, and wrought so Regular
> In evry Lock of Individual Hair.
> Who would imagine, That it should be Portal
> To th' Inward man, and unconforming Mortal?
> And yet it was: And did no less Dissent
> From its own Judgment, then the Government;
> And in the Church did equally Detest
> What it held forth in Private, and Profest;
> Was Peremptory, and did abhom[in]ate
> The least conformity in Church or State.
> And like an Hypocritique selfish Brother
> Profest one thing in words, and Did another;
> As all things where th' are most of all Profest,
> Are found Regarded, and Considerd least.

Who could believe it should be Portall
To unconforming inward Mortall?
And yet it was, and did dissent
No less from it's own Government
Then from the Churches, and detest
That which he held forth and profest;
Did equally abhominate
Conformity in Church and State;
And, like an Hypocritique Brother,
Profest one thing, and did another;
As all things, where th' are most profest,
Are found to be regarded least.

His Eares extended Large, and Flat,
Upon the Pillory of a Hat;
The Tru Philactry of the Scotch
Presbytery, and Classique Dutch.

No Barber with his Crisping Irons, and Cissors,
Could ever Rayse, so Curiously, mens whiskers;
But for the Dagger Part upon his Chin,
'Twas Brought t' a Poynt too subtle to be seen.
And Rubd to a sharpnes, by a Pumis-stone,
That Nicest Chymiques strove to work upon.

Although He Had an Artificial Case
For Laying-up his Beard in, and his Face;
And when the Art was discomposed: 'twas harder
Then Farrer-watches, to be Put in order.
That Berenices famous Head of Haire
Was not so neatly drest into a Star.
The Roman Beards that govern'd all the world
Were not so curiously cut and curld.

And [when] the State had orderd all the Churches
To Preach and Feast, This Beard was cut of Purpose
That Lachesis that Spin's the Threds of Fate,
Could nere have drawn it out, more Delicate,
Nor Vulcan file a curiouser Gin
To catch himself an open Cuckold in.

Prologue to the Queen of Arragon... [Habington's Queen of Arragon was performed before the Duke and Duchess of York on 14 October 1668.] *Printed from* The Genuine Remains.

Epilogue Upon the same... *Printed from* The Genuine Remains.

An Epistle to a Friend. *Printed from Butler's MS.*
p. 145, l. 9. of.

To Thomas....... *Printed from Butler's MS.*

NOTES

p. **146**, l. 7. Thy *omitted*. l. 18. of.

Triplets upon Avarice. *Printed from Butler's MS. Published for the first time by Thyer.*

p. **147**, l. 1. *Thyer prints* Misers.

Epigram on a Club of Sots. *Printed from* The Genuine Remains.

p. **148.** *Alt. reading:*

> All the Members of a Club
> Are Hoop'd together like a Tub;
> And in a Close alliance linke
> For nothing else, but to hold drink.

Description of Holland. *Printed from Butler's MS. Published for the first time by Thyer.*

p. **149**, l. 1. Draw. l. 4. *Thyer prints* Lake. l. 7. *Thyer prints* aground.

POETICAL THESAURUS

The portion of this volume which I have called *Poetical Thesaurus*, after Thyer, is printed from the Butler MSS. in the British Museum. The passages already published in Thyer's *Genuine Remains* or in the edition of 1822 are expressly indicated as such.

p. **153**, ll. 1–4. *Printed by Thyer.*

p. **154**, ll. 13–18. *Printed by Thyer.* l. 18. of. l. 21. Rust.

p. **155**, l. 4. the. ll. 5–8. *Printed by Thyer who reads:*

> Too much or too little wit.

l. 33. Greates.

p. **156**, ll. 3–16 *and* 27–32. *Printed by Thyer.* l. 27. *Thyer reads* Those.
l. 32. *Thyer reads* Then those.

p. **158**, l. 5. *Alt. reading:*

> Some think there['s] Nothing worthy to be known
> Until it has been Puzzeld long upon.

ll. 17–30. *Printed by Thyer.* l. 24. to. l. 30. *Alt. reading:*

> one.
> And confidence is never so strong
> As when 'tis certaine to be in the wrong.

p. **159**, l. 10. God. l. 15. conclude. l. 17. thing.

p. **160**, ll. 3–12. *Printed by Thyer.* l. 17. Reason. ll. 31–34 *and* 36–38.
Printed by Thyer. l. 32. *Thyer reads* but Brains.

p. **161**, ll. 1–6. *Printed by Thyer.* l. 2. Irrefragables. *Thyer reads* Irrefragable. l. 7. Staw. l. 13. Thesees. l. 17. Etenity.

NOTES

p. **163**, ll. *24–27 and 30–33*. *Printed by Thyer.*
p. **164**, ll. *1–6*. *Printed by Thyer.*
p. **165**, ll. *5 sqq. Alt. reading:*

> The Formes of Learning (Commonly) Devour,
> No less then in Religion, all the Powr;
> For nothing's more Impertinent then Modes,
> As Plants, can never thrive, that grow in Roades:
> Whence Pædantry at first was Introducd,
> As but the Garbe, and Meene, that Schollers usd:
> But since Inlargd so far, to over-grow
> All that is useful to observe, or know:
> When no Man talks, but Consters, and Embrothers
> His Tawdry Stuff, with Ends of Antique Authors;
> Would rather choose (with Otho) to Resigne
> The Empire, then to be without his Coyn:
> Yet Rather have no Money in their Purses
> Then not to know the valew in Sesterces;
> Or take the Rate of any Forrain Coyn:
> And not Reduce it to the Attique Mine.
> Would Scorn to understand the Age of Moones,
> Unles by th' antient Calends, Ides, and Nones;
> But valew nothing, til by time Reducd
> To Reliques of the Age in which 'twas usd:
> For Antiquarys use to understand
> And Judge of all things at the Fifty[th] hand;
> Are Passionate Admirers, and Wellwillers
> Of th' Antique Hieroglyphiques of Seths Pillers;
> And Revrence the Memory of Samboscer,
> Who had been Adams Tutor, and Eves usher.
> When th' are but Brokers of Antiquitys,
> That Botch and Turn and Dress their Fripperys.

l. 13. But *omitted.*   l. 19. Imbrthers.   ll. 25 sqq. *Alt. reading:*

> More tawdry then a Taylers Fizling-Cushion,
> He sings, and Botches, with his Legs across-on.
> But when it is his Fortune to Translate,
> 'Tis well it Happens not, above his Rate:
> For All Translators are but Interceders
> Between a writer, and his Gentle Readers,
> That worse then Botchers, do's but turn, and Dress
> (The wrong-side outward) sevral Languages:
> Is not Allowd to write, or understand
> (As Authors use) But at the Second Hand,
> But Keep's an Office of Intelligence
> Between the Language of a Booke, and Sense:
> To correspond with Forainers, and Carrys
> Advertisments twixt works and Dictionarys.

NOTES

p. 165, *last line. Alt. reading:*

> So some great Ingeneres of Latin Pens
> Take all words in an æqual sober Sense
> And what was meant, for Rallery, and Sport,
> Expresse in matters, of Profound Import.
> Whence Modern Styles are Commonly Patcht up,
> With Affectations of some Idle Fop.
> Which th' Antique Poets only Introducd
> Not to be Imitated, but Abusd;
> And for no other Cause, nor Need affect
> A Partycullord, Tawdry Dialect.
> Will Quote a Sentence, or an Ende of verse
> To bring a single word in by maine force,
> And by the Quantity of Syllables
> Take an Accompt of all Mens Learning else:
> And when the Accent of a word is mist
> Condemn the most Polite Philologist.

Another copy reads after Import:

> As if the Fustian Ribaldry of Gnato
> Did best become the Gravity of Cato,
> And for no other Cause, nor need, affect
> A Botchers Fizling-cussion Dialect
> Patchd up of Particoulled Scraps as Tawdry
> As Drugget or Mock-velvet Imbrodry;
> Until the most Phantastique Idioms
> Smel Rank of thumping Desks, and Byting Thumbs:
> Whence Great Philologists, that take Delight
> In Raritys, Mistake the Wrong for Right.
> And Quote a Sentence, or an End of verse,
> Although the Sense be ever so Averse,
> To bring a Single word in, by maine Force
> As much against the Grain of the Discourse,
> And show the Authors Brains were more Intent
> Upon the Language, then the Argument.

p. 167, ll. 1–8. *Printed by Thyer.*   l. 15. Glasse.

p. 169, l. 22. *Alt. reading:*

> Of Scandalous and Borrowd Imitations.

p. 170, l. 10. Were *omitted.*   l. 24. Mad.

p. 172, l. 5. Adulerous.   l. 20. sligh.   l. 28. Of *omitted.*

p. 173, l. 2. hey.   l. 3. e Patriarch.   l. 4. hat.   l. 21. How *omitted.*
   ll. 19–36 sqq. *Printed by Thyer.*

p. 174, l. 10. Person.   l. 23. mad.   l. 26. of.   l. 27. And two.

p. 176, ll. 7–10. *Printed by Thyer.*   l. 8. ticke.   l. 12. men a.
   ll. 15–20. *Printed by Thyer.*   ll. 21–24. *Printed in Ed.* 1822.

p. 177, l. 5. bee.   l. 18. between teeth.

NOTES

p. **179**, ll. 1–18. *Printed by Thyer.* l. 6. *Thyer reads* And free.
l. 26. *Alt. reading:*

But False No-Body, chant to Disagree.

ll. 27–30. *Printed by Thyer.* l. 28. woodd.

p. **180**, ll. 1–16. *Printed from* The Genuine Remains.

p. **181**, l. 28. the impertinently.

p. **182**, ll. 1–6, 19–24, 29–30, *and* 37 sqq. *Printed by Thyer.*

p. **184**, ll. 9–14. *Printed in Ed.* 1822. l. 12. Braine. l. 32. Family.

p. **186**, l. 13. Patient. l. 15. Pretender. l. 16. the. l. 20. when lets.
ll. 31 sqq. *Printed by Thyer.*

p. **189**, l. 1. Distesses. l. 14. violentstst.

p. **190**, l. 7. of. l. 30. But without.

p. **193**, l. 10. of.

p. **194**, ll. 21–28. *Printed by Thyer.* ll. 22 sq. *Alt. reading:*

The Conqu'ring Fury of the Floud
And taught the world a way to save....

p. **196**, l. 7. Manitude. ll. 9–14. *Printed from Thyer's MS.* l. 16. destry's.
l. 27. thefore. l. 28. of. ll. 31–36. *Printed by Thyer.*

p. **199**, l. 7. Especiall. l. 12. to Disciferd. l. 26. Costantly.

p. **200**, ll. 13–20. *Printed by Thyer.*

p. **201**, l. 6. Pedict.

p. **202**, l. 2. takd.

p. **203**, l. 11. Delusion.

p. **204**, l. 14. the the Thickest. l. 18. should hangd.

p. **205**, ll. 13–22. *Printed in Ed.* 1822. ll. 23–28. *Printed by Thyer.*

p. **206**, ll. 1–8. *Printed in Ed.* 1822. l. 12. come.
ll. 17–26. *Printed in Ed.* 1822.

p. **207**, ll. 1–6. *Printed in Ed.* 1822. l. 10. *Alt. reading:*

As eating sower Fruit dos teeth.

l. 33. f Love.

p. **208**, ll. 1–10. *Printed by Thyer.* l. 1. to. l. 32. sligh. l. 34. wit.
l. 35. see. ll. 32–35. *Printed by Thyer.*

p. **209**, ll. 5–14. *Printed in Ed.* 1822.
ll. 27–34. *Printed by Thyer.* l. 33. of wind *omitted.*
ll. 35–36. *Written in the Margin opposite the preceding lines.*

p. **211**, ll. 1–24. *Printed from Thyer's MS. Alt. reading:*

Adam who was but Accessary t' his wife,
Was doomd to Dig and Drudge for't al his life,
While she, subornd by the Devil to betray him,
Was senten[ce]d but to Love and to obey him,

Which made her Punishment become the worse,
Because she's ty'd to do it as a Curse,
And he at Liberty, to Love or hate her,
Upon her Good Behavior, or ill Nature,
Who is not bound to do it, but at wil,
Though she has usd him, ere so wel, or il:
For there's no slavery so Desperate
And hard, as to b' obligd to Love or hate.
No sooner are they made one Flesh,
And both compounded int' a Mesh,
But Sexes Prove the next Debate,
And who has right to this or that;
Or whether Slavry or Dominion
Belong to that of Men, or women;
Until the Issue has been try'd,
And found most frequent for the Bride,
Who can Reduce the greatest Brave
To be her Utensil and Slave;
To Husband taks him during life,
And makes but Helper to his wife.

p. **211**, l. 32. Burryd but.

p. **212**, ll. 17–24. *Printed by Thyer*. l. 26. Carry. ll. 33 sqq. *Printed by Thyer*. l. 33. *Thyer prints* Most Virgins.

p. **213**, ll. 35 sqq. *Printed by Thyer*.

p. **214**, l. 18. cloath. l. 26. As as.

p. **215**, l. 6. Inhumanit.

p. **216**, ll. 16–19 *and* 22–31. *Printed in Ed.* 1822.

p. **217**, ll. 11–38. *Printed from Thyer's MS*.

p. **218**, ll. 1–16. *Printed from Thyer's MS*.

p. **219**, l. 8. Disconted.

p. **220**, ll. 11–28. *Printed by Thyer*. l. 14. Facuty.

p. **222**, l. 15. suffe. l. 19. Bartlew.

p. **223**, l. 5. Seraglo. l. 18. Chrstian.

p. **224**, l. 2. Jugler Spell.

p. **225**, ll. 31 sqq. *Printed by Thyer*. The same subject had been treated in short verse by Butler, fol. 40 v:

All Generous Creatures live of Course
As if they Joynd for bett'r or worse:
The Lion's Constant to his miss
And never leaves his Liones,
And she's as tru to him agen
As virtuous Ladys are to men;
The Chast and Docile Elephant
T' his only Femal is Gallant,

NOTES

And shee as Constant to his Bed
That first injoyd her Maydenhead;
But Paultry Rams, and Buls, and Goates
Are more Insatiate then Stotes
And other vermine of all Sorts
That spend their time in making Courts,
As all Pultrones Delight to Range
And, though but for the worse, to change.

p. **227**, ll. 7–12. *Printed by Thyer.* l. 7. once *was added by Thyer.*
p. **228**, l. 14. *Alt. reading:*

Such Barbarous Inhumanitys dare.

ll. 15–24. *Printed by Thyer.* l. 16. *Thyer reads* but Patience.
l. 24. *Thyer here added these two lines:*

As Beasts are hunted for their Furs
Men for their Virtues fare the worse. See p. 472, ll. 17–18.

l. 31. fruite shows.
p. **229**, l. 8. serve. l. 15. remain. ll. 23–28. *Printed by Thyer.*
l. 30. would go.
p. **230**, l. 2. mourn *omitted.* l. 22. Epitaph. l. 23. that' lost.
p. **231**, ll. 1–32. *Printed by Thyer.* l. 17. of.
p. **232**, ll. 3–12. *Printed by Thyer.* l. 10. *Thyer reads* Vices.
p. **233**, ll. 1–20 *and* 31 sqq. *Printed by Thyer.* l. 31. *Thyer reads* As in all great. l. 33. of.
p. **234**, ll. 19–26. *Printed from* The Genuine Remains.
p. **235**, ll. 1–8 *and* 18–21. *Printed by Thyer.*
p. **236**, ll. 1–10. *Printed by Thyer.* l. 1. Dame *was added by Thyer.* l. 11. Fortun. ll. 21–22. *Printed by Thyer.* l. 23. An. l. 25. lik. l. 26. they they. ll. 27 sqq. *Printed from Thyer's MS.* l. 29. *Thyer prints* nothing less.
p. **237**, ll. 7–16. *Printed from* The Genuine Remains.
p. **240**, ll. 1–4. *Printed by Thyer.*
p. **241**, l. 34. Dey's.
p. **242**, ll. 7 sqq. *Alt. reading:*

Authors,
Their Judgment, Reason, and their Inclinations
To all their own Opinions and Perswations;
Take measure of themselves in al th' appear
T' extol in others, but designe to wear,
And therefor, nere consider what is Fit
To match another mans but their own wit;
As yeards and Inches first were taken from
The Standard of King Edward[s] arme and thumb.

NOTES

p. **243**, ll. 1–4. *Printed by Thyer.*

p. **244**, ll. 1–16. *MS. slightly damaged.* ll. 9–20. *Printed by Thyer.*
l. 11. *Thyer reads* And those.

p. **245**, ll. 11 sq. *Alt. reading:*

> For every Curious Line is drawn so small
> 'Tis not but by sharp eies discernd at all.

l. 18. An. ll. 19–36. *Printed by Thyer.* ll. 27 sqq. *Alt. reading:*

> For those that use to write in Authors Prayses
> 'Tis but to give themselves, not them, their voyces;
> And tho in Privat th' are not to be hinted,
> In Publique may b' assumd and ownd and Printed:
> For those that Prayse the weake and Ignorant
> Give them like Begging Presents what they want,
> And therefore in their fawning Dedications,
> Provide for all their Necessary Occasions.

l. 31. *Thyer reads* that's due, do give.

p. **246**, ll. 1–24. *Printed by Thyer.* l. 3. *Thyer reads* Streight other.
l. 11. *Thyer reads* the Students. l. 24. *Thyer reads* That's of.

p. **247**, l. 26. of. l. 34. of.

p. **248**, ll. 1–10 *and* 15–20. *Printed by Thyer.*

p. **250**, ll. 1–4, 9–12 *and* 27–32. *Printed by Thyer.*

p. **251**, ll. 7–14. *Printed by Thyer.* l. 7. *Thyer reads* What else does.

p. **252**, ll. 7–14. *Printed by Thyer.* ll. 13–14. *Alt. reading:*

> And brought about with Greatest Art
> By those wh' have but the mere Mechanique Part.

l. 20. Art obtain. ll. 33–36. *Printed by Thyer.* l. 35. Tyrant.

p. **253**, ll. 9–30. *Printed by Thyer.* l. 16. one.

p. **254**, ll. 5–12. *Printed by Thyer.* l. 5. *Thyer reads* Authority intoxicates. l. 6. *Thyer reads* mere Sots. l. 8. *Thyer reads* giddy, proud.
l. 12. *Thyer reads* Base submit. ll. 21–38. *Printed by Thyer.* l. 21. *Thyer
reads* Those that. l. 30. Then *omitted.*

p. **255**, l. 1. Commoner. ll. 15–20. *Printed by Thyer.* l. 17. *Thyer
reads* The Law. ll. 21–30 sqq. *Printed in Ed.* 1822.

p. **256**, l. 1. desere. l. 12. Moun. l. 17. Tuf. l. 28. of.
ll. 31–36. *Printed by Thyer.* l. 31. Law *was added by Thyer.*

p. **257**, ll. 1–16. *Printed from* The Genuine Remains.

p. **258**, ll. 27 sqq. *Printed by Thyer who begins with these lines:*

> Old Laws have not been suffer'd to be pointed,
> To leave the Sense at large the more disjointed,
> And furnish Lawyers, with the greater Ease,
> To turn and wind them any way they please.

l. 36. *Thyer reads* exactly.

NOTES

p. 259, l. 2. *Thyer reads* The Court directs. ll. 11–22 *and* 27–36. *Printed by Thyer.* l. 26. Scores. l. 27. *Thyer prints* Dame Justice. l. 29. like Antique. l. 36. *Thyer reads* leave the Sense at large.

p. 261, l. 5. whe. ll. 15–20. *Printed by Thyer.* l. 15. *Thyer reads* All those. l. 16. *Thyer reads* Court. ll. 27–28. *Printed by Thyer.*

p. 262, ll. 1–16. *Printed by Thyer.*

p. 263, ll. 19–28. *Printed by Thyer.*

p. 264, l. 10. Trick. ll. 13–16. *Printed by Thyer.* l. 17. Probationes. l. 19. no. l. 30. Burglarer.

p. 265, l. 4. the.

p. 266, ll. 9–12. *Printed by Thyer.*

p. 267. *Printed in Ed.* 1822.

p. 268, ll. 1–12 *and* 15–38. *Printed in Ed.* 1822. l. 4. valiant's.

p. 269, ll. 1–8. *Printed in Ed.* 1822. *Last line* keeping Distance.

p. 270, ll. 1–13. *Printed in Ed.* 1822.

p. 271, ll. 1–4 *and* 12–19. *Printed by Thyer.* l. 1. *Thyer reads* Far. l. 4. Was. l. 12. *Thyer reads* There is nothing our Felicities.

p. 272, l. 5. of Childens.

p. 273, ll. 27 sqq. *Printed by Thyer.*

p. 275, ll. 1–4, 7–8, *and* 24–27. *Printed by Thyer.* l. 8. Trad. l. 20. wing. l. 27. The.

p. 276, ll. 9–10. *Printed by Thyer.* l. 10. of. l. 13. Jabbers. l. 14. Labourrs. l. 18. Bandyng.

p. 278, ll. 3–4. *Printed by Thyer.* l. 7. themsevs. l. 20. genly. l. 31. Probationer.

p. 279, l. 8. ther. l. 19. abolish.

p. 280, l. 31. sacre.

p. 281, l. 10. Prases.

p. 282, ll. 1–6 *and* 13–18. *Printed by Thyer.*

p. 284, ll. 1–34. *Printed by Thyer.* l. 1. *Thyer reads* Your wise. l. 4. *Thyer reads* All Pleasure. l. 18. when, how.

p. 285, ll. 9–16. *Printed by Thyer.* l. 12. the.

p. 286, ll. 7–16. *Printed in Ed.* 1822.

p. 287, ll. 7–20. *Printed from Thyer's MS.*

p. 288, l. 12. Epicopacy. l. 13. Jursdiction.

p. 290, ll. 21–38. *Printed by Thyer.* l. 24. *Thyer reads* a Title.

p. 291, ll. 1–4 *and* 9–14. *Printed by Thyer.* l. 8. *Alt. reading:*

Perpetually flock to Jubilies.

l. 9. *Thyer reads* the Ark.

NOTES

p. **292**, ll. 5–6. *Printed by Thyer.* l. 5. As *omitted by Thyer.* l. 6. *Thyer reads* clean Shift. l. 11. Civility. l. 12. but avoyd. l. 17. Relig. l. 25. of. l. 29. Intrest, Dominion.

p. **294**, l. 9. thoug.

PROSE PAMPHLETS AND IMITATIONS

Mola Asinaria....*Printed from the edition of* 1659.

That this amusing piece of Parody is Butler's work is not to be doubted. Anthony Wood unhesitatingly gives him as the author of it, and William Prynne, indeed, was one of our satirist's favourite victims. See *Hudibras, William Prynne's Answer to John Audland,* and, among many other humorous lines referring to the same subject, this allusion to Prynne's ears (Butler's MS. fol. 81 v):

> One that at any time would Freely hange
> For th' opportunity t' Harangue,
> Whose Eares for Large Extent and Space
> Were of the Tru Arcadian Race,
> And might with Pryns for large and wide
> I' th' State of Innocence have viede.

Two Speeches made in the Rump-Parliament... *Printed from* The Genuine Remains.

p. **309**, l. 29. too.

A Speech made at the Rota. *Printed from* The Genuine Remains.

Two Letters, One from John Audland a Quaker...**The Other, William Prynnes Answer**... *Printed from the edition of* 1672. *Thyer reprinted them in* The Genuine Remains.

p. **331**, l. 3. Task-master, of. l. 10. evil and. l. 19. *Thyer prints* the other, who has. l. 29. question I.

p. **332**, l. 30. Playes, for.

p. **333**, l. 6. rod. l. 8. Superstitions. l. 9. Remitter, how. l. 11. Salutation. l. 14. filty. dist. l. 15. Rabble rout. l. 39. Rhim.

p. **334**, l. 6. *Thyer prints* informd; but when. l. 9. *Thyer prints* those he. l. 12. screw, his. l. 19. Gentleman of the House,. l. 20. again, as you know) they once did at midnight,. l. 32. Dieted (like.

p. **335**, l. 29. are.

p. **336**, l. 4. *Thyer prints* induce. l. 7. Supertious. l. 10. *Thyer prints* Where thou. l. 13. thereof *omitted by Thyer.* l. 27. stuff.

p. **337**, l. 5. *Thyer prints* pag. 220. l. 11. puting. l. 34. beginning, whereof.

p. **338**, l. 20. *Thyer prints* even ye. l. 24. *Thyer prints* 1200. l. 30. blows.

NOTES

p. 339, l. 14. *Thyer prints* Potion. l. 19. *Thyer prints* asham'd of, or sorry for or abased. l. 21. reason *omitted by Thyer*. l. 26. *Thyer prints* Now.

p. 340, l. 1. Speculum Iefact. l. 14. Girdle, turn'd. behind *omitted by Thyer*. l. 18. *Thyer prints* in thy *and* conce. l. 32. subject,.

An Occasional Reflection on Dr. Charlton's feeling a Dog's Pulse at Gresham-College. By R.[obert] B.[oyle] Esq. *Printed from* The Genuine Remains.

See Thyer's note (I, 404): *The Title*—An Occasional Reflection *is the same that* Boyle *has given to a little Rhapsody of his printed in his* Seraphic Love; *and the Name* Lyndamore, *to which this is addressed, is the same that is made use of in that Book, which begins*—My dearest Lyndamore.

POLITICAL OBSERVATIONS AND REFLECTIONS

Mercurius Menippeus.... *Printed from the edition of* 1682, *with the addition of the verses published when reprinted in* The Second Volume of the Posthumous Works Of Mr Samuel Butler...1715. pp. 73–110, *under the title* Memoirs of the Years 1649 and 1650.

That these observations are Butler's work, in spite of their being published as "Written by an unknown Hand," is made clear, not only from the fact that many out-of-the-way expressions, similes and ideas are met here that were used and developed later in *Hudibras* (for it might be maintained that *Mercurius Menippeus* was written after the famous mock-epic and is merely an imitation of it), but also because many unusual expressions, similes and ideas found in *Mercurius Menippeus* are met in the MSS. of Samuel Butler, which were still unpublished in 1682 and 1715.

p. 349, l. 8. *See* Characters, p. 100, l. 13. l. 10. *Post. Works:* whipt, yet. ll. 11–12. *See* Poetical Thesaurus, p. 176, ll. 5–6.

p. 350, l. 11. *See* Hudibras, p. 8, l. 28. l. 23. *Post. Works:* for Powder Treason. l. 24. *Post. Works:* Suters. l. 36. greedily savagely.

p. 351, l. 1. *Post. Works:* Underminer. l. 6. his Funeral. l. 32. *Post. Works:* Tillin's.

p. 352, l. 19. *Post. Works:* Dr Gooding. ll. 20–22. *See* Characters, p. 150, ll. 6 sqq. *and* p. 295: "The Turkes accompt mad men Saints, and the Christians despise them for it and yet esteem the greatest Madness in the world Sanctity." *See also* Upon an hypocritical Nonconformist, *supra*, p. 91, ll. 224 sq., The Answer of William Prynne, p. 338, ll. 11 sqq., *and* Butler's MS. fol. 95 r, *with the following lines:*

> As Lewd as Turks that Fooles for Saints adore,
> When they were greater Saints themselves before.

l. 38. *Post. Works:* between.

p. 353, l. 9. *Post. Works:* never to be heard. *See* Hudibras, p. 121, ll. 4–7. l. 14. *Post. Works:* a Scaffold. l. 19. *Post. Works:* it scorched. l. 20. has almost starved.

p. 354, l. 5. *Post. Works:* that there would have been.

p. **355**, l. 14. is Jew.   l. 18. *Post. Works:* believes his merits.   l. 35. *See* Audland's Letter, p. 331, l. 23 "as the Mahometans (they say) will not admit a Jew to turn Turk, unless he first become a Christian."

p. **356**, ll. 22 sq. *Compare with* Ballad, *supra*, p. 109.   l. 25. *Post. Works:* but his Countenance.

p. **357**, ll. 5 sqq. *See* Hudibras, pp. 10–11.   l. 9. *Post. Works:* with a house. l. 10. *Post. Works:* both serve.   l. 16. *Post. Works:* Because 'tis laid. l. 20. *Post. Works:* St Christopher.

p. **358**, l. 18. *Post. Works:* overthrow.   l. 29. *Post. Works:* on the same tune.

p. **359**, l. 7. *Post. Works:* Loyalists.   l. 33. *Post. Works:* for the question. l. 35. *Post. Works:* may.

p. **360**, l. 5. *Post Works:* could not discover.   l. 13. Rebels?.

p. **361**, l. 1. *Post. Works:* have not by this time.   l. 4. *Post. Works:* They will at least perceive.   l. 6. *Post. Works:* Libellers.   l. 9. *We find the same joke in* Butler's MS. fol. 34 v:

> Retaynd Wil Prin and Dorislaus,
> The Learned Counsel of the Cause,
> The one a Martyr, the other lesser,
> A Paultry Auricular Confesse[r].

l. 36. *Post. Works:* all their Treaty.

p. **362**, l. 4. *Post. Works:* No Money.   l. 19. *Post. Works:* by the Conqueror.   l. 37. *Post. Works:* his king.

p. **363**, l. 24. *Post. Works:* may be acted, *and* admit no Scaffold.

p. **364**, l. 5. *Post. Works:* The Thief's best Play is.   l. 12. *Post. Works:* odliest.   l. 16. *Post. Works:* But still he showed more.   l. 18. *See* Hudibras, p. 280, ll. 8 sqq. *See also* A Speech made at the Rota, p. 325, ll. 27 sqq. *and* Butler's MS. fol. 2 v:

> When a Bee has lost his Sting,
> With which he gets his Harvest in,
> The only Engine, that Supplys
> And loads the Carriadge of his thighs,
> The Rest from their Dominions drive
> Exild the Territory of the Hive.

l. 21. stay.

p. **365**, l. 11. *Post. Works:* more freely.

The Case of King Charles I. truly stated... *Printed from* The Genuine Remains. [The Preface to the Reader printed from the edition of 1691.]

See Thyer's note (1, 326): *This and*...[John Audland's Letter to William Prynne, and William Prynne's Answer] *are the only Prose Works of* Butler *already printed which can, upon any sufficient grounds, be asserted to be genuine. The former I find in Manuscript in his own Hand; and of the two latter, I meet with several Fragments, besides Passages in his common-Place Collection, which indubitably confirm their Originality and Genuineness.*

NOTES

p. 366, l. 20. these.

p. 367, l. 5. pairiot.

p. 368, l. 5. Sovereignty. l. 11. *Ed.* 1691 *reads* your.

p. 369, l. 1. Bita-Sheep. l. 4. Patrons. l. 8. *Ed.* 1691 *reads* which should seem. l. 31. whether.

p. 370, l. 33. *Ed.* 1691 *reads* for but.

p. 371, l. 5. *Ed.* 1691 *reads* vulgas. l. 26. *Ed.* 1691 *reads* he gave his assent. l. 28. *Ed.* 1691 *reads* profitable. l. 34. the Absence.

p. 372, l. 17. the may sit. *Ed.* 1691 *reads* sit still. l. 21. possibly. l. 24. Injustice believe. l. 27. forget.

p. 373, l. 13. pretend. l. 16. *Ed.* 1691 *reads* You do.

p. 374, l. 24. *Ed.* 1691 *reads* profitable, any. l. 28. Ways. l. 35. Voice to.

p. 375, l. 17. *Ed.* 1691 *reads* you have mistaken. l. 18. *Ed.* 1691 *reads* Right of Cause.

p. 376, l. 20. Reasons.

p. 377, l. 7. *Ed.* 1691 *reads* proving he fought for. a Power. l. 11. *Ed.* 1691 *reads* cannot. l. 34. think these.

p. 379, l. 21. Speech, is...Purpose: There. l. 23. omitted, and. l. 30. *Ed.* 1691 *reads* to the authority of that.

p. 380, l. 28. *Ed.* 1691 *reads* with alive yourself. l. 29. *Ed.* 1691 *reads* Storm.

p. 381, l. 24. *Ed.* 1691 *reads* at the Alteration.

p. 382, l. 6. *Ed.* 1691 *reads* what Judgment and Conscience we are to expect....Ground for.

p. 383, l. 19. *Ed.* 1691 *reads* as he was. l. 28. they sold. l. 31. *Ed.* 1691 *reads* as prove. l. 37. *Ed.* 1691 *reads* mark.

p. 385, l. 13. Insolence. l. 23. experienced. l. 33. used.

p. 386, l. 31. *Ed.* 1691 *reads* to live long: so long.

Observations upon the Long Parliament of Charles the First. *Printed from* The Genuine Remains.

Beneficial Reflections upon Milford-Haven. *Printed from* The Genuine Remains.

p. 396, l. 7. Cheptow.

APPENDIX

The Appendix is printed from the Butler MSS. in the British Museum.

p. 400, l. 19. Mechaiques. l. 38. *Alt. reading:* On even terms.

p. 401, ll. 23–28. *Printed in Ed.* 1822. l. 26. *Ed.* 1822 *prints* discover.

NOTES

p. **402**, l. 20. Hands.   l. 21. Mad.   l. 26. his His.   ll. 29 sqq. *Alt. reading:*

> Mistake the Real valew of its worth
> Like Epictetus Candle-stick of Earth,
> That to some Stoiques of his Tribe was sold
> And Purchacd for it[s] we[i]gh[t] in ready Gold.

p. **403**, l. 1. *Alt. reading:* Absurdities.   l. 23. underd.

p. **404**. *Printed from Thyer's MS.*   l. 13. *Alt. reading:* wonderfully *or* critically.

p. **405**, ll. 1–26. *Printed from Thyer's MS.*   l. 29. Scholles.
ll. 43 sqq. *Alt. reading:*

> For some have understood, How Separate Soules
> Between the Artique, and Antartique Poles
> Do Ply through all the Regions of Aire
> Their Subtle vehicles to get a Fare,
> That's bound for th' Earth to waft 'em down for Guests
> And Sojorners to Fish, and Foul, and Beasts.
> And with them Carry Letters down of Credence
> To be Deliverd to their Friends the Pedants,
> That use to write stupendious Narratives
> Of all the Strange Adventures of their Lives,
> Tell what they use to Drink, and what to Eate,
> And what they Suffer in the Cold or Heat,
> And with what violence a Separate Ghost
> In Furious Storms and Hurricanes is Tost.
> And are the only Natural Historians
> Below the moone of th' Antique Pythagoreans,
> Know what makes Forme and Matter stick together
> As Boys lift Heavy weights with scraps of Leather.

p. **406**, l. 1. Narrative.   l. 21. not Deaf.   ll. 23 sq. *Alt. reading:*

> And treat 'em like Pythagoras his Followrs
> That for five yeares, in Silence, bred his Schollers.

p. **407**, l. 28. The.

p. **409**, l. 1. Elephant.   l. 8. Apply.   l. 39. Pacquet-male.

p. **410**, l. 35. prove.   l. 36. As *omitted.*

p. **411**, l. 4. bee.

p. **413**, l. 32. Better.

p. **416**, l. 18. then.

p. **417**, l. 3. Thound.   l. 24. Enogh.

p. **420**, l. 15. Avice.   l. 33. of had.

p. **421**, l. 27. Parcel.

p. **422**, l. 11. though.   l. 13. Alitudes.

p. **423**, l. 37. Suble.

p. **424**, l. 19. Nighborhood.

p. **425**, l. 14. the.   l. 24. th.

NOTES

p. 426, l. 14. need.   l. 19. Atients.   l. 22. forsaken *omitted*.

p. 427, ll. 1–8 *and* 33–42. *Printed in Ed.* 1822.

p. 428, ll. 1–10 *and* 25–32. *Printed in Ed.* 1822.   l. 28. Sort.
ll. 39 sqq. *MS. slightly damaged*.

p. 429, l. 33. Who *omitted*.

p. 431, l. 1. Hospitaler-knight.   l. 11. Who.

p. 432, l. 5. he the.   l. 45. of.

p. 434, l. 35. Punishment.

p. 437, l. 3. fit *omitted*.   l. 4. *MS. slightly damaged*.   l. 6. of.

p. 438, l. 13. Beast.   l. 41. of.

p. 439, l. 8. *Alt. reading:* Atlantique Ile.

p. 440, l. 5. of.   l. 21. Beast.

p. 441, ll. 10–15. See Waller's Poem on a Lady singing a Song of his composing: *That Eagles Fate and mine are one.*

p. 444, l. 4. could streit.   l. 14. Are.   l. 18. hs.   l. 20. of.

p. 446, l. 13. Saint.   l. 28. Preact.

p. 449, l. 29. Especilly.

p. 450, l. 1. Papist.

p. 451, l. 22. uttermost an.

p. 453, l. 9. se.

p. 455, ll. 1–6 *and* 13–38. *Printed in Ed.* 1822.   l. 29. No.

p. 456. *Printed in Ed.* 1822.   l. 13. slough.   l. 36. A I t' appear.
l. 38. make, when.

p. 457. *Printed in Ed.* 1822.   l. 34. Soudest.

p. 458. *Printed in Ed.* 1822.

p. 459. *Printed in Ed.* 1822.   l. 10. Cok.

p. 460, ll. 1–10 *and* 35–40. *Printed in Ed.* 1822.

p. 461, ll. 1–6 *and* 13–44. *Printed in Ed.* 1822.   l. 11. Cracks.
l. 39. Pupose.   l. 42. Mary.

p. 462, ll. 1–34. *Printed in Ed.* 1822.   l. 29. long-tayd.   l. 36. of.

p. 463, ll. 5–40. *Printed in Ed.* 1822.   *Last line.* of.

p. 464. *Printed in Ed.* 1822   l. 14. Stays.   l. 16. *Alt. reading:*

Or Highway-men t' injure a Neck.

CAMBRIDGE: PRINTED BY WALTER LEWIS, M.A., AT THE UNIVERSITY PRESS